ZEITGEIST IN BABEL

ZEITGEIST IN BABEL

The Postmodernist Controversy

EDITED BY

INGEBORG HOESTEREY

INDIANA UNIVERSITY PRESS

Bloomington and Indianapolis

The paper used in this publication meets the minimum requirements of American
National Standard for Information Sciences—Permanence of Paper for Printed
Library Materials, ANSI Z39.48-1984.

∞™

Manufactured in the United States of America

Library of Congress Cataloging-in-Publication Data

Zeitgeist in Babel : the postmodernist controversy / edited by
Ingeborg Hoesterey.
p.   cm.
Includes bibliographical references.
ISBN 0-253-32835-7 (alk. paper).—ISBN 0-253-20611-1 (pbk. :
alk. paper)
1. Postmodernism.   I. Hoesterey, Ingeborg.
B831.2.Z45   1991
190'.9'04—dc20
89-46333
CIP

1 2 3 4 5   94 93 92 91 90

CONTENTS

ACKNOWLEDGMENTS

I wish to thank Anya Peterson Royce, Dean of Faculties, and other offices of Indiana University for financial support received in the final stages of preparing this collection of essays for publication. Stephen L. Wailes, chair of Germanic Studies, made it possible to employ the computer wizardry of doctoral student John Blair, who heroically labored over post-scanner editing and also joined me for proofreading. A grant from the American Council of Learned Societies enabled me to attend conferences on postmodernism in Europe, one having been co-organized by Matei Calinescu, who generously gave of his advice throughout the development of the project. Last but not least I am grateful for the fine performance on the part of the staff at Indiana University Press and the pleasant professional atmosphere in which the volume could take shape.

I. H.

INTRODUCTION
Postmodernism As Discursive Event

Ingeborg Hoesterey

Periodization, the naming of a historical era or style, has been shown by E. H. Gombrich and others to emerge as the result of discursive convention, often after the term in question has been tossed about as a rhetorical commodity with dramatic shifts in value over a considerable length of time.[1] Examples from the histories of art and literature come easily to mind. Gothic architecture, for instance, was considered to be an expression of northern barbarism and violence before eighteenth-century taste granted the style the status of high artistic achievement.[2] In European literary history the concept of romanticism underwent amazing discursive mood swings in the first half of the nineteenth century, with French critics vehemently contesting what they perceived to be an English–German conspiracy, to put it briefly but bluntly.[3] Presently we may witness one such stormy genealogy of periodization *in statu nascendi;* for never before has the advent of a linguistic sign, potentially harboring an epochal signified, received the widespread interdisciplinary and international attention paid to the idea of "postmodernism."

The last decade saw the new concept employed with increasing frequency and intensity in artistic practice, related criticism, and general critical theory. Its dissemination in popular culture has been extensive. Thus if one undertakes a cognitive mapping of the many tongues and shapes of postmodernism and does so from a midatlantic position, one is confronted with a complex constellation of greatly differing discourse formations, each attempting to define the concept of postmodernism according to its respective horizon of expectations. The term may designate a positive, progressive development for one interpretative community, while another assigns it a decidedly negative value. "Postmodernism" may connote liberation from the constraints of a specific modernism as it does for those involved in the making and scholarly analysis of American and British literature as well as for many active in visual arts practices and criticism. Or postmodernism may signal cultural decline and the end of the sociopolitical "project of modernity" as it does for certain circles concerned with critical theory on both sides of the Atlantic. Furthermore, the term has amassed a host of usages: it makes for an effective rallying point where a new departure within a system is needed; it serves as a heuristic tool to redefine a particular modernism; or it functions as the object of desire, signifying a state of being "with it" at any price. (Note the many titles of conference papers that feature the concept as bait and then neglect to thematize it.) All of these articulations can be perceived as competing sign systems in a discursive field where hegemonial claims are asserted and propositions collide while their proponents are trying to appropriate postmodernism as *Epochenschwelle*, as epochal threshold.

It is this Babylonian quality exhibited by the assembly of advocates for and critics of the concept of postmodernism in the second half of the eighties that prompted the compilation of essays at hand. The choice reflects a discourse-analytical approach to the phenomenon of postmodernism, conceiving of the latter as being concretized in the dialogical space where the different discourses meet, clash, or exist in a modus vivendi. By no means an ideal space—for we recognize, with Foucault, that discursive practices do create realities. The latter fact can easily be perceived in those postmodern programs that have already accumulated a sizable history, such as the Americanist project or the "language of postmodern architecture."

Given the particular perspective governing the collection, the sequence of articles was determined in order to throw light upon the genealogy of postmodernism as a working concept in inquiries of major status. And since the earlier history of the term, in its various independent origins, has been documented in a number of studies already, it need not concern us here.[4] Our interest leads us back to that point in time, namely to the mid-seventies, when the concept acquired almost overnight the identity of an energizing force for a number of communicative systems of culture. In 1976 the American edition of Charles Jencks's *The Language of Post-Modern Architecture* was published in New York and came to be appropriated by the New York art scene with a vengeance. Consequently, antimodernist directions in art, beginning around 1960 with Pop Art and followed by Photorealism, Postminimalism, Concept Art, Performance, Video Art, Feminist Art, etc. qualified for consideration under the portmanteau label "postmodernism."

As a tribute to that discursive rupture in 1976, architect and architectural historian Charles Jencks opens our critical anthology with a recent study concerned with the confusion of "late-modern" and "postmodern" architecture by both a sophisticated public and theoreticians in other fields. As he documents this confusion of styles, Jencks establishes the principle of "double coding," which he perceives also in Eco's work, as the most important postmodern marker. The currency of the "death of modernism" topos has moved the criticism of Greenberg into a new focus. For the rebellion of the artists and their commentators against "high modernism" as the "terror of formalism" entailed, and still does entail, an attack against the mastermind of American visual modernism, against Greenberg as the mentor of the Abstract Expressionist movement, which gave birth to what we now know as the New York School. Donald B. Kuspit's piece is representative of the reaction against Greenberg and his modernism as a "purism." A few years later Rosalind E. Krauss, who had criticized Greenbergian aesthetics as early as 1972, inserted an immediately seminal article into the discussion, whose major theme, the ideology of the notion of originality in visual modernism, is now echoed in other circles. Studies of intertextuality in literature and culture have likewise dismantled the originality of authorship, stressing the intertextual status of the author, his writing under the supervision of the tradition and in the *perpetuum mobile* of "inspiring" discourses. Clement Greenberg's own position is represented in his polemical dismissal of the "postmodern." Not surprisingly, the art critic holds onto the idea of modernism, however, for reasons entirely different from those of, for instance, Jürgen Habermas, which are the topic of two essays in the philosophical segment of the book (see below).

The Americanists were actively fashioning a literary postmodernism by the late sixties (and earlier).[5] Though Pop Art was as influential for literary developments as it was for Robert Venturi's manifesto of 1966, marking the beginning of the postmodern movement in architecture, the two discourse formations did not overtly intersect.[6] The Americanist program quickly became internationalized in the seventies, the almost singlehanded achievement of Ihab Hassan and his traveling schedule, but remained very much within the discipline. Of late, comparative literature has shown itself to be an active satellite, acknowledging the canon of stylistic features worked out by Americanists as typical for the postmodern text, especially narrative. Since this canon as well as other guidelines to aesthetic postmodernism have been extensively portrayed in a number of recent research publications (Fokkema/Bertens eds., Hassan/Hassan eds., Calinescu/Fokkema eds., Hutcheon, McHale), we chose to bring instead a metacritical contribution dealing with the problematics of the discourse formation in Americanist studies. C. Barry Chabot's article is a critique from within the field; one might add that criticism has also been waged from outside of American literary studies. For some of the structures of the Americanist postmodern text have been hailed for decades as typically modernist in other philologies. Narrative self-reflexivity, for instance, has usually been considered a *modern* trait by German and French scholars.[7] While delineating potentially postmodern semiotics of the theatre, Erika Fischer-Lichte likewise points to the "overwhelming" similarities of modernism and postmodernism.

Even though it was a philosopher of history, Arnold Toynbee, who used the term "postmodernism" as early as the late forties, not until the late seventies of this waning century did philosophers begin to actively pursue the notion. Jean-François Lyotard's *La condition postmoderne* of 1979 is the rhetorical watershed and is followed by the much-acclaimed as well as disdained enterprise of Frankfurt School protagonist Jürgen Habermas to rehabilitate the "project of modernity" by positing it as incomplete. For the latter philosopher and his community, both in Europe and in the United States, postmodernity is synonymous with the threat of a potential reign of poststructuralist positions. Poststructuralism is seen to embrace a discourse of irrationality poised to displace the tradition of rationality initiated by the Enlightenment—the epoch said to have brought forth a politically progressive idea of modernity. Thus in Habermasian thought poststructuralism equals neoconservatism (compare its somewhat different status in a current neo-Marxism, the New Historicism). Martin Jay, a historian of the Frankfurt School, and the pragmatist Richard Rorty have examined the debate ensuing from the dialogical constellation Habermas–Lyotard–Derrida virulent in critical theory circles.

What situates discussions of Derrida's work as postmodernist thought in Babel is the fact that the philosopher himself rejects the term.[8] The teleological linearity of a modernism/postmodernism dialectic is not in the interest of the deconstructive operation, which favors a stratified concept of history. Derrida's "Interventions" thus are called upon to act as wedges throughout the volume. In contrast to this skeptical gesture, the contributions of Susan R. Suleiman and Matei Calinescu assert aspects of the debate that for many now constitute a positively conceived postmodern project: pluralism in contemporary thought and practices, with feminism as a major political consequence in the move away from monism. Peter Koslowski, on the other hand, lets the paradigm of the postmodern emerge from a notion of an already plural modernism—to be exact, from various modernisms. Koslowski is part of a group of West German philosophers, including Robert Spaemann and Wolfgang Welsch, who have developed alternative models to the Habermasian position.

The third part of our collection of essays is less metacritical in character. It concentrates on discourse formations in which the concept of postmodernism has only recently been adopted as a topic of inquiry, as in musicology. Though it is true that Philip Glass speaks freely of himself as a postmodern composer, others such as the composer Charles Boone are more hesitant to engage the term. Further reservations are polemically heightened in the piece by the cultural historian Jost Hermand. Similarly Maureen Turim approaches the sequence modernism/postmodernism with regard to film with rather mixed feelings; much of what would be termed postmodern from the perspective of fields such as American literature, namely a certain type of formal experimentation, has maintained modernist status in film criticism. It is conceivable, however, that a comparative study of the arts might find a number of formal features that "avant-garde" films share with literary texts or visual art practices, devices that clearly contribute to the establishment of postmodernism as a stylistic category. One could easily name a general predilection for hybrid forms and intermedial junctures, for the foregrounding of historical references as quotations, for a fusion of high and low art, for irony executed by a camp sensibility, for a dadaistic attitude—a catalogue that finds multiple variations in the critical contributions at hand.

Much of the confusion that surrounds the concept in question is in fact due to the common conflation of postmodernism as an epoch, involving a general change of societal and cultural paradigms, and postmodernism as a period style in the arts visibly distinct from modernism. In architecture, for instance, the postmodern has concrete presence in a now twenty-year-old history of buildings that can be distinguished clearly from a bauhaus-type modernism. In fact, postmodern architecture has already experienced such widespread popularization, frequently in watered-down versions of innovative examples by leading artists, that recent directions such as "deconstruction" practiced by American, Japanese, and German architects function to historicize the earlier breakthrough as well as the "classical" phase of the new style. Postmodernity as an epoch following modernity is a much more problematic proposition, since the concept of modernity surfaces as early as the fifth century and continues to connote postantiquity until the Enlightenment rewrites it as a social utopia, a technological program, and so on.

Scholarly approaches such as *Geistesgeschichte* in the twenties made it their virtue to subsume all artistic and philosophical discourses under one label that would embrace the *Geist der Zeit*, the spirit of the time. The terms "Baroque" and "Romantic" underwent this type of semantic enlargement which in the latter case turned even Hegel into a Romantic philosopher. Here, indeed, the notions of historical period and artistic period style are treated as identical. Neo-Marxist approaches, e.g., those of Frederic Jameson and Jürgen Habermas, likewise tend toward generalizations and totalizations assimilating a medium such as architecture into their specific sociopolitical horizon of expectations, without paying due heed to the systemic features of "the other art."[9]

The discourse-analytical approach to postmodernism that informs this volume of essays is not interested in forging a unified vision of the postmodern phenomenon. Rather it has been our intention to acquaint the reader with as many different concretizations of postmodernism as space permitted and the adventure of gathering relevant material finally yielded. Such programmatic disunity renders any claims to the "truth" of postmodernism, as voiced by some research communities, illusory.

When we aligned the notion of Zeitgeist in the title with the mythical locus of linguistic confusion, Babel, we did so with deconstructive intent. Zeitgeist in Babel is, to be sure, a paradox. For according to the most prominent definition of Zeitgeist, Hegel's, the general drift of thought and feeling is the expression of the *Weltgeist*, the objective principle of historical evolution. Hegel imbued the "spirit of the times" with telos, linearity, totalization. The latter objective underlies the *Geistesgeschichte* method, which tended to bring all directions in the arts of a given period into an organic unity as in H. A. Korff's *Geist der Goethezeit* (spirit of the time of Goethe), disregarding differences in medium or type of discourse, e.g., literature versus philosophy. The New Criticism naturally rejected the Zeitgeist cult of earlier phases of criticism; recently the notion has made a comeback.

The revival is understandable, and not only because of a renewed affinity between literary criticism and philosophy. As an expression, Zeitgeist denotes vagueness of definition, and with the openness of its referent seems to match the characteristics of the postmodern as perceived from an impressionistic perspective: fuzziness, lack of clarity. Zeitgeist is used negatively by Neo-Marxists such as Peter Bürger to denounce a troublesome poststructuralist invasion and to register a change of paradigm that is not one's own.

With this reaction the author of the much-quoted *Theory of the Avant-Garde* (1984) picks up again the negative strand of Zeitgeist semantics that can already be found with Goethe and is continued by Kierkegaard and others. Today's frequent negative invocation of the term can be read as an unacknowledged gesture of resignation toward a present that is unsurveyable in its pluralism of cultural narratives and values. An aesthetically oriented perspective, by contrast, is more likely inclined to admit that something is going on which can be felt in many areas of artistic practice and above all in the discourses fashioning the "Lebenswelt"—rock culture, fashion, design. Stylistic pluralism and eclecticism, a fusion of art and kitsch as camp are the most visible signs of a postmodern popular culture and structurally not unsimilar to the developments in the finer arts.

To a certain degree, then, the "hesitancies, confusions, and contradictions" (Chabot) associated with the concept of postmodernism are countered by a communality in general aesthetic and cultural sensibilities which may, however, arise from different ontological foundations. The postmodern *fin de siècle* aesthetics in Europe flourish within and beside a discourse of catastrophe, not exactly an American preoccupation. In America Baudrillard's theory of simulation, positing the threat of a nuclear catastrophe as the real, has been less central to the discussion than his notion of *simulacrum*, naming the unreal nature of our technological reality. And Americanists have continued to point out that it is an increased ontological insecurity in the face of a multitude of discourses and a resulting lack of center that is the moving force behind a literary postmodernism which draws on the literature of the absurd. French texts in turn show themselves to be quite differently postmodern in style, one example being Philippe Sollers's *H*, analyzed by David Hayman as a radically dialogical novel. Unconcerned about plot, it moves from image cluster to image cluster, voice to voice—a polylogue obsessed with writing as existential intertextuality. Hayman compares the "discursive charges" to Joyce's *Finnegans Wake*, a work that Umberto Eco in his inspired and inspiring "conversation" with Stefano Rosso terms postmodern. That *Ulysses* should be seen as a modernist text and *Finnegans Wake* as postmodern or that Dada figures as the postmodern Other to the modernism of Cubism and abstract art leads us one more time into Borges's "Library of Babel" with its unlimited and cyclical referentiality. Nothing prevents the interpreter from calling any previous stylistic occurrence resembling contemporary structures postmodern. It would certainly be preferable if these designatory practices brought the syllable "proto-" back into fashion.

The diverging claims concerning the "birth" of postmodernism remain likewise puzzling. Arnold Toynbee's negatively conceived postmodern age starts in 1875; scholars of English literature have suggested 1939, using the outbreak of World War II and the publication of *Finnegans Wake* as markers. American literature critics and creative writers have convened to set the advent of postmodernism as *following* World War II, an agreement elevated to dictionary status.[10] The visual arts community has more or less settled on the above-mentioned rupture in 1960 (see also Jencks), whereas from a Habermasian perspective the rise of the postmodern syndrome would have to be associated with the emergence of numerous poststructuralist writings in the late sixties. Contemplating this forest of origins, one is reminded of Foucault's reflections on the displacements and transformations of concepts: "the history of a concept is not wholly and entirely that of its progressive refinement, its continuously increasing rationality . . . but that of its various fields of constitution and validity, that of its successive rules of use, that of the many theoretical contexts in which it developed and matured."[11]

NOTES

1. E. H. Gombrich, *Norm and Form* (London: Phaidon, 1966).

2. Lionello Venturi, *History of Art Criticism*, trans. Charles Marriott (New York: Dutton, 1964), 166f.

3. Lilian Fürst, *Romanticism* (London/New York: Methuen, 1969).

4. See Michael Köhler, "Postmodernismus: Ein begriffsgeschichtlicher Überblick," *Amerikastudien* 22, no. 1 (1979) 8–18; Matei Calinescu, *Five Faces of Modernity: Modernism, Avant-Garde, Decadence, Kitsch, Postmodernism* (1977; Durham: Duke University Press, 1987) 132–44; Hans Bertens, "The Postmodern *Weltanschauung* and Its Relation with Modernism: An Introductory Survey," in *Approaching Postmodernism* ed. Douwe Fokkema and Hans Bertens (Amsterdam/Philadelphia: John Benjamins, 1986) 9–51.

5. E.g., Irving Howe's essay, "Mass Society and Postmodern Fiction," *Partisan Review* 26 (1959), 420–36.

6. Robert Venturi, *Complexity and Contradiction in Architecture* (New York: Museum of Modern Art, 1966).

7. See Ingeborg Hoesterey, *Verschlungene Schriftzeichen: Intertextualität von Literatur und Kunst in der Moderne/Postmoderne* (Frankfurt: Athenäum, 1988), 130–47.

8. In conversation.

9. Habermas erroneously identifies architectural postmodernism with nineteenth-century eclecticism, and Jameson does not see that the Bonaventura Hotel in Los Angeles is *late-modern* rather than postmodern. See the contributions by Jencks and Chabot.

10. M. H. Abrams, *A Glossary of Literary Terms* (New York: Holt, Rinehart and Winston, 1985), 109.

11. Michel Foucault, *The Archaeology of Knowledge* (New York: Pantheon, 1982), 4.

ZEITGEIST IN BABEL

I.

Revisiting Constitutive Discursive Practices

Architecture, Americanist Literary Criticism, the Anti–Greenbergian Art Scene

The principle of taxonomic disorder can give rise to reasoned and ordered translations or else to comic collapses, which can sometimes be glimpsed in some course descriptions, in blurbs, sometimes in books. It is the serialization of things which are as heterogeneous but nonetheless in a relationship of contaminating and teratological coincorporation as psychoanalysis, poststructuralism, postmodernism, feminism, Marxism, etc. The teratology is our normality.

J.D.

POSTMODERN VS. LATE-MODERN

Charles Jencks

Postmodernism, like modernism, varies for each art both in its motives and time-frame, and here I shall define it just in the field with which I am most involved—architecture. The responsibility for introducing it into the architectural subconscious lies with Joseph Hudnut who, at Harvard with Walter Gropius, may have wished to give this pioneer of the modern movement a few sleepless nights. At any rate, he used the term in the title of an article published in 1945 called "the post-modern house" (all lower case, as was Bauhaus practice), but didn't mention it in the body of the text or define it polemically. Except for an occasional slip here and there, by Philip Johnson or Nikolaus Pevsner, it wasn't used until my own writing on the subject which started in 1975.[1] In that first year of lecturing and polemicizing in Europe and America, I used it as a temporizing label, as a definition to describe where we had left rather than where we were going. The observable fact was that architects as various as Ralph Erskine, Robert Venturi, Lucien Kroll, the Krier brothers and Team Ten had all departed from modernism and set off in different directions which kept a trace of their common departure. To this day I would define postmodernism as I did in 1978 as double coding—the combination of modern techniques with something else (usually traditional building) in order for architecture to communicate with the public and a concerned minority, usually other architects. The point of this double coding was itself double. Modern architecture had failed to remain credible partly because it didn't communicate effectively with its ultimate users—the main argument of my book *The Language of Post-Modern Architecture*—and partly because it didn't make effective links with the city and history. Thus the solution I perceived and defined as postmodern: an architecture that was professionally based and popular as well as one that was based on new techniques and old patterns. Double coding to simplify means both elite/popular and new/old and there are compelling reasons for these opposite pairings. Today's postmodern architects were trained by modernists, and are committed to using contemporary technology as well as facing current social reality. These commitments are enough to distinguish

4

them from revivalists or traditionalists, a point worth stressing since it creates their hybrid language, the style of postmodern architecture. The same is not completely true of postmodern artists and writers who may use traditional techniques of narrative and representation in a more straightforward way. Yet all the creators who could be called postmodern keep something of a modern sensibility—some intention which distinguishes their work from that of revivalists—whether this is irony, parody, displacement, complexity, eclecticism, realism, or any number of contemporary tactics and goals. Postmodernism has the essential double meaning: the continuation of modernism and its transcendence.

The main motive for postmodern architecture is obviously the social failure of modern architecture, its mythical "death" announced repeatedly over ten years. In 1968, an English tower block of housing, Ronan Point, suffered what was called "cumulative collapse" as its floors gave way after an explosion. In 1972, many slab blocks of housing were intentionally blown up at Pruitt-Igoe in St Louis. By the mid 1970s, these explosions were becoming a quite frequent method of dealing with the failures of modernist building methods: cheap prefabrication, lack of personal "defensible" space and the alienating housing estate. The "death" of modern architecture and its ideology of progress which offered technical solutions to social problems was seen by everyone in a vivid way. The destruction of the central city and historical fabric was almost equally apparent to the populace and again these popular, social motives should be stressed because they aren't quite the same in painting, film, dance, or literature. There is no similar, vivid "death" of modernism in these fields, nor perhaps the same social motivation that one finds in postmodern architecture. But even in postmodern literature there is a social motive for using past forms in an ironic way. Umberto Eco has described this irony or double coding:

> I think of the postmodern attitude as that of a man who loves a very cultivated woman and knows he cannot say to her "I love you madly," because he knows that she knows (and that she knows that he knows) that these words have already been written by Barbara Cartland. Still, there is a solution. He can say, "As Barbara Cartland would put it, I love you madly." At this point, having avoided false innocence, having said clearly that it is no longer possible to speak innocently, he will nevertheless have said what he wanted to say to the woman: that he loves her, but he loves her in an age of lost innocence. If the woman goes along with this, she will have received a declaration of love all the same. Neither of the two speakers will feel innocent, both will have accepted the challenge of the past, of the already said, which cannot be eliminated, both will consciously and with pleasure play the game of irony. . . . But both will have succeeded, once again, in speaking of love.[2]

Thus Eco underlines the lover's use of postmodern double coding and extends it, of course, to the novelist's and poet's social use of previous forms. Faced with a restrictive modernism, a minimalism of means and ends, writers such as John Barth have felt just as restricted as architects forced to build in the International Style, or using only glass and steel. The most notable, and perhaps the best, use of this double coding in architecture is James Stirling's addition to the Staatsgalerie in Stuttgart. Here one can find the fabric of the city and the existing museum extended in amusing and ironic ways. The U-shaped palazzo form of the old gallery is echoed and placed on a high plinth, or "Acropolis," above the traffic. But this classical base holds a very real and necessary parking garage, one that is ironically indicated by stones which have "fallen," like ruins, to the ground. The resultant holes show the real construction—not the thick marble blocks of the real Acropolis, but a steel frame holding stone cladding which allows the air ventilation required by law. One can sit on these false ruins and ponder the truth of our lost innocence: that we live in an age which can build with beautiful, expressive masonry as long as we make it skin-deep and hang it on a steel skeleton. A modernist would of course deny himself and us this pleasure for a number of reasons: "truth to materials," "logical consistency," "straightforwardness," "simplicity"—all the values and rhetorical tropes celebrated by such modernists as Le Corbusier and Mies van der Rohe.

Stirling, by contrast and like the lovers of Umberto Eco, wants to communicate more and different values. To signify the permanent nature of the museum, he has used traditional rustication and classical forms including an Egyptian cornice, an open-air pantheon, and segmental arches. These are beautiful in an understated and conventional way, but they aren't revivalist either because of small distortions, or the use of a modern material such as reinforced concrete. They say, "We are beautiful like the Acropolis or pantheon, but we are also based on concrete technology and deceit." The extreme form of this double coding is visible at the entry points: a steel temple outline which announces the taxi drop-off point, and the modernist steel canopies which tell the public where to walk in. These forms and colors are reminiscent of De Stijl, that quintessentially modern language, but they are collaged onto the traditional background. Thus modernism confronts classicism to such an extent that both modernists and classicists would be surprised, if not offended. There is not the simple harmony and consistency of either language; instead we are uneasily confronted with the understanding that we live in a complex world where we can't deny either the past and conventional beauty, or the present and current technical and social reality. Caught between this past and present, unwilling to oversimplify our situation, Stirling has produced the most "real" reality of postmodern architecture to date.

As much of this reality has to do with taste as it does with technology. Modernism failed as mass-housing and city building partly because it failed to communicate with its inhabitants and users who might not have liked the style, understood what it meant, or even known how to use it. Hence the double coding, the essential definition of postmodernism, has been used as a strategy for communicating on various levels at once.

James Stirling, Michael Wilford and Associates, Neue Staatsgalerie, Stuttgart, 1977–84. *Photo: Charles Jencks*

Virtually every postmodern architect—Robert Venturi, Hans Hollein, Charles Moore, Robert Stern, Michael Graves, Arata Isozaki are the notable examples—use popular and elitist signs in their work to achieve quite different ends, and their styles are essentially hybrid. To simplify, at Stuttgart the blue and red handrails and vibrant polychromy fit in with the youth that use the museum—they literally resemble their dayglo hair and anoraks—while the classicism appeals more to the lovers of Schinkel. This is a very popular building with young and old, and when I interviewed people there—a group of plein air painters, schoolchildren, and businessmen—I found their different perceptions and tastes were accommodated and stretched. The pluralism which is so often called on to justify postmodernism here became a tangible reality.

This is not the place to recount the history of postmodern architecture, but I want to stress the ideological and social intentions which underlie this history because they are so often overlooked in the bitter debate with modernists.[3] Even traditionalists often reduce the debate to matters of style, and thus the symbolic intentions and morality are overlooked. If one reads the writings of Robert Venturi, Denise Scott Brown, Christian Norberg-Schulz, or myself, one will find the constant notion of pluralism, the idea that the architect must design for different "taste cultures" (in the words of the sociologist Herbert Gans) and for differing views of the good life. In any complex building, in any large city building such as an office, there will be varying tastes and functions that have to be articulated and these will inevitably lead, if the architect follows these hints, toward an eclectic style. He may pull this heterogeneity together under a free-style classicism, as do many postmodernists today, but a trace of the pluralism will and should remain. I would even argue that "the true and proper style" is not, as they said, Gothic, but some form of eclecticism, because only this can adequately encompass the pluralism that is our social and metaphysical reality.

Many people would disagree with this last point and some of them, such as the visionary and urbanist Leon Krier, are almost postmodern. I bring him up as a borderline case and because he shows how different traditions may influence each other in a positive way. Krier worked for James Stirling in the early 1970s and since then has evolved his own form of vernacular classicism. In his schemes for the reconstruction of cities such as Berlin and Washington D.C., he shows how the destroyed fabric of the historic city could be repaired and a traditional set of well-scaled spaces added to this core. The motivations are urbanistic and utopian (in the sense that they are unlikely to be realized). They are also traditional and idealistic in the straightforward manner that postmodernism is not. The way of life implied is paternalistic and monistic, but the plans would entail not the totalitarianism that his critics aver when they compare him with Albert Speer but an integrated culture led by a determined and sensitive elite. In this sense, Krier hasn't lost the innocence which Umberto Eco and the postmodernists believe is gone for good, but has returned to a preindustrial golden age where singular visions could be imagined for everyone. Again, critics will say he's kept his innocence precisely because he hasn't built and faced the irreducibly plural reality.

This may be true and yet Krier has had a beneficent effect on postmodernists, as on others, because his ideal models act as a critique of current planning in the same way as do such surviving fragments as the centers of Siena and Venice. His nostalgia, like that of the French Revolution, is of a very positive and creative kind because it shows what a modern city might be if built with traditional streets, arcades, lakes, and squares. Moreover— and this does make him a postmodernist—his drawing manner, derived equally from Le Corbusier and the Ecole des Beaux-Arts, is based on practical urban knowledge. He is not simply a mannerist, sprinkling biplanes and 1920s technology through the sky, but someone who thinks through all the public buildings and private fabric before he draws. His biplanes are of course ironic postmodern comments on the desirability of technical regression.

There are, inevitably, many more strands of postmodern architecture than the two major ones which the work of Stirling and Krier represent, and I have tried to show the plurality as consisting of six basic traditions or "species." There is some overlap between these identifiable species, within the evolutionary tree of my diagram (*What Is Postmodernism?* 23), and architects, unlike animals, can jump from one category to another, or occupy several strands at once. The diagram shows two fundamental aspects which have to be added to our former definition of postmodernism: it is a movement that starts roughly in 1960 as a set of plural departures from modernism. Key definers are a pluralism both philosophical and stylistic, and a dialectical or critical relation to a pre-existing ideology. There is no one postmodern style, although there is a dominating classicism, just as there was no one modern mode, although there was a dominating International Style. Furthermore, if one is going to classify anything as complex as an architectural movement, one has to use many definers: Anthony Blunt, in a key text on Baroque and Rococo, shows the necessity for using ten definers, and in distinguishing postmodernism from modern and late-modern architecture, I have used thirty.[4] Most of these definers concern differences over symbolism, ornament, humor, technology, and the relation of the architect to existing and past cultures. Modernists and late-modernists tend to emphasize technical and economic solutions to problems, whereas postmodernists tend to emphasize contextual and cultural additions to their inventions.

Many of these points could be made about postmodern art. It also started roughly in 1960 with a succession of departures from modernism—notably Pop Art, Hyperrealism, Photorealism, Allegorical and Political Realism, New Image Painting, La Transavanguardia, Neoexpressionism and a host of other more or less fabricated movements. Pressure from the art market to produce new labels and synthetic schools has, no doubt, increased the tempo and heat of this change. And the influence of the international media, so emphasized as a defining aspect of the postindustrial society, has made these movements cross over national boundaries. Postmodern art, like architecture, is influenced by the "world village" and the sensibility that comes with this: an ironic cosmopolitanism. If one looks at three Italian postmodernists, Carlo Maria Mariani, Sandro Chia and Mimmo Paladino, one sees their "Italianness" always in quotation marks, an ironic fabrication of their roots made as much for the New York they occasionally inhabit as from inner necessity. Whereas a mythology was given to the artist in the past by tradition and by patron, in the postmodern world it is chosen and invented.

Mariani, in the mid 1970s, created his fictional academy of eighteenth-century peers—Goethe, Winckelmann, Mengs, etc.—and then painted some missing canvases to fill out a mythic history. In the early 1980s he transferred this mythology to the present day and painted an allegory of postmodern Parnassus with friends, enemies, critics and dealers collected around himself in the center—a modern-day version of Raphael's and Meng's versions of the traditional subject. We see here a series of texts lay-

Carlo Maria Mariani, *La Mano Ubbidisce all'Inteletto*, 1983. Oil
on canvas, 78½" x 69". *Courtesy of Sperone Westwater. Photo:
Zindman/Fremont*

ered one on top of another as an enigmatic commentary, like the structure of
a myth. Is it serious, or parody, or more likely, the combination ironic allegory? The facial expressions and detail would suggest this double reading.
Mariani both solemn and supercilious sits like Ganymede being abducted to
heaven by Zeus: Ganymede is not only the beautiful boy of Greek mythology being captured in the erotic embrace of the eagle Zeus, but a portrait of
the performance artist Luigi Mariani, hence the hoop and stick. To the right,
Francesco Clemente gazes at a canvas held by Sandro Chia; Mario Merz is
Hercules in an understated bathtub; a well-known New York dealer waddles
to the water personified as a turtle; critics write and admire their own
profiles. All this is carried out in the mock heroic style of the late eighteenth
century, the style of la pittura colta which Mariani has made his own. No
one who gives his "cultured painting" an extended analysis would call it
eighteenth-century, or straight revivalist, although many critics unsympa-
thetic to postmodernism have again branded the work as "fascist." The representational conventions had been dismissed by modernists as taboo, as
frigid academic art.

If Mariani adapts and invents his mythology then so do many post-modernists who are involved in allegory and narrative. This concern for content and subject matter is in a sense comparable to architects' renewed concern for symbolism and meaning. Whereas modernism and particularly late-modernism concentrated on the autonomy and expression of the individual art form—the aesthetic dimension—postmodernists focus on the semantic aspect. This generalization is true of such different artists as David Hockney, Malcolm Morley, Eric Fischl, Lennart Anderson, and Paul Georges, some of whom have painted enigmatic allegories, others a combination of sexual and classical narratives. The so-called "return to painting" of the 1980s is also a return to a traditional concern with content, although it is content different from premodern art.

First, because these postmodernists have had a modern training, they are inevitably concerned with abstraction and the basic reality of modern life, that is, a secular mass culture dominated by economic and pragmatic motives. This gives their work the same complexity, mannerism, and double coding present in postmodern architecture, and also an eclectic or hybrid style. For instance Ron Kitaj, who is the artist most concerned with literary and cultural subject matter, combines modernist techniques of collage and a flat, graphic composition with Renaissance traditions. His enigmatic allegory "If Not, Not" is a visual counterpart of T.S. Eliot's "The Wasteland," on which it is partly based. Survivors of war crawl through the desert toward an oasis, survivors of civilization (Eliot himself) are engaged in quizzical acts, some with representatives of exotic culture. Lamb, crow, palm tree, turquoise lake, and a Tuscan landscape consciously adapted from the classical tradition resonate with common overtones. They point toward a Western and Christian background overlaid by modernism, the cult of primitivism and disaster. The classical barn/monument at the top, so reminiscent of Aldo Rossi and postmodern face buildings, also suggests the death camps, which it represents. Indeed the burning inferno of the sky, the corpse and broken pier, the black and truncated trees all suggest life after the Second World War: plural, confused, and tortured on the whole, but containing islands of peace (and a search for wholeness). The title, with its double negative—"If Not, Not"— was taken from an ancient political oath which meant roughly: if you the King do not uphold our liberties and laws, then we do not uphold you. Thus the consequences of broken promises and fragmented culture are the content of this gripping drama, one given a classical gravitas and dignity.

Examples could be multiplied of this type of hidden moralistic narrative: Robert Rauschenberg, David Salle, Hans Haacke, Ian Hamilton Finlay, and Stephen McKenna all make use of the classical tradition in portraying our current cultural situation. Their political and ethical views are often opposed, but their intention to revive the tradition of moralistic art is shared. Thus the definition of postmodernism that I've given above for architects also holds true for artists and, I believe, such literary figures as Umberto Eco, David Lodge, John Barth, John Gardner, and Jorge Luis Borges among many others.

It does not hold true, however, for so many artists lumped together under a postmodern label for whom there are much better appellations.

The Modern Movement, as I've suggested, was in architecture a Protestant Reformation putting faith in the liberating aspects of industrialization and mass democracy. Le Corbusier pursued his "crusade," as he called it, for "a new spirit," as he also called it, and his reformed religion was meant to change the public's attitude toward mass-production. So convinced was this prophet of the beneficent effects of his well-designed environment that he ended his bible—*Towards a New Architecture*—with the exhortation: "Architecture or Revolution. Revolution can be avoided." Walter Gropius, another militant saint of the Design Reformation, founded the Bauhaus as a "cathedral of the future" and in 1923 declared the standard doctrine: "art and technology: a new unity." Mies van der Rohe made any number of pleas to the Spirit of the Age, the Zeitgeist of the new industrialization, and proclaimed that it could solve all our problems, even "social, economic, and artistic" ones.[5]

In short, the three leading modern architects didn't just practice a common, Protestant style, but also believed that if their faith were to govern industrialization then it could change the world for the better, both physically and spiritually. This religion of modernism triumphed throughout the globe as it was disseminated by the saints and proselytizers—Sir Nikolaus Pevsner, Sir James Richards, Sir Leslie Martin, with the bible according to Siegfried Giedion, *Space, Time and Architecture*. Modern academies were formed at the major universities such as Cambridge and Harvard and from there the Purist doctrines of John Calvin Corbusier, Martin Luther Gropius and John Knox van der Rohe were dispersed. Their white cathedrals, the black and white boxes of the International Style, were soon built in every land, and for a while the people and professors kept the faith. Ornament, polychromy, metaphor, humor, symbolism, and convention were put on the Index and all forms of decoration and historical reference were declared taboo. We are all well acquainted with the results—"the architecture of good intentions"—as Colin Rowe termed them, and there are a lot of pleasant white housing estates and machine-aesthetic hospitals to prove that the intentions were not all misguided.

The reigning religion of architectural modernism could be called pragmatic amelioration, that is, the belief that by "doing more with less" as Buckminster Fuller said, social problems would slowly disappear. Technical progress, in limited spheres such as medicine, seems to bear out this ideology, still a dominant one of late-modernists.

Thus we might define modern architecture as the universal, international style stemming from the facts of new constructional means, adequate to society, both in its taste and social make-up. But there is an anomaly in this modernism which is both overwhelming and missed by commentators on the subject. It is the direct opposite of the more widespread modernism in the other arts and philosophy; for these are not optimistic and progressivist

at all. Think of Nietzsche, Goedel, Heisenberg, Heidegger, and Sartre—
closer to nihilism than to the positivism of Fuller. Or think of Yeats, Joyce,
Pound, T. S. Eliot, or De Chirico, Picasso, Duchamp, and Grosz—hardly
liberal, not very socialist, and certainly not optimistic. Whereas modernism
in architecture has furthered the ideology of industrialization and progress,
modernism in most other fields has either fought these trends or lamented
them. In two key areas, however, the various modernisms agree and that is
over the value of abstraction and the primary role of aesthetics, or the perfection of the expressive medium. Modernism as Clement Greenberg has
defined it always has this irreducible goal: to focus on the essence of each art
language. By doing this, he argues, standards are kept high in an age of
secularization, where there are few shared values and little left of a common
symbolic system. All one can do in an agnostic age of consumer pluralism is
sharpen the tools of one's trade, or "purify the language of the tribe," as
Mallarmé and T. S. Eliot defined the poet's role.

This idea relates closely to the nineteenth-century notion of the avant-
garde, and modernism is based, of course, on the myth of a romantic advance guard setting out before the rest of society to conquer territory, new
states of consciousness and social order. The metaphor of an avant-garde as
a political and artistic military was formulated in the 1820s. Although there
were very few artists who were politically active, like Gustave Courbet, and
even fewer that were agitating politically, like Marinetti, the myth of social
activism sustained an elevated role for what was becoming a patronless
class. Artists, like architects, were often unemployed and at the mercy of a
heartless, or at least uninterested, economic system. Where before they had a
defined social relationship to a patron—the State, Church, or an individual—now they related to a marketplace that was competitive and agnostic.

One can thus see modernism as the first great ideological response to this
social crisis and the breakdown of a shared religion. Faced with a post-
Christian society, the intellectuals and the creative elite formulated a new
role for themselves, inevitably a priestly one. In their most exalted role, they
would heal society's rifts; in "purifying the language of the tribe," they could
purify its sensibility and provide an aesthetic-moral base—if not a political
one. From this post-Christian role developed two positions and a contradiction between them that has caused much confusion. To deal with this confusion I shall resort, as others such as Frank Kermode and Robert Stern have
done, to two technical terms, because the word "modern" hides at least two
different meanings.[6]

There is the healing role of the artist, that of overcoming the "split between thinking and feeling" which T. S. Eliot and Siegfried Giedion located
in the nineteenth century, and this leads to what has been called "Heroic
Modernism." Then there is the subversive and romantic role of the artist to
conquer new territory, "to make it new," to make art different, difficult, self-
referential, and critical: what I would call "Agonistic Modernism." These
two meanings relate to what Stern labels "traditional versus schismatic mod-

ernism," humanism versus agonism, continuity versus "the shock of the new," optimism versus nihilism, and so on. For Stern and other writers such as Ihab Hassan, the second of the traditions—schismatic or resistant modernism—has itself mutated into schismatic postmodernism. Thus Hassan writes: "Post-Modernism, on the other hand, is essentially subversive in form and anarchic in its cultural spirit. It dramatizes its lack of faith in art even as it produces new works of art intended to hasten both cultural and artistic dissolution."[7]

As examples Hassan mentions the literature of Genet and Beckett—what George Steiner calls the "literature of silence"—the self-abolishing art of Tinguely and Robert Morris, the mechanistic and repetitive art of Warhol, the non-structural music of John Cage, and the technical architecture of Buckminster Fuller.[8] All of this takes Early Modernism and its notion of radical discontinuity to an extreme leading to the hermeticism of the 1960s and 1970s. Because this later tradition was obviously different from the Heroic Modernism of the 1920s quite a few critics loosely applied the prefix "post." For instance the popular critics Paul Goldberger and Douglas Davis used it in the *New York Times* and *Newsweek* to discuss the ultramodern work of Hardy, Holzman and Pfeiffer, Cesar Pelli and Kevin Roche, all of which exaggerates the high-tech work of Mies and Le Corbusier.[9] The art critic Edward Lucie-Smith, like others, even applied it to Piano and Rogers's Pompidou Center.[10] In short, postmodern meant everything that was different from high modernism, and usually this meant skyscrapers with funny shapes, brash colors, and exposed technology. That such architects were against the pluralism, ornament, and convention of postmodernism was missed by these critics. They just adopted a current phrase for discontinuity and lumped every departure under it.

The same permissive categorization was practiced in artistic theory and criticism and so when conferences were held on the subject artists were confused as to whether they were supporting the postmodern, or against it.[11] In fact a whole book, *The Anti-Aesthetic: Essays on Postmodern Culture*, was dedicated to this confusion.[12] Here the editor Hal Foster uses it to mean a cultural and political resistance to the status quo. For one of the contributors, Craig Owens, it is the critical use of postindustrial techniques (computers and photography) in art and the "loss of master narratives" (he follows J. F. Lyotard in this). Frederic Jameson uses it as an umbrella term to cover all reactions to high modernism (again John Cage and William Burroughs), the leveling of distinctions between high- and mass-culture and two of its "significant features"—pastiche and schizophrenia. Jean Baudrillard refers to it as epitomizing our era and its "death of the subject" caused basically by television and the information revolution. ("We live in the ecstasy of communication. And this ecstasy is obscene."[13]) Most of the remaining authors use it in different ways, some of which have a relation to resisting or "deconstructing" the common assumptions of our culture. In short, it means almost everything and thus nearly nothing.

Before I discuss this "Nothing Postmodernism" where very little is at stake, I'd like to mention one of its causes: the view that the word can be appropriated to mean any rupture with high modernism. Rosalind Krauss's essay "Sculpture in the Expanded Field" printed in Foster's and another anthology on postmodern art shows this appropriation.[14] Her elegant and witty essay seeks to define all departures from sculpture that appear to break down the category of modernist sculpture—let us say Brancusi's *Endless Column*—and expand them to include such things as Christo's *Running Fence* and wrapped buildings, Robert Smithson's use of earth-covered mirrors in the Yucatan, a wooden maze by Alice Aycock constructed in 1972, and various earthworks and "marked sites" such as a sunken, framed hole in the ground executed by Mary Miss in 1978.

Krauss uses a structuralist diagram to draw this expanded field of sculpture—the objects that are *not* architecture, *not* landscape, indeed *not* sculpture, and her wit consists in making the diagram itself expand to include a lot of combined "nots." The strategy is not dissimilar to the modernist practice of defining things by what they are not, in order to maximize their differences and essentiality, but she presents their expansion as a "rupture" with modernism: "One after another Robert Morris, Robert Smithson, Michael Heizer, Richard Serra, Walter de Maria, Robert Irwin, Sol LeWitt, Bruce Nauman (between 1968 and 1970) had entered a situation the logical conditions of which can no longer be described as modernist."[15] In her diagrammatical, logical terms this is quite true, but then she goes on to make a false inference: "In order to name this historical rupture and the structural transformation of the cultural field that characterizes it, one must have recourse to another term. The one already in use in other areas of criticism is postmodernism. There seems no reason not to use it."

Oh yes there is *not*, to use the not-way of not-definition, for if one thing is not obscure it is that you can't define things usefully by what they are not. All the things in a room that are not men are not necessarily women: there is a near infinity of other classes of things. And those artists she mentions are not postmodernists, but really late-modernists. Why? Because like ultra- or neomodernists they take modernist disjunction and abstraction to an extreme. Essentially their practice goes against the thirty or so definers of postmodernism I have mentioned—all those connected with semantics, convention, historical memory, metaphor, symbolism, and respect for existing cultures. Their work is much closer to Agonistic Modernism, except it is more extreme, exaggerated—in short, "late."

Indeed this brings us to the essential definition of late-modernism: *in architecture it is pragmatic and technocratic in its social ideology and from about 1960 takes many of the stylistic ideas and values of modernism to an extreme in order to resuscitate a dull (or clichéd) language.*[16] Late-modern art is also singly coded in this way and like the modernism of Clement Greenberg tends to be self-referential and involved with its art-specific language, even minimalist in this concentration, as so many critics such as Umberto Eco have pointed out.[17]

Schismatic postmodernism is late-modernism. What I'm suggesting here is not a minor shift in nomenclature, but a complete reshuffling of categories: that is, to redefine as mostly "late" what Davis, Goldberger, Foster, Jameson, Lyotard, Baudrillard, Krauss, Hassan, and so many others often define as "post." It is mostly "late" because it is still committed to the tradition of the new and does not have a complex relation to the past, or pluralism, or the transformation of Western culture—a concern with meaning, continuity, and symbolism. I don't for a moment believe that these writers will agree with me, but I do believe that what is at stake is more than a pedantic distinction. It is a difference of values and philosophy. To call a late-modernist a postmodernist is tantamount to calling a Protestant a Catholic because they both practice a Christian religion. Or it is to criticize a donkey for being a bad sort of horse. Such category mistakes lead to misreadings, and this may be very fruitful and creative—the Russians read Don Quixote as a tragedy—but it is ultimately violent and barren.

Try to read Norman Foster's recently completed Hongkong Shanghai Bank as a postmodern building and you will get as far as the "non-door" where the two escalators are shifted at an angle to accommodate the Chinese principle of *Feng Shui*. Is it contextual or related to the buildings surrounding it and the vernaculars of Hong Kong and China? Only in the most oblique sense that it is "high-tech" and one side has a thin, picturesque group of towers. Is it involved with the "taste-cultures" of the inhabitants and users? Only in the subliminal sense that its "skin and bones" suggest muscle power. According to the permissive definitions of "Nothing Postmodernism" it should be a member of this class, because it is a "rupture" with modernism and fully committed to the tradition of the new. Indeed most of its parts, adopted from airplane and ship technology, were purpose-built in different parts of the globe precisely to be new. It is the first radical "multinational" building—parts were fabricated in Britain, Japan, Austria, Italy and America—resolved by all the technologies of the postindustrial society, including of course the computer and instant world communication, and therefore according to the definitions of J. F. Lyotard and others it should be a prime example of postmodernism. But it isn't, and if it were it would be a failure.

No, it is to be judged as the latest triumph of late-modernism and celebrated for what it intends to be, namely, the most powerful expression of structural trusses, lightweight technology, and huge open space stacked internally in the air. The cost of the building—and it is called the most expensive building in the world—directly reflects these intentions, for it turns out that the money went on the bridge-like structure and the superb use of finishing materials, surprising areas to take up so much of a budget. Thus, I don't mean only to criticize the building for its postmodern shortcomings, but to support it for its late-modern virtues. There are, as usual, the imaginative and consistent use of the technical language of architecture. The morality of late-modernism consists in this integrity of invention and usage; like

Clement Greenberg's defense of modernist morality the work has to be judged as a hermetic, internally related world where the meanings are self-referential. Literally, does the high-tech fit together and work, visually, poetically, and functionally? The answers to all these questions appear to be positive, although it is too soon to be sure.

The concept of postmodernism is often confused with late-modernism because they both spring from a postindustrial society. Of course there is a connection between these two "posts," but not the simple and direct one that the philosopher Jean-François Lyotard implies. He opens his book *The Postmodern Condition: A Report on Knowledge* with the elision of the two terms:

> The object of this study is the condition of knowledge in the most highly developed societies. I have decided to use the word postmodern to describe that condition. . . . I define postmodern as incredulity toward metanarratives. . . . Our working hypothesis is that the status of knowledge is altered as societies enter what is known as the postindustrial age and cultures enter what is known as the postmodern age.[18]

Lyotard's study is mostly concerned with knowledge in our scientific age, in particular the way it is legitimized through the "grand narratives" such as the liberation of humanity, progress, the emancipation of the proletariat, and increased power. These "master narratives," he contends, have gone the way of previous ones such as religion, the nation-state and the belief in the destiny of the West; they've become noncredible and incredible. Indeed all beliefs, or master narratives, become impossible in a scientific age, especially the role and ultimate legitimacy of science itself. Hence the nihilism, anarchism, and pluralism of "language games" which fight each other, hence his belief that postmodern culture entails a "sensitivity to differences" and a "war on totality."[19] Postmodern is then defined as "a period of slackening," a period in which everything is "delegitimized." Given this nihilism and the sociological jargon, one can understand why our Sunday reporter at *Le Monde* was so upset by the specter about to descend, like a fog of waffle, onto the breakfast table. Lyotard has almost defined postmodernism as this "slackening" relativity. But in another section he amazingly defines the "postmodern" as pre-modern: "What space does Cézanne challenge? The Impressionists. What object do Picasso and Braque attack? Cézanne's. . . . A work can become modern only if it is first postmodern. Postmodernism thus understood is not modernism at its end but in the nascent state, and this state is constant."[20]

This crazy idea at least has the virtue of being original and it has led to Lyotard's belief in continual experiment, the agonism of the perpetual avant-garde and continual revolution. This also led to his exhibition of experiments with the media at the Pompidou Center called *Les Immatériaux* which, from reports, appears to have been mislabeled postmodernist. I'm not sure, since I haven't seen the exhibition, but it is clear that Lyotard continues in his writing to confuse postmodernism with the latest avant-gardism, that is late-modernism. It's embarrassing that postmodernism's first philosopher should be so fundamentally wrong.

However it is not surprising, because the "mistake" has such a long pedigree, predating Ihab Hassan's work, on which Lyotard rests for so much of his cultural evidence. Thus we are at a "crisis" point—to use one of his concepts of legitimation—over whether to go on using the word postmodern to encompass two opposite meanings and diverging traditions. It is literally nonsense to continue with this linguistic confusion. Furthermore, I would argue that the meanings and definitions I have proposed—dichotomizing late- and postmodern—gain in power precisely to the extent that they are used together, because they elucidate opposite intentions, traditions of art and architecture which are fundamentally opposed to each other. Lyotard, because he is a philosopher and sociologist of knowledge and not a historian or critic of these cultural trends, is not finely tuned to their differences.

Having stated this case for a fundamental distinction between post- and late-modernism, one should, however, add some refinements which modify an absolute difference. Both traditions start about 1960, both react to the wane of modernism, and some artists and architects—for instance David Salle, Robert Longo, Mario Botta, Helmut Jahn, and Philip Johnson—either vacillate between or unite the two. This overlap, or existential mixing of categories, is what we would expect in any period after the Renaissance when, for instance, an artist such as Michelangelo could move from Early Renaissance to Mannerist and Baroque solutions of sculptural and architectural problems. So there are indeed many artists whom Hal Foster et al. include in their corpus as "postmodernists of resistance" who should also be included as postmodernists: Robert Rauschenberg, Laurie Anderson, some feminist art which uses conventional subject matter in an ironic way, Hans Haacke and others who might be termed "Agonistic" or combative. But they should be so classified only in so far as their intention was to communicate with society and its professional elites through the use of double coding. And even if such artists are termed postmodern, this doesn't guarantee their value, which must depend, as always, on the imaginative transformation of a shared symbolic system. The role of the critic must first be to define the field—that is, the very real traditions which are evolving—and then make distinctions of quality and value, a process I have started with an evolutionary tree showing the five main postmodern classical strands of art: the metaphysical, narrative, allegorical, and realist classicists, and those who share a classical sensibility (*What Is Postmodernism?* 37). We can see in this return to the larger Western tradition a slow movement of our culture, now worldwide, back to a "center which could not hold" (to misquote Yeats). The return has various causes, but among the most important is the idea that the value of any work must depend partly on tradition, both for its placement and quality. The tradition of the new made such a fetish of discontinuity that now a radical work of quality is likely to have a shock of the old.

Modern (1920–60)	Late-modern (1960–)	Postmodern (1960–)
IDEOLOGICAL		
1 one international style, or "no style"	unconscious style	double coding of style
2 utopian and idealist	pragmatic	"popular" and pluralist
3 deterministic form, functional	loose fit	semiotic form
4 *Zeitgeist*	late-capitalist	traditions and choice
5 artist as prophet/healer	suppressed artist	artist/client
6 elitist/for "everyman"	elitist professional	elitist and participative
7 holistic, comprehensive redevelopment	holistic	piecemeal
8 architect as savior/doctor	architect provides service	architect as representative and activist
STYLISTIC		
9 "straightforwardness"	supersensualism/slick-tech/high-tech	hybrid expression
10 simplicity	complex simplicity—oxymoron, ambiguous reference	complexity
11 isotropic space (Chicago frame, Domino)	extreme isotropic space (open office planning, "shed space"), redundancy, and flatness	variable space with surprises
12 abstract form	sculptural form, hyperbole, enigmatic form	conventional and abstract form
13 purist	extreme repetition and purist	eclectic
14 inarticulate "dumb box"	extreme articulation	semiotic articulation
15 machine aesthetic, straightforward logic, circulation, mechanical, technology, and structure	2nd machine aesthetic, extreme logic, circulation, mechanical, technology, and structure	variable mixed aesthetic depending on context; expression of content and semantic appropriateness toward function
16 anti-ornament	structure and construction as ornament	pro-organic and applied ornament
17 anti-representational	represent logic, circulation, mechanical, technology, and structure, frozen movement	pro-representation
18 anti-metaphor	anti-metaphor	pro-metaphor
19 anti-historical memory	anti-historical	pro-historical reference

20 anti-humor	unintended humor, malapropism	pro-humor
21 anti-symbolic	unintended symbolic	pro-symbolic
DESIGN IDEAS		
22 city in park	"monuments" in park	contextual urbanism and rehabilitation
23 functional separation	functions within a "shed"	functional mixing
24 "skin and bones"	slick skin with Op effects, wet-look distortion, sfumato	"Mannerist and Baroque"
25 *Gesamtkunstwerk*	reductive, elliptical gridism, "irrational grid"	all rhetorical means
26 "volume not mass"	enclosed skin volumes, mass denied; "all-over form"—synecdoche	skew space and extensions
27 slab, point block	extruded building, linearity	street building
28 transparency	literal transparency	ambiguity
29 asymmetry and "regularity"	tends to symmetry and formal rotation, mirroring, and series	tends to asymmetrical symmetry (Queen Anne Revival)
30 harmonious integration	packaged harmony, forced harmonization	collage/collision

CLASSIFYING MOVEMENTS ACCORDING TO THIRTY VARIABLES *Architects usually classify movements according to a few stylistic categories, but here a more extended list of variables is used to bring out the complexity of the situation: the overlap, contradictions, and differences among movements*

Table from Charles Jencks, *Architecture Today.*

NOTES

1. My own writing and lecturing on postmodernism in architecture started in 1975 and "The Rise of Post-Modern Architecture" was published in a Dutch book and a British magazine: *Architecture—Inner Town Government* (Eindhoven, 1975), and *Architecture Association Quarterly* 4 (1975). Subsequently Eisenman and Stern started using the term and by 1977 it had caught on. For a brief history see the "Footnote on the Term" in *The Language of Post-Modern Architecture*, 4th ed. (New York: Academy Editions, London/Rizzoli, 1984), 8.

2. Umberto Eco, *Postscript to the Name of the Rose* (New York: Harcourt Brace Jovanovich, 1984), 67–68.

3. Besides my own *The Language of Post-Modern Architecture* and *Current Architecture* (New York: Academy Editions, London/Rizzoli, 1982), and *Modern Movements in Architecture*, 2nd ed. (Harmondsworth: Penguin Books, 1985), see Paolo

Portoghesi, *After Modern Architecture* (New York: Rizzoli, 1982), and its updated version, *Postmodern* (New York: Rizzoli, 1983), and *Immagini del Post-Moderno* (Venice: Edizioni Chiva, 1983). See also Heinrich Klotz, *Die Revision der Moderne, Postmoderne Architektur, 1960–1980* and *Moderne und postmoderne Architektur der Gegenwart 1960–1980* (Braunschweig/Wiesbaden: Friedr. Vieweg & Sohn, 1984). We have debated his notion of postmodern architecture as "fiction" and this has been published in *Architectural Design* July 8, 1984, *Revision of the Modern*. See also my discussion of user and abuser of Post-Modern in "La Bataille des étiquettes," *Nouveaux plaisir d'architecture* (Paris: Centre Georges Pompidou) 1985, 25–33.

4. Anthony Blunt, *Some Uses and Misuses of the Terms Baroque and Rococo As Applied to Architecture* (Oxford, 1973); Charles Jencks, *Late-Modern Architecture* (New York: Academy Editions, London/Rizzoli, 1980), 32.

5. Ludwig Mies van der Rohe, "Industrialized Building" (1924), reprinted in *Programmes and Manifestos on 20th Century Architecture* (London: Lund Humphries, 1970), 81.

6. The two basic strands of modernism are discussed by many critics. See for instance Renato Poggioli, *The Theory of the Avant-Garde* (Cambridge, Mass.: Harvard University Press, 1968). The discussion of Bradbury and McFarlane is particularly relevant; see their "The Name and Nature of Modernism," in *Modernism 1890–1930*, ed. Malcolm Bradbury and James McFarlane (Harmondsworth: Penguin Books, 1976), 40–41, 46; Frank Kermode, "Modernisms," in *Modern Essays* (London, 1971). For architecture the best discussion is Robert Stern, "The Doubles of Post-Modern," *The Harvard Architectural Review* 1 (Spring 1980), although, as my text makes clear, I would use the term late-modern for his "Schismatic Post-Modern."

7. Ihab Hassan, "Joyce, Beckett, and the Postmodern Imagination," *Tri-Quarterly* 34 (Fall 1975): 200.

8. Ihab Hassan, *Paracriticisms: Seven Speculations of the Times* (Urbana: University of Illinois Press, 1975), 55–56.

9. For references see *The Language of Post-Modern Architecture*, p. 8.

10. The work of Achigram and Richard Rogers was often termed postmodern in the late 1970s before critics began to understand the term and its distinction from high-tech. Edward Lucie-Smith followed this usage in his book on modernism published around this time.

11. "Post-Modernism," a symposium at the Institute for Architecture and Urban Studies, 1981, attended by Christian Hubert, Sherrie Levine, Craig Owens, David Salle, and Julian Schnabel, later published in *Reallife* (30 March 1981).

12. *The Anti-Aesthetic: Essays on Postmodern Culture*, ed. Hal Foster (Port Townsend, Wash.: Bay Press, 1983).

13. Ibid., 130.

14. Ibid., 31–42. See also, *Theories of Contemporary Art*, ed. Richard Hertz (Englewood Cliffs: Prentice-Hall, 1985), 215–25. Postmodernism is discussed by various authors in a loose way in this anthology.

15. *Anti-Aesthetic*, 39.

16. The essential definitions of modern, late-modern, and postmodern were initially proposed by me in *AD News* (July 1981), published later in "Post-Modern Architecture: The True Inheritor of Modernism," *Transactions* 3, RIBA (1983), 37–40.

17. Eco, *Postscript to the Name of the Rose*, 66–67, note 9.

18. Jean-François Lyotard, *The Postmodern Condition: A Report on Knowledge* (Manchester: Manchester University Press, 1984), pp. xxiii, xxiv, 3. The book was first published in French in 1979.

19. Ibid., xxv, 82.

20. Ibid., 79.

THE PROBLEM OF THE POSTMODERN

C. Barry Chabot

During the past fifteen years we have increasingly heard and read about something variously termed "fabulism" (Scholes), "metafiction" (McCaffery), "surfiction" (Federman), and, with growing unanimity, "postmodernism." The former terms were typically developed in efforts to account for apparent changes of direction and emphasis within recent fiction. "Postmodernism," on the other hand, is a broader term and has been pressed into service to describe developments throughout the arts; it is even said that we live in a postmodern society. Any number of people obviously believe that a cultural rupture of some moment has occurred, and that its mark is discernible across the range of our cultural activities. There seems to be little agreement, however, about the precise nature and timing of the supposed break, and even less about how we can most adequately characterize its effects upon our cultural products.

I remain doubtful that a rupture of such magnitude has occurred and want here to register a minority report. Our lack of an adequate and widely accepted understanding of literary modernism makes many arguments for the postmodern initially plausible, but much of what has been termed postmodern derives quite directly from the work of earlier writers. In order to demonstrate the hesitancies, confusions, and contradictions within and between various characterizations of the postmodern, I want to investigate the work of several representative critics. For the sake of focus, I shall concentrate initially upon characterizations of our recent novel; if my conclusions are valid, they should apply as well to comparable accounts of our recent poetry and drama.

I

When Ihab Hassan writes in *Paracriticisms* that the "change in Modernism may be called Postmodernism," he emphasizes the continuity between these literary movements (43). He locates the origins of the latter in 1938, with the publication of Sartre's *La Nausée* and Beckett's *Murphy*, but he is not primarily attempting to define the sensibilities of entire eras. "Modernism," he writes, "does not suddenly cease so that Postmodernism may begin: they now coexist" (47). Modernism and postmodernism for Hassan thus provide competing visions of the contemporary predicament, and it is as likely that a particular work will be informed by the one as by the other. Hassan does not completely neglect the temporal dimension implied by the terms themselves. He understands both as responses to the character of life and thought in the twentieth century. If individuals earlier in the century had reason to be apprehensive about the possibilities then available for perpetuating viable forms of life, there has subsequently been even more reason for disquiet. Modernism and postmodernism, respectively, represent the literary equivalents of such more pervasive concerns. "Postmodernism," writes Hassan, "may be a response, direct or oblique, to the Unimaginable which Modernism glimpsed only in its most prophetic moments" (53). Such sentences award the primacy of vision to postmodernism, but its perceptiveness is largely the product of its times, which have made the awful possibilities we face only too clear.

Hassan defines neither modernism nor postmodernism. Instead he offers a catalogue of characteristic modernist concerns—urbanism, technologism, dehumanization, primitivism, eroticism, antinomianism, and experimentalism; he then glosses each, providing instances of the forms it takes within postmodernism. In regard to primitivism, for instance, Hassan writes that its modernist forms represented a use of ritual and myth to structure contemporary experience, whereas its postmodernist forms move away "from the mythic, toward the existential," initially in the work of the Beats and later "the post-existential ethos, psychedelics (Leary), the Dionysian ego (Brown), Pranksters (Kesey), madness (Laing), animism and magic (Castaneda)" (56). As his examples make clear, for Hassan postmodernism is not exclusively a literary phenomenon; rather, it represents a broad cultural response to pressing contemporary issues, and is as likely to emerge within social practices as within artistic products.

Despite the potential importance of the postmodernist program, and despite his own desire to stay in sympathy with whatever is most current, Hassan's assessment of postmodernism is finally ambiguous. He concedes that modernists frequently resorted to questionable means in shoring up such artistic authority as they could muster, citing Hemingway's code as an example, but observes that postmodernism "has tended toward artistic Anarchy in deeper complicity with things falling apart—or has tended toward Pop" (59). The choice between authoritarianism and anarchy seems a devil's choice, and it is not altogether clear, to Hassan at least, that the latter is unmistakably the course of wisdom. Finally, however, Hassan's reservations about a postmodern aesthetic go much deeper. It releases new imaginative energies, but Hassan worries that we might now have entered a time when no art "can help to engender the motives we must now acquire; or if we can

long continue to value an art that fails us" (59). I am not sure how to take
this reservation—does it imply that our needs are too pressing for us to
fiddle with art, or that our art already fails to provide us with the necessary
direction? In the end, Hassan suggests that postmodernism is in danger of
being overwhelmed by the very cultural crisis that originally called it into
existence.

Jerome Klinkowitz accepts Hassan's designation of postmodernism, and
thus needs another term to designate work manifesting what he takes to be
an independent and more recent impulse. He offers several—"Post-Contemporary," "disruptivist," "Superfiction," and most recently "self-apparent"—
but there are reasons to assimilate Klinkowitz's efforts within the broader
attempt to define postmodernism.[1] Klinkowitz has assumed the role of apologist for a relatively small group of recent fiction writers; he is, accordingly,
eager to differentiate their particular virtues from those of other writers.
Among readers of contemporary fiction, Klinkowitz is almost alone in believing that his writers form an identifiable school distinct from postmodernism.
Hassan, for instance, cites several writers Klinkowitz would term disruptivists when developing his own understanding of postmodernism. I shall
return to this question later, and shall assume for the present that, despite
his intentions, Klinkowitz is struggling to define a version of postmodernism.

Klinkowitz locates the emergence of disruptivist fiction "with the publishing season of 1967-68, when for the first time in a long time a clear trend in
literary history became apparent" (ix). Disruptivist fiction is particularly ada-
mant about the need to abandon the mimetic aspirations of the traditional
novel. "If the world is absurd," writes Klinkowitz, "if what passes for reality
is distressingly unreal, why spend time representing it" (32). Such statements suggest that the disruptivists believe the world is not now worth
representing, whereas others suggest that representation is not possible and
has always been a misplaced aspiration. Whatever the rationale, on
Klinkowitz's account disruptivists are concerned with "not just the reporting
of the world, but [with] the imaginative transformation of it" (32). The transformative power of the imagination enters this fiction in two ways. First, at
the thematic level, it figures in the plot, as in Vonnegut's use of time-travel in
Slaughterhouse-Five. More importantly, however, it appears in the self-
reflexiveness of its characters (who frequently know that they are fictive
constructs) and narrators (who frequently comment on the difficulties they
are having in constructing the piece at hand). Such narrative shifts frustrate
whatever tendencies readers might have to suspend disbelief and take the
work at hand as a representation of some common world; in the same way,
they perform the instructive function of demonstrating the ways and means
by which readers too make their worlds.

Hassan's postmodern always hovers on the edge of despair and enerva-
tion, but Klinkowitz's disruptivist fiction is almost programmatically playful
and energetic. "The writers we're discussing are out to create a good time,"
writes Klinkowitz in the prologue to *The Life of Fiction* (4). These qualities are

not ancillary to disruptivist fiction, and their absence is sufficient reason to read writers out of the disruptivist camp. Thus Klinkowitz terms Barth and Pynchon "regressive parodists," and apparently believes that the former's influential essay, "The Literature of Exhaustion," has retarded appreciation of the disruptivists (ix). Barth's self-reflexive characters typically feel caught in and by their self-consciousness. It is a condition they would escape, whereas in disruptivist fiction it is perceived precisely as the condition of imaginative freedom. Exuberance is also what obviously differentiates disruptivist fiction from the French New Novel. In each of his books Klinkowitz approvingly quotes Barthelme's observation that the French New Novel " 'seems leaden, selfconscious in the wrong way. Painfully slow-paced, with no leaps of the imagination, concentrating on the minutiae of consciousness, these novels scrupulously, in deadly earnest, parse out what can safely be said' " (174). Barthelme's description of the New Novel seems a catalogue of characteristics that disruptivist fiction on Klinkowitz's account is at pains to avoid.

Hassan's postmodernism and Klinkowitz's disruptivist fiction are similar in the emphasis each places on the transformative potential of the imagination. This similarity might account for Hassan's running together of writers from Beckett to Sukenick into a pervasive postmodernism; Klinkowitz, on the other hand, believes that to "the newer writers, Beckett is as traditional as Joyce" (LF 2), and accordingly would differentiate sharply among modern, postmodern, and disruptivist fiction. Hassan locates postmodernism within a general sense of cultural crisis and potential calamity; although he has written a cultural history, *The American 1960s*, Klinkowitz concentrates on the writers in question and rarely alludes to larger cultural issues. This difference in the ways they situate their work might account for a corresponding difference in tone: Hassan is prophetic, edgy, uncertain that the imagination will prove equal to the tasks at hand; Klinkowitz can be as bouncy as the authors he values, and since he sets the imagination no particular problems to solve he need not doubt its adequacy.

Alan Wilde also finds an affirmation at the core of what he terms postmodernism, but its character is far less exuberant and has quite different sources. *Horizons of Assent: Modernism, Postmodernism, and the Ironic Imagination* is a closely reasoned study of the shift in the novel during this century from modernism, through what Wilde terms "late modernism," to postmodernism. Wilde pays particular attention to the characteristic uses and meanings of irony; he argues that these shift as the century progresses and that each of his three phases corresponds to a characteristic form of irony.

For Wilde modernism is characterized by what he terms disjunctive or absolute irony, "the conception of equal and opposed possibilities held in a state of total poise, or, more briefly still, the shape of an indestructible, unresolvable paradox" (21). Wilde distinguishes absolute irony from an earlier and more pervasive form, which he terms "mediate irony." It "imagines a world lapsed from a recoverable . . . norm" (9) and has as its goal the recovery of that earlier wholeness. The modern ironist, by way of contrast, confronts a world apparently in such fundamental disarray that no recovery of previous states seems possible. The modern ironist nonetheless attempts to impose a shape or order, and for his efforts achieves "not resolution but closure—an aesthetic closure that substitutes for the notion of paradise regained an image . . . of a paradise fashioned by man himself" (10). Since the order achieved by the modern writer is exclusively aesthetic, he ends at a remove from the world he would make cohere. With no course of action clearly preferable to any other, in the end the modern ironist is finally inactive as well as detached, unable to commit himself to the world without thereby destroying the order he has struggled to create.

Wilde illustrates his definition of the modernist program primarily through references to the novels of E. M. Forster and Virginia Woolf. In the work of other and generally younger writers, especially those who come to attention during the thirties, he sees a subtle shift indicative of what he terms the "late modern" sensibility. His chief examples of the late-modern are Christopher Isherwood and Ivy Compton-Burnett. These writers are typically less concerned with depth than with surfaces; as a result, the relations between language and world are thought to be less problematic than among the modernists, and appearances are again held to be valuable in understanding people and events. The obvious pleasure that Isherwood and his narrators take in some aspects of their worlds not only contrasts with the discomfort typical of the modernists, it also implies that they have partially overcome the detachment characteristic of the latter.

In their participation in their worlds, the late-modernists anticipate what Wilde terms postmodernism. Although he calls Woolf's *Between the Acts* "still the most impressive of *postmodern* novels" (48), Wilde argues that postmodernism "is essentially an American affair" (12).[2] On Wilde's account, postmodernists typically deploy "suspensive irony." It involves the perception of "experience as random and contingent . . . rather than—the modernist view—simply fragmented" (27). Nonetheless, postmodernism does not press for or impose order, even one limited to the aesthetic realm; instead, the contingent world is simply accepted. Modernist paradox thereby gives way "to quandary, to a low-keyed engagement with a world of perplexities and uncertainties, in which one can hope, at best, to achieve what Forster calls 'the smaller pleasures of life' and Stanley Elkin, its 'small satisfactions' " (10).

Wilde isolates two strands within postmodernism. The first consists roughly of Klinkowitz's disruptivists, especially Ronald Sukenick and Raymond Federman, but Wilde attends less to their statements of intention than the effects of their practice. On Wilde's reading, Sukenick and Federman, for all their overt hostility to modernism, end by unintentionally reproducing, in an attenuated form, many modernist dilemmas; "they are," he writes, "Modernism's lineal descendants (or perhaps its illegitimate sons), patricides manqués" (144). Wilde's other strand of postmodernism employs "generative irony: the attempt, inspired by the negotiations of self and world, to create tentatively and provisionally, anironic enclaves of value in the face of—but not in place of—a meaningless universe" (148). The world envisioned in these works is even more contingent than that found in modernist fiction, but its narrators and characters accede to that condition, recognizing that it cannot be redressed. Instead, they recognize that their worlds contain pleasures as well as pains, and therefore choose not to distance themselves, in the manner of their predecessors, from the phenomenal world. Elkin's *The Living End*, Apple's "The Oranging of America" and "Disneyad," and several of Barthelme's later stories serve as Wilde's primary examples of this postmodernism. It embodies "a vision that lacks the heroism of the modernist enterprise but that, for a later and more disillusioned age, recovers its humanity" (165).

Wilde's characterization of postmodernism does not, like those by Hassan and Klinkowitz, place a premium upon the imagination. For Hassan, the postmodern imagination must redeem a world on the brink of calamity, and its prospects for success are at best problematic; for Klinkowitz, the world similarly requires redemption, but he apparently has no doubt that the postmodern imagination is equal to the task. On Wilde's account, postmodern writers find the world fully as contingent, but he finds in them a willingness to endure the random and a capacity to identify sources of gratification within it. Both Klinkowitz and Wilde believe that an affirmative moment defines postmodern fiction, but they identify its sources differently. For Klinkowitz, what is affirmed is finally the supposedly transformative power of the imagination; for Wilde, on the other hand, it is the phenomenal world itself, which, amidst its various turnings, upon occasion throws up gratifying possibilities.

II

The efforts by Hassan, Klinkowitz, and Wilde to define postmodernism are representative of many others, and display many of the same strengths and weaknesses. They bring contemporary writers to our attention, provide insights into their particular ambitions, and begin to place them within the strands of literary and cultural history. Each defines postmodernism, however, in ways that are not only distinct but in the end mutually exclusive. Wilde's late-modern, for instance, is not the same as Hassan's postmodern, even though both are located in the thirties; and Hassan links the fiction of Beckett and Sukenick, whereas Klinkowitz sees the latter as being in rebellion against the former. The primary difficulties in the way of the very concept of postmodernism, in other words, involve its definition and inclusiveness.

As the term suggests, postmodernism is invariably defined vis-à-vis modernism—postmodernism is what comes after and in opposition to modernism. But there is little agreement about the nature of modernism, many characterizations of it enjoying some degree of currency within the profession. In Wilde's account, for instance, modernism is equivalent to the use of a particular form of irony, what he terms absolute irony. I have no quarrel with his readings of Forster and Woolf, but I find it difficult to extend the term so defined to cover the work of other writers typically termed modernists, such as Fitzgerald and Hemingway, or Stevens and Hart Crane. One wonders, in other words, if Wilde's postmoderns would seem equally distinct from modernism if they were read within the context of earlier American instead of British writers. Perhaps the differences that Wilde finds derive as much from differences between the national literary traditions, differences obscured by his framework, as from any supposed change in the literary sensibility that has occurred over time. Although I frequently find Wilde's readings of individual works compelling, such doubts leave me with questions about the history he constructs from them.

Unlike Wilde, Klinkowitz does not venture detailed accounts of the succession of literary sensibilities during the century. His conception of disruptivist or self-apparent fiction is the most narrow of the three surveyed. It identifies writers of a particular school, but then claims that it represents an entire generation of writers come of age during 1967–68. In *Literary Disruptions* he writes of a "generational gap" between Barth and Barthelme, which "has obstructed the critical understanding of new fiction" (175). When he reduces the relations between disruptivist and other fiction to the terms of generational conflict, Klinkowitz introduces several difficulties. One of his disruptivists, Kurt Vonnegut, is in fact eight years older than John Barth, and his first novel was published in 1952, four years before Barth's *The Floating Opera*; Klinkowitz is thus in the anomalous position of having a rebellious son who in fact arrives on the scene earlier than the figurative father. Such local anomalies, however, are the least of Klinkowitz's conceptual difficulties. I want to discuss three that particularly disable his argument.

First, Klinkowitz is concerned largely with younger or at least recently arrived writers who clearly feel a need to make a space for themselves on the literary scene. They do so in part by issuing manifestos and granting interviews in which they attempt to differentiate their own efforts from those of earlier and already established writers. As an apologist for these writers, Klinkowitz takes them at their word, rarely questioning either their announced goals, the measure of their success in meeting them, or their statements concerning the position of their own work in regard to that of other writers. A curiously naive species of literary history is the result, especially when one considers that Klinkowitz writes at the same time that Harold Bloom and others have been demonstrating how complicated the relations among writers can be. Klinkowitz's literary sons (and they are all sons) overcome their literary fathers with little difficulty, and the latter never survive to disfigure the former's efforts. We now know to be suspicious of such characterizations of literary succession, where literary influence is conceived purely as a negative affair and breaks between literary generations appear absolute.

Second, Klinkowitz, like the writers he admires, is so intent upon celebrating this generation that he fails to recognize the ways in which it simply continues or modifies the literary heritage. Wilde, for instance, observes that "the Surfictionists recall ('in attenuated form') nothing so much as the aesthetic manifestos of the earlier decades of the century" (144). When Sukenick and Federman engage in polemics against the novel as currently practiced and invent neologisms to identify themselves, they continue the tradition and rhetoric of Pound, Breton, and other poets earlier in the century. Indeed, one way of understanding these writers involves recognizing the extent to which they have adapted to the writing of fiction many of the practices common to poets during the teens and twenties. Fitzgerald, Hemingway, and Faulkner did not issue manifestos, nor did they devote much energy to berating other novelists to their own advantage. Poets of that time, especially those who self-consciously considered themselves part of the avant-garde, did engage in such activities, and the Surfictionists seemingly follow their example, simply adapting it to the conditions of another time and genre. This adaptation is particularly clear in the case of Sukenick, who wrote a dissertation and first book on the poetics of Wallace Stevens. In his own subsequent fiction Sukenick adapts Stevens's poetics to the condition of the contemporary novel, but large portions of the poet's work survive the adaptation virtually unaltered. Klinkowitz simply passes over such borrowings, either because he does not notice them, because they weaken his case, or because he believes the transportation of poetic doctrines and practices to fiction in itself constitutes a significant innovation. Whatever the reason, the neglect of such continuities with writers earlier in the century casts doubt upon Klinkowitz's account of the disruptivists.

Although Wilde does not use the language of generations and is characteristically more cautious in suggesting the kinds of departures that constitute postmodernism, his own account of the phenomenon encounters similar problems. Stanley Elkin is one of Wilde's exemplary postmoderns. Elkin wrote a dissertation on Faulkner and has said in an interview that Saul Bellow is probably the writer who has influenced him most strongly. "To the extent that I imitate anyone," he continued, "I think I may—in dialogue—imitate Saul Bellow" (140). Few people, including Bellow himself, would consider Bellow a postmodern writer, and Faulkner is certainly one of the foremost American modernists. Like Faulkner and Bellow, Elkin writes an extremely rhetorical prose. Although each possesses a distinctive voice and puts it to distinctive ends (consider, for instance, the differences between Faulkner's Flem Snopes and Elkin's Ben Flesh in *The Franchiser*), it seems excessive to posit an additional difference between them of the kind usually associated with the transition between modern and postmodern.

Modernism, in its usual usage, is a fairly capacious term, one covering a range of literary practices. A final difficulty in the way Klinkowitz and others typically propose definitions of the postmodern involves their violation of modernism in this larger sense. "Modernism" is not a term equivalent to "Imagism," "Futurism," "Surrealism," "Vorticism" and the like, which refer to specific literary schools or movements; instead, it is the term invoked to suggest what such particular and divergent programs have in common. It is a *period* concept; and its use involves the claim that in the end, and whatever their obvious differences, the individual energies of the time possess enough family resemblances that it makes sense to refer to them collectively. Modernism refers to whatever Ezra Pound and Wallace Stevens, Ernest Hemingway and William Faulkner, to name only American writers whose credentials as modernists seem beyond question, have in common. By its very nature, then, modernism is a second-order concept.

Since modernism is a period concept, one encompassing many divergent specific movements, it is likely to be surpassed or replaced only by a concept of the same kind and with comparable reach. The emergence of Surrealism, for instance, did not represent the overcoming of modernism so much as the emergence of another dimension within it. When we consider the various claims being made for the emergence of what is being called "postmodernism," we must ask whether the tendencies in question resemble in kind Surrealism or modernism. Klinkowitz, as we have seen, believes that the disruptivists form an identifiable "school" (x); we have also seen that they are unmistakably indebted to modernist poets for their means of self-promotion and their aesthetic. There are thus reasons to believe that these writers represent, like the Surrealists, a late development within modernism rather than its replacement. The rhetoric used in clearing themselves a place, of course, makes larger claims; but I understand the rhetorical intensity as itself in part a legacy from modernism, and in part as deriving from the felt urgency, at this late date, of claiming some necessarily marginal territory as its own.

Unlike Klinkowitz, Hassan recognizes that modernism is a period concept. He acknowledges the diversity of literary modernism when he catalogues its various schools and movements. His lists, however, fall short of providing definitions for either modernism or its supposed successor, because he does not indicate what the items on either list have in common, or what differentiates them from other contemporary cultural phenomena. He provides something of an anatomy without a conception of the whole the various organs and limbs finally compose. His attention is on the immediate future, or better on the question of whether we shall have one, and does not pause over what might be considered academic questions.

The situation in regard to Wilde's characterization of recent literary history and the emergence of the postmodern is somewhat more complicated. Wilde defines modernism narrowly, as the consequences that follow from the use of what he terms absolute irony. The emergence more recently of what Wilde terms suspensive or generative irony provides the grounds for claiming that it constitutes a new or postmodern sensibility. The narrow conception of modernism, in other words, is what lends credence to the claims for postmodernism; but, as mentioned earlier, I doubt the adequacy of Wilde's characterizations of modernism. My doubts take two forms. First, I doubt that it is possible to say that the entire range of modern novelists employ absolute irony. It seems that Wilde has mistaken a form of modernism for modernism itself, much as if he had identified it with, say, Pound's Imagism. Second, even if Wilde could make a reasonable case for the pervasiveness of absolute irony in this body of fiction, I do not believe he would thereby be identifying its most distinctive feature. I do not believe, in other words, that one can define modernism formally, despite its own obvious formal intensities; as a period concept, modernism must be approached more broadly and its distinctive features sought in the relationships it establishes with both the literary tradition and the immediate cultural context.

Horizons of Assent is in most respects the best book now available on our recent fiction, and Wilde's failure to develop a satisfactory account of postmodernism is therefore especially instructive. By its nature the postmodern is conceived in contrast to the modern—the era, sensibility, or set of literary strategies it would supplant. The initial plausibility of Wilde's description of postmodernism turns out to depend upon his prior conception of modernism. When that conception is found wanting, the claims for an emergent postmodernism are simultaneously thrown into doubt. In the absence of an adequate and widely accepted conception of modernism, we shall probably continue to be presented with claims in behalf of an emergent postmodern; but at least for the near term I doubt that upon inspection any will prove any more substantial than those already proposed by Hassan, Klinkowitz, and Wilde.[3]

III

In a series of recent essays, Fredric Jameson has been developing his own conception of postmodernism. It is explicitly a period concept, and thus does not fall prey to the difficulties enumerated above. Jameson believes that postmodernism has become the cultural dominant for the entire social order; accordingly, its force is to be found as much in the economy, the cinema, philosophy, and architecture as in literature itself. Indeed, Jameson says that his own formulation of postmodernism initially took shape in response to the continuing debates concerning the nature of contemporary architecture.[4] Since Jameson's use of the term is so distinctive among literary critics, it will be instructive to see if it proves more adequate to its appointed task.

At crucial points in these essays, after lengthy discussions of various cultural manifestations of what he terms postmodernism, Jameson alludes to its characteristic economic forms. His conception of economic postmodernism clearly derives from Ernest Mandel's *Late Capitalism*. Mandel argues that Western capitalism has evolved through three distinct stages: market capitalism, monopoly capitalism, and since the 1940s, what Jameson calls multinational capitalism. This latest form simultaneously clarifies the logic of capitalism and, to an unprecedented degree, expands its reach, drawing the entire globe within its ambit. In his contribution to *The Sixties without Apology*, Jameson suggests that the upheavals of that period parallel the culminating moments of the transition from monopoly to multinational capitalism, a shift that was largely completed by the early seventies. The postmodern, or so Jameson argues, is the culture appropriate to this last phase of capitalism, just as realism and modernism, respectively, had been appropriate to its earlier forms (78).

Jameson enumerates a number of constitutive features of this postmodern culture—among them, "a new depthlessness," "a consequent weakening of historicity," "a whole new type of emotional ground tone" (58), and the dissolution of the individual subject—but a new sense of space seems to hold a privileged position. The preoccupation of modernism with "the elegiac mysteries of *durée* and of memory" (64) have been replaced within the postmodern by a comparably intense concern with spatial questions. This apparent shift makes Jameson's interest in contemporary architecture especially relevant. He analyzes John Portman's Bonaventura Hotel in Los Angeles as postmodern, and suggests that the building aspires less to be a part of its environment than to be "a total space, a complete world, a kind of miniature city" (81), capable of replacing the city itself. Its interior is a stage for continual movement via escalators and exposed elevators; but what most distinguishes the building is the way it deprives patrons of spatial coordinates so that they are often unable to relocate shops on its balconies. Jameson believes that the confusion felt by the visitor to the Bonaventura Hotel is the architectural equivalent of a more fundamental confusion felt by inhabitants of the postmodern era; namely, our inability "to map the great global multinational and decentered communicational network in which we find ourselves caught as individual subjects" (84). Postmodern architecture, in Jameson's eyes, reproduces the experiential conditions of multinational capitalism.

In a review of two recent novels, Don Delillo's *The Names* and Sol Yurick's *Richard A.*, Jameson illustrates how this difficulty manifests itself within fiction. The latter is a version of the common conspiracy novel (the postmodern, says Jameson, effects a new relation with the forms of popular culture [PC 54–55]); it uses the image of the telephone system to suggest the ways in which people's lives have become interconnected. That image represents Yurick's attempt to conceptualize or map the locations of his characters within a world as disorienting as Portman's hotel. Delillo's narrator is an American abroad, an employee of a risk insurance firm, who is increasingly unable to assess the risks in an increasingly dangerous world. He picks up pieces of information, fragments of puzzling knowledge, but cannot make them cohere into anything resembling a map of his surroundings. Each of these novels, according to Jameson, struggles with the special spatial dilemma of contemporary life: "That dilemma can be schematically described as the increasing incompatibility—or incommensurability—between individual experience, existential experience, as we go on looking for it in individual biological bodies, and structural meaning, which can now ultimately derive only from the world system of multinational capitalism" (116). The solutions found in these works differ markedly: Yurick constructs an image that evokes the interconnections that cannot be directly experienced, whereas Delillo renders the experience of living amidst fragments that, however suggestive of some larger order, resist our effort to piece them together.

Jameson's account of the postmodern is immensely suggestive. He seems to be a person unable to forget or ignore anything; his work, accordingly, invariably contains striking analogies and connections among the most disparate phenomena. I have only sketched a portion of his argument, but it should be clear that his conception of the postmodern differs strikingly from those discussed earlier. In particular, Jameson's postmodern is systematically a period concept, one that reaches not only across various movements and genres, but as well across the various arts and other social institutions in the contemporary world. Its very reach, however, produces an order of difficulties distinct from those discussed in regard to Hassan, Klinkowitz, and Wilde.

As we have seen, Jameson coordinates an apparent preoccupation with space with the establishment of a genuinely multinational economic system. He recognizes, of course, that the economic system became increasingly international throughout the earlier period of monopoly capitalism, as previously isolated cultures were penetrated and opened as markets. Jameson believes, however, that the effects upon local cultures of these earlier penetrations were comparably benign and that they are now being dramatically transformed as the logic of multinational capitalism takes hold on a global scale. I am not in a position to judge the adequacy of such sweeping claims; I do question, however, some of the cultural consequences Jameson would derive from them. In particular, I question his claim that contemporary arts are uniquely concerned with locating the individual within some "postmodern hyperspace" (83). Jameson himself makes substantial use of Kevin Lynch's *The Image of the City*, which argues that the "alienated city is above all a space in which people are unable to map (in their minds) either their own positions or the urban totality in which they find themselves" (89). Such cities and the confusions to which they give rise predate postmodernism, but Jameson nowhere differentiates specifically postmodern forms. Similarly, since at least the early years of this century Western culture has been exploring the implications of an increasingly interconnected world; such explorations have taken various forms, such as the use of artist resources drawn from other cultures, and the depiction of travel through distant and disorienting lands. The culminating achievement of Jameson's most recent book, *The Political Unconscious*, is his reading of Conrad's *Lord Jim*, one of many exemplary works concerned with such issues. Neither experiences of spatial dislocation nor the existence of a multinational world, in other words, are unique to the last decade. The manifestations of both might have changed and become more pronounced, but Jameson would then have to demonstrate how differences in intensity have become differences in kind, such that one can speak of a distinctly postmodern disorientation. I suspect that Jameson's reliance upon Mandel's economic stages compels him to make claims for corresponding cultural transformations that he has not as yet adequately supported.

As we have seen, architecture holds a special place within Jameson's conception of postmodern culture. Not only is it the art primarily concerned with the spaces we inhabit; the recent debates within architecture have also informed Jameson's own formulations in important ways. Within architecture, the claims for postmodernism have developed in an especially clear way, and Jameson has largely appropriated these claims for more sweeping purposes. I believe that the reason postmodernism has emerged with special clarity within architecture has to do largely with the remarkable agreement within that field about the nature of modernism, the aesthetic it would replace. Architectural modernism consists largely of the so-called International Style. The increasingly strident reaction against the main tenets of this style is carried out in the name of postmodernism. The comparative uniformity of architectural modernism lends credibility to the claims of its new rivals that they constitute a genuinely postmodern alternative.

The situation within architecture, in other words, is quite different from that within the other arts, particularly literature. Literary modernism, as we have seen, has been characterized by a great diversity of separate movements and styles. It possesses nothing comparable to the Seagram Building. Since many different and competing aesthetic programs collectively constitute literary modernism, the claims of any particular program to supercede literary modernism per se must be scrutinized with some care; upon inspection, as we have seen, such programs are likely to represent new alternatives within modernism, not alternatives to it. The claims for the emergence of a genuine architectural postmodernism, on the other hand, possess a greater initial credibility due to the more monolithic quality of its predecessor.

Different cultural spheres, then, seemingly require different conceptualizations in terms of periods. By way of explanation, it might be said that different spheres evolve at different paces, depending upon a welter of factors, including both internal dynamics and their locations within the culture as a whole. In the case at hand, however, it is probably more to the point that the parallel between literary and architectural modernism was never more than an analogy. That is, roughly contemporary movements within architecture and literature were both termed modernism, but their contemporaneity and designations were all that they had in common. The mere fact that both have been termed modernism has clearly tempted many to claim more substantial similarities between them, or to see both as manifestations of an overarching cultural shift; but such findings have invariably been metaphoric or analogic: architectural and literary modernism have about as much in common as any two contemporaries named John Smith.

Jameson, in brief, errs in attempting to apply the debate within contemporary architectural circles to contemporary culture generally. What might be true of one art need not be true of others. In particular, a genuine postmodern alternative might be emerging within architecture; but we have less reason to believe that a corresponding phenomenon is occurring within literature, due to the different nature of what is called literary modernism. A rhetoric of postmodernism might be common to both fields, but in the latter it is misplaced, at most a sign of impatience. Since Jameson is attempting to develop a period concept that encompasses all of social life, he presumes that changes occur across a broad front and thus discounts the conditions specific to discrete cultural spheres. As a Marxist, Jameson knows that contending energies are likely to be operative at any particular time, and that resolutions among them achieved in one sphere need not have occurred elsewhere. Social life changes unevenly. In his work on postmodernism, however, Jameson's awareness of these facts remains theoretical; whenever he gets to actual cases, postmodernism seems to be progressing apace in every cultural sphere.

If Jameson sometimes argues that significant changes are occurring within all cultural spheres, at other times his argument for an emergent postmodern culture takes a different form:

> The first point to be made about the conception of periodization in dominance, therefore, is that even if all the constitutive features of postmodernism were identical and continuous with those of an older modernism—a position I feel to be demonstrably erroneous but which only an even lengthier analysis of modernism proper could dispel—the two phenomena would still remain utterly distinct in their meaning and social function, owing to the very different positioning of postmodernism in the economic system of late capital, and beyond that, to the transformation of the very sphere of culture in contemporary society. (PC 57)

Jameson here argues that the conditions under which cultural production and reception take place have so changed that culture itself has been thoroughly transformed. I in fact agree with this assessment, but would not go on to say that we therefore now have a postmodern literary culture. American literary modernism was crucially shaped by its relations with the whole of contemporary social life; but it is best *defined* by the set of strategies it developed in response, and thus by the relations it establishes with the contemporary social order. Consistency would seem to demand that a proper literary postmodernism be defined in the same manner; that is, not alone by the social conditions in which it reaches us, but as well by the strategies it deploys for existing within those conditions.

Jameson is currently embarked upon an anatomy of contemporary culture; literary matters obviously figure in this undertaking, but only in a subsidiary manner. The entire undertaking is prone to the kind of error we have already seen in regard to his generalization of architectural debates. It is instructive to compare the difficulties encountered by Jameson in developing a conception of postmodernism with those encountered by Klinkowitz and Wilde. The latter, as we saw, generated initially plausible definitions of the postmodern by countering it with an impoverished sense of modernism. In particular, they failed to acknowledge that modernism is a second-order, period concept, and thus proposed definitions of postmodernism that could as well or better be conceived as developments within modernism itself. Jameson, on the other hand, knows that modernism is a period concept. His generalization of the situation within architecture, however, provides him with a fairly monolithic modernism against which he can conceive a postmodern alternative. Architectural modernism, in brief, serves the same function in Jameson's formulations that absolute irony serves in Wilde's. Since he conceives postmodernism as a period concept, Jameson then wants to locate parallel developments in other cultural spheres. In the process, however, he typically minimizes crucial differences among the spheres, thereby creating the erroneous appearance of a culture undergoing change in a fairly uniform manner. Jameson knows that cultural change is an uneven affair, but the ambition to describe an entire cultural transformation apparently leads him to pay more attention to claims for cultural change, and then to lend his voice to them, than the available evidence seems to warrant.

IV

Our survey of difficulties encountered in proposing definitions of some emergent postmodernism leads to several proposals. First, before we can speak meaningfully of the postmodern we require an adequate conception of modernism. That conception, at least in regard to literary modernism, must guard against mistaking one of its constitutive movements (Surrealism, for example) for modernism itself; it must, that is, be a period concept, able to clarify what its different and competing movements have in common. That definition, too, should be specific to literature. The existence of something termed modernism in other cultural realms does not mean that these various artistic modernisms have much in common. Different cultural realms have different histories, needs, and opportunities; and these differences combine to assure that "modernism" will mean different things in each. Finally, we should profit from the example of Wilde and at least initially confine our investigations of literary modernism to individual national traditions. Otherwise we too are likely to mistake differences between national literatures for developments within literature itself. Different national literatures differ in the same ways that literature differs from architecture; since at any given time a national literature represents a specific disposition of cultural forces, each reacts uniquely to any attempt to introduce new and necessarily competing aesthetic programs. The distinctive colorations achieved by literary modernism within the British and American traditions are largely due to the native traditions, with their existing relations among competing interests.[5] It seems only prudent, therefore, that we attend to the configuration achieved by literary modernism within single national literatures before venturing more expansive characterizations of it. This research strategy was recently pursued successfully by June Howard, whose *Form and Function in American Literary Naturalism* conceives the work of Jack London and others as responses to the particular disposition of social and literary forces in the United States at the turn of the century. I am suggesting, in short, that we pursue a comparable program in regard to American literary modernism, for until we have an adequate conception of literary modernism, all claims for anything called postmodernism, like those addressed here, are likely to be premature.

It might be argued that these difficulties in establishing the canon and shape of a nascent postmodernism are only to be expected. The argument might invoke the authority of Thomas Kuhn, and claim that such critics are attempting to describe a shift between prevailing paradigms, and that such confusions are characteristic of transitional periods, times that lack the securities provided by stable intellectual coordinates. The tools of the old order are not appropriate to the new, assuring that those who use them will fail; the intellectual tools of the new order, on the other hand, are either unfamiliar or not yet to hand, with the result that their use is uncertain. Such arguments beg the question. They assume that we are in fact witnessing the emergence of some genuinely postmodern culture, whereas I want to question that assumption. It seems to me at least equally plausible that what some are calling postmodernism is actually a late development or mutation within modernism itself. I have presented several arguments to support my contention: (1) that no satisfactory and widely accepted account of postmodernism now exists; (2) that much of what is called postmodern in fact derives directly from modernism; and (3) that most arguments for its existence achieve their initial plausibility largely through impoverished characterizations of modernism, especially characterizations that neglect its nature as a second-order concept.

I suspect that the term's currency has more to do with impatience than with actual conceptual shifts. Modernism has been with us for the better part of the century. Its own restless search for innovation in part informs efforts to move beyond it. Some contemporary writers want to claim for their own efforts as radical a departure from now established strategies as that achieved earlier in the century. All honor seems to belong to the founders, and these writers want to avoid thinking of themselves as like Kuhn's normal scientists, working out the residual problems left them by the true innovators. Comparable motives inspire their academic apologists. In the end, as Frank Kermode has shown, there is considerable satisfaction in believing that one inhabits a cusp between eras, not the least of which is the belief that one is replicating the heroic phase of modernism. We might sympathize with such desires, but it seems to me that we should receive announcements of postmodernism's arrival as skeptically as we do commercials for other new products in the marketplace.

Whatever the merits of my arguments, the term "postmodern" has entered our lexicon and will doubtless continue to be used. Too many factors conspire to keep it in circulation, not least of which is inertia, the tendency for anything once set in motion to continue on its way. At the moment, however, the term is an empty marker. It holds a place in our language for a concept that might one day prove necessary; in the meantime, it is the recipient of the ambitions and apprehensions that our prospects for the future evoke.

NOTES

1. The first two terms appear in *Literary Disruptions*, the third in *The Life of Fiction*, and the last in *The Self-Apparent Word*. Unless otherwise indicated, all quotations of Klinkowitz are from *Literary Disruptions*.

2. This claim obviously puts Wilde's conception of postmodernism at odds with Hassan's and in line with Klinkowitz's and Rother's.

3. The tendency to reduce modernism to some caricature of itself in order to get a definition of postmodernism off the ground is especially strong when critics define both terms simply against each other and in isolation from the implicit series of period concepts; see, for example, Lodge.

4. "Postmodernism" 54. Unless otherwise indicated, all quotations of Jameson are from this essay.

5. Compare the opening sentences of Jeffrey Herf's *Reactionary Modernism*: "There is no such thing as modernity in general. There are only national societies, each of which becomes modern in its own fashion" (1). Herf studies a phenomenon much wider than literary, architectural, or any other specific cultural modernism, but his research strategy resembles my proposals.

WORKS CITED

Barthelme, Donald. "After Joyce." *Location* 1 (1964): 13–16.

Elkin, Stanley. Interview. *Contemporary Literature* 16 (1975): 131–45.

Federman, Raymond. "Surfiction—Four Propositions in Form of an Introduction." In *Surfiction: Fiction Now and Tomorrow*. Ed. Raymond Federman, 5–15. Chicago: Swallow, 1975.

Hassan, Ihab. *Paracriticisms: Seven Speculations of the Times*. Urbana: U. of Illinois Press, 1975.

Herf, Jeffrey. *Reactionary Modernism: Technology, Culture, and Politics in Weimar and the Third Reich*. New York: Cambridge University Press, 1984.

Howard, June. *Form and Function in American Literary Naturalism*. Chapel Hill: U. of North Carolina Press, 1985.

Jameson, Fredric. "Periodizing the Sixties." In *The Sixties without Apologies*. Ed. Sohnya Sayres et al., 178–209. Minneapolis: U. of Minnesota Press, 1984.

_____ "The Politics of Theory: Ideological Positions in the Postmodernism Debate." *New German Critique* 33 (1984): 53–65.

_____ "Postmodernism, or the Cultural Logic of Late Capitalism." *New Left Review* 146 (1984): 53–92.

_____ Review of *The Names*, by Don Delillo, and *Richard A.*, by Sol Yurick. *Minnesota Review* 22 (1984): 116–22.

_____ "Wallace Stevens." *New Orleans Review* 11 (1984): 10–19.

Kermode, Frank. *The Sense of an Ending: Studies in the Theory of Fiction.* New York: Oxford University Press, 1967.

Klinkowitz, Jerome. *The Life of Fiction.* Urbana: U. of Illinois Press, 1977.

_____ *Literary Disruptions: The Making of a Post-Contemporary American Fiction.* Urbana: U. of Illinois Press, 1975.

_____ *The Self-Apparent Word: Fiction As Language / Language As Fiction.* Carbondale: Southern Illinois University Press, 1984.

Lodge, David. *The Modes of Modern Writing: Metaphor, Metonymy, and the Typology of Modern Literature.* Ithaca: Cornell University Press, 1977.

McCaffery, Larry. *The Metafictional Muse: The Work of Robert Coover, Donald Barthelme, and William Gass.* Pittsburgh: U. of Pittsburgh Press, 1982.

Rother, James. "Parafiction: The Adjacent Universe of Barth, Barthelme, Pynchon, and Nabokov." *Boundary 2* 5 (1976): 21–43.

Scholes, Robert. *Fabulation and Metafiction.* Urbana: U. of Illinois Press, 1979.

Wilde, Alan. *Horizons of Assent: Modernism, Postmodernism, and the Ironic Imagination.* Baltimore: Johns Hopkins University Press, 1981.

Structuralism, poststructuralism, postmodernism, Marxism, post-Marxism, or any of the other "new-isms" and "post-isms"? They all make the claim to reinterpret globally the state and their own inscription of and within the state. The formalization of both the past and the future of the state has to be read *in* the present; and the *new* and the *post,* what they announce and what they outdate, give the exact measure and the clear, synchronic, and systemic formulation of that present.

J.D.

THE NOTION OF "POSTMODERN"

Clement Greenberg

"Postmodern" is a rather new term. It's a catchy one, and has been coming up more and more often in talk and writing about the arts and not only about the arts. I'm not clear as to just what it points to except in the case of architecture. There we know more or less definitely what "modern" means, so we're better able to tell what "post" means when prefixed to "modern." Modern architecture means—to put it roughly—functional, geometric rigor and the eschewing of decoration or ornament. Buildings have been put up or projected lately that break with these canons of style, and therefore have gotten called "postmodern." Everybody concerned knows what's meant, including the architects themselves.

Can "postmodern" be identified in an equally agreed-upon way in any of the other arts? I haven't yet seen or heard the term applied in earnest to anything in recent literature. It's come up in connection with music, but haphazardly and with no agreement about what it means there. And from what I can tell, it comes up hardly at all in talk about the dance or the movies. Away from architecture, it's in the area of painting and sculpture that I've mostly heard and seen "postmodern" used—but only by critics and journalists, not by artists themselves.

There are reasons and reasons here. One possible reason is the return to the foreground of figurative or representational pictorial art. But there's been enough precedent, since De Chirico and Surrealism and Neoromanticism, for including figurative art in the modern. There have to be other, less obvious, and at the same time more general reasons for the currency of "postmodern" in talk about recent painting and sculpture. All the more because no critic or journalist I'm aware of who makes free with "postmodern" points to any specific body of work he or she feels really confident in calling that.

Now the "post" in "postmodern" can be taken in a temporal, chronological sense. Anything that comes after something else is "post" that something else. But this isn't quite the way in which "postmodern" is used. It's supposed, rather, to mean or imply art that supersedes, replaces, succeeds the modern in terms of stylistic evolution, the way that the Baroque succeeded

Mannerism and the Rococo succeeded the Baroque. The corollary is that the modern is over and done with, just as Mannerism was over and done with when superseded by the Baroque. But the problem for those who claim this becomes to specify what they mean, not by "post," but by "modern." However, what we usually mean by modern is something considered up-to-date, abreast of the times, and going beyond the past in more than a temporally or chronologically literal sense.

Well, how are you to decide what is and what isn't modern in present-day art in a sense that goes beyond the literal one? There's no rule, no principle, no method. It comes down to a question of taste, or else a terminological quibble. Different stylistic definitions of the modern have been proposed in every generation since the word first came into circulation as applicable to painting and sculpture in more than a merely temporal sense, and none of them have held. Nor have any of those offered by the proponents of the postmodern, whether stylistic or not.

I want to take the risk of offering my own definition of the modern, but it will be more in the nature of an explanation and description than a definition. First of all, I want to change the term in question from "modern" to Modernist—Modernist with a capital M. And then to talk about Modernism instead of the modern. Modernism has the great advantage of being a more historically placeable term, one that designates a historically—not just chronologically—definable phenomenon: something that began at a certain time, and may or may not still be with us.

What can be safely called Modernism emerged in the middle of the last century. And rather locally, in France, with Baudelaire in literature and Manet in painting, and maybe with Flaubert too in prose fiction. (It was a while later, and not so locally, that Modernism appeared in music and architecture, but it was in France again that it appeared first in sculpture. Outside France, later still, it entered the dance.) The "avant-garde" was what Modernism was called at first, but this term has become a good deal compromised by now as well as remaining misleading. Contrary to the common notion, Modernism or the avant-garde didn't make its entrance by breaking with the past. Far from it. Nor did it have such a thing as a program, nor has it really ever had one—again, contrary to the common notion. Nor was it an affair of ideas or theories or ideology. It's been in the nature, rather, of an attitude and an orientation: an attitude and orientation to standards and levels: standards and levels of aesthetic quality in the first and also the last place. And where did the Modernists get their standards and levels from? From the past, that is, the best of the past. But not so much from particular models in the past—though from these too—as from a generalized feeling and apprehending, a kind of distilling and extracting, of aesthetic quality as shown by the best of the past. And it wasn't a question of imitating, but one of emulating—just as it had been for the Renaissance with respect to antiquity. It's true that Baudelaire and Manet talked much more about having to be modern, about reflecting life in their time, than about matching the best of the past. But the need and the ambition to do so shows through in what they actually did, and in enough of what they were recorded as saying. Being modern was a means of living up to the past.

But didn't artists and writers before these two look to the past for standards of quality? Of course. But it was a question of how one looked, and with how much urgency.

Modernism appeared in answer to a crisis. The surface aspect of that crisis was a certain confusion of standards brought on by Romanticism. The Romantics had already looked back into the past, the pre-eighteenth century past, but had made the mistake in the end of trying to re-install it. Architecture was where this attempt became most conspicuous, in the form of revivalism. Romantic architecture wasn't all that slavish, it wasn't the dead loss it's supposed to be, but still it didn't suffice; it may have maintained a look of the past, but not its standards. It wasn't revised enough by later experience, or revised in the right way: as Baudelaire and Manet might have put it, it wasn't modern enough. There ensued finally an academicization of the arts everywhere except in music and prose fiction. Academicization isn't a matter of academies—there were academies long before academicization and before the nineteenth century. Academicism consists in the tendency to take the medium of an art too much for granted. It results in blurring: words become imprecise, color gets muffled, the physical sources of sound become too much dissembled. (The piano, which dissembles its being a stringed instrument, was the Romantic instrument par excellence; but it is as if precisely because it made a point of dissembling that it produced the wonderful music it did in Romantic times, turning imprecision into a new kind of precision.)

Modernism's reaction against Romanticism consisted in part in a new investigating and questioning of the medium in poetry and painting, and in an emphasis on preciseness, on the concrete. But above all Modernism declared itself by insisting on a renovation of standards, and it effected this by a more critical and less pious approach to the past in order to make it more genuinely relevant, more modern. It reaffirmed the past in a new way and in a variety of new ways. And it belonged to this reaffirming that the balance was tipped toward emulation as against imitation more radically than ever before—but only out of necessity, the necessity imposed by the reaffirmed and renovated standards.

Innovation, newness have gotten themselves taken as the hallmark of Modernism, newness as something desired and pursued. And yet all the great and lasting Modernist creators were reluctant innovators at bottom, innovators only because they had to be—for the sake of quality, and for the sake of self-expression if you will. It's not only that some measure of innovation has always been essential to aesthetic quality above a certain level; it's also that Modernist innovation has been compelled to be, or look, more radical and abrupt than innovation used to be or look: compelled by an ongoing crisis in standards. Why this should be so, I can't try to account for here; it would take me too far afield and involve too much speculation. Let it suffice for the moment to notice one thing: how with only a relatively small lapse of time the innovations of Modernism begin to look less and less radical, and how they almost all settle into place eventually as part of the continuum of high Western art, along with Shakespeare's verse and Rembrandt's drawings.

That rebellion and revolt, as well as radical innovation, have been associated with Modernism has its good as well as bad reasons. But the latter far outnumber the former. If rebellion and revolt have truly belonged to Modernism, it's been only when felt to be necessary in the interests of aesthetic value, not for political ends. That some Modernists have been unconventional in their ways of life is beside the point. (Modernism, or the avant-garde, isn't to be identified with bohemia, which was there before Modernism, there in London's Grub Street in the eighteenth century, there in Paris by the 1830s if not before. Some Modernists have been bohemians more or less, many more others haven't been at all. Think of the impressionist painters, of Mallarmé, of Schönberg, of the sedate lives led by a Matisse, a T. S. Eliot. Not that I attach a particular value to a sedate as against a bohemian life; I'm just stating a fact.)

By way of illustration I'd like to go into a little detail about how Modernism came about in painting. There the proto-Modernists were, of all people, the Pre-Raphaelites (and even before them, as proto-proto-Modernist, the German Nazarenes). The Pre-Raphaelites actually foretold Manet (with whom Modernist painting most definitely begins). They acted on a dissatisfaction with painting as practiced in their time, holding that its realism wasn't truthful enough. It seemed to belong to this want of truth that color wasn't allowed to speak out clearly and frankly, that it was being swathed more and more in neutral shading and shadows. This last they didn't say in so many words, but their art itself says it, with its brighter, higher-keyed color, which marks off Pre-Raphaelite painting in its day even more than its detailed realism (to which clearer color was necessary in any case). And it was the forthright, quasi-naive cclor, as well as the quasi-innocent realism, of fifteenth-century Italian art that they looked back to in calling themselves Pre-Raphaelite. They weren't at all the first artists to go back over time to a remoter past than the recent one. In the later eighteenth century David, in France, had done that when he invoked antiquity against the Rococo of his immediate predecessors, and the Renaissance had done that in appealing to antiquity against the Gothic. But it was the urgency with which the Pre-Raphaelites invoked a remoter past that was new. And it was a kind of urgency that carried over into Modernism proper and remained with it.

How much Manet knew of Pre-Raphaelism, I can't tell. But he too, ten years or so later than they, when he was starting out, became profoundly dissatisfied with the kind of painting he saw being done around him. That was toward the end of the 1850s. But he put his finger on what dissatisfied him more "physically" than the Pre-Raphaelites had, and therefore, as I think, to more lasting effect. (From the seventeenth century on the English anticipated ever so much, in culture and the arts as well as in politics and social life, but usually left it to others to follow through on what they'd started.) Seeing a "Velasquez" in the Louvre (a picture now thought to be by Velasquez's son-in-law Mazo), he said how "clean" its color was compared to the "stews and gravies" in contemporary painting—which "stews and gravies" were owed to that same color-muffling, graying and browning, shading and shadowing that the Pre-Raphaelites had reacted against. Manet, in his own reaction, reached back to a nearer past than they had in order to "disencumber" his art of those "half-tones" responsible for the "stews and gravies." He went only as far back as Velasquez to start with, and then even less far back, to another Spanish painter, Goya.

The Impressionists, in Manet's wake, looked back to the Venetians insofar as they looked back, and so did Cézanne, that half-impressionist. Again, the looking back had to do with color, with warmer as well as franker color. Like the Pre-Raphaelites, like so many others in their time, the Impressionists invoked truth to nature, and nature on bright days was luminous with warm color. But underneath all the invocations, the explanations and the rationalizations, there was the "simple" aspiration to quality, to aesthetic value and excellence for its own sake, as an end in itself. Art for art's sake. Modernism settled in in painting with Impressionism, and with that, art for art's sake. For which same sake the successors in Modernism of the Impressionists were forced to forget about truth to nature. They were forced to look even more outrageously new: Cézanne, Gauguin, Seurat, Van Gogh, and all the Modernist painters after them—for the sake of aesthetic value, aesthetic quality, nothing else.

I haven't finished with my exposition and definition of Modernism. The most essential part of it comes, finally, now. Modernism has to be understood as a holding operation, a continuing endeavor to maintain aesthetic standards in the face of threats—not just as a reaction against Romanticism. As the response, in effect, to an ongoing emergency. Artists in all times, despite some appearances to the contrary, have sought aesthetic excellence. What singles Modernism out and gives it its place and identity more than anything else is its response to a heightened sense of threats to aesthetic value: threats from the social and material ambiance, from the temper of the times, all conveyed through the demands of a new and open cultural market, middlebrow demands. Modernism dates from the time, in the mid-nineteenth century, when that market became not only established—it had been long before—but entrenched and dominant, without significant competition.

So I come at last to what I offer as an embracing and perdurable definition of Modernism: that it consists in the continuing endeavor to stem the decline of aesthetic standards threatened by the relative democratization of culture under industrialism; that the overriding and innermost logic of Modernism is to maintain the levels of the past in the face of an opposition that hadn't been present in the past. Thus the whole enterprise of Modernism, for all its outward aspects, can be seen as backward-looking. That seems paradoxical, but reality is shot through with paradox, is practically constituted by it.

It also belongs to my definition of Modernism that the continuing effort to maintain standards and levels has brought about the widening recognition that art, that aesthetic experience, no longer needs to be justified in other terms than its own, that art is an end in itself and that the aesthetic is an autonomous value. It could now be acknowledged that art doesn't have to teach, doesn't have to celebrate or glorify anybody or anything, doesn't have to advance causes; that it has become free to distance itself from religion, politics, and even morality. All it has to do is be good as art. This recognition stays. It doesn't matter that it's still not generally—or rather consciously— accepted, that art for art's sake still isn't a respectable notion. It's acted on—and in fact it's always been acted on. It's been the underlying reality of the practice of art all along, but it took Modernism to bring this out into the open.

But to return to "postmodern." A friend and colleague had been to a symposium about "postmodern" last spring. I asked him how the term had gotten defined at that symposium. As art, he answered, that was no longer self-critical. I felt a pang. I myself had written twenty years ago that self-criticism was a distinguishing trait of Modernist art. My friend's answer made me realize as I hadn't before how inadequate that was as a covering definition of Modernism or the modern. (That I hadn't the presence of mind to ask my friend just how self-critical was only incidental. We both understood, in any case, that it hadn't to do with the difference between abstract and figurative, just as we also understood that the "modern" wasn't confined to particular styles, modes, or directions of art.)

If the definition of Modernism or the modern that I now offer has any quality, then the crucial word in "postmodern" becomes "post." The real, the only real, question becomes what it is that's come after and superseded the modern; again, not in a temporal sense, but a style-historical one. But it's no use, as I said in the beginning, asking the critics and journalists who talk postmodern (which includes my friend); they disagree too much among themselves, and resort too much to cloudy generalizations. And anyhow there's nobody among them whose eye I trust.

In the end I find myself having to presume to tell all these people what I think they mean by their talk about the postmodern. That is, I find myself attributing motives to them, and the attributing of motives is offensive. All the same, I feel forced to do so, by the nature of the case.

As I said, Modernism was called into being by the new and formidable threats to aesthetic standards that emerged, or finished emerging, toward the middle of the last century. The Romantic crisis, as I call it, was, as it now seems, an expression of the new situation, and in some ways an expression of the threats themselves insofar as they worked to bring about a confusion of standards and levels. Without these threats, which come mostly from a new middle-class public, there would have been no such thing as Modernism. Again as I said earlier, Modernism is a holding operation, a coping with an ongoing emergency. The threats persist, they are as much there as they ever were. And right now they may have become even more formidable because more disguised, more deceptive. It used to be the easily identifiable philistines who did the threatening. They are still here, but hardly matter. Now the threats to aesthetic standards, to quality, come from closer to home, from within as it were, from friends of advanced art. The "advanced" used to be coterminous with Modernism, but these friends hold that Modernism is no longer advanced enough, that it has to be hurried on, hurried into the postmodern. That it will fall behind the times if it continues to be concerned with such things as standards and quality. I'm not manipulating the evidence here in order to make a rhetorical point; just take a look at what these postmodern people like and at what they don't like in current art. They happen, I think, to be a more dangerous threat to high art than old-time philistines ever were. They bring philistine taste up to date by disguising it as its opposite, wrapping it in high-flown art jargon. Notice how that jargon proliferates nowadays, in New York and Paris and London if not in Sydney. Realize, too, how compromised words like "advanced," as well as "avant-garde," have become of late. Underneath it all lies the defective taste of the people concerned, their bad eye for visual art.

The making of superior art is arduous, usually. But under Modernism the appreciation, even more than the making, of it has become more taxing, the satisfaction and exhilaration to be gotten from the best new art more hard-won. Over the past hundred and thirty years and more the best new painting and sculpture (and the best new poetry too) have proven a challenge and a trial in their time to the art-lover—a challenge and a trial as they hadn't used to be. Yet the urge to relax is there, as it's always been. It threatens and keeps on threatening standards of quality. (It was different, apparently, before the mid-nineteenth century.) That the urge to relax expresses itself in changing ways does but testify to its persistence. The postmodern business is one more expression of that urge. And it's a way, above all, to justify oneself in preferring less demanding art without being called reactionary or retarded (which is the greatest fear of the new-fangled philistines of advancedness).

The yearning for relaxation became outspoken in presumedly avant-garde circles for the first time with Duchamp and Dada, and then in certain aspects of Surrealism. But it was with Pop art that it became a fully confident expression. And that confidence has stayed in all the different fashions and trends of professedly and supposedly advanced art since then. What I notice is that the succession of these trends has involved, from the first, a retreat from major to minor quality; and a cause for concern about the state of contemporary art is just that: the retreat from the major to the minor: the hailing of the minor as major, or else the claim that the difference between the two isn't important. Not that I look down on minor art, not at all. But without the perpetuation of major art minor art falls off too. When the highest levels of quality are no longer maintained in practice or taste or appreciation, then the lower levels sink lower. That's the way it's always been, and I don't see that way changing now.

The notion of the postmodern has sprouted and spread in that same relaxing climate of taste and opinion in which Pop art and its successors thrive. The notion represents wishful thinking for the most part; those who talk about the postmodern are too ready to greet it. Yes, if the modern, if Modernism, is over and done with, then there'll be surcease, relief. At the same time art history will have been kept going, and we critics and journalists will have kept abreast of it. But I happen to think that Modernism isn't finished, certainly not in painting or sculpture. Art is still being made that challenges the longing for relaxation and relief and makes high demands on taste (demands that are all the more taxing because deceptive: the best new art of latter years innovates in a less spectacular way than the best new art used to under Modernism). Modernism, insofar as it consists in the upholding of the highest standards, survives—survives in the face of this new rationalization for the lowering of standards.

(1980)

THE UNHAPPY CONSCIOUSNESS OF MODERNISM

Donald B. Kuspit

I

Modernism—which I take to be that point of view which sees art as the mastery of purity—involves not so much a loss of tradition as a willing suspension of tradition. It is not so much that tradition is impossible from the perspective of the present as that the very meaning of historicity—its implications of smooth continuity, of the easy inevitability that seems to make events flow into one another—has been bankrupted by a new sense of what it means to be in the present. To be modern, as Jung says, means to be "fully conscious of the present," and that full consciousness is not possible from the point of view of traditionalism which sees all presents as *petites perceptions* of an infinite continuum of events, an uninterrupted flow of history with no particular *telos* but then also with no particular dead ends. There is simply the passage of events into one another in an all-embracing temporality. To be modern is to discover raw possibility giving the present an enormous presence, making it seem the totality of being the very essence of being. As Jung says, man "is completely modern only when he has come to the very edge of the world leaving behind him all that has been discarded and outgrown and acknowledging that he stands before a void out of which all things may grow."[1] I take it that modernism in art is a way of commanding the presence which the present has when viewed from the perspective of modernity—a way of being responsible for the enormous charge of possibility that is concentrated in the pure present, for the sense of complete openness that gives the present its purity. Modernism in art intends to give us the pure present as a complete openness to being, an openness out of which new worlds are likely to emerge. Yet this openness remains bound by presentness, and so—remains an abstract charge making the concrete presence of the artwork more "pregnant," to use Clement Greenberg's word, than it would ordinarily be. And in that tension between abstract charge and concrete presence we catch our first glimpse of the unhappy consciousness of modernism, or presentism as it should properly be called. For the relationship between the abstract charge of possibility, or the aura of openness, and the actuality of material presence—the "closed" factuality of what is given to us in the present—is unresolved and remains unresolved so long as the art is understood to be purely immediate, i.e, completely taken up by its presentness. Presentness is self-defeating, for by consuming all openness—by allowing openness to exist only as a utopian aura to material presence—it depreciates, and with that material presence itself must be depreciated. The aura of openness degenerates into a felt void, and material presence fades into matter-of-fact givenness. The work of art becomes an "interesting fact," the dull shadow of a once-substantial present and an echo of its own dream. Modernism collapses; full consciousness of the basic present becomes consciousness of the banally given. Any return to traditionism is precluded by the recognition that no amount of historical consciousness can restore the dream that was lost, can compensate for the abandonment of the sense of an infinite creative potential which proved to be the mask of nihilism. The modernist work of art shrinks to an unresonant finitude.

But there is a more immediate formulation that helps us understand the unhappy predicament that modernism embodies. It has to do with the modernist sense of what is proper to art. Modernism understands the immanence of art in terms which deny it self-transcendence, or rather which subsume its self-transcendence in its immanence. The givenness of a work should be its only effect; this is what it means to speak of the work as pure. Thus when Greenberg acknowledges that the unconscious or preconscious effect of the modernist work of art is as constitutive of its quality as its "literal order of effects," yet never demonstrates how this is so, he implicitly assumes that such an unconscious or preconscious effect is sufficiently unspecifiable as to seem illusory, or else is too negligible in its influence on quality to take serious account of. Paying attention to the modernist work of art's unconscious or preconscious effect distracts from the proper experience of the modernist work, the experience which has to do with the making of art itself. It is that experience which is responsible for the "increasingly literal order of effects in the modernist work." The modernist outlook views art entirely in terms of its making and the literal results of that making. In fact, the modernist outlook carries the Aristotelian sense of art-as-making to an extreme. Modernism represents the absurd argument for an exclusively materialist conception of art, which not only sees the work literally but reduces its "effectiveness" to its literalness so that all it "communicates" is its own givenness. In Greenberg's thought there is a quasi-Marxist aspect to this reduction, with unconscious or preconscious effect seen as a dispensable superstructure or ideological superimposition on the materially literal work of art. Such literalness is indisputable and becomes the basis for common sense agreement about the nature of the work of art, the referent for unequivocal communication about it.

But communication exists in name only, for the materially abstracted work is addressed to no one in particular, and those who find themselves addressed by it are neither transformed by it nor have any transformative effect on it. Their consciousness of it does not help constitute it nor does their consciousness of the modernist ("presentist") work significantly constitute them. Communication then is not assumed by the manifestness or literalness of the modernist work, which requires only that its addressee—who is never more than arbitrarily conceived and is certainly not to be socially rooted, apart from having the leisure to contemplate art—conform to its visible character, acknowledge its givenness. Clearly this is a reversal of the Copernican revolution that Kant effected, in which the object had to conform to the subject rather than vice versa. It is an unacknowledged if sophisticated return to a traditional conception of perception. The sophistication comes in with the concept of literalness, and above all with its effect on the subject who is forced back on his own literalness, subtly cut off from his own history, the fluidity of his own experience. Pure or modernist art thus seems to succeed, where even religion never completely did, in liberating us from the limits of our own experience—by limiting us to our literalness.

The question, of course, is what it means for both the work and its serious contemplator to seem unencumbered by any other meaning than that of their own being—which hardly seems a meaning at all, since it is not a horizon by which either is framed. Self-framing, without context, both the modernist work and the modernist contemplator appear absolute by virtue of their literalness. But is not such absolute literalness an illusion—as much of an illusion from the point of view of unconscious or preconscious effect, as they are from its point of view? Is not the impulse to purity, however cultivated and elevated, the sign of a general attitude and as such fraught with social meaning? The reduction to the literal implies a search for the unchangeable in a field of rapidly changing historical experience, for the secular equivalent of the sacred in an unredeemably profane field of experience. The literal is seen as the holy grail, the unequivocally and divinely "communicable," in a world of highly equivocal, changeable communication—a world full of misunderstandings, in which the ground of communication seems like quicksand, and even seems to call itself into question. From another closely related point of view, giving allegiance to literalness, limiting art to literalness is a way—like that of the ostrich who buries his head in the sand—of precluding, or at least seeming to escape, the expanded consciousness of reality in the modern world. The rhetoric of literalness that modernism asserts—fanatically advocates—not only seems a kind of know-nothingness in the face of an expanded knowledge of reality, but the articulation of an unselfcontradictory knowledge in a situation in which knowledge inevitably becomes self-contradictory, in an expanded, one might say Faustian, field of experience which seems to demand self-contradiction if it is even minimally to be mastered.

In analyzing the concept of modernism we begin to realize that purity is defined as much by what it negates as by what it affirms, and that its self-certainty or affirmative character rests on a foundation of uncertainty, a shaky negation. The concretely felt is always haunted by the vaguely known; the explicit experience of art is always hemmed in by the implicit experience of the historical world—our sense of the literalness of art must always struggle against our sense of its metaphoric relation with life. Our sense of the effectiveness of art must always struggle with our sense of our effect on it, with what we read into it to make it effective in our lives. Oscar Wilde summarizes the situation brilliantly in his account of "the highest kind of criticism," the criticism which "treats the work of art simply as a starting point for a new creation" and "does not confine itself to discovering the real intention of the artist and accepting that as final." As Wilde says:

> the meaning of any beautiful created thing is, at least, as much in the soul of him who looks at it, as it was in his soul who wrought it. Nay, it is rather the beholder who lends to the beautiful thing its myriad meanings, and makes it marvellous for us, and sets it in some new relation to the age so that it becomes a vital portion of our lives, and a symbol of what we pray for, or perhaps of what, having prayed for, we fear that we may receive.[2]

Clearly, the modernist does not want the kind of imaginative intimacy with the work of art which would give it an identity beyond itself, an existence beyond its pure or literal presence, and which would make it seem, as a whole, communicative of anything beyond the sum of its material parts. And yet modernism is unhappy with being merely literal, and is haunted by the desire to communicate beyond itself, to have effect that is more than itself. It knows, though, it can never communicate an effective whole of meaning, for it is too self-conscious of the conditions of communication. This self-consciousness is forced upon it by the state of communication today. For to be modern or fully conscious of the present, to take the present as the only perspective, means to acknowledge the bankruptcy not only of historicity, but of communicativeness. The easy inevitability of neither can be assumed today, and the dissection of the language of art which modernism implies—and which goes hand in hand with the rejection of historicity—carries with it an implicit acknowledgment of the difficulty of communication. This difficulty is ironically confirmed by our impatient expectation of achieving full communication—of the great possibilities of communication which an understanding of the mechanisms of communication seems to offer, but only in a utopian way, as an unrealized creative potential. Wilde is again a help to our understanding of modernist unhappy consciousness, the consciousness that is divided between a sense of the language of art and an awareness of its uselessness for communication. Speaking of the Mona Lisa, Wilde writes:

> Do you ask me what Leonardo would have said had anyone told him of this picture that "all the thoughts and experience of the world had etched and moulded therein that which they had of power to refine and make expressive

the outward form, the animalism of Greece, the lust of Rome, the reverie of the Middle Age with its spiritual ambition and imaginative loves, the return of the Pagan world, the sins of the Borgias?" He would probably have answered that he had contemplated none of these things, but had concerned himself simply with certain arrangements of lines and masses, and with new and curious colour-harmonies of blue and green.

Modernism is caught between these two points of view. And even though modernism means to take the artist's side in the dichotomy, and has only a shrunken sense of the meaning that a work of art might have in even the most active imagination, it is driven to do so not only by its own desire for purity but also in part by its effort to escape the situation of meaning that art, and all understanding, finds itself in by being modern.

The modernist predicament is epitomized, although without awareness that it is a predicament, in Greenberg's assertion that

> Only by reducing themselves to the means by which they attain virtuality as art, to the literal essence of their medium, and only by avoiding as much as possible explicit reference to any form of experience not given immediately through their mediums, can the arts communicate that sense of concretely felt, irreducible experience in which our sensibility finds its fundamental certainty.[3]

Greenberg puts this even more strongly and particularly:

> It follows that a modernist work of art must try, in principle, to avoid communication with any order of experience not inherent in the most literally and essentially construed nature of its medium. Among other things, this means renouncing illusion and explicit subject matter. The arts are to achieve concreteness, "purity" by dealing solely with their respective selves—that is, by becoming "abstract" or nonfigurative. Of course, "purity" is an unattainable ideal. Outside music, no attempt at a "pure" work of art has ever succeeded in being more than an approximation and compromise (least of all in literature). But this does not diminish the crucial importance of "purity" or concrete "abstractness" as an orientation and aim.[4]

The allusion to music brings to mind, not inappropriately, Valéry's sense of music "appreciation," which in fact Greenberg quotes with approval: "I conclude that the real connoisseur in this art is necessarily he to whom it suggests nothing."[5] Greenberg generalizes from this point of view; art as such suggests nothing, but rather presents itself. There are no hidden connotations within its denotation of its own making. In Kantian language, there is no synthesis of the work of art beyond the unity of its own making, the suggestive aura around it being nothing but the illusion—we would say projection—of our own needs. The position that the making of the work of art might have something to do with the satisfaction of our needs is of course not considered by the modernist, who rejects the notion, as Greenberg says, that there is any higher purpose to art, any "spiritual" point to its production. That there might be a lower purpose—and that even the spiritual might have something to do with this lower purpose—escapes him despite his obsessive, inconclusive interest in the emotional density of the modernist work of art. In all of this there is a refusal to consider the work of art as anything more than the material and work that went into it, with little interest in why the effect should be made, and in fact with a strong interest in beating back any such interest, as detrimental to an understanding of the immediate presence of the work.

From the modernist point of view, the aura of allusion that surrounds the work can never synthesize into a coherent consciousness of the work. It remains unavoidably incoherent and stammering, because the work speaks clearly only when it speaks literally, i.e., as a particular presence that can never be generalized by any emotional or spiritual use to which we might put it. Its stubborn particularity resists appropriation even by the aura of meaning it seems to adduce, for that aura finally seems to be no more than a sign of our own insecurity with meaning in general—with what anything might finally mean, might finally communicate beyond its own being. Indeed modernism seems to tell us that acceptance of the work of art as indifferent to and so in a sense beyond questions of meaning and the communication of meaning is a way of securing oneself against the general chanciness of communication and uncertainty of meaning that become apparent the moment one begins to question the conventions of both. Part of what modernism tells us is that one inevitably does begin to question those conventions in even the most ordinary circumstances, because, from the perspective of the present, conventions always seem to be arbitrary and to interfere with creative potential, the expanded sense of possibility that comes with trying to be totally present. The presentness of the modernist work of art is one important—presumably unique—way of being secure in the present. And yet taking the point of view of the present exclusively was what made one insecure in the first place. The pure presence of the work of art seems to be an antidote to the poison that pure existential presentness let loose, yet it seems also to be another, more insidious, version of that poison.

There is then in the Greenberg quotations, the pseudodialectical structure typical of the unhappy consciousness. The structure is "pseudo" in part because it is unconscious of itself, unaware that the positive artistic presence it proposes is premised on a negative sense of artistic presence as failed communication. The structure is also "pseudo" because recognizing that an unwillingness, almost an inability, to communicate is the hidden condition of art's purity, and implies a division within the very structure of art that cannot be reconciled. For modernism, the reconciliation of art with itself—the happiness of art—can be imagined only in terms which put all the weight of reconciliation on the one changeless—pure—term in art, i.e, only in terms of a false consciousness of art. Thus there is pure or literally given art, whose integrity—the easy integrity that literalness gives—is conceived as entirely independent of its communicative potential. Such "renunciation" of communication is, implicitly, the first line of defense against the flux of historical experience and the relativity of meaning and communication that comes with that flux. Giving attention to literalness seems to stop the flux of relativity, or at least functions like a kind of breakwater that keeps it under control. Yet the weight of literalness as such is important in the pseudo-dialectical structure that means to reconcile art to itself, for any use to which literalness can be put implies the divided, "communicative" nature of art, and as such shows its unhappiness. However, Greenberg himself implies that modernism, with its emphasis on literalness for the sake of literalness, cannot help but reveal an unhappy consciousness when, in his notion of "art-adoration," he suggests that the pursuit of purity implies a pathological sense of experience. Attention to literalness for its own sake can indicate "moral or intellectual failing" in the face of experience, even an incapacity for experience, which implies a disorder of the will, a collapse or degeneration of being.

Yet what Greenberg calls "aesthetic transposition"—the starting point for the pursuit of purity—is an inextricable part of historical experience. Whatever the aesthetic might seem to be in itself, it is a transposition of experience, i.e., it seems to offer a perspective on experience. The problem with the aesthetic perspective on experience is that it remains bound to the most immanent, untransposable aspect of experience—sense experience—which seems almost impossible to get a perspective on. Aesthetic transposition fearlessly presents what is perhaps the central epistemological paradox. Modernism, without realizing it, falls into the trap of this paradox, this double bind, and suffers the unhappy consciousness that is implied by the paradox. The need to have a perspective on experience, to transpose it into the control of some form of clarity, implies the canceling of the impact of its presentness or literalness. But it seems that the need can only be satisfied, perspective can only be gained, after plunging the depths of presentness. Indeed, gaining a perspective on experience as a whole sometimes seems to be the direct consequence of immersion in presentness, complete abandonment to sensory literalness. The aesthetic perspective, aesthetic clarity about experience seems inseparable from perpetual bondage to the most intimate and uncontrollable experience, the sense-certainty of presentness. Indeed, the aesthetic perspective may be a way of loosening the bonds of involuntary submission to sensory literalness, of making the sense-certainty of presentness more devious, without denying it. The paradox of the aesthetic is that it seems to carry us deep into one kind of experience while promising to deliver us from all experience. The aesthetic, in fact, seems the most difficult perspective to sustain, if the easiest to come by. Deeply dependent on the presentness of experience—it implies that experience will always be "modern"—the aesthetic becomes the most tentative transposition of experience, the weakest demonstration of the inevitable generation of a perspective on experience, from experience. "High art"—aesthetically pure art—offers a perspective on experience that refuses to function as one.

Instead, in the act of monumentalizing presentness, it monumentalizes itself thereby in effect self-destructing and showing its uselessness as a perspective on experience. High art epitomizes the paradox of the aesthetic, which implies the inadequacy of the aesthetic to the experience. In modernist high art we see this inadequacy at its most acute. We see how the search for the unchangeable, which Hegel notes is characteristic of the unhappy consciousness, leads to the dead end of presentness. This is accompanied by a dead end conception of present experience as excruciatingly literal. This is also typical of the unhappy consciousness, which, according to Hegel, finds the unchangeable in the literally particular, so that the unchangeable has no general credibility, and the search for it reveals itself to be a regressive form of understanding.

Communication demands and imposes perspective, but to offer presentness as the ground of certainty of communication—as the ultimate perspective—is to play a bad joke on communicative potential. Presentness is so narrow a ground of experience as such that when it is conceived as the ground of communication it becomes absurd beyond the usual reduction to absurdity. And the communication about presentness inherent in the aesthetic, particularly in the modernist aesthetic, adds to the absurdity. Presentness is so insecure a footing that it begins to seem a delusion. The "aesthetic" narrowing of experience that presentness and communication about presentness imply does not so much intensify experience as cancel it into a fictional finality. The hypostatized present or pure presence is the most null concept of experience imaginable. And while superficially it is the most communicable experience, it stands outside communication, which means that it stands outside experience, as a myth of what experience ought to be. But then we must ask, why should experience become aesthetically present, why might it be expected to be pure?

II

We can begin to answer this question by examining modernism's obsession with the ineffability of art, which is an acknowledgment that art stands outside communication. We immediately find that such an examination immerses us in the larger cultural issues at stake in modernism, particularly the struggle between conformity and nonconformity. These are the terms in which the unhappy consciousness of modern society works, the terms in which, in Hegel's words, the modern "Alienated Soul" reveals its "divided nature," its "doubled and merely contradictory being." The myth of pure presence, of an absolute experience of presentness, originates in an effort to impose unity on this contradictory being, or rather, to present the higher unity of pure presence as the secret goal of alienation. It is presumably the goal in the name of which inner nature divides itself and suffers self-division, advocates and patiently endures a form of self-loss. The soul is to reconstitute itself in the light of pure presence—to achieve and become such presence. But its doubleness is more evident, even seems primordial. This is nowhere more evident than in art, and in just that art which means to be pure, to be sublimely modern.

Valéry and Barthes give us clues as to how this is so, how the doubleness works, why it should be so necessary as to seem primordial, the very essence of inner nature, the irreducible and ineradicable core of selfhood. Valéry remarks:

> Just as the thinker tries to defend himself from the platitudes and set phrases which protect the mind from surprise at everything, and make practical living possible, so the painter can try, by studying formlessness, or rather *singularity* of form, to rediscover his own singularity, and with it the original and primitive state of coordination between hand and eye, subject and will.[6]

There is a conformist language, largely practical in import—a useful language, which unifies people in their enterprise—and then the singular language of the wondering thinker, the language of wonder and surprise at being a language able to recover the freshness of being and so itself be fresh. There is the artist who puts himself outside the form of vision to which all other eyes conform, and not so much creates his own form of vision as re-creates vision from the start, restores it to a kind of elemental state, in which it is full of surprises—in which anything seen is an elemental surprise. The thinker makes a fresh start, the artist makes a fresh start. Both are visionaries in the pursuit of the fresh start. But the pursuit of the mythical fresh start, with its sense of surprising being—the surprise of being which the idea of pure presence embodies—generates a contradiction, even originates in a contradiction. For the fresh start implies the abandonment of the old history, which is far from mythical, and more certain than the surprise of being. Platitudes and set phrases—familiar form in general—is a more definite location in being, than the formlessness that seems to recover its originality, the singularity of form that seems to encode, in a strong echo, the surprise of being. Sedimented being seems to be more substantial than surprising being. Clearly, the shift from familiar platitude to singular form, from a historical and conforming to an ahistorical and nonconforming language of vision—in effect, from an overly collective to a highly individual apprehension of being—implies the alienation of art from itself. The escape from what Valéry calls "the Nondescript" to surprise clearly implies the divided nature of experience itself, the shifting ground of response to being, which now seems stale, now fresh. Whether fresh language can induce fresh experience of being, or fresh experience of being generate fresh language is beside the point. What is crucial is the inherent doubleness of experience, which makes language difficult, insecure, so ultimately uncertain as to demand platitudes and set phrases as if to ballast experience—indeed, being itself. The nondescript is necessary to make surprise possible, and while the surprise, as

Valéry writes, is not that of "shock which breaks with convention or habit," but rather a renewal of the "fresh look,"[7] it nonetheless presupposes convention or habit as the ground of the nondescript, the inert ground of history which, paradoxically, is the catalyst of surprise. It seems that one does not need to break with convention or habit to generate the surprise of the fresh look, but, on the contrary, must embed oneself all the more deeply in convention and habit for the surprise of the fresh look to spring forth spontaneously. The more inert convention and habit are, then, the more inevitable and spontaneous the fresh look is, the more singular are the final results of understanding experience, the more intuitive is the relationship one has to being. By deliberately planting roots deep in convention and habit, by conforming willingly to tradition, the artist almost guarantees himself a fresh look, or guarantees that the forms he offers will look singular to the viewer who has lost the sense of the singularity of experience and comes to art to restore it, and finally to restore the sense of the uniqueness of being as such.

Now this kind of surprise, the surprise of the fresh look, the surprise of the unconventional and nonhabitual, the surprise of singular form is ineffable, however much its point of departure is an all too obvious, all too historical and used language. As Valéry writes, "We must not forget that a thing of great beauty leaves us *mute* with admiration." The thing of great beauty—the singular form—is mute because it is in no danger of becoming a platitude or set phrase, of being taken up by the collective historical language. That is why we are mute before it. We cannot use it, either for our practice of history or theory of being; our muteness before it is an implicit rejection of its usefulness, an explicit affirmation of its nonconformity. We admire, we pay homage to its singularity, but we want and can have nothing to do with it until that singularity is assimilated into a set phrase, becomes familiar and even overfamiliar. Then it acquires collective historical value, and then—and this is perhaps the truly crucial point—it might catalyze a surprise, seem to encode a fresh look at experience, generate an intuitive grasp of being. As long as its singularity seems absolute, the artistic fresh look is beyond language, beyond communication, and seems to be surrounded by an "impenetrable neutral zone," to use the phrase by which Valéry characterized Mallarmé's "immensely refined politeness." This politeness was a sanctuary, within which Mallarmé retained the sanctity of his "notion of an absolute work of imagination," a work which at every turn was full of the kind of "indefinable yet powerful" surprises Valéry sought.[8] This "immensely refined politeness," this "impenetrable neutral zone," which initially terrorized Valéry, as he notes—until he learned it—is the aura of the ineffable around the singular. It is the inarticulate existence of radically individual form, the languagelessness of absolutely literal, unique language, the artlessness of the all too artful. It is the zone of speechlessness that surrounds highly individual speech, the sublime speechlessness that accompanies sublimely singular speech. Mallarmé's "immensely refined politeness" is the ornamental form of this speechlessness, an attempt to socialize the ineffable.

It is a kind of midway zone between absolute speechlessness and practical language, the unhappy meeting ground of the ineffable and the useful, the ultimately artistic and the ultimately inartistic. Ornamental, polite speech, while it is a matter of set phrases, is also, when refined or elaborated, unsettling, for then the way it verges on speechlessness becomes evident. Mallarmé's "immensely refined politeness" transformed the nondescript language of conformist sociality into singular form, making it ineffable, or at least an avoidance of practical communication. Mallarmé, in other words, made polite speech into a tentative art form so as to keep intact his dream of an absolute art form, one whose singularity was conceived from the start, i.e., one whose ahistorical nonconformity does not spring from historical conformist language.

A retort to such singularity—to speechless singularity of form in general, whether such pure form be as in Mallarmé's dream, parthenogenetically, or, as is more common, pure by reason of nonconformity to some conformist mode of speech and being—comes to mind from Barthes, who remarks the "opiate-like philosophies" by means of "which one gets rid of intellectuals by telling them to run along and get on with the emotions and the ineffable." This attitude implies, as Barthes says, a "reservation about culture," and thus "means a terrorist position."[9] Modernism, with its insistence on purity, and the ineffability of purity, and the correlation of this ineffability with what Gauguin called "transcendental emotivity," is a species of terrorism, and an opiate of the intellectuals. The proper experience of art, or the experience proper to art, as Greenberg calls it, is the means by which intellectuals distract themselves from the improper experiences the world inflicts on them and on everyone, and the gross impropriety that depth analysis of the world and experience unavoidably becomes. The refinement of purity, the release from speech into ineffability, and the great relief this affords, is intended to be an antidote to, and a reprieve from, the crudeness of experience and the indecency forced upon us by our analysis of experience. Instead pure form functions as an opiate dulling any sense of the extent and intensity of experience, interfering with even the most nominal analysis of experience and pointedly giving us a new sense of the pristine decorousness and disinterestedness of art. Even more crucially, pure form precludes the clear emergence of any horizon of meaning, the frame of reference which alone makes the analysis of experience possible. Pure form makes all horizons of meaning seem negligible, collapses every perspective by which one might achieve an overview of the world of experience. All meaning and perspective are absorbed in the literalness of pure form. Every meaningful perspective is reduced to an evasive nuance of such form, or rather dissipated by its pursuit. Meaningful perspective seems at once a possibility offered by pure form and an actuality dismissed by it. This self-contradictoriness is another expression of the paradox of the aesthetic.

In any case the critic of modernism must assume that pure form implies a world of experience, though it does so in the most inchoate way possible. He must try to reinstate the world of experience that pure form implies, taking pure form as a clue to a buried consciousness of experience, a lost horizon of meaning. From what Robert Pincus-Witten calls "signature material" the singularity of the world of experience—of which the singularity of the artist is only an instance—must be recovered. It is as though the pure presence of signature material were the dust of a world—the very fact that pure form can be regarded as signature material tells us that it must be—and, like a visionary, the critic of modernism, to complete his criticism, must gain a perspective on the world of experience from its dust, from pure art. The criticism of modernism must in fact offer a vision of the world that can have a vision of purity.

The criticism of modernism completes itself, restores the implicit vision of the modern world that underlies the concept of modernist art, when it recognizes the dialectic of conformity and nonconformity that underlies that concept. Such a recognition restores an important sense of what it means to say the world is modern, but it does not give us any stable perspective on that modern world, for it cannot itself transcend the dialectic of conformity and nonconformity. But a fuller exploration of this dialectic as it appears in art gives us a kind of perverse perspective on modernity, on presentness itself, permitting us to transcend it without forfeiting it—to effect a standoff with it. Barthes offers us this avenue of exploration. The value of modernist works, he writes, is in "their duplicity," which means "that they always have two edges." They have an obedient conformist, plagiarizing edge— Valéry's platitudes and set phrases—and a subversive edge—"the place where the death of language is glimpsed."[10] This is the place of what Valéry calls formlessness, and the death of language is the source of what he calls surprise. In fact the death of language is a positive resource—perhaps the only resource—for the sense of freshness of being and experience. The death of language is the source of singularity of form, and singularity of form generates the transcendent illusion of freshness of being, and the real feeling of freshness of experience—that restoration of subjectivity, that momentary sense of having an undivided nature, which is reflected in the sense of freshness of experience.

Modernism assumes that language must necessarily die, that it can no longer be the ground of unity between speakers, but only, through its death, the ground for a possible unity of self, for a radical or singular sense of self. The singularity of form achieved through the subversion and death of language is emblematic of a radically individualized self. It is the form of the nonconformist self, the self that finds its unity in the dividedness of language, and that in a sense recovers its unity from the false, collective unity implied by historical, conformist language. In another sense, it recovers its authenticity from inauthentic language, using language against itself to break its hold on consciousness, and finally on being. Modernism not only comes to assume that language has died, that singularity of form is inevitable, that there is no need for plagiarizing conformity, that pure presence does not have to be achieved by the subversion of practical existence, but that it arises spontaneously from the very being of things, is innate to historical experience. Hence Duchamp's Readymades and Pincus-Witten's conception of signature material, and the credo of honesty to material that has dominated the production of much of modern art, and continues to be the ideology behind a good deal of contemporary abstract art. Carl Andre is perhaps the clearest representative of this ideology. (One might note that the reverse approach, which might be described as the romanticism—dandyism—of today assumes that language, and by implication social "practice," can never die, or even appear to die, but has and will always exist in banal, nondescript, platitudinous form, which can be manipulated to bring certain obscured horizons of meaning to life. Robert Morris perhaps best exemplifies this attitude.)

Reaching this position, emphasizing pure presence as an absolute, modernism becomes unexpectedly paradoxical, in a self-destructive way. It contradicts itself, it becomes exactly the opposite of what it intends. It endures what Barthes calls the "novelistic instant"—in the case of modernism, the novelistic instant of communication. Despite all appearances to the contrary, despite the aura of ineffability that surrounds pure presence, it conveys the sense of inner communication with its viewer, who as it were hears what it has to say through an inner communion with it. It becomes like the demonic voice Socrates heard, compelling him to an unexpected sense of existence—a kind of sibylline voice speaking an unknown tongue and, just for that reason, a voice that is presumed to be saying something profound. Its message must be interpreted, its very sound has hieroglyphic connotations, i.e., the purity of its presence has meaning, however indeterminate. Felt meaning here is not simply the sign of a compulsive relationship to the pure work of art, but indicative of a belief that pure presence is divinely communicative, and communicates like all divine beings, in a perverse way—that is, by using our own being as its medium. Pure presence induces in us a sense of exalted communication—communication at once elevated and subliminal, out of reach yet felt, and so, effective. Such exalted communication becomes evident through the sense of self-communication and self-possession that pure presence induces, catalyzes. This sense is reflected in Greenberg's notion of the " 'sensation' of exalted cognitiveness—exalted because it transcends cognition as such," that taste affords. It is "as though," writes Greenberg, "for the instant, [one] were in command, by dint of transcendent knowing, of everything that could possibly affect [one's] consciousness, or even [one's] existence." In this "state of consciousness, not of a gain to consciousness. . . . consciousness revels in the sense of itself (as God revels in the sense of himself, according to some theologians)."[11] The "instant" described seems, on reflection, the "purely *novelistic* instant so relished by Sade's libertine when he manages to be hanged and then to cut the rope at the very moment of his orgasm, his bliss," in Barthes's words.[12] This moment is "the cut, the deflation, the *dissolve* which seizes the subject in the midst of bliss." In the midst of the bliss of pure presence, reaching that orgasm that only pure presence can give, one is deflated by a kind of coming to one's senses, a refusal of self-loss in pure presence, of the death that pure presence implies. This refusal takes the form of communication about oneself which seems to come from pure presence, and seems to enhance the bliss that one has in the presence of the pure work of art. But what is really discovered here is pure presence, for its silence is broken, its ineffability mocked, by attributing to it a communication of the fundamental nature of one's own existence. What is deflated in the novelistic instant that pure presence is unavoidably subjected to by consciousness is the ineffability, the quality of being beyond communication, of pure work of art. Pure presence is dissolved in the communication of consciousness with itself, which is the most primordial communication. While it looks as though pure presence triggered this communication, in fact this communication came to the fore of consciousness, became a powerful presence, because of the absence of communicative potential in the pure work of art. Consciousness came to itself to fill the void of literalness, to give it some magic, to make it meaningful, to get a perspective on it. The appeal to self-reference made by consciousness when it is faced with the pure work of art—the implicit appeal of consciousness to the higher self that its own self-awareness seems to generate—is a last-ditch attempt to fill a void, to end the emptiness of pure presence by giving it the seemingly global, though subliminal, fullness of self-consciousness. Self-consciousness is an underworld projected onto pure presence to give it a significance it does not otherwise have—to make it signify, with however limited a semaphore. The pure work of art is encoded in such a way that it becomes narcissistic, which is still to socialize it beyond all expectations. The sense of narcissistic communication that pure presence supposedly affords makes it collectively accessible, for it seems to echo the self-consciousness that is at the root of every consciousness. Each of us can know pure presence from within, where it seems to speak of that unity of being, that self-recognition, which otherwise evades us, in our usual state of self-contradiction.

Of course, the bliss of self-communion that is supposedly what pure presence communicates is another symptom of self-contradiction, is a transcendental illusion that seems to heal the relationship one has with oneself (which is unavoidably dialectical), and to put one in a "natural" relationship with others, i.e., demonstrate one's inclusion in a collectivity. But in fact this bliss of self-communion, this "communication" carried out by pure presence, confirms the Babel-like collapse of the conformist collective language into singular forms that are mutually incomprehensible. It confirms, in other words, the death of language and effective society. The monad-like character of singular form reflects the atomization of society into a realm of hyperindividuals, answerable ultimately only to themselves. But the monadic hyperindividual, because his sense of self is premised on nonconformity, can hardly begin to know what it means to be fully answerable to himself, i.e., to have a self to conform to. The hyperindividual's purity of self is premised on the conformity of other selves and his own nonconformity, just as the pure presence of the modernist work of art is premised on the assumption of conformist communication within the world and its own nonconformist "communication." The nonconformist's only sense of responsibility is to his own nonconformity, to his own singularity of form. To sustain this singularity and remain nonconformist, he finally must become arbitrarily self-contradictory, i.e., root out any suspicion of self-conformity. Indeed, gratuitous nonconformity, a restless shifting of grounds of selfhood— becoming what Robert Jay Lifton calls the protean self—has become a fetish in our hyperindividualist society.

The production of modern art seems to depend on institutionalized non-conformity, a deliberate process of contradiction of or alienation from a collective style, regarded by Nicolas Calas as generating the tradition of the new. This institutionalized nonconformity is also the end result for selfhood of the secularization of reality as pure fact. Modernism represents that secularization for art, i.e., the sense of the entirely matter-of-fact presence of the work of art, as being nothing but a material making. This seemingly demystifying emphasis on fact bogs down when it comes to dealing with individuality, and what finally emerges is a sense of the radical uniqueness of each individual fact. To sustain this idea of uniqueness, any one fact must be shown to be radically different from every other fact, to carry its own logic within itself as it were—thus making it a monad. The literal becomes the individual—becomes, in the last analysis, a logic in itself. And thus we arrive, in Greenberg's words, at the literal order of effects as the only significant order of effects, meaning the only order that will communicate the radical individuality of facts. But if literalness communicates singularity and singularity becomes, in a completely secular world, the only substance of individuality and communication, then we are in a position that can only be described as narcissistic nonconformity. This is narcissism with a difference, the neonarcissism prevalent in our world of exaggerated individuality. Modernism represents the narcissistic nonconformity in art, for it claims that the work of art's pure manner of presence, its self-possession is a matter of its accepted nonconformity, a high tolerance for the individuality it achieves by abandoning any commitment to communication. It is quite possible that modernist art is admired just because it is able to mute itself in a world in which nothing is mute. It has out-individualized all the individuals who achieve their individuality by communication, for out of the opposite it has created a new way of being individual, of nonconforming. This, too, is proving to be a collective nonconformity.

NOTES

1. C. G. Jung, *Modern Man in Search of a Soul* (New York: Harcourt, Brace and World, 1966 [1933]), 197.

2. Oscar Wilde, "The Critic As Artist, Part I," *Intentions* (New York, 1905), 142–43.

3. Clement Greenberg, "The New Sculpture," *Partisan Review*, June 1949, 637.

4. Clement Greenberg, "Sculpture in Our Time," *Arts Magazine*, June 1958, 22.

5. Clement Greenberg, "Irrelevance versus Irresponsibility," *Partisan Review*, May 1948, 574.

6. Paul Valéry, "Degas, Dance, Drawing," *Degas Manet Morisot* (New York: Pantheon Books, 1960), 45.

7. Valéry, 87.

8. Valéry, 28–29.

9. Roland Barthes, *Mythologies* (New York, 1975), 35.

10. Roland Barthes, *The Pleasure of the Text* (New York: Hill and Wang, 1975), 6–7.

11. Clement Greenberg, "Seminar One," *Arts Magazine*, November 1973, 45.

12. Barthes, *The Pleasure of the Text*, 7.

THE ORIGINALITY OF THE AVANT-GARDE
A POSTMODERNIST REPETITION

Rosalind E. Krauss

In the summer of 1981 the National Gallery in Washington installed what it proudly describes as "the largest Rodin exhibition, ever." Not only was this the greatest public gathering of Rodin's sculpture, but it included, as well, much of his work never before seen. In certain cases the work had not been seen because it consisted of pieces in plaster that had lain on the shelves in storage at Meudon since the artist's death, closed off to the prying eyes of scholars and public alike. In other instances the work had not been seen because it had only just been made. The National Gallery's exhibition included, for example, a brand new cast of *The Gates of Hell*, so absolutely recent that visitors to the exhibition were able to sit down in a little theater provided for the occasion to view a just completed movie of the casting and finishing of this new version.

To some—though hardly all—of the people sitting in that theater watching the casting of *The Gates of Hell*, it must have occurred that they were witnessing the making of a fake. After all, Rodin has been dead since 1918, and surely a work of his produced more than sixty years after his death cannot be the genuine article, cannot, that is, be an original. The answer to this is more interesting than one would think; for the answer is neither yes nor no.

When Rodin died he left the French nation his entire estate, which consisted not only of all the work in his possession, but also all of the rights of its reproduction, that is, the right to make bronze editions from the estate's plasters. The Chambre des Deputés, in accepting this gift, decided to limit the posthumous editions to twelve casts of any given plaster. Thus *The Gates of Hell*, cast in 1978 by perfect right of the State, is a legitimate work: a real original we might say.

But once we leave the lawyer's office and the terms of Rodin's will, we fall immediately into a quagmire. In what sense is the new cast an original? At the time of Rodin's death *The Gates of Hell* stood in his studio like a mammoth plaster chessboard with all the pieces removed and scattered on the floor. The arrangement of the figures on *The Gates* as we know it reflects the most current notion the sculptor had about its composition, art arrangement documented by numbers penciled on the plasters corresponding to numbers located at various stations on *The Gates*. But these numbers were regularly changed as Rodin played with and recomposed the surface of the doors; and so, at the time of his death, *The Gates* were very much unfinished. They were also uncast. Since they had originally been commissioned and paid for by the State, they were, of course, not Rodin's to issue in bronze, even had he chosen to do so. But the building for which they had been commissioned had been canceled; *The Gates* were never called for, hence never finished, and thus never cast. The first bronze was made in 1921, three years after the artist's death.

So, in finishing and patinating the new cast there is no example completed during Rodin's lifetime to use for a guide to the artist's intentions about how the finished piece was to look. Due to the double circumstance of there being no lifetime cast and, at time of death, of there existing a plaster model still in flux, we could say that all the casts of *The Gates of Hell* are examples of multiple copies that exist in the absence of an original. The issue of authenticity is equally problematic for each of the existing casts; it is only more conspicuously so for the most recent.

But, as we have constantly been reminding ourselves ever since Walter Benjamin's "Work of Art in the Age of Mechanical Reproduction," authenticity empties out as a notion as one approaches those mediums which are inherently multiple—"from a photographic negative, for example," Benjamin argued, "one can make any number of prints; to ask for the 'authentic' print makes no sense."

For Rodin, the concept of the "authentic bronze cast" seems to have made as little sense as it has for many photographers. Like Atget's thousands of glass negatives for which, in some cases, no lifetime prints exist, Rodin left many of his plaster figures unrealized in any permanent material, either bronze or marble. Like Cartier-Bresson, who never printed his own photographs, Rodin's relation to the casting of his sculpture could only be called remote. Much of it was done in foundries to which Rodin never went while the production was in progress, he never worked on or retouched the waxes from which the final bronzes were cast, never supervised or regulated either the finishing or the patination, and in the end never checked the pieces before they were crated to be shipped to the client or dealer who had bought them. From his position deep in the ethos of mechanical reproduction, it was not as odd for Rodin as we might have thought to have willed his country posthumous authorial rights over his own work.

The ethos of reproduction in which Rodin was immersed was not limited, of course, to the relatively technical question of what went on at the foundry. It was installed within the very walls, heavy with plaster dust—the blinding snow of Rilke's description—of Rodin's studio. For the plasters that form the core of Rodin's work are, themselves, casts. They are thus potential multiples. And at the core of Rodin's massive output is the structural prolif-eration born of this multiplicity.

In the tremulousness of their balance, *The Three Nymphs* compose a figure of spontaneity—a figure somewhat discomposed by the realization that these three are identical casts of the same model; just as the magnificent sense of improvisatory gesture is strangely bracketed by the recognition that *The Two Dancers* are not simply spiritual, but mechanical twins. *The Three Shades*, the composition that crowns *The Gates of Hell*, is likewise a produc-tion of multiples, three identical figures, triple-cast, in the face of which it would make no sense—as little as with the nymphs or dancers—to ask which of the three is the original. *The Gates* themselves are another example of the modular working of Rodin's imagination, with the same figure com-pulsively repeated, repositioned, recoupled, recombined. If bronze casting is that end of the sculptural spectrum which is inherently multiple, the forming of the figurative originals is, we would have thought, at the other end—the pole consecrated to uniqueness. But Rodin's working procedures force the fact of reproduction to traverse the full length of this spectrum.[1]

Now, nothing in the myth of Rodin as the prodigious form-giver prepares us for the reality of these arrangements of multiple clones. For the form-giver is the maker of originals, exultant in his own originality. Rilke had long ago composed that incantatory hymn to Rodin's originality in describing the profusion of bodies invented for *The Gates*:

> bodies that listen like faces, and lift themselves like arms; chains of bodies, garlands and single organisms; bodies that listen like faces and lift tendrils and head clusters of bodies into which sin's sweetness rises out of the roots of pain. . . . The army of these figures became much too numerous to fit into the frame and wings of *The Gates of Hell*. Rodin made choice after choice and eliminated everything that was too solitary to subject itself to the great totality; everything that was not necessary was reject.[2]

This swarm of figures that Rilke evokes is, we are led to believe, composed of different figures. And we are encouraged in this belief by the cult of originality that grew up around Rodin, one that he himself invited. From the kind of reflexively intended hand-of-God imagery of Rodin's own work, to his carefully staged publicity—as in his famous portrait as genius progenitor by Edward Steichen—Rodin courted the notion of himself as form-giver, creator, crucible of originality. Rilke chants, "one walks among these thou-sand forms, overwhelmed with the imagination and the craftsmanship which they represent, and involuntarily one longs for the two hands out of which this world has risen. . . . One asks for the man who directs these hands."[3] Henry James, in *The Ambassadors*, has added, "With his genius in his eyes, his manners on his lips, his long career behind him and his honors and rewards all round, the great artist affected our friend as a dizzying prodigy of type . . . with a personal lustre almost violent, he shone in a constellation." What are we to make of this little chapter of the *comédie humaine,* in which the artist of the last century most driven to the celebration of his own originality and of the autographic character of his own kneading of matter into formal life, that artist, should have given his own work over to an afterlife of mechanical reproduction? Are we to think that in this peculiar last testimony Rodin acknowledged the extent to which his was an art of reproduction, of multiples without originals?

But at a second remove, what are we to make of our own squeamishness at the thought of the future of posthumous casting that awaits Rodin's work? Are we not involved here in clinging to a culture of originals which has no place among the reproductive mediums? Within the current photography market this culture of the original—the vintage print—is hard at work. The vintage print is specified as one made "close to the aesthetic moment"—and thus an object made not only by the photographer himself, but produced, as well, contemporaneously with the taking of the image. This is of course a mechanical view of authorship—one that does not acknowledge that some photographers are less good printers than the printers they hire; or that years after the fact photographers reedit and recrop older images, sometimes vastly improving them; or that it is possible to re-create old papers and old chemical compounds and thus to resurrect the look of the nineteenth-century vintage print, so that authenticity need not be a function of the history of technology.

But the formula that specifies a photographic original as a print made "close to the aesthetic moment" is obviously a formula dictated by the art historical notion of period style and applied to the practice of connoisseurship. A period style is a special form of coherence that cannot be fraudulently breached. The authenticity folded into the concept of style is a product of the way style is conceived as having been generated: that is, collectively and unconsciously. Thus an individual could not, by definition, consciously will a style. Later copies will be exposed precisely because they are not of the period; it is exactly that shift in sensibility that will get the chiaroscuro wrong, make the outlines too harsh or too muddy, disrupt the older patterns of coherence. It is this concept of period style that we feel the 1978 cast of *The Gates of Hell* will violate. We do not care if the copyright papers are all in order; for what is at stake are the aesthetic rights of style based on a culture of originals. Sitting in the little theater, watching the newest *Gates* being cast, watching this violation, we want to call out, "Fraud!"

Now why would one begin a discussion of avant-garde art with this story about Rodin and casts and copyrights? Particularly since Rodin strikes one as the very last artist to introduce to the subject, so popular was he during his lifetime, so celebrated, and so quickly induced to participate in the transformation of his own work into kitsch.

The avant-garde artist has worn many guises over the first hundred years of his existence: revolutionary, dandy, anarchist, aesthete, technologist, mystic. He has also preached a variety of creeds. One thing only seems to hold fairly constant in the vanguardist discourse and that is the theme of originality. By originality, here, I mean more than just the kind of revolt against tradition that echoes in Ezra Pound's "Make it new!" or sounds in the futurists' promise to destroy the museums that cover Italy as though "with countless cemeteries." More than a rejection or dissolution of the past, avant-garde originality is conceived as a literal origin, a beginning from ground zero, a birth. Marinetti, thrown from his automobile one evening in 1909 into a factory ditch filled with water, emerges as if from amniotic fluid to be born—without ancestors—a futurist. This parable of absolute self-creation that begins the first Futurist Manifesto functions as a model for what is meant by originality among the early twentieth-century avant-garde. For originality becomes an organicist metaphor referring not so much to formal invention as to sources of life. The self as origin is safe from contamination by tradition because it possesses a kind of originary naiveté. Hence Brancusi's dictum, "When we are no longer children, we are already dead." Or again, the self as origin has the potential for continual acts of regeneration, a perpetuation of self-birth. Hence Malevich's pronouncement, "Only he is alive who rejects his convictions of yesterday." The self as origin is the way an absolute distinction can be made between a present experienced *de novo* and a tradition-laden past. The claims of the avant-garde are precisely these claims to originality.

Now, if the very notion of the avant-garde can be seen as a function of the discourse of originality, the actual practice of vanguard art tends to reveal that "originality" is a working assumption that itself emerges from a ground of repetition and recurrence. One figure, drawn from avant-garde practice in the visual arts, provides an example. This figure is the grid.

Aside from its near ubiquity in the work of those artists who thought of themselves as avant-garde—their numbers include Malevich as well as Mondrian, Leger as well as Picasso, Schwitters, Cornell, Reinhardt, and Johns as well as Andre, LeWitt, Hesse, and Ryman—the grid possesses several structural properties which make it inherently susceptible to vanguard appropriation. One of these is the grid's imperviousness to language. "Silence, exile, and cunning," were Stephen Dedalus's passwords: commands that in Paul Goodman's view express the self-imposed code of the avant-garde artist. The grid promotes this silence, expressing it moreover as a refusal of speech. The absolute stasis of the grid, its lack of hierarchy, of center, of inflection, emphasizes not only its antireferential character, but—more importantly—its hostility to narrative. This structure, impervious both to time and to incident, will not permit the projection of language into the domain of the visual, and the result is silence.

This silence is not due simply to the extreme effectiveness of the grid as a barricade against speech, but to the protectiveness of its mesh against all inclusions from outside. No echoes of footsteps in empty rooms, no scream

of birds across open skies, no rush of distant water—for the grid has col-
lapsed the spatiality of nature onto the bounded surface of a purely cultural
object. With its proscription of nature as well as of speech, the result is still
more silence. And in this new-found quiet, what many artists thought they
could hear was the beginning, the origins of Art.

For those for whom art begins in a kind of originary purity, the grid was
emblematic of the sheer disinterestedness of the work of art, its absolute
purposelessness, from which it derived the promise of its autonomy. We
hear this sense of the originary essence of art when Schwitters insists, "Art is
a primordial concept, exalted as the godhead, inexplicable as life, indefinable
and without purpose." And the grid facilitated this sense of being born into
the newly evacuated space of an aesthetic purity and freedom.

While for those for whom the origins of art are not to be found in the idea
of pure disinterest so much as in an empirically grounded unity, the grid's
power lies in its capacity to figure forth the material ground of the pictorial
object, simultaneously inscribing and depicting it, so that the image of the
pictorial surface can be seen to be born out of the organization of pictorial
matter. For these artists, the grid-scored surface is the image of an absolute
beginning.

Perhaps it is because of this sense of a beginning, a fresh start, a ground
zero, that artist after artist has taken up the grid as the medium within which
to work, always taking it up as though he were just discovering it, as though
the origin he had found by peeling back layer after layer of representation to
come at last to this schematized reduction, this graph-paper ground, were *his*
origin, and his finding it an act of originality. Waves of abstract artists "discover" the grid; part of its structure one could say is that in its revelatory
character it is always a new, a unique discovery.

And just as the grid is a stereotype that is constantly being paradoxically
rediscovered, it is, as a further paradox, a prison in which the caged artist
feels at liberty. For what is striking about the grid is that while it is most
effective as a badge of freedom, it is extremely restrictive in the actual exercise of freedom. Without doubt the most formulaic construction that could
possibly be mapped on a plane surface, the grid is also highly inflexible.
Thus just as no one could claim to have invented it, so once one is involved
in deploying it, the grid is extremely difficult to use in the service of invention. And thus when we examine the careers of those artists who have been
most committed to the grid, we could say that from the time they submit
themselves to this structure their work virtually ceases to develop and becomes involved, instead, in repetition. Exemplary artists in this respect are
Mondrian, Albers, Reinhardt, and Agnes Martin.

But in saying that the grid condemns these artists not to originality but to
repetition, I am not suggesting a negative description of their work. I am
trying instead to focus on a pair of terms—originality and repetition—and to
look at their coupling unprejudicially; for within the instance we are examining, these two terms seem bound together in a kind of aesthetic economy,

interdependent and mutually sustaining, although the one—originality—is the valorized term and the other—repetition or copy or reduplication—is discredited.

We have already seen that the avant-garde artist above all claims originality as his right—his birthright, so to speak. With his own self as the origin of his work, that production will have the same uniqueness as he; the condition of his own singularity will guarantee the originality of what he makes. Having given himself this warrant, he goes on, in the example we are looking at, to enact his originality in the creation of grids. Yet as we have seen, not only is he—artist x, y, or z—not the inventor of the grid, but no one can claim this patent: the copyright expired sometime in antiquity and for many centuries this figure has been in the public domain.

Structurally, logically, axiomatically, the grid *can only be repeated*. And, with an act of repetition or replication as the "original" occasion of its usage within the experience of a given artist, the extended life of the grid in the unfolding progression of his work will be one of still more repetition, as the artist engages in repeated acts of self-imitation. That so many generations of twentieth-century artists should have maneuvered themselves into this particular position of paradox—where they are condemned to repeating, as if by compulsion, the logically fraudulent original—is truly compelling.

But it is no more compelling than that other, complementary fiction: the illusion not of the originality of the artist, but of the originary status of the pictorial surface. This origin is what the genius of the grid is supposed to manifest to us as viewers: an indisputable zero-ground beyond which there is no further model, or referent, or text. Except that this experience of originariness, felt by generations of artists, critics, and viewers is itself false, a fiction. The canvas surface and the grid that scores it do not fuse into that absolute unity necessary to the notion of an origin. For the grid *follows* the canvas surface, doubles it. It is a representation of the surface, mapped, it is true, onto the same surface it represents, but even so, the grid remains a figure, picturing various aspects of the "originary" object: through its mesh it creates an image of the woven infrastructure of the canvas; through its network of coordinates it organizes a metaphor for the plane geometry of the world; through its repetition it configures the spread of lateral continuity. The grid thus does not reveal the surface, laying it bare at last; rather it veils it through a repetition.

As I have said, this repetition performed by the grid must follow, or come after, the actual, empirical surface of a given painting. The representational text of the grid however also precedes the surface, comes before it, preventing even that literal surface from being anything like an origin. For behind it, logically prior to it, are all those visual texts through which the bounded plane was collectively organized as a pictorial field. The grid summarizes all these texts: the gridded overlays on cartoons, for example, used for the mechanical transfer from drawing to fresco; or the perspective lattice meant to contain the perceptual transfer from three dimensions to two; or the matrix on which to chart harmonic relationships, like proportion; or the millions of acts of en-framing by which the picture was reaffirmed as a regular quadrilateral. All these are the texts which the "original" ground plane of a Mondrian, for example, repeats—and, by repeating, represents. Thus the very ground that the grid is thought to reveal is already riven from within by a process of repetition and representation; it is always already divided and multiple.

What I have been calling the fiction of the originary status of the picture surface is what art criticism proudly names the opacity of the modernist picture plane, only in so terming it, the critic does not think of this opacity as fictitious. Within the discursive space of modernist art, the putative opacity of the pictorial field must be maintained as a fundamental concept. For it is the bedrock on which a whole structure of related terms can be built. All those terms—singularity, authenticity, uniqueness, originality, original— depend on the originary moment of which this surface is both the empirical and the semiological instance. If modernism's domain of pleasure is the space of autoreferentiality, this pleasure dome is erected on the semiological possibility of the pictorial sign as nonrepresentational and nontransparent, so that the signified becomes the redundant condition of a reified signifier. But from our perspective, the one from which we see that the signifier can-not be reified; that its objecthood, its quiddity, is only a fiction; that every signifier is itself the transparent signified of an already-given decision to carve it out as the vehicle of a sign—from this perspective there is no opac-ity, but only a transparency that opens onto a dizzying fall into a bottomless system of reduplication.

This is the perspective from which the grid that signifies the pictorial surface, by representing it, only succeeds in locating the signifier of another, prior system of grids, which have beyond them, yet another, even earlier system. This is the perspective in which the modernist grid is, like the Rodin casts, logically multiple: a system of reproductions without an original. This is the perspective from which the real condition of one of the major vehicles of modernist aesthetic practice is seen to derive not from the valorized term of that couple which I invoked earlier—the doublet, *originality/repetition*— but from the discredited half of the pair, the one that opposes the multiple to the singular, the reproducible to the unique, the fraudulent to the audience, the copy to the original. But this is the negative half of the set of terms that the critical practice of modernism seeks to repress, *has* repressed.

From this perspective we can see that modernism and the avant-garde are functions of what we could call the discourse of originality, and that that discourse serves much wider interests—and is thus fueled by more diverse institutions—than the restricted circle of professional art-making. The theme of originality, encompassing as it does the notions of authenticity, originals, and origins, is the shared discursive practice of the museum, the historian, and the maker of art. And throughout the nineteenth century all of these institutions were concerted, together, to find the mark, the warrant, the certi-fication of the original.[4]

That this would be done despite the ever-present reality of the copy as the *underlying condition of the original* was much closer to the surface of consciousness in the early years of the nineteenth century than it would later be permitted to be. Thus, in *Northanger Abbey* Jane Austen sends Catherine, her sweetly provincial young heroine, out for a walk with two new, rather more sophisticated friends; these friends soon embark on viewing the countryside, as Austen says, "with the eyes of persons accustomed to drawing, and decided on its capability of being formed into pictures, with all the eagerness of real taste." What begins to dawn on Catherine is that her countrified notions of the natural—"that a clear blue sky" is for instance "proof of a fine day"— are entirely false and that the natural, which is to say, the landscape, is about to be constructed for her by her more highly educated companions:

> a lecture on the picturesque immediately followed, in which his instructions were so clear that she soon began to see beauty in everything admired by him. . . . He talked of fore-grounds, distances, and second distances—side-screens and perspectives—lights and shades;—and Catherine was so hopeful a scholar that when they gained the top of Beechen Cliff, she voluntarily rejected the whole city of Bath, as unworthy to make part of a landscape.[5]

To read any text on the picturesque is instantly to fall prey to that amused irony with which Austen watches her young charge discover that nature itself is constituted in relation to its "capability of being formed into pictures." For it is perfectly obvious that through the action of the picturesque the very notion of landscape is constructed as a second term of which the first is a representation. Landscape becomes a reduplication of a picture which preceded it. Thus when we eavesdrop on a conversation between one of the leading practitioners of the picturesque, the Reverend William Gilpin, and his son, who is visiting the Lake District, we hear very clearly the order of priorities.

In a letter to his father, the young man describes his disappointment in the first day's ascent into the mountains, for the perfectly clear weather insured a total absence of what the elder Gilpin constantly refers to in his writings as effect. But the second day, his son assures him, there was a rainstorm followed by a break in the clouds.

> Then what effects of gloom and effulgence. I can't describe [them]—nor need I—for you have only to look into your own store house [of sketches] to take a view of them—It gave me however a very singular pleasure to see your system of effects so compleatly confirmed as it was by the observations of that day—wherever I turned my eyes, I beheld a drawing of yours.[6]

In this discussion, it is the drawing—with its own prior set of decisions about effect—that stands behind the landscape authenticating its claim to represent nature.

The 1801 supplement to Johnson's Dictionary gives six definitions for the term "picturesque," the six of them moving in a kind of figure eight around the question of the landscape as originary to the experience of itself. According to the Dictionary the picturesque is: 1) what pleases the eye; 2) remarkable for singularity; 3) striking the imagination with the force of paintings; 4) to be expressed in painting; 5) affording a good subject for a landscape; 6) proper to take a landscape from.[7] It should not be necessary to say that the concept of singularity, as in the part of the definition that reads, "remarkable for singularity," is at odds semantically with other parts of the definition, such as "affording a good subject for a landscape," in which a landscape is understood to mean a type of painting. Because that pictorial type—in all the formulaic condition of Gilpin's "effects"—is not single (or singular) but multiple, conventional, a series of recipes about roughness, chiaroscuro, ruins and abbeys, and therefore, when the effect is found in the world at large, that natural array is simply felt to be repeating another work—a "landscape"—that already exists elsewhere.

But the singularity of the Dictionary's definition deserves even further examination. *Gilpin's Observations on Cumberland and Westmorland* addresses this question of singularity by making it a function of the beholder and the array of singular moments of his perception. The landscape's singularity is thus not something which a bit of topography does or does not possess; it is rather a function of the images it figures forth at any moment in time and the way these pictures register in the imagination. That the landscape is not static but constantly recomposing itself into different, separate, or singular pictures, Gilpin advances as follows:

> He, who should see any one scene, as it is differently affected by the lowering sky, or a bright one, might probably see two very different landscapes. He might not only see distances blotted out; or splendidly exhibited; but he might even see variations produced in the very objects themselves; and that merely from the different times of the day in which they were examined.[8]

With this description of the notion of singularity as the perceptual-empirical unity of a moment of time coalesced in the experience of a subject, we feel ourselves entering the nineteenth-century discussion of landscape and the belief in the fundamental, originary power of nature dilated through subjectivity. That is, in Gilpin's two-different-landscapes-because-two-different-times-of-day, we feel that the prior condition of landscape as being already a picture is being let go of. But Gilpin then continues, "In a warm sunshine the purple hills may skirt the horizon, and appear broken into numberless pleasing forms; but under a sullen sky a total change may be produced," in which case, he insists, "the distant mountains, and all their beautiful projection may disappear, and their place be occupied by a dead flat." Gilpin thus reassures us that the patent to the "pleasing forms" as opposed to the "dead flat" has already been taken out by painting.

Thus what Austen's, Gilpin's, and the Dictionary's picturesque reveals to

us is that although the simular and the formulaic or repetitive may be semantically opposed, they are nonetheless conditions of each other: the two
logical halves of the concept landscape. The priorness and repetition of pictures is necessary to the singularity of the picturesque, because for the beholder singularity depends on being recognized as such, a re-cognition made
possible only by a prior example. If the definition of the picturesque is beau-
tifully circular, that is because what allows a given moment of the perceptual
array to be seen as singular is precisely its conformation to a multiple.

Now this economy of the paired opposition—singular and multiple—can
easily be examined within the aesthetic episode that is termed the Picturesque, an episode that was crucial to the rise of a new class of audience for
art, one that was focused on the practice of taste as an exercise in the recognition of singularity, or—in its application within the language of romanticism—originality. Several decades later into the nineteenth century,
however, it is harder to see these terms still performing in mutual interdependence, since aesthetic discourse—both official and nonofficial—gives
priority to the term originality and tends to suppress the notion of repetition
or copy. But harder to see or not, the notion of the copy is still fundamental
to the conception of the original. And nineteenth-century practice was concerted toward the exercise of copies and copying in the creation of that same
possibility of recognition that Jane Austen and William Gilpin call taste.
Thiers, the ardent Republican who honored Delacroix's originality to the
point of having worked on his behalf in the awarding of important government commissions, had nevertheless set up a museum of copies in 1834.
And forty years later in the very year of the first impressionist exhibition, a
huge Musée des Copies was opened under the direction of Charles Blanc,
then the director of France's Ministry of Fine Arts. In nine rooms the museum housed 156 newly commissioned full-scale oil copies of the most important masterpieces from foreign museums as well as replicas of the Vatican
Stanze frescoes of Raphael. So urgent was the need for this museum, in
Blanc's opinion, that in the first three years of the Third Republic, *all* monies
for official commissions made by the Ministry of Fine Arts went to pay for
copyists.[9] Yet, this insistence on the priority of copies in the formation of
taste hardly prevented Charles Blanc, no less than Thiers, from deeply ad-
miring Delacroix, or from providing the most accessible explanation of advanced color theory then available in print. I am referring to the *Grammar of
the Art of Design*, published in 1867, and certainly the obvious text in which
the budding impressionists could read about simultaneous contrast, comple-
mentarity, or achromatism, and be introduced to the theories and diagrams
of Chevreul and Goethe.

This is not the place to develop the truly fascinating theme of the role of
the copy within nineteenth-century pictorial practice and what is emerging
as its necessity to the concept of the original, the spontaneous, the new.[10] I
will simply say that the copy served as the ground for the development of an
increasingly organized and codified sign or seme of spontaneity—one that

Gilpin had called roughness, Constable had termed "the chiaroscuro of nature"—by which he was referring to a completely conventionalized overlay of broken touches and flicks of pure white laid in with a palette knife—and Monet later called instantaneity, linking its appearance to the conventionalized pictorial language of the sketch or pochade. Pochade is the technical term for a rapidly made sketch, a shorthand notation. As such, it is codifiable, recognizable. So it was both the rapidity of the pochade and its abbreviated language that a critic like Chesnaud saw in Monet's work and referred to by the way it was produced: "the chaos of palette scrapings," he called it.[11] But as recent studies of Monet's impressionism have made explicit, the sketchlike mark, which functioned as the *sign* of spontaneity, had to be prepared for through the utmost calculation, and in this sense spontaneity was the most fakable of signifieds. Through layers of underpainting by which Monet developed the thick corrugations of what Robert Herbert calls his texture-strokes, Monet patiently laid the mesh of rough encrustation and directional swathes that would signify speed of execution, and from this speed, mark both the singularity of the perceptual moment and the uniqueness of the empirical array.[12] On top of this constructed "instant," thin, careful washers of pigment establish the actual relations of color. Needless to say, these operations took—with the necessary drying time—many days to perform. But the illusion of spontaneity—the burst of an instantaneous and originary act—is the unshakable result. Rémy de Gourmont falls prey to this illusion when he speaks in 1901 of canvases by Monet as "the work of an instant," the specific instant being "that flash" in which "genius collaborated with the eye and the hand" to forge "a personal work of absolute originality."[13] The illusion of unrepeatable, separate instants is the product of a fully calculated procedure that was necessarily divided up into stages and sections and worked on piecemeal on a variety of canvases at the same time, assembly-line style. Visitors to Monet's studio in the last decades of his life were startled to find the master of instantaneity at work on a line-up of a dozen or more canvases. The production of spontaneity through the constant overpainting of canvases (Monet kept back the Rouen Cathedral series from his dealer, for example, for three years of reworking) employs the same aesthetic economy of the pairing of singularity and multiplicity, of uniqueness and reproduction, that we saw at the outset in Rodin's method. In addition, it involves that fracturing of the empirical origin that operates through the example of the modernist grid. But as was true in those other cases as well, the discourse of originality in which impressionism participates represses and discredits the complementary discourse of the copy. Both the avant-garde and modernism depend on the repression.

What would it look like not to repress the concept of the copy? What would it look like to produce a work that acted out the discourse of reproductions without originals, that discourse which could only operate in Mondrian's work as the inevitable subversion of his purpose, the residue of representationality that he could not sufficiently purge from the domain of his painting? The answer to this, or at least one answer, is that it would look like a certain kind of play with the notions of photographic reproduction that begins in the silkscreen canvases of Robert Rauschenberg and has recently flowered in the work of a group of younger artists whose production has been identified by the critical term *pictures*.[14] I will focus on the example of Sherrie Levine, because it seems most radically to question the concept of origin and with it the notion of originality.

Levine's medium is the pirated print, as in the series of photographs she made by taking images by Edward Weston of his young son Neil and simply rephotographing them, in violation of Weston's copyright. But as has been pointed out about Weston's "originals," they are already taken from models provided by others; they are given in that long series of Greek kouroi by which the nude male torso has long ago been processed and multiplied within our culture.[15] Levine's act of theft, which takes place, so to speak, in front of the surface of Weston's print, opens the print from behind to the series of models from which it, in turn, has stolen, of which it is itself the reproduction. The discourse of the copy, within which Levine's act must be located has, of course, been developed by a variety of writers, among them Roland Barthes. I am thinking of his characterization, in *S/Z*, of the realist as certainly not a copyist from nature, but rather a "pasticher," or someone who makes copies of copies. As Barthes says: "To depict is to . . . refer not from a language to a referent, but from one code to another. Thus realism consists not in copying the real but in copying a (depicted) copy. . . . Through secondary mimesis [realism] copies what is already a copy."[16]

In another series by Levine in which the lush, colored landscapes of Eliot Porter are reproduced, we again move through the "original" print, back to the origin in nature and—as in the model of the picturesque—through another trap door at the back wall of "nature" into the purely textual construction of the sublime and its history of degeneration into ever more lurid copies.

Now, insofar as Levine's work explicitly deconstructs the modernist notion of origin, her effort cannot be seen as an extension of modernism. It is, like the discourse of the copy, postmodernist. Which means that it cannot be seen as avant-garde either.

Because of the critical attack it launches on the tradition that precedes it, we might want to see the move made in Levine's work as yet another step in the forward march of the avant-garde. But this would be mistaken. In deconstructing the sister notions of origin and originality, postmodernism establishes a schism between itself and the conceptual domain of the avant-garde, looking back at it from across a gulf that in turn establishes a historical divide. The historical period that the avant-garde shared with modernism is over. That seems an obvious fact. What makes it more than a journalistic one is a conception of the discourse that has brought it to a close. This is a complex of cultural practices, among them a demythologizing criticism and a

truly postmodernist art, both of them acting now to void the basic propositions of modernism, to liquidate them by exposing their fictitious condition.
It is thus from a strange new perspective that we look back on the modernist
origin and watch it splintering into endless replication.

NOTES

1. For a discussion of Rodin's figural repetition, see my *Passages in Modern Sculpture* (New York: Viking, 1977), chap. 1; and Leo Steinberg, *Other Criteria* (New York:
Oxford University Press), 322-403.

2. Rainer Maria Rilke, *Rodin*, trans. Jessie Lemont and Hans Frausil (London: Grey
Walls Press, 1946), 52.

3. Ibid., 2.

4. On the discourse of origins and originals, see Michel Foucault, *The Order of
Things* (New York: Pantheon, 1970), 328–35: "But this thin surface of the original,
which accompanies our entire existence . . . is not the immediacy of a birth; it is
populated entirely by those complex mediations formed and laid down as a sediment
in their own history by labor, life and language so that . . . what man is reviving
without knowing it, is all the intermediaries of a time that governs him almost to
infinity."

5. Jane Austen, *Northanger Abbey*, 1818, vol. 1, chap. 14.

6. In Carl Paul Barbier, *William Gilpin* (Oxford: Clarendon Press, 1963), 111.

7. See Barbier, 98.

8. William Gilpin, *Observations on Cumberland and Westmorland* (Richmond: Richmond Publishing Co., 1973), vii. The book was written in 1772 and first published in
1786.

9. For details, see Albert Boime, "Le Musée des Copies," *Gazette des Beaux-Arts* 64
(1964): 237–47.

10. For a discussion of the institutionalization of copying within nineteenth-century artistic training, see Albert Boime, *The Academy and French Painting in the Nineteenth Century* (London: Phaidon, 1971).

11. Cited by Steven Z. Levine, "The 'Instant' of Criticism and Monet's Critical
Instant," *Arts Magazine* 55, no. 7 (Mar. 1981): 118.

12. See Robert Herbert, "Method and Meaning in Monet," *Art in America* 67, no. 5
(Sept. 1979): 90–108.

13. Cited by Levine, 118.

14. The relevant texts are by Douglas Crimp; see his exhibition catalogue *Pictures*
(New York: Artists Space, 1977); and "Pictures," *October* 8 (Spring 1979): 75–88.

15. See Douglas Crimp, "The Photographic Activity of Postmodernism," *October*
15 (Winter 1980): 98–99.

16. Roland Barthes, *S/Z*, trans. Richard Miller (New York: Hill and Wang,
1974), 55.

II.

*The Debate in Philosophy and
More Politics of Discourse*

Play of titles: "From One Newism to Another through Some Post-isms (New Criticism, Postmodernism, Post-Marxism, Poststructuralism, New Historicism") or "Estates General of the Quotation Market," or else "Inverted Commas Auctioned Off."

The demarcation by quotation marks or inverted commas means that these labels have the exchange value of currencies meant to circulate and make possible the circulation of goods, the allocation of places, the situation and evaluation of pieces on a chessboard or in some Wall Street of the academy (that is, in a place of quotations on the stock exchange as well as in the linguistic sense "cotations" and quotations), but without ever allowing anybody to appropriate them or make claims for them as a monopoly. And above all without any Central Bank or Federal Reserve Bank or First Interstate Bank ever guaranteeing the issue of titles. Those titles are always declared as the discourse of the other. They always have the doxographic value of a quasi-quotation, of the mention "the so-called."

J.D.

HABERMAS AND LYOTARD ON POSTMODERNITY

Richard Rorty

In *Knowledge and Human Interests* Habermas tried to generalize what Marx and Freud had accomplished by grounding their projects of "unmasking" in a more comprehensive theory. The strand in contemporary French thought which Habermas criticizes as "neoconservative" starts off from suspicion of Marx and Freud, suspicion of the masters of suspicion, suspicion of "unmasking." Lyotard, for example, says that he will

> use the term "modern" to designate any science that legitimates itself with reference to a metadiscourse of this kind [i.e., "a discourse of legitimation with respect to its own status, a discourse called philosophy"] making an explicit appeal to some grand narrative, such as the dialectics of the Spirit, the hermeneutics of meaning, the emancipation of the rational or working subject, or the creation of wealth.[1]

He goes on to define "postmodern" as "incredulous towards metanarratives" (PC, xxiv), and to ask "Where, after the metanarratives, can legitimacy reside?" (PC, xxiv–xxv). From Lyotard's point of view, Habermas is offering one more metanarrative, a more general and abstract "narrative of emancipation" (PC, 60) than the Freudian and Marxian metanarratives. For Habermas, the problem posed by "incredulity towards metanarratives" is that unmasking only makes sense if we "preserve at least one standard for [the] explanation of the corruption of all reasonable standards."[2] If we have no such standard, one which escapes a "totalizing self-referential critique," then distinctions between the naked and the masked, or between theory and ideology, lose their force. If we do not have these distinctions, then we have to give up the Enlightenment notion of "rational criticism of existing institutions," for "rational" drops out. We can still, of course, have criticism, but it will be of the sort which Habermas ascribes to Horkheimer and Adorno: "they abandoned any theoretical approach and practiced ad hoc determinate negation. . . . The praxis of negation is what remains of the 'spirit of . . .

unremitting theory' " (EME, 29). Anything that Habermas will count as retaining a theoretical approach will be counted by an incredulous Lyotard as a "metanarrative." Anything that abandons such an approach will be counted by Habermas as "neoconservative," because it drops the notions which have been used to justify the various reforms which have marked the history of the Western democracies since the Enlightenment, and which are still being used to criticize the socioeconomic institutions of both the Free and the Communist worlds. Abandoning a standpoint which is, if not transcendental, at least "universalistic," seems to Habermas to betray the social hopes which have been central to liberal politics.

So we find French critics of Habermas ready to abandon liberal politics in order to avoid universalistic philosophy, and Habermas trying to hang on to universalistic philosophy, with all its problems, in order to support liberal politics. To put the opposition in another way, the French writers whom Habermas criticizes are willing to drop the opposition between "true consensus" and "false consensus," or between "validity" and "power," in order not to have to tell a metanarrative in order to explicate "true" or "valid." But Habermas thinks that if we drop the idea of "the better argument" as opposed to "the argument which convinces a given audience at a given time," we shall have only a "context-dependent" sort of social criticism. He thinks that falling back on such criticism will betray "the elements of reason in cultural modernity which are contained in . . . bourgeois ideals," e.g., "the internal theoretical dynamic which constantly propels the sciences—and the self-reflexion of the sciences as well—*beyond* the creation of merely technologically exploitable knowledge" (EME, 18).

Lyotard would respond to this last point by saying that Habermas misunderstands the character of modern science. The discussion of "the pragmatics of science" in *The Postmodern Condition* is intended to "destroy a belief that still underlies Habermas's research, namely that humanity as a collective (universal) subject seeks its common emancipation through the regularization of the 'moves' permitted in all language games, and that the legitimacy of any statement resides in its contribution to that emancipation" (PC, 66). Lyotard claims to have shown that "consensus is only a particular state of discussion [in the sciences], not its end. Its end, on the contrary, is paralogy" (PC 65–66). Part of his argument for this odd suggestion is that "Post-modern science—by concerning itself with such things as undecidables, the limits of precise control, conflicts characterized by incomplete information, 'fracta,' catastrophes, and pragmatic paradoxes—is theorizing its own evolution as discontinuous, catastrophic, non-rectifiable and paradoxical" (PC, 60).

I do not think that such examples of matters of current scientific concern do anything to support the claim that "consensus is not the end of discussion." Lyotard argues invalidly from the current concerns of various scientific disciplines to the claim that science is somehow discovering that it should aim at permanent revolution, rather than at the alternation between normality and revolution made familiar by Kuhn. To say that "science aims" at piling paralogy on paralogy is like saying that "politics aims" at piling revolution on revolution. No inspection of the concerns of contemporary science or contemporary politics could show anything of the sort. The most that could be shown is that talk of the aims of either is not particularly useful.

On the other hand, Lyotard does have a point, the point he shares with Mary Hesse's criticism of Habermas's Diltheyan account of the distinction between natural science and hermeneutic inquiry. Hesse thinks that "it has been sufficiently demonstrated [by what she calls "post-empiricist" Anglo-American philosophy of science] that the language of theoretical science is irreducibly metaphorical and unformalizable, and that the logic of science is circular interpretation, re-interpretation, and self-correction of data in terms of theory, theory in terms of data."[3] This kind of debunking of empiricist philosophy of science is happily appropriated by Lyotard. Unfortunately, however, he does not think of it as a repudiation of a bad account of science but as indicating a recent change in the nature of science. He thinks that science used to be what empiricism described it as being. This lets him accuse Habermas of not being up to date.

If one ignores this notion of a recent change in the nature of science (which Lyotard makes only casual and anecdotal attempts to justify), and focuses instead on Lyotard's contrast between "scientific knowledge" and "narrative," that turns out to be pretty much the traditional positivist contrast between "applying the scientific method" and "unscientific" political or religious or common-sensical discourse. Thus Lyotard says that a "scientific statement is subject to the rule that a statement must fulfill a given set of conditions in order to be accepted as scientific" (PC, 8). He contrasts this with "narrative knowledge" as the sort which "does not give priority to the question of its own legitimation, and . . . certifies itself in the pragmatics of its own transmission without having recourse to argumentation and proof." He describes "the scientist" as classifying narrative knowledge as "a different mentality: savage, primitive, under-developed, backward, alienated, composed of opinions, customs, authority, prejudice, ignorance, ideology" (PC, 27). Lyotard, like Hesse, wants to soften this contrast and to assert the rights of "narrative knowledge." In particular, he wants to answer his initial question by saying that once we get rid of the metanarratives legitimacy resides where it always has, in the first-order narratives:

> There is, then, an incommensurability between popular narrative pragmatics, which provides immediate legitimation, and the language game known as the question of legitimacy. . . . Narratives . . . determine criteria of competence and/or illustrate how they are to be applied. They thus define what has the right to be said and done in the culture in question, and since they are themselves a part of that culture, they are legitimated by the simple fact that they do what they do. (PC, 23)

This last quotation suggests that we read Lyotard as saying: the trouble with Habermas is not so much that he provides a metanarrative of emancipation as that he feels the need to legitimize, that he is not content to let the narratives which hold our culture together do their stuff. He is scratching where it does not itch. On this reading, Lyotard's criticism would chime with the Hesse-Feyerabend line of criticism of empiricist philosophy of science, and in particular with Feyerabend's attempt to see scientific and political discourse as continuous. It would also chime with the criticisms offered by many of Habermas's sympathetic American critics, such as Bernstein, Geuss, and McCarthy. These critics doubt that studies of communicative competence can do what transcendental philosophy failed to do in the way of providing "universalistic" criteria.[4] They also doubt that universalism is as vital to the needs of liberal social thought as Habermas thinks it. Thus Geuss, arguing that the notion of an "ideal speech situation" is a wheel which plays no part in the mechanism of social criticism, and suggesting that we reintroduce a position "closer to Adorno's historicism," says: "If rational argumentation can lead to the conclusion that a critical theory [defined as 'the "self-consciousness" of a successful process of emancipation and enlightenment'] represents the most advanced position of consciousness available to us in our given historical situation, why the obsession with whether or not we may call it 'true'?"[5]

Presumably by "rational argumentation" Geuss means not "rational by reference to an extra-historical, universalistic, set of criteria" but something like "uncoerced except in the ways in which all discourse everywhere is inevitably coerced—by being conducted in the terms and according to the practices of a given community at a given time." He is dubious that we need a theoretical account which gets behind that vocabulary and those conventions to something "natural" by reference to which they can be criticized. As Geuss says, the "nightmare which haunts the Frankfurt School" is something like Huxley's Brave New World, in which "agents are actually content, but only because they have been prevented from developing certain desires which in the 'normal' course of things they would have developed, and which cannot be satisfied within the framework of the present social order."[6] To take the scare-quotes out from around "normal," one would have to have just the sort of metanarrative which Lyotard thinks we cannot get. But we think we need this only because an overzealous philosophy of science has created an impossible ideal of ahistorical legitimation.

The picture of social progress which Geuss's more historical line of thought offers is of theory as emerging at dusk, the belated "self-consciousness" of emancipation rather than a condition for producing it. It thus has links with the antirationalist tradition of Burke and Oakeshott, as well as with Deweyan pragmatism. It departs from the notion that the intellectuals can form a revolutionary vanguard, a notion cherished even by French writers who claim to have dispensed with Marx's metanarrative. On this account of social change, there is no way for the citizens of *Brave New World* to work their way out from their happy slavery by theory, and, in particular, by studies of communicative competence. For the narratives which go to make up their sense of what counts as "rational" will see to it that such studies produce a conception of undistorted communication which accords with the desires they presently have. There is no way for us to prove to ourselves that we are not happy slaves of this sort, any more than to prove that our life is not a dream. So whereas Habermas compliments "bourgeois ideals" by reference to the "elements of reason" contained in them, it would be better just to compliment those untheoretical sorts of narrative discourse which make up the political speech of the Western democracies. It would be better to be frankly ethnocentric.

If one is ethnocentric in this sense, one will see what Habermas calls "the internal theoretical dynamic which constantly propels the sciences . . . beyond the creation of technologically exploitable knowledge" not as a theoretical dynamic, but as a social practice. One will see the reason why modern science is more than engineering, not as an ahistorical teleology—e.g., an evolutionary drive toward correspondence with reality, or the nature of language—but as a particularly good example of the social virtues of the European bourgeoisie. The reason will simply be the increasing self-confidence of a community dedicated to (in Blumenberg's phrase) "theoretical curiosity." Modern science will look like something which a certain group of human beings invented in the same sense in which these same people can be said to have invented Protestantism, parliamentary government, and Romantic poetry. What Habermas calls the "self-reflection of the sciences" will thus consist not in the attempt to "ground" scientists' practices (e.g., free exchange of information, normal problem-solving, and revolutionary paradigm-creation) in something larger or broader, but rather of attempts to show how these practices link up with, or contrast with, other practices of the same group or of other groups. When such attempts have a critical function, they will take the form of what Habermas calls "ad hoc determinate negation."

Habermas thinks that we need not be restricted, as Horkheimer and Adorno were, to such merely sociohistorical forms of social criticism. He views Horkheimer, Adorno, Heidegger, and Foucault as working out new versions of "the end of philosophy":

> no matter what name it [philosophy] appears under now—whether as fundamental ontology, as critique, as negative dialectic, or genealogy—these pseudonyms are by no means disguises under which the traditional [i.e., Hegelian] form of philosophy lies hidden; the drapery of philosophical concepts more likely serves as the cloak for a scantily concealed end of philosophy.[7]

Habermas's account of such "end of philosophy" movements is offered as part of a more sweeping history of philosophy since Kant. He thinks that Kant was right to split high culture up into science, morality, and art and

that Hegel was right in accepting this as "the standard (*massgebliche*) interpretation of modernity" (I-17). He thinks that "the dignity specific to cultural
modernism consists in what Max Weber has called the stubborn differentiation of value-spheres" (EME, 18). He also thinks that Hegel was right in
believing that "Kant does not perceive the . . . formal divisions within culture . . . as diremptions. Hence he ignores the need for unification that
emerges with the separations evoked by the principle of subjectivity" (I-17).
He takes as seriously as Hegel did the question "How can an intrinsic ideal
form be constructed from the spirit of modernity, that neither just imitates
the historical forms of modernity nor is imposed upon them from the outside?" (I-18).

From the historicist point of view I share with Geuss, there is no reason to
look for an intrinsic ideal that avoids "just imitating the historical forms of
modernity." All that social thought can hope to do is to play the various
historical forms of modernity off against one another in the way in which,
e.g., Blumenberg plays "self-assertion" off against "self-grounding."[8] But
because Habermas agrees with Hegel that there is a "need for unification" in
order to "regenerate the devastated power of religion in the medium of
reason" (I-18), he wants to go back to Hegel and start again. He thinks that
in order to avoid the disillusionment with "the philosophy of subjectivity"
which produced Nietzsche and the two strands of post-Nietzschean thought
which he distinguishes and dislikes (the one leading to Foucault, and the
other to Heidegger), we need to go back to the place where the young Hegel
took the wrong turn (III-30). That was the place where he still "held open
the option of using the idea of uncoerced will formation in a communication
community existing under constraints of cooperation as a model for the reconciliation of a bifurcated civil society" (III-15). He thus suggests that it was
the lack of a sense of rationality as social that was missing from "the philosophy of the subject" which the older Hegel exemplified (and from which he
believes the "end-of-philosophy" thinkers have never really escaped—see
III-30).

But whereas Habermas thinks that the cultural need which "the philosophy of the subject" gratified was and is real, and can perhaps be fulfilled by
his own focus on a "communication community," I would urge that it is an
artificial problem created by taking Kant too seriously. On this view, the
wrong turn was taken when Kant's split between science, morals, and art
was accepted as a *donnée*, as *die massgebliche Selbstauslegung der Moderne*.
Once that split is taken seriously, then the *Selbstvergewisserung der Moderne*,
which Hegel and Habermas both take to be the "fundamental philosophical
problem" (see I-12), will indeed seem urgent. For once the philosophers
swallow Kant's "stubborn differentiation," then they are condemned to an
endless series of reductionist and antireductionist moves. Reductionists will
try to make everything scientific ("positivism"), or political (Lenin), or aesthetic (Baudelaire, Nietzsche). Antireductionists will show what such attempts leave out. To be a philosopher of the "modern" sort is precisely to be

unwilling either to let these spheres simply coexist uncompetitively, or to reduce the other two to the remaining one. Modern philosophy has consisted in forever realigning them, squeezing them together, and forcing them apart again. But it is not clear that these efforts have done the modern age much good (or, for that matter, harm).

Habermas thinks that the older Hegel "solves the problem of the self-reassurance of modernity too well," because the Philosophy of Absolute Spirit "removes all importance from its own present age . . . and deprives it of its calling to self-critical renewal" (II-28). He sees the popularity of "end-of-philosophy" thought as an overreaction to this over-success. But surely part of the motivation for this kind of thought is the belief that Hegel too was scratching where it did not really itch. Whereas Habermas thinks that it is with Hegel's own over-success that philosophy becomes what Hegel himself called "an isolated sanctuary" whose ministers "form an isolated order of priests . . . untroubled by how it goes with the world," it is surely possible to see this development as having been Kant's fault, if anybody's, and precisely the fault of his "three-sphere" picture of culture. On this latter view, Kant's attempt to deny knowledge to make room for faith (by inventing "transcendental subjectivity" to serve as a fulcrum for the Copernican revolution was provoked by an unnecessary worry about the spiritual significance, or insignificance, of modern science. Like Habermas, Kant thinks that modern science has a "theoretical dynamic," one which can be identified with (at least a portion of) "the nature of rationality." Both think that by isolating and exhibiting this dynamic, but distinguishing it from other dynamics (e.g., "practical reason" or "the emancipatory interest"), one can keep the results of science without thereby disenchanting the world. Kant suggested that we need not let our knowledge of the world *qua* matter-in-motion get in the way of our moral sense. The same suggestion was also made by Hume and Reid, but unlike these pragmatical Scotchmen, Kant thought that he had to back up this suggestion with a story which would differentiate and "place" the three great spheres into which culture must be divided. From the point of view common to Hume and Reid (who disagreed on so much else) no such metanarrative is needed. What is needed is a sort of intellectual analogue of civic virtue—tolerance, irony, and a willingness to let spheres of culture flourish without worrying too much about their "common ground," their unification, the "intrinsic ideals" they suggest, or what picture of man they "presuppose."

In short, by telling a story about Kant as the beginning of modern philosophy (and by emphasizing the difference between modern and premodern philosophy) one might make the kind of fervent end-of-philosophy writing Habermas deplores look both more plausible and less interesting. What links Habermas to the French thinkers he criticizes is the conviction that the story of modern philosophy (as successive reactions to Kant's diremptions) is an important part of the story of the democratic societies' attempts at self-reassurance. But it may be that most of the latter story could be told as the history of reformist politics, without much reference to the kinds of theoretical backup which philosophers have provided for such politics. It is, after all, things like the formation of trade unions, the meritocratization of education, the expansion of the franchise, and cheap newspapers, which have figured most largely in the willingness of the citizens of the democracies to see themselves as part of a "communicative community"—their continued willingness to say "us" rather than "them" when they speak of their respective countries. This sort of willingness has made religion progressively less important in the self-image of that citizenry. One's sense of relation to a power beyond the community becomes less important as one becomes able to think of oneself as part of a body of public opinion, capable of making a difference to the public fate. That ability has been substantially increased by the various "progressive" changes I have listed.

Weber was of course right in saying that some of these changes have also worked the other way (to increase our sense of being controlled by "them"). But Habermas is so preoccupied with the "alienating" effects of such changes that he allows himself to be distracted from the concomitant increase in people's sense of themselves as free citizens of free countries. The typical German story of the self-consciousness of the modern age (the one which runs from Hegel through Marx, Weber, and Nietzsche) focuses on figures who were preoccupied with the world we lost when we lost the religion of our ancestors. But this story may be both too pessimistic and too exclusively German. If so, then a story about the history of modern thought which took Kant and Hegel less seriously and, for example, the relatively untheoretical socialists more seriously, might lead us to a kind of "end-of-philosophy" thinking which would escape Habermas's strictures on Deleuze and Foucault. For these French writers buy in on the usual German story, and thus tend to share Habermas's assumption that the story of the realignment, assimilation, and expansion of the three "value-spheres" is essential to the story of the *Selbstvergewisserung* of modern society, and not just to that of the modern intellectuals.

In order to interpret this problem of the three spheres as a problem only for an increasingly "isolated order of priests," one has to see the "principle of the modern" as something other than that famous "subjectivity" which post-Kantian historians of philosophy, anxious to link Kant with Descartes, took as their guiding thread. One can instead attribute Descartes's role as "founder of modern philosophy" to his development of what I earlier called "an overzealous philosophy of science"—the sort of philosophy of science which saw Galilean mechanics, analytic geometry, mathematical optics, and the like, as having more spiritual significance than they in fact have. By taking the ability to do such science as a mark of something deep and essential to human nature, as the place where we got closest to our true selves, Descartes preserved just those themes in ancient thought which Bacon had tried to obliterate. The preservation of the Platonic idea that our most distinctively human faculty was our ability to manipulate "clear and distinct ideas," rather than to accomplish feats of social engineering, was Descartes's most important and most unfortunate contribution to what we now think of as "modern philosophy." Had Bacon—the prophet of self-assertion, as opposed to self-grounding—been taken more seriously, we might not have been struck with a canon of "great modern philosophers" who took "subjectivity" as their theme. We might, as J. B. Schneewind puts it, have been less inclined to assume that epistemology (i.e., reflection on the nature and status of natural science) was the "independent variable" in philosophical thought and moral and social philosophy the "dependent variable." We might thereby see what Blumenberg calls "self-assertion"—the willingness to center our hopes on the future of the race, on the unpredictable successes of our descendants—as the "principle of the modern." Such a principle would let us think of the modern age as defined by successive attempts to shake off the sort of ahistorical structure exemplified by Kant's division of culture into three "value-spheres."

On this sort of account, the point I claimed Lyotard shared with Feyerabend and Hesse—the point that there are no interesting epistemological differences between the aims and procedures of scientists and those of politicians—is absolutely fundamental. The recovery of a Baconian, non-Cartesian attitude toward science would permit us to dispense with the idea of "an internal theoretical dynamic" in science, a dynamic which is something more than the "anything goes that works" spirit which unites Bacon and Feyerabend. It would break down the opposition between what Habermas calls "merely technologically exploitable knowledge" and "emancipation," by seeing both as manifestations of what Blumenberg calls "theoretical curiosities." It would free us from preoccupation with the purported tensions between the three "value-spheres" distinguished by Kant and Weber, and between the three sorts of "interests" distinguished by Habermas.

In the present space, I cannot do more than gesture toward the various rosy prospects which appear once one suggests that working through "the principle of subjectivity" (and out the other side) was just a side-show, something which an isolated order of priests devoted themselves to for a few hundred years, something which did not make much difference to the successes and failures of the European countries in realizing the hopes formulated by the Enlightenment. So I shall conclude by turning from the one issue on which I think Lyotard has a point against Habermas to the many issues about which Habermas seems to me in the right.

The thrust of Habermas's claim that thinkers like Foucault, Deleuze, and Lyotard are "neoconservative" is that they offer us no "theoretical" reason to move in one social direction rather than another. They take away the dynamic which liberal social thought (of the sort represented by Rawls in America and Habermas himself in Germany) has traditionally relied upon, viz., the need to be in touch with a reality obscured by "ideology" and disclosed by "theory." Habermas says of Foucault's later work that it replaced the model of repression and emancipation developed by Marx and Freud with a pluralism of power/discourse formations. These formations intersect and succeed one another and can be differentiated according to their style and intensity. They cannot, however, be judged in terms of validity, which was possible in the case of the repression and emancipation of conscious as opposed to unconscious conflict resolutions. (EME, 29)

This description is, I think, quite accurate, as is his remark that "the shock" which Foucault's books produce "is not caused by the flash of insight into a confusion which threatens identity" but instead by "the affirmed de-differentiation and by the affirmed collapse of those categories which alone can account for category mistakes of existential relevance." Foucault affects to write from a point of view light-years away from the problems of contemporary society. His own efforts at social reform (e.g., of prisons) seem to have no connection with his exhibition of the way in which the "humane" approach to penal reform tied in with the needs of the modern state. It takes no more than a squint of the inner eye to read Foucault as a stoic, a dispassionate observer of the present social order, rather than its concerned critic. Because the rhetoric of emancipation—the notion of a kind of truth which is not one more production of power—is absent from his work, he can easily be thought of reinventing American "functionalist" sociology. The extraordinary dryness of Foucault's work is a counterpart of the dryness which Iris Murdoch once objected to in the writing of British analytic philosophers.[9] It is a dryness produced by a lack of identification with any social context, any communication. Foucault once said that he would like to write "so as to have no face." He forbids himself the tone of the liberal sort of thinker who says to his fellow-citizens: "We know that there must be a better way to do things than this; let us look for it together." There is no "we" to be found in Foucault's writings, nor in those of many of his French contemporaries.

It is this remoteness which reminds one of the conservative who pours cold water on hopes for reform, who affects to look at the problems of his fellow-citizens with the eye of the future historian. Writing "the history of the present," rather than suggestions about how our children might inhabit a better world in the future, gives up not just on the notion of a common human nature, and on that of "the subject," but on our untheoretical sense of social solidarity. It is as if thinkers like Foucault and Lyotard were so afraid of being caught up in one more metanarrative about the fortunes of "the subject" that they cannot bring themselves to say "we" long enough to identify with the culture of the generation to which they belong. Lyotard's contempt for "the philosophy of subjectivity" is such as to make him abstain from anything that smacks of the "metanarrative of emancipation" which Habermas shares with Blumenberg and Bacon. Habermas's socialization of subjectivity, his philosophy of consensus, seems to Lyotard just one more pointless variation on a theme which has been heard too often.

But although disconnecting "philosophy" from social reform—a disconnection previously performed by analytic philosophers who were "emotivist" in metaethics while being fiercely partisan in politics—is one way of expressing exasperation with the philosophical tradition, it is not the only way. Another would be to minimize the importance of that tradition, rather than seeing it as something which urgently needs to be overcome, unmasked, or genealogized. Suppose, as I suggested above, one sees the wrong turn as having been taken with Kant (or better yet, with Descartes) rather than (like Habermas) with the young Hegel or the young Marx. Then one might see the canonical sequence of philosophers from Descartes to Nietzsche as a distraction from the history of concrete social engineering which made the contemporary North Atlantic culture what it is now, with all its glories and all its dangers. One could try to create a new canon—one in which the mark of a "great philosopher" was awareness of new social and religious and institutional possibilities, as opposed to developing a new dialectical twist in metaphysics or epistemology. That would be a way of splitting the difference between Habermas and Lyotard, of having things both ways. We could agree with Lyotard that we need no more metanarratives, but with Habermas that we need less dryness. We could agree with Lyotard that studies of the communicative competence of a transhistorical subject are of little use in reinforcing our sense of identification with our community, while still insisting on the importance of that sense.

If one had such a de-theoreticized sense of community, one could accept the claim that valuing "undistorting communication" was of the essence of liberal politics without needing a theory of communicative competence as backup. Attention would be turned instead to some concrete examples of what was presently distorting our communication—e.g., to the sort of "shock" we get when, reading Foucault, we realize that the jargon we liberal intellectuals developed has played into the hands of the bureaucrats. Detailed historical narratives of the sort Foucault offers us would take the place of philosophical metanarratives. Such narratives would not unmask something created by power called "ideology" in the name of something not created by power called "validity" or "emancipation." They would just explain who was currently getting and using power for what purposes, and then (unlike Foucault) suggest how some other people might get it and use it for other purposes. The resulting attitude would be neither incredulous and horrified realization that truth and power are inseparable nor Nietzschean *Schadenfreude*, but rather a recognition that it was only the false lead which Descartes gave us (and the resulting overvaluation of scientific theory which, in Kant, produce "the philosophy of subjectivity") that made us think truth and power were separable. We could thus take the Baconian maxim that "knowledge is power" with redoubled seriousness. We might also be made to take seriously Dewey's suggestion that the way to re-enchant the world, to bring back what religion gave our forefathers, is to stick to the concrete. Much of what I have been saying is an attempt to follow up on the following passage from Dewey:

We are weak today in ideal matters because intelligence is divorced from aspiration. . . . When philosophy shall have cooperated with the force of events
and made clear and coherent the meaning of the daily detail, science and
emotion will interpenetrate, practice and imagination will embrace. Poetry
and religious feeling will be the unforced flowers of life.[10]

I can summarize my attempt to split the difference between Lyotard and
Habermas by saying that this Deweyan attempt to make concrete concerns
with the daily problems of one's community—social engineering—the substitute for traditional religion seems to me to embody Lyotard's postmodernist "incredulity towards metanarratives" while dispensing with the
assumption that the intellectual has a mission to be avant-garde, to escape
the rules and practices and institutions which have been transmitted to him
in favor of something which will make possible "authentic criticism."
Lyotard unfortunately retains one of the left's silliest ideas—that escaping
from such institutions is automatically a good thing, because it insures that
one will not be "used" by the evil forces which have "co-opted" these
institutions. Leftism of this sort necessarily devalues consensus and communication, for insofar as the intellectual remains able to talk to people outside
the avant-garde he "compromises" himself. Lyotard exalts the "sublime,"
and argues that Habermas's hope that the arts might serve to "explore a
living historical situation" and to "bridge the gap between cognitive, ethical
and political discourses," (PC, 72) shows that Habermas has only an "aesthetic of the beautiful" (PC, 79). On the view I am suggesting, one should
see the quest for the sublime, the attempt (in Lyotard's words) to "present
the fact that the unpresentable exists" (PC, 82), as one of the prettier unforced blue flowers of bourgeois culture. But this quest is wildly irrelevant to
the attempt at communicative consensus which is the vital force that drives
that culture.

More generally, one should see the intellectual *qua* intellectual as having a
special, idiosyncratic, need—a need for the ineffable, the sublime, a need to
go beyond the limits, a need to use words which are not part of anybody's
language-game, any social institution. But one should not see the intellectual
as serving a social purpose when he fulfills this need. Social purposes are
served, just as Habermas says, by finding beautiful ways of harmonizing
interests, rather than sublime ways of detaching oneself from others' interests. The attempt of leftist intellectuals to pretend that the avant-garde is
serving the wretched of the earth by fighting free of the merely beautiful is a
hopeless attempt to make the special needs of the intellectual and the social
needs of his community coincide. Such an attempt goes back to the Romantic period, when the urge to think the unthinkable, to grasp the uncondi-
tioned, to sail strange seas of thought alone, was mingled with enthusiasm
for the French Revolution. These two, equally laudable, motives should be
distinguished.

If we do distinguish them, then we can see each as a distinct motive for the kind of "end of philosophy" thinking Habermas deplores. The desire for the sublime makes one want to bring the philosophical tradition to an end because it makes one want to cut free from the words of the tribe. Giving these words a purer sense is not enough; they must be abjured altogether, for they are contaminated with the needs of a repudiated community. Such a Nietzschean line of thought leads to the kind of avant-garde philosophy which Lyotard admires in Deleuze. The desire for communication, harmony, interchange, conversation, social solidarity, and the "merely" beautiful, wants to bring the philosophical tradition to an end because it sees the attempt to provide metanarratives, even metanarratives of emancipation, as an unhelpful distraction from what Dewey calls "the meaning of the daily detail." Whereas the first sort of end-of-philosophy thinking sees the philosophical tradition as an extremely important failure, the second sort sees it as rather unimportant excursus.[11] Those who want sublimity are aiming at a postmodernist form of intellectual life. Those who want beautiful social harmonies want a postmodernist form of social life, in which society as a whole asserts itself without bothering to ground itself.[12]

NOTES

1. Jean-François Lyotard, *The Postmodern Condition: A Report on Knowledge*, trans. Geoff Bennington and Brian Massumi (Minneapolis, 1984), xxiii. Further references to this book will be included in the text of the essay as "PC."

2. Jürgen Habermas, "The Entwinement of Myth and Enlightenment: Re-reading *Dialectic of Enlightenment*," *New German Critique* 26 (1982): 28. Further references to this essay will be included in the text as "EME."

3. Mary Hesse, *Revolutions and Reconstructions in the Philosophy of Science* (Bloomington, 1980), 173.

4. See, for example, Thomas McCarthy, "Rationality and Relativism: Habermas' 'Overcoming' of Hermeneutics," in *Habermas: Critical Debates*, ed. John B. Thompson and David Held (Cambridge, Mass., 1982).

5. Raymond Geuss, *The Idea of a Critical Theory: Habermas and the Frankfurt School* (Cambridge, 1982), 94.

6. Ibid., 83.

7. Jürgen Habermas, *Paris Lectures*, III, 3. In the spring of 1983, Habermas gave four lectures in Paris on the theme of modernity. These lectures form part of a book on modernity entitled *Der philosophische Diskurs der Moderne* (Frankfurt: Suhrkamp, 1985). References are to a typescript translation of the lectures by Thomas McCarthy and will be referred to in the text as lectures I, II, III, and IV.

8. Hans Blumenberg, *The Legitimacy of the Modern Age*, trans. Robert M. Wallace (Cambridge, Mass., 1983), 184.

9. See Murdoch, "Against Dryness," reprinted (from *Encounter*, 1961) in *Revisions*, ed. Stanley Hauerwas and Alasdair MacIntyre (Notre Dame, Indiana, 1983).

10. John Dewey, *Reconstruction in Philosophy* (Boston, 1957), 164.

11. I pursue this contrast in a discussion with Derrida called "Deconstruction and Circumvention," *Critical Inquiry* 11 (1984): 1–21.

12. I wrote this essay while enjoying the hospitality of the Center for Advanced Study in the Behavioral Sciences, and while being supported in part by National Sciences Foundation Grant no. BNS 820-6304. I am grateful to both institutions, and also to Prof. Martin Jay of the University of California at Berkeley who made several very helpful comments on the first version of the essay.

HABERMAS AND POSTMODERNISM

Martin Jay

In the burgeoning debate over the apparent arrival of the postmodern era (or over the implications of a discourse that claims such an era has arrived), no contributor has been as forthright and unflinching a defender of the still uncompleted project of modernity as Jürgen Habermas. In several recent works, *Der philosophische Diskurs der Moderne, Die neue Unübersichtlichkeit,* and his response to the essays collected by Richard Bernstein in *Habermas and Modernity,*[1] he has expanded his critique far beyond the first, tentative essays he published in the early 1980s.[2] These initial efforts, in part because of their imperfect command of the French intellectual scene and in part because of their controversial attribution of a conservative political implication to postmodernism, proved a lightning rod for criticism. In many quarters, Habermas was pilloried as a naively one-dimensional celebrant of an outdated liberal, Enlightenment rationalism. His attempt to formulate a theory of social evolution was damned as a new version of a discredited objectivist philosophy of history.

Although the relation of Habermas's critique to the specific context out of which it emerged, that of the cynically antipolitical *Tendenzwende* in the West Germany of the late 1970s, was on occasion acknowledged,[3] by and large, he was chided with having superficially reversed the profound analysis of the Enlightenment's failure offered by the older generation of the Frankfurt School. Indeed, because he has been understood as a staunch defender of universalist, totalizing reason, his work has been accused of being only the most recent and subtle version of an intellectual tradition which inadvertently fostered the authoritarian political uniformity it claimed to resist. Habermas, the passionate defender of democratically achieved consensus and generalized interest, was thus turned into the terrorist of coercive reason *malgré lui.*

Whether or not his more recent works will dispel this caricature remains to be seen. From all reports of the mixed reception he received in Paris when he gave the lectures that became *Der philosophische Diskurs der Moderne,* the odds are not very high that a more nuanced comprehension of his work will prevail, at least among certain critics. At a time when virtually any defense of rationalism is turned into a brief for the automatic suppression of otherness, heterogeneity, and nonidentity, it is hard to predict a widely sympathetic hearing for his complicated argument. Still, if such an outcome is to be made at all possible, the task of unpacking his critique of postmodernism and nuanced defense of modernity must be forcefully pursued. One way to start this process is to focus on a particularly central theme in his work, which has hitherto been relatively ignored. Because it concerns an issue closely related to his similar critique of poststructuralism, it will also illuminate Habermas's no less virulent hostility to the other leading "post" phenomenon of our no longer modern world.

The theme in question is what might be called the opposition between differentiation and *différance*. The latter term, a neologism coined by Jacques Derrida in a seminal essay now twenty-one years old, doubtless needs little introduction to contemporary readers of cultural criticism. I would only like to emphasize that Derrida specifically emphasizes its distance from differentiation. "Among other confusion," he notes, "such a word would suggest some organic unity, some primordial and homogeneous unity, that would eventually come to be divided up and take on difference as an event. Above all, formed on the verb 'to differentiate,' this word would annul the economic signification of detour, temporalizing delay, 'deferring.'"[4] Differentiation, in other words, implies for Derrida either nostalgia for a lost unity or conversely a utopian hope for a future one. Additionally, the concept is suspect for deconstruction because it implies the crystallization of hard and fast distinctions between spheres, and thus fails to register the supplementary interpenetrability of all subsystems, the effaced trace of alterity in their apparent homogeneity, and the subversive absence undermining their alleged fullness or presence.

Now, although deconstruction ought not to be uncritically equated with postmodernism, a term Derrida himself has never embraced, one can easily observe that the postmodernist temper finds *différance* more attractive than differentiation as a historical or, better put, posthistorical conceptual tool. The metanarrative of a process of original unity progressively articulating itself into a series of increasingly autonomous and internally homogeneous subsystems is far less compelling to it than an antinarrative of heterogeneous but interpenetrating movements that flow in no discernible historical or evolutionary direction. Even though the prefix "post" implies temporal irreversibility, it has become a favorite pastime to find the postmodern already evident in such earlier figures as Gustave Flaubert.[5] Postmodernists like Jean-Francois Lyotard explicitly eschew any yearning for the restoration of a predifferentiated unity or the construction of a dedifferentiated totality in a reconciled future. Instead, they valorize a fluid network of proliferating and incommensurable *différances*, which escape reduction to a finite number of common denominators. In the neo-Wittgensteinian language Lyotard adopted in *The Postmodern Condition* (but later abandoned as too anthropocentric in *Le Différend*), he contends that "there is no possibility that language games can be unified or totalized in any meta-discourse."[6] But if unity or totality is denied, so too is the apparent necessity of those binary oppositions that characterize traditional thought. Thus, the recent postmodernist "non-exhibition" staged at the Centre Pompidou in Paris by Lyotard was called "Les Immatériaux" to stress the overturning of the rigid separation between mind and matter, subject and object, consciousness and body, even life and death.[7] Furthermore, as Jacques Bouveresse, one of Lyotard's most persistent critics, notes in his recent diatribe *Rationalité et Cynisme*, "the deliberate effacement of conventional frontiers that exist for the moment among sciences, philosophy, literature and art is the shibboleth (*mot d'ordre*) par excellence, it seems to me, of postmodernity."[8]

If we also look more closely at the aesthetic dimension of the postmodern condition, we will see the same antidifferentiating impulse at work. Thus, the art critic Suzi Gablik notes in *Has Modernism Failed?* that a great deal of performance art in particular makes us anxious because "it violates our sense of boundaries; no distinction is made between public and private events, between real and aesthetic emotions, between art and self."[9] As such, postmodernism can be seen in part as the nonutopian anticlimax to what Peter Bürger has defined as the avant-garde, as opposed to the modernist project: the abolition of the separate institution of art and its reabsorption into the life-world out of which it originally came.[10] Typical of this postmodernist penchant for violating boundaries is the breakdown of the differences between high and low art, culture and kitsch, and the sacred space of the museum and the profane world without. In architecture in particular, which has been widely recognized as the cutting edge of the postmodernist offensive, what Charles Jencks called "radical eclecticism"[11] has meant the disruption of the time-honored distinctions between different styles, as well as the breakdown of the hierarchical superiority of "serious" architecture over a more popular and vulgar vernacular, such as that celebrated by Robert Venturi in his defense of Las Vegas.[12]

What is, however, important to recognize in all of these transgressions of various frontiers is the abandonment of any hope for a new totalization in the sense of a dialectical *Aufhebung* or sublation. Instead, an untotalized network of supplementary *différances* is posited as the superior alternative to the seemingly rigid and unyielding dichotomies of modernist differentiation. Georges Bataille's model of a carnivalesque disruption of all hierarchies in the sacred and ecstatic community of expenditure can be found lurking behind much poststructuralist social theorizing. The postmodernist sensibility has also borrowed a great deal from that dimension of feminist thought which rejects the abstract universalism underlying any homogenizing humanist discourse, while also remaining suspicious of the essentializing opposition between the sexes so much a part of patriarchal culture.[13]

Now, because Habermas has been outspoken in his distrust of both poststructuralist and postmodernist theories, and has heretofore not really absorbed the feminist critique of the Western tradition,[14] he has variously been accused of hoping for a utopian totalization based on the universal power of rationality and rigidly holding on, like a typically German anal-compulsive, to the existent differentiations of a modernization process still worth salvaging. The first charge is exemplified by Lyotard's complaint that "what Habermas requires from the arts and the experiences they provide is, in short, to bridge the gap between cognitive, ethical and political discourses, thus opening the way to a unity of experience."[15] Habermas, he believes, still remains hostage to the fantasy of "humanity as a collective (universal) subject"[16] seeking a perfect consensus in a metalanguage game transcending all others.

The second and in some ways contrary criticism is typified by the Derridean argument of Dominick LaCapra, who concedes Habermas's strong distaste for Hegelian or other metasubjects, but still questions his alternative:

> The problem, however, is whether, in rejecting reductionism and dialectical synthesis, Habermas goes to the extreme of analytic dissociation which is itself constitutive of a logic of domination. Habermas does not directly see how his own analytic distinctions, which are useful within limits, may be rendered problematic, especially when they are taken as categorical definitions of realms of thought or action.[17]

As an antidote, LaCapra urges Habermas to pay more attention to the supplementary and carnivalesque play of language, which would undermine the apparently rigid differentiations posited in various ways during the development of his work. More recent deconstructionist critics of Habermas like Michael Ryan and Jonathan Culler have echoed this advice, in each case defending *différance* as superior to categorical distinctions.[18]

A more patient reading of Habermas's demanding corpus than is evident in these critiques would, I want to suggest, allow us to appreciate the virtues of defending a certain notion of differentiation against postmodernist *différance*. First, it is clear that although the very early Habermas may have espoused the position attributed to him by Lyotard, that of believing in a metasubjective species being capable of achieving a universal consensus, at least as early as 1972 and possibly even during the positivist dispute of the 1960s, he had explicitly abandoned this position.[19] Repudiating the idea of a Hegelian-Marxist universal subject as a residue of a discredited consciousness philosophy, he began to call instead for the nurturing of a plurality of intersubjectively grounded speech communities. In fact, his main complaint against poststructuralism is that it merely inverts consciousness-philosophy by denying the subject, and thus ironically, is as holistic as the logocentric traditions it opposes. Rather than calling for a unity of experience, as Lyotard contends, Habermas has scrupulously defended the value of distinctive forms of interaction, not merely among human beings, but also between human beings and nature. In fact, his skepticism toward the project of reconciling humanity and the natural world has brought him under fire from such advocates of a more Marcusean or Blochian strain in Western Marxism, such as Thomas McCarthy, Joel Whitebook, and Henning Ottmann.[20] Instead of holding out hope for a utopian reenchantment of our disenchanted world, Habermas has resolutely acknowledged humanity's disembeddedness, that is, differentiation from the natural world.

But second, while valorizing differentiation, Habermas has fully recognized that the process has been plagued by severe difficulties. Even as he has called modernity an uncompleted project worth carrying forward, he has been very sensitive to the deep discontents it has spawned. Unlike the more sanguine defenders of modernization who peopled the American and West German academies in the postwar era, he has always been enough of a student of Max Horkheimer and Theodor Adorno's *Dialectic of Enlightenment* to recognize that the mere refinement of analytic categories and the increased complexity of modern society are by no means emancipatory in themselves.

Habermas's attitude toward differentiation is, thus, a highly complicated one. To do justice to it would require tracing its origins in at least two traditions, sociological and philosophical. To make sense of the former would mean beginning with Herbert Spencer and Emile Durkheim in the nineteenth century and passing on to twentieth-century theorists like Max Weber, Talcott Parsons, Niklas Luhmann and Wolfgang Schluchter, all of whom are critically appropriated in Habermas's massive *Theory of Communicative Action* and elsewhere.[21] We would then have to reconsider the heated sociological controversies over evolutionism and functionalism and make distinctions among segmental, stratified, and functionalist forms of differentiation. And finally, we would have to consider the responses of such contemporary sociologists as Anthony Giddens to Habermas's reading of the tradition.[22]

To probe the second, philosophical tradition, we would have to go back at least as far as Immanuel Kant and examine his three critiques with their separation among forms of judgment. We would then have to trace efforts to undo Kant's differentiations, beginning perhaps with Hegel and continuing up through the Western Marxist struggle to articulate a defensible concept of totality.[23] And we would have to conclude with a consideration of Habermas's recent exchanges with Hans-Georg Gadamer and other defenders of a radical hermeneutics, who try to provide a new foundationless foundation for a holistic approach to understanding.

Rather than attempt so ambitious and foolhardy a reconstruction of the roots of Habermas's attitude toward differentiation, let me simply point to the major implications he has drawn from his contact with these disparate sources. Habermas's rational reconstruction of the evolution of Western societies posits a relatively undifferentiated society of hominids who became what can be called human through both the division of labor and the development of kinship structures.[24] At the very beginning of the evolutionary process, as he conceptualizes it, there is thus already a form of differentiation between subsystems of the whole. Similarly, the distinction between labor and language means that any universal explanation of human development, say, a vulgar Marxist productivism or a vulgar deconstructionist paritextualism, must be rejected as reductionist. For the process of evolution takes place on several levels, which roughly can be grouped under two rubrics. The first, which Habermas calls system integration, derives from an instrumental relationship between humanity and its natural environment. Initially generated by the dialectic of labor, system integration spawns steering mechanisms, like money and bureaucratic power, which achieve a certain autonomy of their own. The second level, which Habermas calls social integration, refers to norms and values, which are derived from a communicative rather than instrumental relationship among actors, who have the capacity to be active agents rather than mere bearers of structural forces. It is only in the modern period beginning in the eighteenth century, so Habermas contends, that the distance between system and social integration becomes especially evident with the differentiation of subsystems of economics and administration, the decentering of world views (what Weber calls the "disenchantment of the world"), and the uncoupling of law from morality.

Unlike more complacent functionalist theorists of evolutionary differentiation, Habermas recognizes the potential for radical distress in this process. In particular, he is sensitive to the disproportionately advanced development of system as opposed to social integration in modern capitalist and bureaucratic socialist societies. Both types of integration can be understood as emerging against the background of a life-world in which rationalization takes place when communicative argumentation supplants more authoritarian and coercive forms of social coordination. System rationalization, however, entails means-ends rationalism, whereas social or communicative rationalization involves other forms of reciprocal intersubjective integration. In the modern world, the former has revealed itself as more powerful than the latter, leading to what Habermas calls the "colonization" of the life-world by system or instrumental rationality. Hostility to this trend has expressed itself in many ways, including the derogation of all forms of reason as dominating and coercive. It is, however, Habermas's contention that unless we carefully distinguish among types of rationalization, we risk regressing beyond the genuine achievements of moderation. Thus, he writes, the deconstructionist critique of logocentrism becomes legitimate when it understands its target, "not as an excess, but as a deficit of reason"[25] because of the partiality of the subject-centered, instrumental rationality it misidentifies with reason *tout court*. It is illegitimate, however, when it rejects any rational adjudicating of competing truth claims because of the inherent undecidability of all language, a belief whose practical consequences is an irrationalist decisionism.

Following Weber and before him Kant, Habermas stipulates a differentiation among three basic types of reason in the sphere of values: cognitive (or scientific), moral, and aesthetic. The Enlightenment had hoped that the emancipatory potential of each of these spheres could ultimately be harnessed for practical purposes. "The twentieth century," Habermas admits, "has shattered this optimism. The differentiation of science, morality and art has come to mean the autonomy of the segments treated by the specialist and at the same time their splitting off from the hermeneutics of everyday communication. This splitting off is the problem that has given rise to those efforts to "negate" the culture of expertise."[26] Although understanding the motivation behind these attempts to dedifferentiate and thus end the alienation of the separate spheres from each other and from the everyday life-world, Habermas is nonetheless very reluctant to abandon the Enlightenment project entirely. For with it came the refinement of rationalization itself, which resists the reduction of modern life to any one common denominator, rational or otherwise.

Habermas's argument in this regard is worth following in some detail, because it has so often been misconstrued by those who see him as the advocate of a terroristically universal form of reason. First of all, although Habermas sees each sphere as having undergone a variant of what can be called rationalization, he nonetheless explicitly rejects the idea that reason means the same thing in each case. In an earlier essay on his attitude toward modernism, I challenged him in particular to clarify what he meant by rationality in the aesthetic sphere.[27] Was he claiming in the manner of, say, Suzi Gablik in her book on *Progress in Art* that Jean Piaget's developmental cognitive categories could be applied to aesthetics, as he argued they could to cognitive and moral development? His reply was that art criticism, which arose with the differentiation of autonomous art from its religious-ceremonial context,

> has developed forms of argumentation that specifically differentiate it from the forms of theoretical and moral-practical discourse. As distinct from merely subjective preference, the fact that we link judgments of taste to a criticizable claim presupposes non-arbitrary standards for judgment of art. As the philosophical discussion of "artistic truth" reveals, works of art raise claims with regard to their unity (harmony: *Stimmigkeit*), their authenticity, and the success of their expressions by which they can be measured and in terms of which they may fail.[28]

Thus, in the discourse about art, there is an argumentative rationality that resists reduction to moral or scientific reason.

Not only does aesthetic discourse reveal such a rationalization, Habermas continues, so too does art immanently considered. In art itself, there is a type of learning process, which is cumulative. "What accumulates are not epistemic contents," Habermas contends, "but rather the effects of the inner logical differentiation of a special sort of experience: precisely those aesthetic experiences of which only a decentered, unbound subjectivity is capable."[29] The increasingly decentered and unbounded subjectivity of artistic experience has an ultimately emancipatory potential, for it "dictates an increased sensitivity to what remains unassimilated in the interpretive achievements of pragmatic, epistemic, and moral mastery of the demands and challenges of everyday situations; it effects an openness to the expurgated elements of the unconscious, the fantastic, and the mad, the material and the bodily."[30] Thus, "art becomes a laboratory, the critic an expert, the development of art the medium of a learning process—here, naturally, not in the sense of an accumulation of epistemic contents, of an aesthetic 'progress'—which is possible only in individual dimensions—but nonetheless in the sense of concentrically expanding, advancing exploration of a realm of possibilities opened up with the autonomization of art."[31] In short, instead of providing a straightjacket for transgressive, heterogeneous experiences, as those who formulate a simple opposition between art and reason assume, aesthetic rationalization—in the dual sense of critical and productive learning processes—allows, indeed encourages, a proliferation of artistic stimuli to a widened consciousness. Only the modernist autonomization of art, its differentiation as an institution of its own, makes such a rationalization possible.

The extreme autonomization of both esoteric art and hermetic aesthetic criticism does, to be sure, create pressures for their reintegration with the life-world out of which they originally emerged. Here Habermas admits to a certain ambivalence. On the one hand, he rejects what he sees, following Adorno, as the premature, forced, and impotent *Aufhebung* of art and life in such movements as Surrealism. Yet on the other hand, he recognizes that too rigid and inflexible a detachment of art from life courts the danger of forfeiting art's ultimate capacity to reinvigorate the life-world by giving it a higher level access to those expurgated experiences it normally marginalizes or suppresses. Too radical a break between art and life also threatens to cause the wellsprings of aesthetic expression themselves to run dry. He hesitates to affirm an immediate reintegration, however, because he contends that the utopian dedifferentiation of art *by itself* is insufficient to undo the pathologies of modernization. A new constellation of the separate value spheres with their expert rationalized discourses and the communicative life-world of everyday experience is needed in order to maximize the emancipatory potential in the project of modernity. This neither necessitates the collapse of all of these now distinct realms into one universal language game, as Lyotard accuses him of advocating, nor the rigid maintenance of the boundaries of the differentiated spheres, as his deconstructionist critics aver he upholds. Instead, a more nuanced mediation of relatively, but not absolutely commensurable realms is a preferable alternative.[32]

In a recent essay on "Modern and Postmodern Architecture,"[33] Habermas spells out the implications of this argument in the aesthetic field that is now at the cutting edge of the debate. Modernist architecture, he points out, was at once functional and formalist, following both the socially progressive imperatives of, say, early Bauhaus radicalism and the antiornamental purism of constructivist abstraction. In both ways, it sought to break with a sterile traditionalism and use the methods and materials of the modern world. As such, it was based on a mediated interaction between nonaesthetic needs and the development of immanent aesthetic reflexivity. The postmodernists are right, Habermas admits, in recognizing that the utopian social intentions of the early modernists went awry when the international style became the emblem of corporate capitalism and the excuse for alienating an impersonal mass housing. But here the problem was not so much the Enlightenment ambition at the root of the modernist quest, as its distorted application in terms more of instrumental, system rationality than communicative, social rationality.

The postmodernists go too far, Habermas suggests, in reaction to this failure by seeking to separate formalist and functional imperatives entirely. Either they retreat into an eclectic celebration of historical styles, which conservatively affirms all of them merely because they once existed, or "like surrealist stage designers," they "utilize modern design methods in order to coax picturesque effects from aggressively mixed styles."[34] Any attempt, moreover, to generate a vitalist architecture, which would immediately restore all severed ties with the life-world—here perhaps Habermas is thinking of the Heideggerian-inspired call for a Critical Regionalism by Kenneth Frampton and others[35]—risks turning into an antimodernist nostalgia for a predifferentiated form of life. An immanent critique of the limitations of modernist architecture, acknowledging its achievements as well as its failures, is thus preferable to a wholesale turning of the page, which offers only pseudo-solutions to the pathologies of modern life.

Premature dedifferentiation is, in fact, one of the most troubling of those false answers, which Habermas sees as legitimated by the postmodernist discourse of *différance*. In his latest book, *Der philosophische Diskurs der Moderne*, he criticizes Michel Foucault, Derrida, and also Adorno for their undifferentiated critique of modernity: "Enlightenment and manipulation, conscious and unconscious, forces of production and forces of destruction, expressive self-realization and repressive desublimation, freedom-guaranteeing and freedom-eliminating effects, truth and ideology—all of these moments are confused with each other."[36] The dedifferentiation of the value spheres of modernity are, moreover, purchased at the cost of the tacit elevation of one of them, aesthetics, understood in an essentially irrationalist sense.

For Habermas, the current fascination with Friedrich Nietzsche betrays this inclination, for the new Nietzscheanism "represents the differentiation of science and morality as the developmental process of a reason that at the same time usurps and stifles the poetic, world-disclosing power of art,"[37] which it seeks to resurrect. But in making art somehow prior to differentiation, in assuming that rhetoric is somehow more fundamental than philosophy,[38] it fails to see that the very sphere of art itself is the result of a process of differentiation. In other words, it is mistaken to offer an aesthetic colonization of the life-world as an antidote to its instrumental rational counterpart produced by the hypertrophy of science and system integration in modern capitalism.

Similarly, Foucault's effort to collapse cognition and power is based on a problematic dedifferentiation of the will to knowledge and the will to power, which reduces all the human sciences to little more than subtle instruments of discipline and normalizing control. Likewise, Derrida's critique of J. L. Austin fails to register the linguistic differentiations of the communicative life-world in which fictional discourse has been usefully distinguished from other language games.[39] In short, much postmodernist analysis has been vitiated by a confusingly ahistorical failure to recognize that certain patterns of differentiation have emerged in ways that defy the attempt to say that they are always already undermined. And moreover, it is precisely the separate rationalizations of the distinct spheres that must be defended as a way to avoid a holism of indiscriminate *différance* that merely turns on its head the logocentric holism of reductive sameness. Albrecht Wellmer puts Habermas's alternative cogently when he writes,

> we have to distinguish between those irreversible differentiation processes, which signify the end of traditional society and the emergence of specifically modern, universalist conceptions of rationality, freedom, and democracy on the one hand, and the specific form in which these differentiation processes have been articulated and institutionalized in capitalist societies. It is obviously to the latter only that the ideas of a sublation of formal law, politics, or art can meaningfully apply. What they can mean is what could be called a new "permeability" of the relatively autonomous subsystems or cultural spheres for each other.[40]

Such an answer may, to be sure, raise a few questions of its own. How can we tell, for example, when a healthy balance has been struck between permeability and boundary maintenance? If, on the one hand, the boundaries become too fluid, aren't we forced into a postmodernist *différance* in which supplementarity reigns supreme? If, on the other, they have become too rigid, might it no longer be possible to assume even the partial commensurability that is at the root of Habermas's guarded optimism about the modernist project? How can we, moreover, be certain that it is only the specific differentiations of the Western modernization process that possess enough rationality to be worth defending? As Thomas McCarthy points out in questioning Habermas's debt to Luhmann's systems theory, it is important to insure that "the possibility of democratization as dedifferentiation of economy and state not be metatheoretically ruled out of court by systems-theoretic borrowing. Here again, the question arises of whether it should be superseded by some non-regressive form of dedifferentiation."[41] The same question arises for the other forms of articulation defended by Habermas in his eagerness to avoid abandoning the modern project before its emancipatory potential is fully tapped. It is perhaps not by chance that *différance* has often come to be the rallying cry for many who feel excluded by the dominant forms of rationality in our culture.

And yet, after having acknowledged all of these questions, it still seems justifiable to conclude by stressing the value of Habermas's alternative to postmodernist *différance*. A recent critic of his position, Peter Uwe Hohendahl, complains,

> It is not quite evident why Habermas is not willing to use the critical force of deconstruction against the logic of differentiated systems. It seems that Habermas overstates his case when he describes deconstruction as a purely literary approach without concern for problem-solving in the realm of the life-world. Thus my suggestion would be: if we want to free the life-world from the constraints of the overarching system and its institutions, there is room for the project of deconstructive criticism, precisely because it questions the logic of systems.[42]

The answer to this complaint is that for Habermas, the differentiation of systemic institutions cannot be construed solely as a constraint on an oppressed life-world, but rather as the source of certain rationalizations that are worthy of continued presentation. It would therefore be dangerous to turn deconstruction from an essentially literary approach into a more universal solvent of all structures and systems, in the hope of reconvening the sacred community of Bataille's ecstatic general economy. For the result would be a night of endless *différance* in which all cows were piebald, which is as deceptive as the old idealist trick of turning them all black. Instead, we should be more sensitive to the enlightening as well as obscuring implications of a much-maligned modernity whose promise is still greater than is assumed by those who counsel a leap into the postmodernist dark.

NOTES

1. Jürgen Habermas, *Der philosophische Diskurs der Moderne* (Frankfurt: Suhrkamp, 1985); *Die neue Unübersichtlichkeit* (Frankfurt, 1985); "Questions and Counterquestions," in *Habermas and Modernity*, ed. Richard Bernstein (Cambridge, Mass., 1985).

2. Jürgen Habermas, "Modernity versus Postmodernism," *New German Critique* 22 (Winter, 1981); "The Entwinement of Myth and Enlightenment: Re-reading *Dialectic of Enlightenment*," *New German Critique* 26 (Spring-Summer, 1982).

3. Andreas Huyssen, "Mapping the Postmodern," *New German Critique* 33 (Fall, 1984): 30.

4. Jacques Derrida, "Différance," in *Speech and Phenomena and Other Essays on Husserl's Theory of Signs*, trans. David Allison (Evanston, 1973), 143.

5. See, for example, *Flaubert and Postmodernism*, ed. Naomi Schor and Henry F. Majewski (Lincoln, 1984).

6. Jean-François Lyotard, *The Postmodern Condition: A Report on Knowledge*, trans. Geoff Bennington and Brian Massumi (Minneapolis, 1984), 36.

7. *Les Immatériaux* was presented at the Centre Pompidou from March 28 to July 15, 1985. For a selection of texts reflecting on it, see the simultaneously published *Modernes et Après: Les Immatériaux*, ed. Elie Théofilakis (Paris, 1985). It should be acknowledged that in certain of his writings, Lyotard himself emphasizes the impermeability of boundaries between radically incommensurable spheres. See, for exam-

ple, his dialogue with Jean-Loup Thébald, *Just Gaming,* trans. Wlad Godzich (Minneapolis, 1985). In the afterword to the volume by Samuel Weber, Lyotard is in fact criticized from a more rigorously Derridean perspective for being too obsessed with the purity and specificity of discrete language games. Instead, Weber asks him to be aware of their ambiguous interpenetration, that is, of the very ubiquity of *différance,* which is privileged by the postmodern temper.

8. Jacques Bouveresse, *Rationalité et Cynisme* (Paris, 1985), 163.

9. Suzi Gablik, *Has Modernism Failed?* (New York, 1984), 48.

10. Peter Bürger, *Theory of the Avant-garde,* trans. Michael Shaw (Minneapolis, 1984).

11. Charles Jencks, *The Language of Post-Modern Architecture* (New York, 1984), 127f.

12. Robert Venturi et al., *Learning from Las Vegas* (Cambridge, 1977).

13. Craig Owens, "The Discourse of Others: Feminists and Postmodernism," in *The Anti-Aesthetic: Essays on Postmodern Culture,* ed. Hal Foster (Port Townsend, Washington, 1983).

14. For a feminist-deconstructionist critique of Habermas, see Gayatri Chakravorty Spivak, "Three Feminist Readings: McCullers, Drabble, Habermas," *Union Seminary Quarterly Review* 35 (Fall 1979–Winter 1980). For a feminist critique closer to his own position, see Nancy Fraser, "What's Critical about Critical Theory? The Case of Habermas and Gender," *New German Critique* 35 (Spring/Summer, 1985).

15. Lyotard, *The Postmodern Condition,* p. 72. This characterization of Habermas is also taken for granted by Philippe Lacoue-Labarthe in his 1982 discussion with Lyotard at Cerisy-la-Salle. See the transcript, "Talks," in *Diacritics* 14 (Fall 1984): 26.

16. Ibid., 66.

17. Dominic LaCapra, *Rethinking Intellectual History: Texts, Contexts, Language* (Ithaca, 1983), 178–79.

18. Michael Ryan, *Marxism and Deconstruction: A Critical Articulation* (Baltimore, 1982), 112f; Jonathan Culler, "Communicative Competence and Normative Force," *New German Critique* 35 (Spring/Summer, 1985).

19. For an account of Habermas's break with the idea of a metasubject, see Martin Jay, *Marxism and Totality: The Adventures of a Concept from Lukács to Habermas* (Berkeley, 1984), chap. 15.

20. Thomas McCarthy, "Rationality and Relativism: Habermas's 'Overcoming' of Hermeneutics," in *Habermas: Critical Debates,* ed. John B. Thompson and David Held (Cambridge, Mass., 1982); Joel Whitebook, "The Problem of Nature in Habermas," *Telos* 40 (Summer, 1979); Henning Ottmann, "Cognitive Interest and Self-Reflection," in Thompson and Held, *Habermas: Critical Debates.*

21. Jürgen Habermas, *Theory of Communicative Action,* trans. Thomas McCarthy, 2 vols. (Cambridge, Mass., 1985).

22. Anthony Giddens, "Reason without Revolution? Habermas's *Theorie des kommunikativen Handelns,*" in Bernstein, *Habermas and Modernity.*

23. Jay, *Marxism and Totality.*

24. Jürgen Habermas, *Communication and the Evolution of Society,* trans. Thomas McCarthy (Boston, 1979), 130f.

25. Habermas, *Der philosophische Diskurs der Moderne,* 361.

26. Habermas, "Modernity versus Postmodernity," 9. Translation amended.

27. Martin Jay, "Habermas and Modernism," in Bernstein, *Habermas and Modernity;* reprinted here as chap. 9.

28. Habermas, "Questions and Counterquestion," 200.

29. Ibid.

30. Ibid., 201.

31. Ibid. For another recent consideration of the issue of aesthetic rationality that draws in part on Habermas, see Martin Seel, *Die Kunst der Entzweiung: Zum Begriff der*

ästhetischen Rationalität (Frankfurt, 1985). Ironically, the inflationary expansion of different aesthetic experiences has itself been connected to postmodernism by Charles Newman. See his *The Post-Modern Aura: The Act of Fiction in an Age of Inflation* (Evanston, 1985). Quantitative increase may not in fact be a fully satisfactory criterion of rationalization.

32. Ironically, despite his opposition to Habermas, Lyotard can perhaps be read against the grain as expressing hope for something similar. Thus, Cecile Lindsay recently writes, "By meticulously unmasking the operations of the various types of metanarratives, by turning the conditions of any narrative back upon itself, Lyotard's work points to a powerful potential for a dialogic situation among genres of discourse that have been kept separate and hierarchized." See her "Experiments in Postmodern Dialogue," *Diacritics* 14 (Fall, 1984): 61. It is of course in a similar direction—without the overly intersubjectivist notion of dialogue—that Weber wants to turn Lyotard in the afterword to *Just Gaming* cited above. But because Lyotard, like Habermas, is interested in preserving boundary maintenance to a greater extent than the more rabid deconstructionist, he preserves the hope for some sort of actual dialogue. For unless there is a sense of relatively autonomous language games capable of interacting, then all we have is an undifferentiated soup of homogeneous heterogeneity, a kind of absolute concreteness that paradoxically turns itself into pure abstraction.

33. Jürgen Habermas, "Modern and Postmodern Architecture" in *Critical Theory and Public Life*, ed. John Forester (Cambridge, Mass: MIT Press, 1985).

34. Ibid., 328.

35. See Frampton's "Toward a Critical Regionalism: Six Points for an Architecture of Resistance," in Hal Foster, *The Anti-Aesthetic*. Frampton, to be sure, is no friend of postmodernism and acknowledges a debt to the Frankfurt School, as well as to Heidegger and Hannah Arendt.

36. Habermas, *Der philosophische Diskurs der Moderne*, 392.

37. Ibid., 393.

38. Jonathan Culler, in "Communicative Competence and Normative Force," chides Habermas for marginalizing literature and rhetoric in the name of philosophy. One might reply that the deconstructionist impulse in postmodernism is open to the reverse charge.

39. Habermas, *Der philosophische Diskurs der Moderne*, 240.

40. Albrecht Wellmer, "Reason, Utopia and the *Dialectic of Enlightenment*," in Bernstein, *Habermas and Modernity*, 62–63.

41. Thomas McCarthy, "Complexity and Democracy, or the Seducements of Systems Theory," *New German Critique* 35 (Spring/Summer, 1985): 50.

42. Peter Uwe Hohendahl, "The Dialectic of Enlightenment Revisited: Habermas' Critique of the Frankfurt School," *New German Critique* 35 (Spring/Summer, 1985): 25.

FEMINISM AND POSTMODERNISM
A QUESTION OF POLITICS

Susan Rubin Suleiman

> . . . and to this day young authors sally
> forth in fiction like majestic—indeed,
> divinely ordained!—picaros to discover,
> again and again, their manhood.
>
> Robert Coover

> To write a quality cliché you have to come
> up with something new.
>
> Jenny Holzer

Contrary to what some recent commentators on postmodernism seem to think, there was life before Jean-François Lyotard.[1] The term "postmodernism," designating a cultural sequel and/or challenge to modernism (however one defined that term) existed well before the publication of *La condition postmoderne* (1979).[2] It is ironic that Lyotard's book, or rather its English translation, *The Postmodern Condition* (1981), should have become the required starting point for all current discussions of postmodernism by American and English critics, when Lyotard himself, in what I have called elsewhere a "rare instance of 'reverse importation' in the French-American theoretical marketplace," credited his use of the term to American critics, notably to Ihab Hassan.[3]

One would not be altogether wrong to see in this displacement, whereby the French philosopher "takes the place of" all his American predecessors, a sign of what Fredric Jameson diagnosed as the absence of historical consciousness in postmodern culture—as if the memory of those who discuss postmodernism in the 1980s did not extend beyond the confines of the decade itself; or perhaps, more ironically, to see in it a sign of the snob appeal of "genuine French imports" (or what are mistakenly thought to be such) in a

111

certain sector of American intellectual life. But if this view would not be altogether wrong it would not be altogether right either, for although Lyotard's book did not initiate the discourse on postmodernism, it did place it on a new theoretical and philosophical footing. Most notably, it articulated the links between French poststructuralist philosophy and postmodern cultural practices ("culture" being understood to include science and everyday life as well as the arts), so that the latter could be seen—at least in the ideal sketched by Lyotard—as an instantiation of the former.

All of the concepts Lyotard invoked to define the innovative aspects of postmodern knowledge—the crisis of legitimation and the refusal of "grand narratives," the choice of models of dissent and heterogeneity over models of consensus and systemic totality, the view of cultural practices as overlapping language games with constantly shifting rules and players—are concepts grounded in poststructuralist thought, as the latter was elaborated in France in the 1960s and 1970s by Lyotard, Derrida, Foucault and others. *The Postmodern Condition* can thus be read as a poststructuralist manifesto or "manifesto of decentered subjectivities," expressing the optimism for the future that the manifesto genre requires. Although Lyotard is aware of the nightmarish possibilities offered by the "computerization of society" (his model of postmodern knowledge invokes and seeks to generalize the new technologies and conceptualizations—such as Mandelbrot's fractals—made possible by the computer), he emphasizes instead its potentialities as a positive dream. The dream is of a society in which knowledge would consist of language games that would be "non-zero-sum games," where there would be no losers or winners, only players in a constantly evolving process; where openness would be the rule, with information and data banks available to all; where instability and "temporary contracts" would lead neither to alienation nor to anarchy, but to "a politics that would respect both the desire for justice and the desire for the unknown" (Lyotard, 67).

In short, a utopian—or cautiously utopian, if such a thing is possible— version of Babel, a positive counterargument to the pessimistic views being elaborated, during the same post-1968 decade, by Jean Baudrillard. Lyotard was seeing the same things as Baudrillard, but interpreting them differently: what to Baudrillard appeared as the increasingly horrifying world of simulacra evacuating the real, indeed evacuating the very concept of a difference between the simulacrum and the real, appeared to Lyotard—at least potentially—as a world of increasing possibilities for innovation, brought about precisely by the breakdown of stable categories like "the real." Where Baudrillard saw the "postmodern condition" (a term he did not use) as the end of all possibility for (real) action, community, resistance, or change, Lyotard saw it as potentially a whole new game, whose possibilities remained open.[4]

That difference marked one of the stakes in what was soon to become, with the entry of Jürgen Habermas into the fray, the best-known version of the "modernism-postmodernism debate."[5] Since then, the debate has shifted again: What is now in question is not so much whether postmodernism constitutes a totally new development or "break" in relation to modernism (most people, it seems to me, have now accepted that as a given, even if they don't agree on all the details of why and how), but rather the current significance and future direction of the new development as such.

What does all this have to do with women or feminism? And with the earlier American discourses about postmodernism, which I accused other recent commentators of ignoring and then proceeded to ignore myself? Obviously, this is not the place to undertake a full-scale history of discourses on the postmodern.[6] Suffice it to say that, like a number of other important "isms," (romanticism, modernism, classicism), postmodernism has functioned as both a formal/stylistic category and a broadly cultural category. From the start, the most provocative discussions have been those that linked the formal or stylistic to the broadly cultural. Irving Howe's 1959 essay, for example, "Mass Society and Postmodern Fiction," which is generally credited with first use of the term "postmodern" in its current sense, saw in the emergence of a new kind of American fiction (roughly, that of the Beat generation) both a stylistic sequel to modernism—exemplified by Joyce, Mann, and Kafka as well as Hemingway and Fitzgerald—and a cultural symptom of the transformations that had occurred in Western countries after the Second World War.[7] A similar argument, although adopting a different, more positive judgment on these transformations and on the literature that accompanied them, was made by Leslie Fiedler a few years later; it was also suggested, again in positive terms, by Robert Venturi and Denise Scott Brown around the same time regarding architecture, in the essay that was to become the basis for their famous (or infamous) manifesto of postmodern architecture, *Learning from Las Vegas.*[8]

A few years ago, I argued that as far as literature was concerned, it made no sense to try and establish clearcut formal differences between the "modernist" and the "postmodernist," for such an attempt invariably involved oversimplification and flattening out of both categories.[9] Although I would now want to change some of the premises of that earlier argument, I still believe that the effort to define postmodernism chiefly as a formal (or even as a formal and thematic) category and to oppose it as such to modernism is, even when successful, of limited interest.[10] If postmodernist practice in the arts has provoked controversy and debate, it is because of what it "does" (or does not do), not because of what it "is." In other words, it is as an object "to be read," an intervention in the sense of an action or a statement requiring a response, rather than as an object of descriptive poetics, that postmodernism, whether in literature or in the other arts, strikes me as significant today.

This position, whether explicitly stated or not, seems to me to be shared by all those who are currently involved in the "postmodernism debate." Where is postmodernist practice going? Can it be political?—should it be? Does it offer possibilities for opposition, critique, resistance to dominant ideologies? Or is it irremediably compromised by its complicity with the market, with mass culture, capitalism, commercialism? Familiar questions, questions that have been asked in one form or another, at one time or another, about every avant-garde movement and experimental practice since Impressionism. Which does not make them less significant when asked about postmodernism, though it suggests that no definitive answers may be forthcoming.

And women? And feminism?

Discourses on the Postmodern and the Emergence of Feminist Postmodernism

It should come as no surprise, knowing what we know about earlier avant-garde movements and their historians, to learn that the first writings about postmodernism made absolutely no mention of the work of women. One could argue that if early commentators like Irving Howe and Leslie Fiedler, whose prime examples of the postmodern were the Beats (Fiedler also mentioned Pop Art in the visual arts), did not mention women's work, it was because there was little or no such work around to be mentioned at the time. This would mean that the Beats and the Pop Artists were male avant-gardes similar to certain earlier movements like Surrealism, excluding women during their most dynamic period.[11] In fact, there were some women active in both movements, if not at the very beginning, then close enough to it (Diane Di Prima among the writers, Marisol among the painters). Still, as in the case of Surrealism, one can ascribe the early critics' silence not only to ordinary sexism ("not seeing" women who are there), but also to a real scarcity of women's work in those movements.

Critics who started to write about postmodernism in the 1970s or 1980s had less of an excuse for excluding the work of women; for in what I take to be a genuinely *new* (*inédit*, as they say on bookcovers in Paris) historical development, women's participation in experimental literary and visual work during those two decades reached a level, both in terms of quantity and quality, that could no longer be ignored. Some critics, of course, even among the most brilliant, managed to ignore it, as late as the mid 1980s; others, less brilliant, went so far as to theorize its absence. (A few years ago, I received a letter from a European doctoral student who asked whether I agreed with her professor that "women have not produced any postmodernist fiction," and if so, to what I attributed that lack. I replied that the lack may have been in the beholder rather than in the object.)

In the 1980s women's work began to be mentioned, and even featured, in academic discussions of postmodernism, especially in the visual arts. Rosalind Krauss's important 1981 article, "The Originality of the Avant-Garde: A Postmodernist Repetition," which made a strong, polemically "pro-postmodernist" case for the difference between postmodernism and its modernist or historical avant-garde predecessors (the difference residing, according to Krauss, in postmodernism's "radical questioning of the concept of origin . . . and originality"), cited as exemplary postmodernist works the photographs of Sherrie Levine; two years earlier, in the pages of the same journal, Douglas Crimp had argued for the innovativeness (originality?) of postmodernist "pictures" and cited, among other examples, the photographs of Levine and Cindy Sherman.[12]

To discuss the work of women as part of a new movement, trend, or cultural paradigm one is defending is undoubtedly a desirable thing. As Renato Poggioli showed, every avant-garde has its critical defenders and explicators;[13] their work, in turn, becomes a basis on which the movement, once it goes beyond its "scandalous" phase, is integrated into the standard literary and cultural histories. It is quite another thing, however, to take into account not only the existence of women's work, but also its (possibly) feminine or feminist specificity; and to raise, furthermore, the question of how the specificity, whether sexual or political, of women's work within a larger movement affects one's understanding of the movement itself.

In his 1983 essay, "The Discourse of Others: Feminists and Postmodernism," Craig Owens made one of those conceptual leaps that later turn out to have initiated a whole new train of thought. Simply, what Owens did was to theorize the political implications of the intersection between the "feminist critique of patriarchy and the postmodernist critique of representation."[14] He was not the first to suggest the political potential of poststructuralism (which, in the preceding sentence and in Owens's argument, is virtually interchangeable with postmodernism); the ideological critique of the "unified bourgeois subject" and of classical representation had been a continuing theme in French poststructuralist writing from the late 1960s on, and had been part of the political platform of *Tel Quel* in its most revolutionary period.[15] Nor was the linking of the feminist critique of patriarchy with poststructuralism surprising, since French feminist theory had from the beginning acknowledged its link to deconstruction, and even proclaimed it in its famous portmanteau word, "phallogocentrism." The novelty, indeed the pathbreaking quality of Owens's essay was that it placed the feminist issue at the center of the debate on postmodernism (which was also, if one wishes, a debate on poststructuralism), as that debate was unfolding in the United States (and, with a bit of delay, in England) after the publication of Lyotard's *The Postmodern Condition.*[16]

On the one hand, Owens quite rightly criticized the major players in the debate for ignoring both the "insistent feminist voice" in postmodern culture and the whole issue of sexual difference in their discussions of postmodernist practices: thus even those critics who, like Crimp, Krauss, and Hal Foster (and Owens himself, in an earlier essay), discussed women's work as an important part of postmodernist art, could be faulted for ignoring the specifically feminist—or even "feminine"—meanings of that work (Owens, 73–77). On the other hand, Owens suggested that if the feminist/critical aspect of postmodernist work was taken into account, there would result a new and more politically sharpened view of postmodernism itself—for feminism, after all, is not only a theory or an aesthetics, it is also a politics.

By linking feminist politics with postmodernist artistic practice, Owens provided the pro-postmodernists in the debate with a precious argument, whose advantages they were quick to grasp. Feminism provided for postmodernism a concrete political edge, or wedge, that could be used to counter the accusatory pessimism of a Baudrillard or a Jameson: for if there existed a genuinely feminist postmodernist practice, then postmodernism could no longer be seen only as the expression of a fragmented, exhausted culture steeped in nostalgia for a lost center. Indeed, such a view of postmodernism, with its sense of irremediable decline and loss, could now itself be shown to be implicated in the Western, patriarchal logic of the "grand narratives"— the very logic that feminism, and feminist postmodernism, contested. As Hal Foster, in a 1984 essay that I read as a response to and development of Owens's argument, eloquently noted:

> Here, then we begin to see what is at stake in [the] so-called dispersal of the subject. For what is this subject that, threatened by loss, is so bemoaned? For some, for many, this may indeed be a great loss, a loss which leads to narcissistic laments and hysterical disavowals of the end of art, of culture, of the west. But for others, precisely for Others, it is no great loss at all.[17]

Andreas Huyssen, around the same time, was arguing that feminism and the women's movement, together with anti-imperialism, the ecology movement, and the growing awareness of "other cultures, non-European, non-Western cultures," had created a new "postmodernism of resistance" that would "satisfy the needs of the political and those of the aesthetic."[18] Most recently, following up on these arguments, Linda Hutcheon has spoken of the overlapping agendas between postmodernism and "ex-centrics": blacks, women, and other traditionally marginalized groups.[19]

In short, feminism brings to postmodernism the political guarantee postmodernism needs in order to feel respectable as an avant-garde practice. Postmodernism, in turn, brings feminism into a certain kind of "high theoretical" discourse on the frontiers of culture, traditionally an exclusively male domain.[20]

If this summary sounds cynical, the effect is only partly intended. There is, I believe, an element of mutual opportunism in the alliance of feminists and postmodernists, but it is not necessarily a bad thing. The opportunism operates not so much, or perhaps not at all, in the actual practice of feminist postmodernist artists, but rather in the public discourse about that practice: influential critics who write about the work of feminist postmodernists, especially in the realm of the visual arts, are both advancing their own reputations as "high theorists" and contributing to—or even creating—the market value of those artists' work, while other, less fashionable feminist work may go unnoticed. And once it becomes valuable on the market, the feminist postmodernist work may lose its critical edge.

This is not a new problem, as I have already suggested and will suggest again. In a world in which everything, even the discourse of high post-modernist theory, has an exchange value, should one reject the advantages of the feminist-postmodernist alliance for the sake of an ideal of aesthetic or intellectual purity? If every avant-garde has its public defenders and promoters, why not feminist postmodernism?

Oh dear oh dear, now I do sound excessively cynical. Let me therefore quickly affirm that I take the theoretical arguments advanced by Owens, Foster, Huyssen, and Hutcheon in favor of the feminism/postmodernism alliance extremely seriously, and indeed subscribe to them (mostly); that I believe it is important to look for the critical and political possibilities of avant-garde practices in general, and of postmodernism in particular; and that I think women and feminists rightfully belong in the center of such discussions and practices—in the middle of the margin, as it were.[21] As I said earlier, with postmodernism we have arrived at a totally new situation for women artists: for the first time in the history of avant-gardes (or in history *tout court*), there exists a critical mass of outstanding, innovative work by women, both in the visual arts and in literature.[22] Simone de Beauvoir's complaint, in *The Second Sex,* that women artists lacked genius—that is, the audacity to take real risks and to carry "the weight of the world on their shoulders"—is no longer true, if it ever was. Today, thanks in part to the existence of predecessors like Beauvoir, there are women artists who possess genius in her sense—and who are aware at the same time that "genius," like every other abstract universal category, is determined by particulars: race, sex, nationality, religion, history. As Christine Brooke-Rose has recently noted, "genius" has the same Indo-European root as gender, genre, and genesis.[23]

Still, it would be unwise to celebrate postmodernism, even more so feminist postmodernism, without keeping one's ears open to dissenting voices, or without acknowledging things that don't "fit." Feminist postmodernism, like postmodernism in general, must confront anew some of the dilemmas that have plagued every successful avant-garde for the past century or more: the dilemma of political effectiveness versus stylistic indirection and innovation, numbingly familiar to students of the 1930s; or the dilemma of the market and the avant-garde's relation to mass culture, which dominated, as Andreas Huyssen has shown, the "Greenberg and Adorno decades" after the Second World War. In addition, feminist postmodernism must confront the specific questions and challenges posed to it from within the feminist movement, notably as concerns the political status of the "decentered subject."

Not a short order, in sum. Enough to fill a whole book, in fact. But I shall fill only a few more pages, with thoughts and notes for future reflection and work, whether by me or others.

Opposition in Babel? The Political Status of
(Postmodern, Ironic) Intertextuality

> Then I shall enter with my hypotheses and
> sweep the detritus of civilization.
>
>   Christine Brooke-Rose,
>   *Amalgamemnon*

> The vital thing is to have an alternative so
> that people will realise that there's no such
> thing as a true story.
>
>   Jeanette Winterson,
>   *Boating for Beginners*

The appropriation, misappropriation, montage, collage, hybridization, and general mixing up of visual and verbal texts and discourses, from all periods of the past as well as from the multiple social and linguistic fields of the present, is probably the most characteristic feature of what can be called the "postmodern style." The question, as it has emerged in the debate on postmodernism, is: Does this style have a critical political meaning or effect, or is it—in Fredric Jameson's words—merely "blank parody," a "neutral practice" devoid of any critical impulse or historical consciousness?[24]

There is not much point in looking for a single "right" answer to that question, since it is precisely the object of the debate. One can, however, try to refine and clarify the question; and one must, sooner or later, state one's own position on it. What, then, does it mean to talk about the political effect of a novel or painting or photograph? If one means that in a particular historical circumstance an art work can be used for political ends, well and good: Picasso's *Guernica*, exhibited in major European and American capitals between 1937 and 1939, earned a lot of sympathy as well as material support for the Spanish Republic before coming to rest for a few decades in the Museum of Modern Art. If one means that the work elicits a political response, whether in the form of public commentaries or private reactions, including the production of other art works that build on it (*Guernica* is again a good example), that is also well and good.[25] What seems to me wrong-headed, or at the very least problematic, is to talk about the political effect or meaning of a work—especially of a self-conscious, insistently intertextual, often multiply ironic work—as if that meaning were clear, immutable, and immanent to the "text," rather than determined by its interpretive context.

Political readings—indeed, all interpretations—tend to speak of works as if their meanings and effects were immanent; in order to convince someone else of the validity of one's reading, one has to claim, or at least imply, that it is the best reading, the reading most closely corresponding to the "work itself." When Jameson made his often-quoted claim that postmodern pastiche "is a neutral practice of . . . mimicry, without any of parody's ulterior motives, amputated of the satiric impulse, devoid of laughter and of any conviction that . . . some healthy linguistic normality still exists," implicit in the claim (which was used to support his general argument that postmodernism lacked authentic historical awareness) was the assumption that works of art determine their own meaning and reading. Linda Hutcheon, who strongly criticizes Jameson for not citing any examples, and offers many examples of her own to show that postmodern parody does not lack the "satiric impulse" and is not apolitical or ahistorical, is no doubt justified in her critique; but as the very act of citing counterexamples shows, she shares Jameson's assumption that political meanings reside in works, not in their readings.

As the by now familiar theories of "reader-oriented criticism" have shown, however, this assumption is extremely problematic, and probably downright wrong. Stanley Fish and others have argued that every reading of a text, no matter how personal or "quirky," can be shown to be part of a collective discourse and analyzed historically and ideologically as characteristic of a group, or what Fish has called an interpretive community.[26] It is a matter of having learned, in the classroom or through scholarly exchange, or through more informal modes of communication, certain shared ways of approaching a text: asking certain questions of it, and elaborating a language and an interpretive "strategy" for answering those questions.

Displacing the political effect from the work to its reading has the advantage of moving the debate from the question of what postmodernism "is" to the question of what it does—in a particular place, for a particular public (which can be a public of one, but as I have just suggested, every individual is part of a larger interpretive community) at a particular time. That displacement does not, however, alter the basic questions about the politics of intertextuality or of irony, or more generally about the relation between symbolic action and "real" action in the world. It merely . . . displaces them, from the work to its readings and readers.

Jameson, reading postmodernist intertextuality as an expression of advanced capitalism, "a field of stylistic and discursive heterogeneity without a norm," calls it "blank parody, a statue with blind eyeballs" (p. 65). But postmodernist intertextuality (is it the "same" one?) can also be thought of, for example in the British artist Mary Kelly's terms, as a sign of critical commitment to the contemporary world. According to Kelly, this commitment distinguished British postmodernist art of the 1970s and early 1980s from its American counterpart: whereas the Americans merely "purloined" previous images and "pilfered" the contemporary world's "cultural estate," the British were "exploring its boundaries, deconstructing its centre, proposing the decolonisation of its visual codes and of language itself."[27]

It is not clear from Kelly's comparison how one can distinguish, objectively, "mere pilfering" from political deconstruction and decolonization. Similarly, Jameson's recent attempt to distinguish the "ahistorical" postmodernism he deplores from its "homeopathic critique" in the works of E. L. Doctorow, works he admires and finds salutary, strikes me as dubitable at best.[28] So, for that matter, do all the other attempts that have been made to distinguish a "good" postmodernism (of resistance) from a "bad" postmodernism (what Lyotard calls the "anything goes" variety).[29]

It seems a good bet that almost any given work can be shown to belong to either of those categories, depending on how one reads it. Cindy Sherman's early work, the series of *Untitled Film Stills* from nonexistent Hollywood films, which the artist interprets as being "about the fakeness of role playing as well as contempt for the domineering 'male' audience who would read the images as sexy,"[30] and which some critics have read in those terms as a form of feminist ironic critique, have been read by other critics as works that play up to the "male gaze" for the usual profit: "the work seems a slicked-up version of the original, a new commodity. In fact, much of this work has proved quite salable, easy to show, easy to write about, easy to sell."[31] Even the "Third World" and "women of color," those brave new banners under which (together with feminism) the postmodernism of resistance has sought its political credentials, can be shown, if one is so inclined, to be caught up in the logic of the simulacrum and in the economics of multinational capitalism. In today's world, one can argue, there are no more places outside; the Third World too is part of the society of the spectacle.

Perhaps it all comes down, in the end, to how one understands Christine Brooke-Rose's evocative phrase about "sweeping the detritus of civilization." Does (can?) the sweeper hope to clear the detritus, or is she merely making new patterns with it and thus adding to the heap? And if the latter, should the sweeper put away her broom?

Yet another twist: If postmodernist intertextuality can be read both ways, that fact itself is open to interpretation. For Linda Hutcheon, it proves that postmodernist works are ambivalent and contradictory, "doubly encoded," and that they therefore constitute not a "break" but a "challenge to culture from within."[32] For Craig Owens, it proves that postmodernism is the true art of deconstruction, for it recognizes the "unavoidable necessity of participating in the very activity that is being denounced precisely in order to denounce it."[33] On the other hand, one could call this apology for postmodernism itself part of a strategy of "anything goes," with the added proviso: "as long as I recognize that I am not innocent." This was already, in an ethical and existential perspective, the strategy of Camus's "penitent judge" in *La Chute* (1956). Clamence is more than willing to admit his own guilt, as long as it allows him to denounce everyone else. But Clamence is not exactly an admirable character. . . .

And so it goes—the twists may be unending.

Does that mean we should no longer play?

Martha Rosler, who calls her work "didactic" but not "hortatory," and whom critics consider a political postmodernist, worries that if the ironic work is not "derived from a process of politicization, although it claims a politics," it will simply end up in the art-critical establishment, where even feminist work—which has been affiliated with a politics—may become no more than "just a competing style of the sixties and seventies . . . outdated by fashion."[34] I recognize in Rosler's worry the outlines of two old but apparently inexhaustible arguments: can art which claims an oppositional edge take the risk of entering a museum? Can it afford to be negative and individualistic, rather than offering a positive, collective "alternative vision" of "how things might be different" (Rosler, 72)?

Related to these arguments is the question of the symbolic versus the real. Meaghan Morris recently criticized the facile uses that apologists for postmodernism have made of the verb "appropriate":

> it outrages humanist commitments, adds a little frisson of impropriety and risk by romanticizing as violation the intertextual *sine qua non* of all cultural activity, and semantically guarantees a politics to practitioners by installing predation as the universal rule of cultural exchange. . . . All energies become seizures and we all get a piece of the action.[35]

Morris's critique is both humorous and apt: it *is* too easy to endow metaphorical appropriation with the power of real takeovers, and one *should* look for connections between "the politics of culture and the politics of politics" (Morris, 125). One should also, however, not belittle the value of symbolic interventions in the field of the real. Is it necessary to belabor the fact that language is part of the world (the "real world") and plays a non-negligible part in shaping both our perceptions of it and our actions in it?

And then there are those who believe only a certain kind of "real" can be political. Laura Kipnis, who identifies herself as a video artist and critic, dismisses all "first-world" writing that is not concerned with immediate political action—for example, French feminist theory—as an elitist luxury: "real shifts in world power and economic distribution have little to do with jouissance, the pre-Oedipal, or fluids," she notes sarcastically.[36] (Sarcasm, as we know, is not to be confused with "blank" postmodern pastiche.) For Kipnis, if I read her right, the true postmodernist critique is an act of international terrorism in which "retaliation is taken, as has been announced, for 'American arrogance,'" and a truly new form of political struggle, which the West in its blindness has not recognized, is one "in which civilian tourists are held responsible for the actions of their governments" (Kipnis, 163).

This position, for all its hard-nosed charm, strikes me as too close for comfort to the murderous anti-intellectualism of commissars and other ayatollahs—or, since Kipnis is neither, to the traditional self-hatred of intellectuals who dream of getting their hands dirty.

Jeanette Winterson's *Boating for Beginners* is an outrageously blasphemous rewriting of the Flood story from Genesis. It is also very funny. Has it escaped the censorious eyes of those who picket Scorsese's *Last Temptation of Christ* because it is "only a novel," by an author who is not a household name? Or because it is not "serious"? And yet, what could be more serious than the realization (if indeed it is true) that "there is no such thing as a true story"?

Postmodernism for postmodernism, politics for politics, I'd rather be an ironist than a terrorist.

To Market, to Market: Oppositional Art in Mass Culture

> The whole world is constrained to pass through the filter of the culture industry.
>
> Max Horkheimer and Theodor Adorno,
> *Dialectic of Enlightenment*

Horkheimer and Adorno's pessimistic analysis of the power of the culture industry has become so much a part of contemporary intellectual discourse (to the point that it is almost itself a cliché, part of an anonymous "general wisdom") that one may wonder whether there is any new way to conceptualize the relation between authentic art and degraded entertainment, or between genuine thought and the manipulated thought-control of advertising and the mass media.[37] It is not that their argument hasn't been criticized for its elitism—it has been, most recently by Andreas Huyssen. Furthermore, it can be criticized as a "grand narrative," explaining all of contemporary culture in terms of a single paradigm: the culture industry, in their analysis, appears to be a monolithic mechanism whose effects are omnipresent and inescapable.

Yet, the argument still has power; it is hard to get around. One possible conclusion to which their analysis leads has been stated by Thomas Crow, concerning the deep logic of innovative art since the mid-nineteenth century: "the avant-garde serves as a kind of research and development arm of the culture industry."[38] According to Crow (whose rich and complex argument would be worth following in detail), there exists a predictable pattern from Impressionism on, in which the avant-garde "appropriates" certain dynamic oppositional practices from "below," from marginal groups or subcultures (here Crow differs significantly from Horkheimer and Adorno); these practices, transformed into avant-garde invention, become, after a moment of productive tension between the "high" and the "low" (or between the oppositional and the institutional), simply a part of "high" art, but are eventually recuperated by the culture industry and returned to the lower zone of mass culture—in a form, however, where the avant-garde invention is "drained of its original force and integrity"

(Crow, 258). This cycle, alternating between "moments of negation and an ultimately overwhelming recuperative inertia" (Crow, 259), accounts for the chronically problematic status of avant-garde art movements, which claim to want to have a real effect in the world but are always, in the end, "domesticated."

What hope is there for postmodernism, and specifically for feminist postmodernism, as an oppositional avant-garde practice? Quite possibly, not much—or not more than for previous avant-gardes. But that does not mean that the attempt is not worth making. Rozsika Parker and Griselda Pollock suggest that "feminism explores the pleasures of resistance, of deconstruction, of discovery, of defining, of fragmenting, of redefining."[39] Is it possible that such pleasures can be experienced by more than a privileged few and still maintain their critical charge? I think it is significant that a number of politically motivated experimental women artists working today have found some unexpected ways to use technologies associated with the culture industry.[40] Jenny Holzer's use of electronic signs in airports and other public places—such as the Spectacolor Board in Times Square, which flashed her message in huge letters (part of a series titled *Truisms*): PRIVATE PROPERTY CREATED CRIME—is one well-known example; Barbara Kruger, who has used billboards to display some of her photomontages has also used the Spectacolor Board, to display the message: I AM NOT TRYING TO SELL YOU ANYTHING.

In an interview in 1985, Holzer explained: "My work has been designed to be stumbled across in the course of a person's daily life. I think it has the most impact when someone is just walking along, not thinking about anything in particular, and then finds these unusual statements either on a poster or on a sign."[41] In the same interview, Holzer mentioned her discovery that "television is not prohibitively expensive. . . . You can buy thirty seconds in the middle of 'Laverne & Shirley' for about seventy-five dollars, or you can enhance the CBS Morning News for a few hundred dollars. The audience is all of Connecticut and a little bit of New York and Massachusetts, which is enough people" (Siegel, 297). Barbara Kruger has expressed a similar view. While harboring no illusions about the alienating effects of television ("TV is an industry that manufactures blind eyes"), Kruger, like Holzer, seeks new ways to use it: for Kruger it is in the very "site of the stereotype," characteristic of TV representations, that "the rules of the game can be changed and subtle reformations can be enacted."[42]

The hope expressed in such statements is that it is possible to find openings even in the monolithic mechanism of the culture industry; that it is possible for innovative, critical work to reach a large audience without passing through the "upward and downward" cycle analyzed by Crow, where what reaches the mass public is always already "evacuated cultural goods," deprived of force and integrity.

I am sure there must exist arguments to deflate this hope. But I will not look for them here.

Of Cyborgs and (Other) "Women": The Political Status of Decentered Subjects

> What kind of politics could embrace partial, contradictory, permanently unclosed constructions of personal and collective selves and still be faithful, effective—and, ironically, socialist feminist?
>
> Donna Haraway,
> "A Manifesto for Cyborgs"

The question asked by Donna Haraway sums up, as well as any could, what is at stake in the feminist embrace, but also in the feminist suspicion, of postmodernism.[43] Haraway, proposing the technological cyborg as an "ironic political myth" to take the place of earlier, naturalistic myths of the goddess, celebrates the postmodernist model of "identity out of otherness and difference"; she proclaims herself antiessentialist, antinaturalist, antidualist, antimaternal, utopically "for a monstrous world without gender" (Haraway, 100). All of this ironically, and politically to boot.

Next to such inventiveness, those feminists who want to hang on to a notion of feminine specificity may look (in Naomi Schor's ironic self-characterization) like "wallflowers at the carnival of plural sexualities."[44] But the differences between worshipers of the goddess and celebrants of the cyborg may themselves need to be put into question.

"If authenticity is relational, there can be no essence except as a political, cultural invention, a local tactic," writes James Clifford.[45] Which makes me think that sometimes it is politic to "be" a goddess, at other times a cyborg— and at still other times, a laughing mother[46] or an "alone-standing woman"[47] who sweeps the detritus of civilization.

Julia Kristeva's recent book, an exploration of what it means to be "foreign," reached the bestseller list in France—a country, Kristeva writes, which is both the best and the worst place to be an *étranger*. It is the worst, because the French consider everything that is not French "an unpardonable offense to universal taste;"[48] it is the best, because (as Kristeva, being herself one, knows) in France a foreigner is a constant object of fascination, loved or hated, never ignored.

Of course it makes a difference (nor would Kristeva suggest otherwise) whether one feels loved or hated. It also makes a difference if one is actively persecuted for being "different." Still, for yet another ironic myth, I feel much drawn to her evocation of the "happy cosmopolitan," foreign not to others but to him or herself, harboring not an essence but a "pulverized origin." Such a person "transmutes into games what for some is a misfortune and for others an untouchable void" (Kristeva, 57). Which may not be a bad description of a feminist postmodernist.

As for politics, I don't hesitate to make my own ("appropriate" is the word) a message I recently found on a card sold at the Centre Georges Pompidou. The card is by Jamie Reid, the British artist whose work appeared on posters and jacket covers for the short-lived punk rock group the Sex Pistols. I bought it at the Paris opening (February 1989) of the exhibition on Situationism, a revolutionary movement of the 1960s that spurned museums (their chief spokesman was Guy Debord—he was not at the opening). Some of Reid's other work, ironic and anti-Thatcher, is shown in the exhibit.

The card is quite expensive, as cards go, and comes wrapped in cellophane; it is sold only in the museum. The picture on the cover shows Delacroix's *Liberty Leading the People*, against a background formed by four tilted modernist skyscrapers. The message reads (not exactly in this order): "Live in the Present. Learn from the Past. Look to the Future."

NOTES

1. This essay is a shortened version of the last chapter of my book, *Subversive Intent: Gender, Politics, and the Avant-Garde* (Cambridge, Mass.: Harvard University Press, 1990). Besides the people I mention in specific notes, I wish to thank Ingeborg Hoesterey and Mary Russo for their careful reading and very useful suggestions regarding this essay.

2. Jean-François Lyotard, *La condition postmoderne: rapport sur le savoir* (Paris: Editions de Minuit, 1979). English translation: *The Postmodern Condition: A Report on Knowledge*, trans. Geoff Bennington and Brian Massumi (Minneapolis: University of Minnesota Press, 1981); hereafter cited parenthetically in the text.

3. Suleiman, "Naming and Difference: Reflections on 'Modernism versus Postmodernism' in Literature," in *Approaching Postmodernism*, ed. Douwe Fokkema and Hans Bertens (Amsterdam and Philadelphia: John Benjamins, 1986), 255. As I note in that essay, the first footnote in Lyotard's book cites Hassan's *The Dismemberment of Orpheus: Toward a Postmodern Literature* (New York: Oxford University Press, 1971) as a source for his use of the term "postmodern"; in the introduction to his book, Lyotard justifies his choice of "postmodern" to characterize "the condition of knowledge in the most highly developed societies," by noting that "the word is in current use on the American continent among sociologists and critics" (*The Postmodern Condition*, xxiii).

Recent works on postmodernism that use Lyotard as an obligatory reference and make virtually no mention of any work before his on the subject include: *Universal Abandon? The Politics of Postmodernism*, ed. Andrew Ross (Minneapolis: University of Minnesota Press, 1988); *Postmodernism and Its Discontents*, ed. E. Ann Kaplan (London: Verso, 1988); "Modernity and Modernism, Postmodernity and Postmodernism," special issue of *Cultural Critique* 5 (Winter 1986–87); "Postmodernism," special issue of *Social Text* 18 (Winter 1987–88). This may be a specifically American, or Anglo-American phenomenon, I should add; Richard Martin informs me that in Germany, where he teaches, Lyotard's book is known but Hassan's work remains the starting reference. I wish to thank Richard Martin for his careful reading and very useful criticisms of this essay.

4. Lyotard situates himself explicitly in opposition to Baudrillard early on in *The Postmodern Condition*, when he notes that the "breaking up of the grand Narratives . . . leads to what some authors analyze in terms of the dissolution of the social bond and the disintegration of social aggregates into a mass of individual atoms thrown into the absurdity of Brownian motion. Nothing of the kind is happening: this point of view, it seems to me, is haunted by the paradisiac representation of a lost 'organic' society" (p. 15). Although he does not name Baudrillard in the text, Lyotard footnotes Baudrillard's 1978 book, *A l'ombre des majorités silencieuses*, as the one example of the analyses he is contesting here. Baudrillard's theory of the simulacrum, to which I referred, dates from 1975: *L'échange symbolique et la mort* (Paris: Gallimard). This theory is much indebted to Debord's theory of the "society of the spectacle," which dates from just before 1968. (Guy Debord, *La société du spectacle* [Paris: Buchet-Chastel, 1967]). In 1988, Debord published a short commentary on his earlier book, which reiterates and reinforces his earlier pessimistic analyses. See his *Commentaires sur la société du spectacle* (Paris: Gérard Lebovici, 1988).

5. Habermas's contribution to the debate was the now famous essay, "Modernity—An Incomplete Project" (1981), reprinted in *The Anti-Aesthetic: Essays on Postmodern Culture*, ed. Hal Foster (Port Townsend, Wash.: Bay Press, 1986), 3–15. Habermas criticized all those, including the French poststructuralists (whom he called "anti-modernist young conservatives"), who argued for a "break" with the "modernist" project of the Enlightenment. Habermas does not seem to have been responding here to Lyotard's book (the essay does not mention Lyotard), and he did not link postmodernism to poststructuralism. Lyotard, however, responded to Habermas in his 1982 essay, "Réponse à la question: qu'est-ce que le postmoderne?" which appears in English as an appendix to *The Postmodern Condition*. It was after that essay that the version of the "modernism-postmodernism" debate associated with the names of Lyotard and Habermas reached full swing. There are other versions of the debate as well. For an American response specifically to this debate, see Richard Rorty, "Habermas and Lyotard on Postmodernity," reprinted in this volume.

6. For a somewhat useful historical overview (as of about 1985), see Hans Bertens, "The Postmodern *Weltanschauung* and Its Relation with Modernism: An Introductory Survey," in *Approaching Postmodernism*, 9–51. My essay in the same volume, "Naming and Difference," distinguishes various discourses on the postmodern in terms of their founding impulse: ideological, diagnostic, or classificatory.

7. Irving Howe, "Mass Society and Postmodern Fiction," in *The Decline of the New* (New York: Harcourt, Brace and World, 1970); first published in *Partisan Review* in 1959. The term *postmodernismo* was, it appears, already used in Spain by Federico de Onis in 1934; however, its meaning was quite different. See John Barth, "Postmodernism Revisited," *The Review of Contemporary Fiction* 8 no. 3 (Fall 1988): 18.

8. Leslie Fiedler, "The New Mutants" (1965), reprinted in *Collected Essays*, vol. 2 (New York: Stein and Day, 1971), 379–400; Robert Venturi, Denise Scott Brown, and Steven Izenour, *Learning from Las Vegas: The Forgotten Symbolism of Architectural Form*, revised edition (Cambridge, Mass.: MIT Press, 1988 [original ed. 1977]). In the preface to the first edition, Brown and Venturi cite their 1968 article, "A Significance for A&P Parking Lots, or, Learning from Las Vegas," as the basis for the book.

9. Suleiman, "Naming and Difference."

10. The most successful effort of this kind so far, I believe, is Brian McHale's *Postmodernist Fiction* (New York and London: Methuen, 1987). Describing his work as an example of "descriptive poetics," McHale makes no attempt to link postmodernist fiction to any contemporary or cultural issues—indeed, he concludes that postmodernist fiction, like all significant literature, treats the "eternal themes" of

love and death. Within its self-imposed formalist parameters, I find McHale's criterion for distinguishing modernist from postmodernist fiction (the former being dominated by epistemological issues, the latter by ontological ones) extremely interesting, and his detailed readings of postmodernist works in terms of the ontological criterion suggestive and persuasive.

11. I develop the argument about Surrealism and analyze the place of women in that movement's history (which, I suggest, differs in significant ways from the place of women in the history of Anglo-American modernism) in chap. 1 of my book, *Subversive Intent,* op. cit.

12. Rosalind Krauss, "The Originality of the Avant-Garde: A Postmodernist Repetition," (1981) reprinted in this volume; Douglas Crimp, "Pictures," *October* 8 (Spring 1979): 75–88, both reprinted in *Art after Modernism: Rethinking Representation,* ed. Brian Wallis (New York and Boston: The New Museum of Contemporary Art and David R. Godine, 1984). Among literary critics, Brian McHale has included some discussion of the work of women, notably Angela Carter and Christine Brooke-Rose, in his *Postmodernist Fiction,* without, however, raising the question of sexual difference. Ihab Hassan, in the new postface to the second edition of *The Dismemberment of Orpheus,* cites Brooke-Rose's name in some of his postmodernist lists (she was not cited in the first edition, 1971). The only general study of postmodernist writing to date which discusses women's work (along with that of other marginal groups) and also makes some attempt to take into account its political specificity is Linda Hutcheon's *A Poetics of Postmodernism: History, Theory, Fiction* (New York and London: Routledge, 1988).

13. Renato Poggioli, *The Theory of the Avant-Garde* (Cambridge, Mass.: Harvard University Press, 1968), chaps. 5 and 8.

14. Craig Owens "The Discourse of Others: Feminists and Postmodernism," in *The Anti-Aesthetic,* ed. Hal Foster, 59. Hereafter cited parenthetically in the text.

15. I discuss the politics of *Tel Quel* as an avant-garde movement in my essay, "As Is," in *A New History of French Literature,* ed. Denis Hollier et al. (Cambridge, Mass.: Harvard University Press, 1989).

16. See note 5 above. The most explicit linking of postmodernism and poststructuralism in the debate was made by Terry Eagleton, in his highly negative Marxist critique, "Capitalism, Modernism and Postmodernism," *New Left Review* 152 (1985): 60–73.

17. Hal Foster, "(Post)Modern Polemics," in *Recodings: Art, Spectacle, Cultural Politics* (Seattle: Bay Press, 1985), 136.

18. Andreas Huyssen, "Mapping the Postmodern," in *After the Great Divide: Modernism, Mass Culture, Postmodernism* (Bloomington: Indiana University Press, 1986), 219–21.

19. Hutcheon, *A Poetics of Postmodernism,* chap. 4.

20. It is true, as Richard Martin reminds me, that some feminists are critical of this "high theoretical" discourse (or of any theoretical discourse closely associated with a male tradition) and would just as soon not participate in it. That raises a whole number of other questions regarding alliances and dialogue between men and women, which I will not attempt to develop here. My own favoring of dialogue and "complication" over separatist and binarist positions is explicitly argued in chaps. 4, 6, and 7 of *Subversive Intent.*

21. The same argument can be made (as Linda Hutcheon's grouping together of "ex-centrics" and Huyssen's and Foster's use of the concept "Others" shows) for the alliance between postmodernism and Third World minorities or Afro-American writers, male and female. Many black American critics (Henry Louis Gates comes especially to mind) have recognized the similarity of concerns and of analytic concepts between feminist criticism and Afro-American criticism. The links between Afro-American writing and postmodernism have also been recognized, notably in the

novels of Ishmael Reed. Black women writers, however, have rarely been called postmodernists, and even less feminist postmodernists. A case can be made for considering Toni Morrison and Ntozake Shange (among others) "black women feminist postmodernists." But the question of priorities (race or gender?) remains.

22. To be sure, there were a number of important women writers and artists associated with Anglo-American modernism and other earlier movements who were ignored or belittled by male critics, as recent feminist scholarship has shown. (See, for example, Sandra Gilbert and Susan Gubar, *No Man's Land*, vol. 1, *The War of the Words* [New Haven: Yale University Press, 1987]). And as I have argued elsewhere, there are significant historical and national differences that must be taken into account when discussing the participation of women in avant-garde movements. My sense is, however, that none of the early movements had the *critical mass of outstanding, innovative work by women, both in the visual arts and in literature* (the phrase is worth restating and underlining) that exists today.

Is naming names necessary? Here, for the doubtful, is a partial list of outstanding English and American women artists working today, who can be (and at some time or other have been) called feminist postmodernists: In performance, Joanne Akalaitis, Laurie Anderson, Karen Finley, Suzanne Lacy, Meredith Monk, Carolee Schneemann; in film and video, Lizzie Borden, Cecilia Condit, Laura Mulvey, Sally Potter, Yvonne Rainer, Martha Rosler; in photography and visual arts, Jenny Holzer, Mary Kelly, Barbara Kruger, Sherrie Levine, Cindy Sherman, Nancy Spero; in fiction, Kathy Acker, Christine Brooke-Rose, Angela Carter, Rikki Ducornet, Emily Prager, Jeanette Winterson. (See also n. 21.) I thank Elinor Fuchs and Judith Piper for sharing their expertise with me about women in postmodern performance. For more on contemporary women performers and visual artists, see the exhibition catalogue (which bears out my point about critical mass), *Making Their Mark: Women Artists Move into the Mainstream, 1970–1985* (New York: Abbeville Press, 1989).

23. Christine Brooke-Rose, "Illiterations," in *Breaking the Sequence: Women's Experimental Fiction*, ed. Ellen G. Friedman and Miriam Fuchs (Princeton: Princeton University Press, 1989), 59.

24. Fredric Jameson, "Postmodernism, or the Cultural Logic of Late Capitalism," *New Left Review* 146 (July–August 1984), 53–92. Subsequent page references refer to this essay.

25. For an excellent collection of responses to *Guernica* and a clear exposition of its history as a "political" painting, see *Picasso's Guernica: Illustrations, Introductory Essay, Documents, Poetry, Criticism, Analysis*, ed. Ellen C. Oppler (New York: Norton, 1988).

26. Stanley Fish, *Is There a Text in This Class?* (Cambridge, Mass.: Harvard University Press, 1980). For an overview of theories of reading, see my introductory essay, "Varieties of Reader-Oriented Criticism," in *The Reader in the Text: Essays on Audience and Interpretation*, ed. Susan R. Suleiman and Inge K. Crosman (Princeton: Princeton University Press, 1980), 3–45.

27. Mary Kelly, "Beyond the Purloined Image" (essay on a 1983 London exhibition with the same title, curated by Kelly), quoted in Rozsika Parker and Griselda Pollock, "Fifteen Years of Feminist Action: From Practical Strategies to Strategic Practices," in *Framing Feminism: Art and the Women's Movement 1970–85* (London and New York: Pandora Press, 1987), 53. Aside from the excellent introductory essays by Parker and Pollock, this book offers a rich selection of written and visual work by women involved in various British feminist avant-garde art movements of the seventies and early eighties.

28. See Anders Stephanson, "Regarding Postmodernism—A Conversation with Fredric Jameson," in *Universal Abandon? The Politics of Postmodernism*, ed. Andrew Ross, 3–30. Jameson suggests that Doctorow's works offer the possibility "to undo postmodernism homeopathically by the methods of postmodernism: to work at dis-

solving the pastiche by using all the instruments of pastiche itself, to reconquer some genuine historical sense by using the instruments of what I have called substitutes for history" (17). The question Jameson does not answer (or raise) is: How does one tell the "fake" (homeopathic) postmodernist pastiche from the "real" one—which is itself a "fake," a substitute for history? The play of mirrors here may strike one as quite postmodernist. . . .

29. Lyotard, "Answering the Question: What is Postmodernism?" trans. Régis Durand, in *The Postmodern Condition*, 77. Huyssen picks up the distinction in *Mapping the Postmodern*, 220. See also Foster, "(Post)Modern Polemics," in *Recodings*.

30. See Sherman's interview with Jeanne Siegel, in *Artwords 2: Discourse on the Early 80's*, ed. Jeanne Siegel (Ann Arbor and London: UMI Research Press, 1988), 272.

31. Martha Rosler, "Notes on Quotes," *Wedge* 2 (Fall 1982): 71. Rosler does not refer to anyone by name, but her critique here appears clearly to be directed at the work of Kruger, Levine, and Sherman.

32. Hutcheon, *A Poetics of Postmodernism*, xiii and passim.

33. Craig Owens, "The Allegorical Impulse: Toward a Theory of Postmodernism," in *Art After Modernism*, ed. Brian Wallis, 235.

34. Rosler, "Notes on Quotes," 72, 73; hereafter cited parenthetically in the text. Rosler's characterization of her work as didactic but not hortatory is in an interview with Jane Weinstock, *October* 17 (Summer 1981): 78.

35. Meaghan Morris, "Tooth and Claw: Tales of Survival and *Crocodile Dundee*," in *Universal Abandon?*, 123; hereafter cited parenthetically in the text.

36. Laura Kipnis, "Feminism: The Political Conscience of Postmodernism?" in *Universal Abandon?*, 162; hereafter cited parenthetically in the text.

37. Max Horkheimer and Theodor W. Adorno, "The Culture Industry: Enlightenment As Mass Deception," in *Dialectic of Enlightenment*, trans. John Cumming (New York: Continuum, 1982), 120–67.

38. Thomas Crow, "Modernism and Mass Culture in the Visual Arts," in *Pollock and After*, 257; hereafter cited parenthetically in the text. I wish to thank Bernard Gendron for bringing Crow's essay, in particular the remark I have quoted about the avant-garde and the culture industry, to my attention; and for his thoughtful reading and criticism of my own essay.

39. Rozsika Parker and Griselda Pollock, "Fifteen years of feminist action: from practical strategies to strategic practices," in *Framing Feminism*, 54.

40. Women postmodernists are not the only ones to have practiced a kind of public intervention, of course; among men doing comparable things, Hans Haacke and Daniel Buren come to mind (though Buren's work questions more the politics of museums than the "politics of politics"). Nor is all of the political work by women exclusively feminist. These considerations do not invalidate my general point; rather, they enlarge it.

41. Interview with Jeanne Siegel, "Jenny Holzer's Language Games," in *Artwords 2*, 286; hereafter cited parenthetically in the text. See also, in the same volume, the interview with Barbara Kruger, where Kruger refers to her use of billboards and of the Times Square Spectacolor Board (299–311).

42. Barbara Kruger, interview with Jeanne Siegel, in *Artwords 2*, 304.

43. Donna Haraway, "A Manifesto for Cyborgs: Science, Technology, and Socialist Feminism in the 1980s," *Socialist Review* 50 (1984): 75; hereafter cited parenthetically in the text.

44. Naomi Schor, "Dreaming Dissymmetry," in *Men in Feminism*, ed. Alice Jardine and Paul Smith (New York and London: Methuen, 1987), 109.

45. James Clifford, *The Predicament of Culture* (Cambridge, Mass.: Harvard University Press, 1988), 12.

46. On the figure of the "Laughing Mother," see Suleiman, *Subversive Intent*.

47. On the figure of the "alone-standing woman"—a fictional creation of Christine Brooke-Rose—as an emblem of postmodernity, see my essay on Brooke-Rose's novel, *Between:* "Living Between, or the Lone(love)liness of the alleinstehende Frau," *The Review of Contemporary Fiction* (Fall 1989): 124–27.

48. Julia Kristeva, *Etrangers à nous-mêmes* (Paris: Fayard, 1988), 58, my translation; hereafter cited parenthetically in the text.

And the more serious and weighty the words
are, the more necessary the mention
"mention" and not "use" becomes. A "don't
use" is from now on attached to each concept,
each word. Don't use that concept, only
mention it. As could be read, above a tap:
don't drink that water, nondrinkable water.
One can make other uses of it, but do not take
it on or in oneself, do not consume it.

J.D.

THE END OF (HI)STORY

Gianni Vattimo

Probably, one of the most important points on which the descriptions of the postmodern condition agree—no matter how different they are from other points of view—is the consideration of postmodernity in terms of "the end of history." Jean-François Lyotard's main thesis in *La condition postmoderne* is that what characterizes this condition is the fact that it is no longer experienced within the framework of any one of the *metarécits* that used to explain and legitimate existence in previous epochs, above all, modern existence, and, specifically, nineteenth-century culture.

Not only Lyotard but also his main critic, Jürgen Habermas, sees postmodernity in these terms. If the notion of a postmodern condition has a meaning at all for Habermas, this meaning is clearly the disappearance of the *metarécits* as ways of legitimation. Of course, Habermas maintains that this is not, nor does it have to be, the case; we are *not* in the postmodern condition; to assume that we are would amount to an abdication of the critical task of reason. Habermas accepts, in a way, Lyotard's description; but in his view, it is not the description of the condition of contemporary man but simply a (wrong) interpretation of this condition that involves a more or less explicitly passive acceptance of the existing disorder of late capitalism, technology, and mass society.

Both Lyotard and Habermas argue on the basis of an interpretation of modern and contemporary history: Lyotard (I refer to one of his more recent texts, the paper published in *Critique* no. 456 [May 1985]) maintains that the *metarécits*—which, in the philosophy of history of the nineteenth and twentieth centuries, were used to describe and legitimize historical existence—have been confuted by decisive events of our time. So the *metarécit* of the rationality of what is real (Hegel) has been confuted by Auschwitz; the *metarécit* of the socialist revolution, by Stalin and his gulags; the *metarécit* of the free-market economy, by the recurrent crisis in capitalist societies; and the *metarécit* of democracy, by May 1968 (see p. 563 of the cited issue of *Critique*). Habermas, of course, does not deny the tragic reality of these facts; simply, he does not believe that they have "confuted" anything; in his view, they simply represent nondefinitive defeats of the project of the Enlightenment—a *metarécit* that Habermas believes in strongly, assuming that it has been continued by Hegel, Marx, and Max Weber's theory of rationality. It would appear that, at the very end, Habermas is not so much interested in maintaining a historicist view of history; in other words, he appears rather as the defender of a sort of Kantian rationality more than as the defender of historicism. I do not think that "reason," in the meaning it had for the Enlightenment and has for Habermas, can be considered apart from the historical project of the *emancipation* of mankind. In very rough terms, I would say that Habermas is not interested in defending reason for the sake of science and of an "objective" knowledge of reality; on the contrary, what he wants is historical emancipation through rational critique and also through science. This simply reflects, in my view, the fact that, in the recent centuries of modernity, reason—at least for Continental philosophy—has always been tied to history. Not only for Hegel, but also, in a different sense, for all modern European philosophy (e.g., positivism) it is true that the only way of experiencing reason as the capacity of reaching a *Grund* on which to "build" is only the capacity for grasping the rationality of historical development. (This is probably simply another implication of the very idea of modernity as a "normative" term: modernity can be defined as the epoch in which being modern is the supreme value; but this can be maintained only on the basis of the identification of the *Grund* with the rationality of historical development, as is visible in its most articulated form in Hegel's metaphysics of history.)

The incapacity of postmodern thought to offer a rational critique of the present conditions of society, and, more generally, to provide a basis for any rational discussion, which is the main reason why Habermas disagrees with Lyotard, is clearly related to the fact that, in postmodernist thought, the *metarécits* have been dissolved. Rationality is equal to historical rationality, that is, to a *metarécit*. The postmodern mind, in the view of Habermas, is incapable of providing the basis for a rational critique because it no longer believes in a possible rational course of history—that is because, for it, the *metarécits* have been confuted. It remains true that, for Habermas as well as for Lyotard, postmodernity can be described mainly in terms of the end of history. (I think this can be also true of Richard Rorty's view of postmodernity. When Rorty says that postmodernity, at the very end, is only "l'oubli graduel d'une certaine tradition philosophique," which involves a diminution of the importance of philosophy in society, a [reductive] readjustment of its position among other social practices [see *Critique* no. 442, 194–97; and no. 456, 580], he should also recognize that the main effect of the change of the position of philosophy in culture is exactly the dissolution of a unifying point of view on history [I think of Nietzsche attributing to Socrates the "invention" of the notion of universal history]. In other words, we can speak of a history only as far as we conceive of humankind as a unique species, developing toward ends, etc.—all ideas that are hardly conceivable outside a philosophical framework.)

Let me briefly summarize these introductory remarks: first, I wanted to point out that there is a general agreement as to the meaning of the very notion of postmodernity. If this notion has a meaning at all, it has to be described in terms of the end of history. What is finished is not simply a certain view (or a set of views) of history but history itself. If the *metarécits* that made it possible for us to think of history as a unitary course have been confuted, as Lyotard assumes, history itself has become impossible. To imagine that history, as a course of events, keeps going on no matter what we feel about the *metarécits* we used to believe in would amount to assuming that the specific *metarécit* that conceives of history as an objective course of events has not been dissolved; or, in other words, that the course of history, as a unitary and continuous course of events, is not "simply" a *metarécit* but the true description of the very reality of history. Now, this is exactly what the *metarécits* used to claim and exactly what postmodern consciousness does not believe any more. This, by the way, is not only an extravagant idea of postmodernist theorists like Lyotard; recent theory of historiography (e.g., the "metahistorical" research of H. White) has clearly pointed out the "rhetorical" character of the schemes by means of which we reconstruct the past. These rhetorical models affect the very substance, as it were, of history—not simply the way we experience it, because the distinction between an objective history and a subjective view of it can be described as a rhetorical scheme as well. . . . Under another point of view, if we think of Nietzsche's critique of *Historismus* and Walter Benjamin's *Theses on the Philosophy of History*, it is easy to see that history as a unitary course has also become inconceivable (and impossible) because of the increasing complexity of the relations between the centers (of power, but also of cultural critique) that collect and order information about what is going on. Once we have discovered the rhetorical and the power-relation implications that lay at the basis of (the notion of) history as a unitary course of events, history becomes impossible, both in its notion and in its pretended objective development. If we do not live any longer within the framework of one or another *metarécit*, we no longer live historically—we have entered into that condition that already A. Gehlen had called *post-histoire* (many traits of which could also be described by developing Marshall McLuhan's idea of the global village and similar themes).

The second point I was trying to make in these introductory remarks was that there seems to be an agreement among theorists (again, both Lyotard and Habermas) that, in the postmodern condition, there is no longer a possibility of arguing and rationally "proving" conclusions. This is indeed the thesis of Habermas, but Lyotard also seems to agree, at least in the sense that he assumes that postmodernity also involves a radical transformation of subjectivity and therefore of the very notion of rationality and of rational critique, too. (This radical transformation is seen by Lyotard as related to the

new conditions of existence which seem to lead toward a new interpenetration of nature and man, which recalls Renaissance naturalism retrieved in a
phenomenological framework. See the exhibition *Les Immatériaux*, planned
and directed by Lyotard at Beaubourg in Spring 1985.) These are then the
two ideas I am going to discuss and elaborate in this paper: that of
postmodernity as the end of history and that of the problems of legitimation
(concerning the possibility of a rationally founded critique), which seem to
be raised by this definition of postmodernity.

Let me take my start from an observation concerning the way Lyotard
argues about the postmodern condition. He says, for instance, in the paper
published in *Critique* I mentioned above, that the *metarécits* have been confuted by the dramatic events that mark our century: so Auschwitz has confuted the Hegelian idea of the rationality of history; Stalin, the idea of the
proletarian revolution, and so on. It seems to me that these events acquire
the capacity of confuting those *metarécits* only if they are included within
the framework of another legitimizing *metarécit*. By themselves, they could
not possibly confute anything. I am not raising the trivial objection of self-
inconsistency against Lyotard. What is important to me is to observe that he
(as well as Habermas, by the way) still uses a procedure of *historical* legitimation in arguing that the *metarécits* have been dissolved. Facts such as
Stalinism or Nazism confute metaphysical philosophies of history only because, paradoxically, they are assumed to belong to a sort of rational development, namely, the development of a postmodern condition. The
dissolution of the *metarécits* is itself a (paradoxical) kind of *metarécit*. To
point out this paradox does not necessarily involve the rejection of Lyotard's
theses. On the contrary: only by recognizing the paradox shall we be in
the position to dissolve Habermas's objections by preparing a solution of the
problem of legitimation that surely has not been completely dissolved by
the dissolution of the *metarécits*.

In the paradox that we must recognize in Lyotard's theory of postmodernity, it seems that postmodern thought simply experiences in its own way
the same "contradiction" that is visible, for instance, in Nietzsche's idea of
the eternal recurrence (which, as K. Loewith has shown, is to be "instau-
rated" by a *historical* decision that is not itself a repetition of the past) or in
Heidegger's view of the relation of postmetaphysical thought to past metaphysics. Unlike these eminent predecessors, Lyotard seems to pay too little
attention to the paradox in which he is captured. He does not see (and would
probably not admit) that his theory of the confutation of the *metarécits* is
itself a *metarécit*. He assumes that this confutation is an accomplished fact,
an event that is completely behind us. The *metarécits* of the past metaphysics
of history have been dissolved, and do not mean anything more to us. In his
paying no attention to the paradox of the (*metarécit* of the) dissolution of the
metarécits, Lyotard reminds me of a page of Nietzsche's *Thus Spoke Zarathustra*, where Zarathustra's animals describe the eternal recurrence in too easy a
form—they sing and dance, chanting, "Everything goes [an anticipation of

Feyerabend's anarchism?], everything comes back, eternally rolls the wheel of being." Zarathustra blames them for having transformed such a terrible and serious idea into a hurdy-gurdy song. The animals, he says, have forgotten all the pain he had to suffer (described in another discourse, of the same third part of the book, "On the Vision and the Riddle") in order to become able to think (or to instaurate, or to accept) the idea of the eternal recurrence (*Thus Spoke Zarathustra*, part 3, "The Convalescent").

It is exactly in authors such as Nietzsche and Heidegger—who, of course, also belong to the theoretical background of Lyotard's theory of postmodernity—that we have to look for a more productive way of paying attention to the paradox on which postmodern theory is based. In this paper I am not developing this discourse as far as Nietzsche is concerned (for this see the last chapter of my book *La fine della modernita* [1985]). I will simply try to show how some key concepts of the late Heidegger—namely, the concepts of *Andenken* and of *Verwindung*—can help us go farther into the meditation on postmodernity and its problem of legitimation.

The problem Heidegger faces in his effort to overcome (*überwinden*) metaphysics is in many senses the same Lyotard is confronted with when he tries to "prove" that we are living in a postmodern condition and that the *metarécits* have been confuted. But while Lyotard, as I suggested above, takes this confutation as an accomplished event which does not require further consideration, and which has put us in a totally new condition, Heidegger explicitly recognizes that metaphysics cannot be left behind us as an error we have got rid of (which, in the terms of Lyotard, would have been confuted). This impossibility is not only a matter of psychological habits (metaphysics as the thought in which we grew up, etc.); nor is it simply the consequence of the lack of a nonmetaphysical language (as Heidegger argues in the *Letter on Humanism* when he explains why *Sein und Zeit* remained unfinished). Both the psychological and cultural difficulty and the lack of a nonmetaphysical language are to be brought back to a more radical reason: metaphysics cannot simply be overcome because to overcome it would mean to perpetuate its methods and structures. To overcome metaphysics would mean to "confute" it, to reject it on the basis of a more adequate foundation, substituting a new truth for the old error: but this would be exactly the way to continue metaphysical thinking. The difficulty that Lyotard reveals in his trying to confute *metarécits* by means of another *metarécit* can be considered a confirmation of this thesis.

Exactly because he is acutely conscious of this difficulty, Heidegger thinks that the only way to step out of metaphysics is not by critical overcoming (or confutation) but by *Verwindung*. I am not going to discuss here all the meanings and implications of Heidegger's use of this word. I just want to point out that it involves a complex set of notions that go from "distortion" (which is the most important for my purpose here) to "healing," "convalescence," "resignation," "acceptance." Metaphysics can only be *verwinden* in all these senses: we can step out of it only by accepting it with resignation, as a sort of illness whose traces we still bring in ourselves; but taking it this way will also be a distortion of its original purposes and claims. If we apply the notion of *Verwindung* to modernity and postmodernity (an application that is justified by the fact that, for Heidegger as well, modernity is just the last result of metaphysics, its "practical" aspect in the moment of its accomplishment), we shall say that postmodernity is the epoch that has a relation of *Verwindung* (in all the sense of the word) to modernity. A postmodern thought, as that of Lyotard, brings in itself the trace of the historicism that characterized modernity; Lyotard can corroborate his argument for the postmodern condition only by bringing in historicist procedures of legitimation, which he should recognize more explicitly; this recognition could help him develop the theory of postmodernity in a more productive way.

In which sense, more precisely, can we say that postmetaphysical (or postmodern) thought is a *Verwindung* of metaphysics (or of modernity)? In what does *Verwindung* consist? Heidegger's late works show how this distortion has to be viewed: what they do is carry on the program of the destruction (or deconstruction) that was already announced in *Sein und Zeit* by the means of the recollection of its turning points, that is, by the means of a retrieval of the whole metaphysical tradition. It would be a mistake to believe that this retrieval or recollection intends to grasp what has remained unthought of in metaphysics, something that has been forgotten and should be remembered, brought back to the presence of representation. What remains un-thought in metaphysical tradition is the *Ereignis* character of Being, Being as an event and not as a stable structure like Plato's *ontos on*. What the recollection achieves is the recovery of this "eventual" character of Being: metaphysics appears to Heidegger as the "series" of the epochs in which Being has opened itself in the form of different *archai*, each one claiming to be a stable (metaphysical) structure while it was "just" an "epochal" openness, a sort of *episteme* in Foucault's sense. This recollection of metaphysics in "archeological" terms (see the recent book by R. Schürman on *Le principe d'anarchie*) is a distortion of it because it deprives metaphysics of its authoritarian character, disregarding its claims to being a knowledge of the stable principles of reality.

Retrieving metaphysics in archeological terms is also what Heidegger calls *An-denken*—recollection, the very essence of postmetaphysical thought. Recollection does not reach any ultimate evidence, any stable foundation. As a matter of fact, Being conceived of as an event cannot be grasped as a presence, as a stable ultimate structure beyond the errors of metaphysics; Being is not, but "happens" (es gibt Sein = Es, Sein, gibt) and can only be "thought" of in the form of recollection, as something that is always already gone. Postmetaphysical thought cannot "overcome" metaphysics through a new foundation; it can only celebrate, in relation to metaphysics, "feasts of memory," as Nietzsche says more or less in the same sense as Heidegger. Being is not presence but *Ereignis*, event, and *Ge-Schick* (the aggregate, *Ge*, of the sending, *Schicken*); therefore, thought is not (is no longer) foundation but

An-denken, recollection. *Andenken* is a distortion because it deprives the metaphysical *archai* of their ultimacy, thinking of them within the framework of the eventuality of Being.

With the emphasis he puts on recollection, Heidegger seems to be very close to much of postmodern sensibility: think of the tendencies toward a free—even arbitrary—revival of the forms of the past; this revival, in architecture and in other artistic fields (the novel, for instance), is not inspired by the idea of an analogy between our epoch and one or the other epoch of the past, an analogy that would justify the evocation of these forms in order to find *adequate* examples for the art of today. Past form and stylistic traits are evoked and revived outside of any kind of foundational motivation; they are just a repertory of rhetoric *exempla* that are not intended as the basis for a more adequate understanding and expression of the present situation.

But, to come to a provisional conclusion, how can we say, as I said before, that this way of referring to the past in a *verwindend* or *andenkend* way can help us solve the problems of legitimation in postmodernity?

The question is also justified because, at least in Heidegger, to whom I especially refer here—but this could also be said of Nietzsche, as far as his thought tends to develop itself in a "genealogical" form—recollection, seen as the "authentic" possibility given to postmetaphysical thought, seems to take totally the place of what, in metaphysics, was the search for the ultimate foundation. Recollection is the form in which thought "corresponds" to Being conceived of in terms of event, *Geschick, Überlieferung* (trans-mission) of historically qualified disclosures. It is an attitude of this kind that Nietzsche describes in *Human, All-Too-Human* as the attitude of the "good tempered man," who, having discovered that all metaphysical, moral, and religious "values" are only the result of the sublimation of impulses, interests, and so on, does not simply reject these values but looks at them with an attitude of "limited" respect, which I think can be described by the Latin term of *pietas; pietas*, in this context, would describe the attitude of devoted attention that we adopt toward the values marked by mortality and finitude. The only kind of foundation that is at our disposal in the age of the end of metaphysics, from a Heideggerian point of view, seems to be this appeal to the inherited "values"—works of art, institutions, language, and so on, more or less what Hegel called the objective spirit—seen as "monuments," that is, as something that lasts and provides us with "valid" ways of approaching experience, but only within the horizon of mortality and perishability. "Was bleibet aber, stiften die Dichter," says Hölderlin as quoted by Heidegger: what lasts is founded by poets. This endurance is not to be conceived in terms of an eternal duration, not even in terms of the perfection of the classical work of art in Hegel's sense (which also involves a certain kind of eternity), but in terms of historical monumentality, which is ultimately related to the notion of trace and of mortality. What remains—traces, monuments, graves, that is, residues in a certain sense—opens itself in poetry.

I think it is easy to see how this conception of the foundation in terms of recollection can claim to be a *Verwindung* of the foundational thought of traditional metaphysics. By implicitly but strongly attributing a normative character to the events that have "confuted" metaphysical *metarécits*, Lyotard was calling for respect and attention toward what *happened*, assuming that it shall be considered a decisive indication for theory and thought. Habermas refuses Lyotard's conclusions, but only by appealing on his side to another course of events that, he assumes, contains another, equally cogent indication for theory. To explicitly substitute recollection and *pietas* for this still-foundational thought means, in the first place, to deprive this "foundation" of its claims to logical cogency and demonstrative power. Nietzsche's words "God is dead" is only the announcement of an event, not the metaphysical description of a structure of being in which God would not possibly "exist."

But, again: does this distortion, or *Verwindung*, of the metaphysical practice of foundation represent a way of solving the problems of legitimation that face postmodern philosophy? It seems that *Verwindung* succeeds indeed in unmasking the still metaphysical character of postmodernist theories, such as that of Lyotard (but it is hard to see how it could provide us with positive alternatives).

In a sense, it is true that there is no alternative solution. This is what is meant by the word *Verwindung*—which is, in my opinion, a key word to describe not only philosophy, but also, for example, the political "chances" of postmodern culture. The only way we have to argue in favor of postmodernist philosophy is still an appeal to history, as those we have seen in Lyotard and Habermas. Only if we recognize this fact explicitly and make it the theme of our reflection, instead of pretending that it is now completely behind us as a *vergangen* event; that is, only if we tell explicitly, again and again, the story of the end of history, shall we be able to change, distort, *verwinden*, its still metaphysical significance. Somebody (K. Rosenkranz, I think, in one of the first works on philosophical anthropology, quoted and discussed by K. Loewith in one of his essays) has observed that the only real way we have to distinguish between sleep and wakefulness is that, when we are awake, we can remember that we have woken up. Nietzsche is right when he says (in *The Twilight of the Idols*) that the true world at the very end became a fable; but fable and simulacra, if they have to be recognized as simulacra and not be given the weight and authority of a new sort of Piatonic *ontos on*, have to be kept in a *verwindend* relation toward the "true" world of metaphysics. If we simply assume, as an indisputable fact, that the events of our time have completely dissolved and liquidated the *metarécits* of metaphysics, we really remain, as Habermas says, without the slightest possibility of a rational critique of the present. On the contrary, if we recognize that, as Heidegger suggests, the end of history belongs to the history of Being, we will still have a criterion—be it paradoxical—for rational arguing and for historical options. Sure, to speak of the history of Being means to appeal again to a cogency of what happened, in the sense that metaphysical historicism (but also Lyotard and Habermas) used to do. We are reviving here a *metarécit*, the *metarécit* of the history of Being. But, contrary to what happened in Lyotard and Habermas, this *metarécit* is recognized as having the sole meaning of the progressive—as it were—dissolution of all the *metarécits*— that is, of the dissolution of Being as a stable structure in favor of Being as an event. To say this is also a way to recognize that Heidegger finally developed a philosophy in which Being (foundation, structure) disappears, takes leave, is gone—and nevertheless he still remained interested in ontology, according to the purpose on which *Sein und Zeit* was based. We can adequately, or authentically, experience the disappearance of Being as an event only within the history of Being; and vice versa. The story of the end of history, in this sense, is both a *Verwindung* (a distorted continuation) of metaphysics (or historicism) and a theory in which the very meaning of the history of Being is *Verwindung,* in all the senses of the word: we could also speak of secularization, de-sacralization (I am thinking here also of R. Girard's idea of Jesus as the unmasker of the "sacred" in its violent implications), God's death in Nietzsche's terms.

As with metaphysical historicism, the *metarécit* of the end of history is also an appeal to correspond to what happened to the history of Being. The distortion, however, consists of the fact that the event that we are to correspond to is a process whose meaning is the dissolution of any *cogency*, as well as the cogency of the history of Being. What we must correspond to is the dissolution of Being itself ("das Sein als Grund fahren lassen," says Heidegger in "Time and Being," a lecture of the sixties). The normativity that thought is faced with, therefore, is a very paradoxical one—but nevertheless, it claims a specific validity. The "process" to which we are to correspond to is the "epochal," self-concealing (or simply nihilistic) essence (*Wesen* being meant here in the verbal sense Heidegger gives to it) of Being; consequently, the "reasons" why we are to correspond to this destiny of Being are also "distorted" reasons, no longer cogent in the sense that belonged to the metaphysical foundation. We are confronted here with a sort of hypothetical imperative that at the very end depends on the *pietas* I was alluding to above. As a matter of fact—and I am thinking here of some recent positions of Rorty's—if thought can no longer be "foundational thought," the reasons we can offer in order to persuade others to accept the thesis of postmodernism (or any other thesis) cannot be based—as pragmatists seem to think—on the need for survival (which would require agreement, playing the social and language games, etc.); if it were so, the need for survival would represent another form of true and ultimate (metaphysical) foundation. Life, to which we can appeal in order to persuade somebody of the validity of a philosophical thesis, is rather, and is perhaps only, a historically and culturally qualified and "charged" form of life; we are hardly interested in pure biological survival, but in surviving within a set of "goods," cultural and human values that constitute our sole being. But the appeal to these historical values is exactly what can be described as *pietas,* in the sense I outlined above.

All this involves plenty of normative content, which can provide the basis for satisfying the reasonable preoccupations of people like Habermas. A postmetaphysical "logic" and "ethics"—not to speak of politics—can be constructed on the notions of *pietas, Andenken, Verwindung.* What seems to be clear from the very beginning are the *negative* criteria with which they provide us: to correspond to the *verwindend* essence of Being and of thought, we have to engage actively in the de(con)struction of all the metaphysical residues that still are alive in our philosophy, psychology, ethics, culture in general. Let me just make an example: in relation to historically decisive phenomena like Khomeini's revolution, or Pope John Paul II's traditionalist interpretation of Catholicism, a postmodernist philosopher would surely be in the condition to choose and judge better than Habermas himself (remember the disastrous mistakes made by left-wing intellectuals in evaluating the meaning of Khomeini's revolution at its beginning). Maybe the initial, purely negative, normative implications of the (paradoxical) postmodernist philosophy of history (because it is actually one) are not much. But they seem to be the only way to open philosophy in a time when foundational thought has become (fortunately) impossible, and Being as *Grund* is (fortunately) gone.

THE (DE-)CONSTRUCTION SITES OF THE POSTMODERN

Peter Koslowski

A limit is not perceptible until it has been transgressed. This transcendental feature of limit-perception applies especially to those limits that form the thresholds of epochs. The shape of an epoch thus cannot be recognized until its acme, the fullest extension of its formation, has been transcended. Today we perceive modernity [*Moderne*], or modern times [*die Neuzeit*], as an epoch that has moved beyond its acme.[T1] The conflict between the modern and the postmodern does not involve this fact. Rather, it is a question of whether modernity has attained its end [*Vollendung*][T2] or whether we can dispense with its completion and turn to more important projects.

I. From the Laws of Conservation to the Principle of Entropy:
The Aging of Modernity

To inquire whether modernity already belongs to the past or whether it has reached its end, involves two different questions that arise from two concepts of the modern. In the first case, modernity is synonymous with modern times, a historical epoch after antiquity and the Middle Ages. Arnold Toynbee, the great universal historian, already claimed thirty years ago that "modern times" have passed into postmodernity.[1] What are the clues that we live on the threshold of a world-historical epoch? Two clues, two shifts in consciousness make such an assumption plausible: the discovery of finitude and the discovery of nonconservation.

The works of Spaemann, Blumenberg, Henrich, and Koyré have demonstrated conclusively that modern times begin with the concepts of the self-preservation of the subject, the conservation of motion and energy, and an open-ended, infinite universe.[2] The significance of the Galileian laws of conservation for the mechanistic, modern world view is well documented. The law of the conservation of energy, the first law of thermodynamics, is the central axiom of modern times. It grounds the assumption of the structural self-identity and self-preservation of being. It underlies moreover all evolutionary approaches to cosmology and biology. The structures of the world become ever more complex, the argument runs, because the energy and former states of increasing complexity are preserved. Increasing complexity, not reduced complexity or regression, defines for modern times the norm because, according to the law of conservation, a previously attained state is maintained over time.

The second law of thermodynamics, namely that structures tend toward the more probable, hence less complex state and that without external influence warmth always flows from the warmer to the colder body, never the other way around, was discovered much later. It did not exert any real influence on modern consciousness until the point that I would like to consider the threshold of a new epoch. The second law of thermodynamics, the "most metaphysical of all natural laws" in the words of Henri Bergson, first became socially effective and relevant in 1972 thanks to the famous study, "The Limits of Growth."[3] Sources of energy and raw materials on earth and in the solar system are finite, the report argues. Forms of energy and matter cannot be infinitely converted and extended because energy cannot be transformed into work or raw materials without producing side-effects on the environment. One could dispute the accuracy of individual prognoses of the Club of Rome study, but one cannot deny that it, together with Fred Hirsch's *Social Limits to Growth*, which appeared four years after the study, revolutionized our "natural" and economic world view.[4] Both works led to a crisis for the metaphor of conservation and for the concepts of growth and progress based on it. Since then, conservation, self-preservation, and constancy of structure have become problematic and hence cannot be simply presupposed as in the beginning of modern times. Regardless of the physical interdependence of the first two laws of thermodynamics, the second, which sees all systems as finite and decadence as more probable than preservation, is the dominant principle of postmodernity, just as the first, the principle of conservation, was the dominant law of modern times. There is thus general consensus that the ecological problems predicted by the second law of thermodynamics have now sealed both the end of man's "unlimited" domination over nature and the end of the utopian aspirations of modern times. The "exhaustion of utopian energies" points to the beginning of the postmodern epoch.

II. Carrying on the Project of Modernity

In spite of the consensus regarding the threshold to a new epoch, postmodernity remains controversial because many authors hold firmly to a project of modernity which is not disproven by ecological limits and the decline of utopias. The phrase "project of modernity" relies on a completely different concept of modernity from the merely historical one. For as epoch, modernity, or modern times, has produced not one but an entire series of projects: Reformation, Counterreformation, Baroque, Enlightenment, German Idealism, Positivism, and Marxism. Jürgen Habermas equates the project of modernity with the program of the Enlightenment.[5] This program consists, according to Habermas, in the process whereby tradition becomes entirely self-reflexive and nothing has natural validity but, rather, everything must be legitimated communicatively before the tribunal of reason. Reason, he continues, thereby becomes the equivalent of the unifying force of religion.[6] Reason appears as the goddess of both modernity and Enlightenment.

The equation, project of modernity = project of Enlightenment does not increase our understanding, however, because the equivocal term modernity is merely equated with the equivocal term Enlightenment. In both cases a proper name is substituted for a concept. The Enlightenment as proper name for an epoch, on the one hand, refers to an epoch in the past. Considered as epoch, the Enlightenment has many meanings and levels.[7] It contains the most divergent directions of idealist and materialist, deistic and atheistic thought and does not fit into Habermas's program. Enlightenment as a generic term, on the other hand, is only meaningful in relation to an object and an addressee, that is as the enlightenment of someone about something. Total enlightenment is not a meaningful term because the individual that is to be enlightened about everything runs the danger of being unable to see anything because of the resultant absolute transparency. To conceive of the project of Enlightenment or modernity in the sense of the *proper name* Enlightenment, however, is just as meaningful and legitimate as today representing the project of High Scholasticism or the Baroque. One can call for the return of an epoch, but one must then represent the historical program with all its faults. In the case of the project of modernity, the historical character of the program becomes veiled by the fact that modernity [*die Moderne*] as proper name for an epoch becomes oddly fused with modernity [*Modernität*] as the concept standing for a property or attribute.

The project of modernity appears as a project that is modern. This is true only if the present, the now, is modernity, and if that which is modern and avant-garde, is modernity. The equivocation between modernity or modern times and modern or contemporary [*neuzeitlich*] can be avoided by a more precise regulation of language usage. Namely, one could equate the term "modern" as attribute with the colloquialism "in" along the lines: "modern" is what is "in." The "moderns" would be those who are "in," and the concept "modernity" would be completely replaced by the concept "modern times" (*Neuzeit*). But since this corrective speech could never be carried out fully, the concept for the historical epoch, modernity, will continue to attach itself parasitically onto the connotations of the attribute "modern." The "project of modernity" profits from the phrase's implicit suggestion of the most advanced state of consciousness, which would be precisely modern consciousness or consciousness of modernity.[8] But this suggestion rests on the mistaken view that there exists such a thing as *one* most advanced consciousness in an epoch and that its realization could become a project that someone could make his own and carry on as its director.

III. The Theory of Modernity As the Theory of the Absolute?

The left-Hegelian foundation of such a view is obvious: Consciousness or reason unfold historically in subjects whose avant-garde forms the highest historical development. The project of modernity is thus in the end a left-Hegelian theory of the absolute, or absolute reason. Reason, in this view, should successively abandon and raise (*aufheben*) its pregiven natural conditions to pure, rational conditions. Reason should become totality. The question remains, however, whether reason can be the absolute.

According to Fichte, the absolute is that which totality is capable of excluding from itself.[9] The early Fichte still understood the absolute as the absolute Ego of the subject. It became clearer to the late Fichte, however, that the Ego of the subject cannot be the absolute because the Ego always remains dependent on an Other: no one gives birth to himself and no one "dies himself." Only the absolute itself is the absolute. It alone is capable of excluding from itself totality as the mere appearance of itself. Reason is not the absolute because, rather than producing reality, reason must always refer to some Other that is not itself. One step removed, reason can only allow reality, which is the appearance of the absolute, to appear. In reason the appearance of the absolute (reality) appears before itself, but reason is not the actual appearing of the absolute.[10]

The absolute reign of reason is a misguided project of modernity because reason is not the absolute and therefore, in raising absolute claims, reason can only dominate, never reconcile itself with, its Other. Recent French postmodern thinkers like Jean-François Lyotard have revealed how this totalitarian character of the domination of reason operates in certain arguments within German Idealism.[11] Their critiques have not yet been given sufficient attention in German philosophical discussions. On the other hand, recent French critical thought has not taken into account the self-criticism of German Idealism presented in the late Fichte, late Schelling, or in Hegel's lectures on the philosophy of religion.

The project of those in contemporary Germany who would carry on and lead the project of modernity is contradictory and reactionary. It is contradictory because the "modernity" that it wants to bring to completion (*vollenden*) is, as the postmodern consciousness demonstrates, no longer "modern." It is reactionary because it tries to keep something past, namely left-Hegelianism, alive. Left-Hegelianism and Marxism, as the discourse of modernity, try to offer a form of gnosis without a transcendental savior: Within the iron frame of history the World Spirit, or productive forces, or discourse, unfold to reveal at each stage a necessary formation. History, however, is not propelled by a World Spirit that unfolds with the force of necessity. There is not *one* discourse behind history, or even *one* modernity, but merely the discourses of different modernisms.

The concept of the postmodern is liberating because it points the way out of the iron frame of history, out of the *heimarmene* (necessity) without divine *pleroma* (plenty) that makes up the philosophy of history, out of the World Spirit that is only a worldly prince. The postmodern points to the recovery of the freedom of (hi)stories and discourses and to a new relationship to that which is not reason, namely to the absolute and to nature. Against the dictatorship of the universal and the collective singular, i.e., those formations that only occur as *singulare tantum*, postmodern thought proposes the plurality of conflicting formations. The *one* discourse, the one consensus, history, progress, evolution, etc. are replaced by discourses, (hi)stories, arrangements, progresses, and evolutions of historical processes and their appearance in the mirror of reason.[T3] For postmodern thought there are only two singulars: the unique individual, like the Leibnizian monad, which is individuated through its entire being and is designated, indeed fixed, by a proper name; and the absolute. Looking back beyond the universality of the Hegelian concept [*Begriff*], postmodern thought links up with Leibniz's theory of the monad and its singularity.[12]

IV. The Temporality of Postmodernism: Buying Time

The concept of the postmodern contains an element of liberation because it can lead us out of the obsessions of modernity, out of the world war between East and West over the correct interpretation of Hegel's philosophy of history. The postmodern points the way out of the entire iron frame of the history of philosophy and its triadic scheme of antiquity, Middle Ages, and modern times. The postmodern thereby effects a temporal postponement.

The triadic scheme is misleading when it is transposed from the divine Trinity to a system of world history. In particular, the Hegelian progression of the kingdom [*Reich*] of the father, kingdom of the son, and kingdom of the spirit, with the latter equated with modern times, comes too close to the image of a Third (and concluding) Reich. If the kingdom of reason promised by the triadic scheme for modernity has still not come to pass after some two hundred years, not only are utopian energies exhausted thereby but there is also great danger that reason will fall into total self-despair.[13] The turn from the triad, antiquity, Middle Ages, modern times, to the postmodern buys time; it produces a temporal gain of a fourth age that fulfills the *tetraktys* (quaternity) of the Pythagoreans. It answers the question of Plato's *Timaeus* and of all Pythagoreans: Where is the fourth?[14] Postmodernity postpones the final decline [*Untergang*][T4] that is supposed to occur after the collapse of the utopian expectations contained in modernism's philosophy of history.

"Mankind's destiny [*Bestimmung*] is to destroy itself. But for that, it must first prove itself worthy. It is not yet so."[15] The epoch of the postmodern is the time remaining to humanity to become worthy of ultimate decline [*Untergang*].

Modernity is characterized just as much by the idolization of, as by despair in, reason. Irrationalism and the flight into violent myths follow the dictatorship of reason like a shadow or an evil twin. Nietzsche's criticism of the West's logocentric history and his appeal to the Dionysian belong to modernity just as much as do the myth of the twentieth century and the neopaganism of Germanic emancipation from the Judeo-Christian tradition attempted in recent history.

Postmodernism partakes in these ruptures of modernity because it adopts its heritage as something that cannot be simply dismissed but must be simultaneously preserved, raised up, and overcome [*aufgehoben und überwunden*]. Whereas modernism grappled with the problem of reconciling past and future, postmodernism must find a new synthesis beyond the opposition rationalism-irrationalism. It is a question of recovering the entire range of intellectual and emotional [*geistigen*] faculties and forms of knowledge, including ones that go beyond communicative competence and analytical reason. Whether the Cartesian dichotomy of spirit and matter, or the body/soul problem, can be overcome by the extension of human consciousness through microelectronics and a new paradigm of man-machine-continuum, as Lyotard and others suggest, remains to be seen.[16] Perhaps the opposition between hardware and software will transcend that between body and soul.

V. The Main Currents of Postmodernism

At present, postmodernism in philosophy and art consists of an open field of competing currents and forces, of which three can be isolated:

1) Late-modernism or transavant-garde
2) Postmodernity as stylistic and intellectual anarchy
3) Postmodernism as postmodern classicism in architecture and postmodern essentialism or "Neoaristotelianism" in philosophy

Postmodernism is late-modernism in the sense of an intensification of modernity, i.e., as the aesthetic of beating the future to the punch by outdoing the ideals of the present. The primacy of novelty demands that modernism overcome itself lest it threaten to become classic. The demon of novelty demands that the new take itself to ever higher heights, lest it threaten to become old. Thus the avant-garde is outdone by the transavant-garde, and the "newest of the new" appear on the scene, *i nuovi-nuovi*, as the Italian group calls itself.[17] In these intensifications one notices both the traces of the dictates of *modernismo* and a certain ironic distance from the compulsion of the new.

The second, anarchistic variation of postmodernism follows Paul Feyerabend's motto, "Anything goes." It introduces both the liberating potential
of aesthetic and philosophical anarchism and the dangers of arbitrariness
and eclecticism which are part of anarchistic pluralism. After the reign of
functionalistic purism in architecture and the methodological straightjacket
[spanischen Stiefeln] of scientistic discourses, the expansion of fields of experience and expression by this new colorfulness has had a tremendous effect.
Of course, arbitrariness becomes a problem for such artists and philosophers
since topics and forms of expression no longer offer any resistance that could
allow them to "work off" [abarbeiten] their subjectivity.

The critique of functionalism in architecture converges today with a critique of functionalism in the social and human sciences. The dogmas of
functionalism—that function determines form and that function alone, not
the means of its achievement, matters—have lost their emancipatory potential in aesthetics. "The repetition a thousand times of the same straight edge
has today lost its aura of enlightenment."[18] Functionalism in design and
construction has lost its once functional role within the framework of a
modernized and more efficient production process. Whereas functionalism
was first necessitated by the streamlining of production in order to reduce
manufacturing costs and thus to allow more consumers to partake in design,
now functionalism has assumed an independent character and, in relation to
the productive forces, it has become an end in itself.[19] A functionalism that
has become self-reflexive and an end it itself, however, is ritualistic in the
worst sense. It is functionalistic without function, ritualistic without purpose
in ritual or cult. Reinhart Maurer wrote in passing: "Perhaps there's a bit of
cult in everything that would seem merely functional."[20] In any case, there is
ritual in every functionalism that is no longer functional.

Postmodern architecture turns from pure stereometric form and shapes
dictated by function back to the expression of material content and pictorial
elements in construction. It once again allows decoration and ornamenta-
tion, symbolic and semiotic expressions on buildings. After the prohibition
against facades and the demand for transparency of the entire structure,
both of which determined postwar architecture in its attempt to escape the
bunker-experience of Nazism, now visible subdivisions, structures, and ex-
teriors on buildings may again be viewed as meaning-bearing signs. The
appearance of a new ostentatiousness, pompous kitsch, and swank in recent
postmodern architecture is the price to be paid for the resemanticization that
charges building structures with significance.

Writers critical of postmodernism often remark with amazement and
head-shaking at the proximity between the postmodern aesthetic-
philosophical anarchism and representatives of both postmodern material
[substantiellen] life-forms and postmodern classicism. The resolution of this
paradox is relatively simple: "One need merely to point out that there exists
a deep-running opposition between fully played-out nihilism and wild anarchy. The struggle between the two boils down to whether the human envi-

ronment should be transformed into a desert or a primeval jungle."[21] The spiritual [*geistiger*] jungle is preferable to the spiritual desert. Out of anarchistic postmodernism grows the chance for an essential and fundamental [*substantielle*] postmodernism that would be in the position to offer new and substantial forms as alternatives to the jargon and aesthetic of inauthenticity.

Modern is: faith in the scientific claims to total explanation, reduction of social life to functions and media of communication, and the hope for utopias in this world. Postmodern is: critique of scientism, functionalism, and utopianism.[22] For postmodern thought, the dissolution of being, be it person or thing, into relations and functions must be opposed by the primacy of essential and entelechial form and the instance of unique individuality in space and time. The postmodern axiom, "The idea determines form," opposes the modernist axiom, "Function determines form." A person or thing that corresponds to its idea always fulfills more than a function and cannot be reduced to its relational determinations. It represents itself and its idea and contains in its form metaphors that refer to the entirety of the cosmos. The most exemplary aspects of *postmodern Essentialism* in art and philosophy adopt the legacy of antiquity and the Middle Ages. It adopts this legacy after having passed through modernism and its principles of subjectivity and individual freedom. Philosophical essentialism is postmodern because it goes beyond the distinctions and differentiations of modernism. That is, it does not take all the inferior products that have resulted from a state in which art, science, and religion are isolated from each other as the final word; rather, it sees them as failed developments that need to be overcome by means of a new integration of these three spiritual spheres of life. This essentialism is postmodern because it strives to avoid two dangers of premodern classicism: academism caused by sterile imitation, and social divisions caused by classicism's inherent class structure. After all, ever since the Romans "classic" has carried with it the aftertaste of class difference and class consciousness.[23] Since we have fought for universal rights to liberty in modernity and since we have to preserve democratic freedoms, human rights, and the legally organized State as achievements of modernity, we can strive for a new synthesis between these modern liberties and the material [*substantiellen*] forms of the aesthetic and social sphere. As Hegel expressed it in unsurpassed form, it's a question of simultaneously thinking the subject as substance and substance as subject. This project of Hegelian philosophy also guides European philosophy.

VI. The Project of Modernity Is Not the Project of Humanity

There is no project of antiquity or modernity. If there is a project that could be binding for all men and for all epochs, modernity as well as postmodernity, it is the project of humanity. This project is not the privilege of one epoch and it is not over with the end of any given epoch. If there is a program of modernity then it must begin with Pythagoras in Greece and with Judaism's Book of Wisdom. Thus Friedrich Schlegel, in his essays of 1795–97, which were to become significant for the theory of modernity, saw Pythagoras as the origin of modernity: "Socrates, or even before him Pythagoras, who was the first to dare to attempt to organize morals and the state according to the ideas of pure reason, stand at the point of origin of recent history, i.e., of the system of infinite perfectability"—and this means at the origin of modernity in the widest sense.[24] According to Schlegel, "it is fundamentally unclear whether some Platonic dialogues are poetic philosophemes or philosophical poems,"[25] and for this reason they are to be considered art works in modern style (using Schlegel's definition). The "sublime urbanity of the Socratic muse" is Romantic irony, which Socrates introduced into the world; it is the mood of recent history and the sign of modernity, "the mood of a higher perspective, infinitely raised above all contingency, even above its own art, virtue, or genius."[26]

The dispute about modernity is not a dispute about reason and the project of humanity but one about a narrow conception of the project of humanity as a historical program of modernism, as a project of *totalizing* reason. A limit to this totalizing and totalitarian reason cannot come from the theory of communicative action. The hope that discourse and communicative praxis could break out of the "compulsion for identity" imposed by conceptual universals (Adorno), as Wellmer and Habermas assume, is fully ungrounded.[27] The logic of domination-free discourse remains too much within the logic of the universal. Particularity and novelty have too little space there. Imagination, the formative power that can give itself new form by projecting itself into an image [*imago*], cannot be contained within deductive logic, which can only subsume, i.e., subjugate the particular under a pregiven universal concept. The imagination and creative knowledge likewise escape the logic of consensus and universal agreement. The new and the creative are, after all, precisely that which must continually challenge, place into question, and destroy the well-established consensus of bourgeois heroism. Habermas's discourse theory cannot provide the answer to Max Weber's question: From where will novelty come in this fossilized world? Discourse theory is not a theory of the discovery of truth or of new truth. It is also not a sufficient theory about the grounding of truth, since it is conceivable that discourse and its consensus, even under the ideal conditions of authenticity, truth, honesty, etc., could produce in their entirety a state of deception, or that some state of deception could permanently prevent the fulfillment of these essential conditions.

Romano Guardini raised the question in his book, *The End of Modern Times* (1950): Why has the optimism of belief in progress entered a crisis? His answer was: "Because one cannot place such confidence in human works as we have done in modern times—any more than one can do so with nature."[28] This necessary skepticism is just as appropriate vis-à-vis human *discourse* since, as Foucault has shown, there is no discourse that is not a discourse of power.[29] Guardini says further that in the time after modern times "danger grows, power grows, but power over power does not grow. What, then, guarantees proper behavior? Nothing. There is no guarantee that freedom will make the correct decisions."[30] Precisely this is true of so-called domination-free discourse, which, under the conditions of human history and finitude, can never be a discourse without power. To quote Guardini again: "The demons take possession of any human power that does not answer to a conscience. . . . There is no form of being that is without domination. Either God, man, or the demons dominate. . . . Modern times have forgotten all this. . . . They have believed that man could have power simply and be secure in its use—thanks to some logic of things that are supposed to act just as dependably in the realm of human freedom as they do in nature."[31] In the end we must side with Adorno and Horkheimer, the older Frankfurt School, against the younger, Habermas and Wellmer: There is no possible source of resistance against the compulsive system of discursive reason without the messianic hope for the absolute, without the thoughtful remembrance [*Eingedenken*] of nature, and without the self-assertion and invulnerability of a centered personhood, what Guardini calls conscience, which is not definable by means of its potential to participate in a discourse.

These three sources of resistance against discursive reason designate the postmodern critique of the project of modernity as a project of continuous enlightenment. Discursive reason is not the totality of human potential. The completion [*Vollendung*] of the project of discursive reason is therefore not at all necessary, indeed not at all possible. History will not come to final completion without the participation of the absolute, without a *concursus divinus*. We are not born of discourses and do not die of our own discourse. Death is the limit of the reconciliation attainable through discursive reason, and it is not without reason that the death of the individual appears as the limit of discursive reconciliation in more recent "critiques of reason."[32] The same is equally true for the beginning of life. Evil "is not at all a mere absence of reason which would then simply yield to rational discourse. One should recall here Goethe's bon mot: Upon being asked how Adam's race would have propagated had the Fall not occurred, Goethe answered: doubtlessly by means of a rational discourse."[33]

The compulsion to reach a final completion [*Vollendungszwang*], which propels both modernity and discursive reason, is opposed not only by the finitude of human existence but also by the right of following epochs to their own projects. Postmodernity will pursue its own projects. This right cannot be taken away from it by a discursive reason that would leave a totalizing imprint on the world. The right of epochs is the right of generations to give their own form to their time and world. We must limit the drive to final completion so that we can be in the position to leave behind ruins, incomplete projects, and open spaces. Indeed, the fact that we cannot bear to see ruins, that we constantly transform all traces of the past into the condition of perfect, shiny restoration, that we consider any open field as a potential site for a structure that needs to be built as soon as possible—this demonstrates that modernity's compulsion to reach a final completion, or totalizing reason's compulsion to modernize, still holds us in its sway. We strive to ban the traces of finitude and temporality from our environment through perfect restoration and modernization. The profundity and age of our world's countenance are erased for the sake of an illusion of completeness. Many ruins need to be kept as testimonies to the greatness and vanity of the past. Their unconstructed remains provide the opportunity to continue construction when their time comes again, the way the Cologne cathedral came to be built again after centuries. Perhaps one will also continue working on the project, or various projects, of modernity at some time in the future. But for now there is something more important than the project of modernity: the numerous (de)construction sites of the postmodern.

Translated by John H. Smith

NOTES

1. Arnold Toynbee, *Study of History* (London: Oxford University Press, 1964), 235. On the definition of the modern, see M. Calinescu, *Faces of Modernity: Avant-Garde, Decadence, Kitsch* (Bloomington: Indiana University Press, 1977) and Hans-Robert Jauss, "Ursprung und Bedeutung der Fortschrittsidee in der 'Querelle des Anciens et des Modernes,'" in *Die Philosophie und die Frage nach dem Fortschritt*, ed. H. Kuhn and F. Wiedemann (Munich: A. Pustet, 1964), 51ff and Jauss, "Literarische Tradition und gegenwärtiges Bewußtsein der Modernität," in *Literaturgeschichte als Provokation* (Frankfurt: Suhrkamp, 1970), 11ff.

2. See the contributions by R. Spaemann, H. Blumenberg, and D. Henrich in *Subjektivität und Selbsterhaltung: Beiträge zur Diagnose der Moderne*, ed. H. Ebeling (Frankfurt: Suhrkamp, 1976) and A. Koyré, *From the Closed World to the Infinite Universe* (Baltimore: Johns Hopkins University Press, 1957).

3. D. and D. Meadows, *Die Grenzen des Wachstums—ein Bericht des Club of Rome zur Lage der Menschheit* (DVA, 1972).

4. Fred Hirsch, *Social Limits to Growth* (Cambridge, Mass.: Harvard University Press, 1976).

5. Jürgen Habermas, "Die Moderne—ein unvollendetes Projekt," in *Kleine politische Schriften* (Frankfurt: Suhrkamp, 1981). See also his more recent study, *Der philosophische Diskurs der Moderne: Zwölf Vorlesungen* (Frankfurt: Suhrkamp, 1985).

6. Jürgen Habermas, "Der Eintritt in die Postmoderne," *Merkur* 421 (1983): 752. For a critique of Habermas, see H. Hesse, "Widersprüche der Moderne. Einwände gegen Habermas' Konzept kommunikativer Rationalität," in *Angesichts objektiver Verblendung: Über die Paradoxien kritischer Theorie*, ed. G. Gamm (Tübingen: Konkursbuchverlag, 1985), 252ff.

7. Already between the years 1785 and 1790 many authors complained about the ambiguity of the concept "enlightenment." For example, J. M. Sailer: "Enlightenment is a word that has become so unstable these days . . . that one can hardly use it without the danger of being misunderstood." Quoted from N. Hinske's entry, "Aufklärung," in the *Staatslexikon* (Freiburg: Herder, 1985), vol. 1, col. 393.

8. On this topos in Adorno, see Peter Bürger, "Das Altern der Moderne," in *Adorno-Konferenz 1983*, ed. L. v. Friedburg and J. Habermas (Frankfurt: Suhrkamp, 1983), 177–97.

9. Johann Gottlieb Fichte, *Grundlage der gesammten Wissenschaftslehre* (1794), ed. I. H. Fichte (Berlin: de Gruyter, 1971), vol. l, 197.

10. Fichte, *Die Wissenschaftslehre* (1812), ibid., vol. 10, 342. On the Ego as the image of the Absolute Ego, see ibid., 484.

11. Jean-François Lyotard, *La condition postmoderne: Rapport sur le savoir* (Paris: Minuit, 1979), trans. Geoff Bennington and Brian Massumi as *The Postmodern Condition: A Report on Knowledge* (Minneapolis: University of Minnesota Press, 1984).

12. See P. Koslowski, "Maximum Coordination of Entelechial Individuals: The Metaphysics of Leibniz and Social Philosophy," *Ratio* 27 (1985): 160–77.

13. See R. Grimminger, "Heimsuchungen der Vernunft," *Merkur* 439/440 (1985): 842–58.

14. Plato, *Timaeus* 17a.

15. Friedrich Schlegel, *Philosophische Fragmente*, Erste Epoche, III, 2nd Fragment, no. 585 (1800). *Kritische Ausgabe*, ed. Ernst Behler (Munich/Zurich: Schöningh-Thomas, 1963), vol. 18, 174.

16. See Jean-François Lyotard et al., *Immaterialität und Postmoderne* (Berlin: Merve, 1985).

17. R. Barilli, F. Irace, F. Alinovi, *Una generazione postmoderna: i nuovi-nuovi, la postarchitettura, la performance vestitia* (Milan: Mazzotta, 1982).

18. H. Klotz, introduction to *Revision der Moderne: Postmoderne Architektur, 1960–1980*, ed. H. Klotz (Munich: Prestel, 1984), 8. See also P. Portoghesi, *Dopo l'architettura moderna* (Roma: Gius. Laterza, 1980), trans. as *Ausklang der modernen Architektur: Von der Verödung zur neuen Sensibilität* (Zurich: Verlag für Architektur Artemis, 1982).

19. See François Burkhardt, in Lyotard et al., *Immaterialität und Postmoderne*, 28.

20. Reinhart Maurer, "Staat, Gesellschaft, Gesellschaftsreligion," in *Die religiöse Dimension der Gesellschaft: Religion und ihre Theorien*, ed., P. Koslowski (Tübingen: J.C.B. Mohr, 1985), 107.

21. E. Jünger, *Auf den Marmorklippen* (Hamburg: Hanseatische Verlagsanstalt, 1941), 106.

22. Jean-François Lyotard, "Beantwortung der Frage: Was ist postmodern?" *Tumult* 4 (1982): 131–42.

23. See Charles Jencks, introduction to "Post-Modern Classicism," Architectural Design 5/6 (1980), guest-edited by Charles Jencks, 5.

24. Friedrich Schlegel, *Vom Wert des Studiums der Griechen und Römer* (1795–96), *Kritische Ausgabe* vol. 1, 636.

25. Friedrich Schlegel, *Über das Studium der griechischen Poesie* (1795–97), *Kritische Ausgabe*, vol. 1, 332.

26. Friedrich Schlegel, *Lyceum: Kritische Fragmente* (1797), *Kritische Ausgabe* vol. 2, 152. On Schlegel's critique of modernity in the narrower sense of contemporary times, see *Über das Studium der griechischen Poesie* (*Kritische Ausgabe*, vol. 1, 256): "The course of modern education and formation, the spirit of our age, and the German national character in particular all do not appear very favorably disposed toward poesy! Could one not think, after all, how tasteless are all institutions and constitutions; how unpoetic all customs, indeed the entire lifestyle of modern men! Everywhere there reigns passionate confusion, despicable conflicts, and a ponderous formalism without life or spirit. My gaze seeks in vain a free fullness, a delicate harmony."

27. A. Wellmer, *Zur Dialektik von Moderne und Postmoderne* (Frankfurt: Suhrkamp, 1985), 88.

28. Romano Guardini, *Das Ende der Neuzeit* (Basel: Hess, 1950), 94.

29. Michel Foucault, *Die Ordnung des Diskurses* (Munich: Hanser, 1974).

30. Guardini, *Das Ende der Neuzeit,* 107.

31. Ibid., 101.

32. W. Schirmacher, "Post-Moderne—Ein Einspruch," *Konkursbuch* 11 (1983): 9–13, and J. Baudrillard et al., *Der Tod der Moderne: Eine Diskussion* (Tübingen: Konkursbuchverlag, 1983), 99ff.

33. F. von Baader, *Über die Behauptung: daß kein übler Gebrauch der Vernunft sein könne* (1807), in *Sämtliche Werke,* ed. F. Hoffmann et al., reprint (Aalen: 1963), vol. 1, 38.

TRANSLATOR'S NOTES

T1. German allows for an equivocation that is not possible in English. Hence, *die Moderne* must be translated as "the modern," "modernity," or "modernism." I generally opt for "modernity" since "modernism" is too narrow and "modern times" is reserved for *Neuzeit*.

T2. The German word *Vollendung*, which occurs in the original subtitle of the essay, means both end and completion/perfection. Its use in Koslowski echoes Heidegger's essay: "Die Vollendung der Philosophie und die Aufgabe des Denkens," which points to the end of a mode of thought in the sense that it has thought itself to its end.

T3. In this list I would replace "arrangements" or "agreements" (*Übereinstimmungen*) with "disputes" (German *Streit* or *Widerstreit*), which would be closer to Lyotard's notion of the "différend."

T4. The play here is on Spengler's *Untergang des Abendlandes (Decline of the West),* where *Untergang* means literally sunset, or collapse.

There is, therefore, no possible theory today which could integrate and take account of its own language without generalizing the practice (either visible or invisible) of quotation marks, going as far as putting in quotation marks the very word "theory." This is the "theory," this is "theory."

J.D.

FROM THE ONE TO THE MANY
PLURALISM IN TODAY'S THOUGHT

Matei Calinescu

I. The New Pluralism: From Absolute Structures to Imperfection

Innovation? Renovation? These are (fortunately) not unambiguous words. In any case, as far as the theme of this essay is concerned, both are relevant and even mutually reinforcing. It is almost a truism to say that modernity was a period dominated by various monistic models of thought, some of them drawing on the cultural prestige of science, and particularly on the materialist-physicalist versions of science, with their built-in passion for reductionism. Perhaps more interestingly, if we see it as an "anti-traditional tradition" (Harry Levin) or as a "tradition against itself" (Octavio Paz), modernity also was, in some of its major philosophical and aesthetic formulations, sharply critical of its own visions of unity, often in the name of a "lost" or "forgotten" or "hidden" or "unrecognizable" Truth. With curiously few exceptions, modernity's movements of radical skepticism confront us with the striking inconsistency that they were premised on monistic assumptions. Would it then not be the case that even modernity's critique of monism was in fact little more than a search (patient or impatient, darkened by despair or illumined by strange millennial hopes) for a new, all-embracing and all-explaining monism? From this vantage point, the contemporary flourishing of pluralist thought has a definitely innovative dimension.

On the other hand, if we abandon the "logic" of linear time, which characterizes modernity's secularized version of Judeo-Christian eschatology, we immediately realize that the recent trends away from monism belong to the realm of renovation rather than innovation. After the One, after its largely absentee reign in the modern period, we are witnessing a return of the Many. The thought of plurality in Western culture goes back straight to antiquity, both religiously (Greek polytheism) and philosophically (was not Empedocles a full-fledged metaphysical pluralist?). Furthermore, pluralist views, although they often had a marginal existence, never completely disappeared—not even in the midst of the modern intellectual crisis, whether this crisis looked for solutions in the direction of a positive (often positivist) monism, or whether it favored a temporarily more fashionable negative monism of absence and derealization. The continuity of pluralism becomes evident if we consider, as far as modernity is concerned, the line of thought that goes from the mid-nineteenth-century reaction against Hegel, through Fechner and Lotze, to William James and his school, not discounting such philosophers with strong pluralistic leanings as John Stuart Mill, C. S. Peirce, Henri Bergson, or John Dewey, to name only a few.[1] In a way, each of these thinkers has paved the way for today's pluralistic renaissance.

In considering innovation or renovation or both (and perhaps the word "both" should be stressed here), the fact of the matter is that most recent Western attempts at defining the major paradigms of today's cultural consciousness show a particularly intense concern for the question of pluralism. This concern can obviously take many forms; but the important thing at this point is simply to take stock of an issue that is, often quite explicitly, at the center of such different works as Ihab Hassan's books, *Paracriticisms* (1975) and *The Right Promethean Fire* (1980); or Paul Feyerabend's *Against Method* (1975) or Michel Benamou and Charles Caramello's *Performance in Postmodern Culture* (1977); or the essays by Ihab Hassan, David Antin, Julia Kristeva, Wallace Martin, Matei Calinescu, Marjorie Perloff, and Charles Russell, included in the *Bucknell Review* special issue, *Romanticism, Modernism, Postmodernism* (1980); or, last but not least, the papers printed in this volume.

It may be noteworthy that the return to pluralism in contemporary thought is by no means confined to authors who identify themselves with, or are sometimes characterized, as "postmodern" (an admittedly confusing but not unuseful label). Advocacies of pluralism often also come from more "traditionalist" quarters. (Parenthetically, I employ the term "traditionalist" in a sense that is both positive and new; this novelty reflects the whole new attitude toward the past that is emerging as a characteristic of our time, an attitude that will be discussed more specifically in the concluding part of this essay.) Chaïm Perelman, for instance, has provided the pluralism of his predecessor at the University Libre of Brussels, Eugène Dupréel, with a new and highly sophisticated basis by returning to Aristotle and rediscovering the philosophical meaning of rhetoric, then developing his own theory of argumentation and founding the school of "la nouvelle rhétorique," whose major historical landmark is the publication (with L. Olbrechts-Tyteca) of *Traité de l'argumentation* in 1958. The significance of Perelman's doctrine of pluralistic argumentation, within the broad context of what I would call "cultural symptomatology," is brought out by the fact that, completely independently and deriving mostly from the post-Wittgensteinian Anglo-American analytic tradition, Robert Nozick, in his *Philosophical Explanations* (1981), asks himself questions and arrives at conclusions that are sometimes similar and often complementary to Perelman's. Thus, to give an example, Perelman's opposition between possibilistic reasoning and demonstrative conviction becomes in Nozick's different language the opposition between "explanation" and "proof," implying a rejection of "coercive philosophy" based on "argumentative bludgeoning."

Closer to the concerns of literary criticism and hermeneutics, however, is Wayne Booth's *Critical Understanding: The Power and Limits of Pluralism* (1979), whose focus is both theoretical and practical. The latter consists of an attentive and discriminating discussion of the work of three quite distinct pluralist critics, Ronald Crane, Kenneth Burke, and M. H. Abrams. Like Crane, a representative of the "Chicago School," Booth clearly arrived at his pluralistic philosophy of literature via Aristotle and a revaluation of the Aristotelian rhetoric of *persuasion* along lines that, although independent, cannot help but remind one of some of Perelman's insights. Booth's central questions deal with both "methodological pluralism" in literary study and with what could be called "hermeneutical pluralism." Is there only one "correct" interpretation of a given text or are there several "valid" or "admissible" interpretations? And, if so, how many? And what are the criteria for distinguishing between an "admissible" and an "inadmissible" interpretation? And what are the criteria for establishing an order or even a hierarchy among the numerous, possibly countless, "valid" but ultimately incompatible interpretations? These are not perhaps the exact terms in which Booth poses the questions; but he addresses them all in one way or another, and his general stance of "limited pluralism" emerges enlighteningly from the unfolding of his dialectic of "understanding" (submission to the text) and "overstanding" (intentional but "just" violation of the text).

This is, not unintentionally, a list of quite heterogeneous names and works. However, there is a not-so-hidden characteristic that is common to them. These and other authors, irrespective of ideological or philosophical commitments, share a certain hostility toward monistic or "totalistic" solutions, however refined and tempting. Not all of them, as we have seen, are complete pluralists; but their implicit table of values is largely pluralist, or at least compatible with pluralism. In the words of one of them, Ihab Hassan, "To think well, to feel well, to read well . . . is to refuse the tyranny of wholes; totalization in any human endeavor is potentially totalitarian." And then, raising the question of models (social but also more general), the same writer goes on to formulate a series of questions that are highly relevant to the theme of this essay: "Model, anti-model, without model? Is a model-in-the-making still a model? Can a model convert, subvert, or pervert its own versions, and so keep itself incomplete? What if various models were set against one another, without dominance of a single model? [One recognizes here the pluralistic-dialogic alternative that will receive more attention later.] How does an under-determined model (anarchic) suddenly become over-determined (totalitarian or utopian)? Or is every model of 'perfection' really an image of the void?"[2] If perfection is indeed "an image of the void," then the poet Yves Bonnefoy should be right when he states, bluntly but how suggestively: "L'imperfection est la cime." The brief poem bearing this title may serve as an introduction to the (postmodern) spirit of our time:

Il y avait qu'il fallait détruire et détruire et détruire,
Il y avait que le salut n'est qu'à ce prix.
Ruiner la face nue qui monte dans le marbre
Marteler toute forme toute beauté.
Aimer la perfection parce qu'elle est le seuil,
Mais la nier sitôt connue, l'oublier morte,
L'imperfection est la cime.[3]

II. Monistic versus Pluralistic Axiologies and the Question of Dialogue

How many worlds are there? How many kinds of worlds? What types of relationships can one establish between the world—if there is only one world—and the plurality of apparent worlds that are its manifestations? And if there are many (actual and possible) worlds, according to what criteria is one to judge and assess them? And is not the mere fact of adopting uniform criteria by which to appraise them a way of positing the existence of a superworld, or a universal model, which would subsume the many worlds? In which case, would such worlds not deserve to be called worlds, but simply aspects, or parts of a larger whole, whose meaning could be understood only in terms of the totality to which they belong? Even from the formulation of such questions we can see how complicated the issue is between monism and pluralism.

The monist says: there is only one real world. The dualist postulates the existence of two worlds or two heterogeneous kinds of reality, separated by an unbridgeable gap. The pluralist says: there are many irreducible principles, and therefore many worlds. The difficulties of each position appear as soon as one tries to "explain" it (in Nozick's sense) with consistency. And these difficulties are only compounded by the highly complex, often contradictory, and almost always overlapping axiological assumptions that are implicit in each of these stances. The monist's assertion of ultimate unity is clearly a value-laden statement: it is based on certain choices of demonstrative strategy (deduction, reduction, and analysis are valued not merely as instruments of truth but also' as weapons against multiplicity and complexity, which are supposed to bow in humility before the final triumph of the One). The monist may welcome the fight and may revel in its tension, insofar as overcome tension gives significance to the victory. In the monist's implicit scale of values, unity, totality, simplicity, and universality obviously rank higher than multiplicity, fragmentation, intricacy, or diversity. The scale of values of the pluralist will be tipped naturally in the opposite direction. But not necessarily so. As suggested by Booth in *Critical Understanding*, the mere assertion of plurality does not preclude the possibility of introducing some kind of hierarchy among the many interpretations (or worlds) whose irreducible existence is recognized. And clearly, with the introduction of hierarchy, axiological monism can creep even into ontological pluralism.

If, from whatever perspective, one or some worlds are superior to others, there is no reason for not focusing attention on the first to the detriment or even the exclusion of the latter.

This brings us to one of the great issues raised by the relation between monism and pluralism. There are monisms which are axiologically pluralistic; there are pluralisms which are axiologically monistic. These possibilities are best illustrated in the case of dualism. The ultimate ontological dualism of Plato, for instance, presents us with one of the most clear-cut versions of axiological monism. The world of movement and flux apprehended by our senses is, in Platonic philosophy, in absolute contrast with the world of changeless and perfect Ideas known by pure intellect. True values can be defined *only* in relation to the latter, and from this exclusive perspective Plato's axiology is of necessity strongly monistic, "totalistic," and, if we accept Karl Popper's argument in his *Open Society and Its Enemies*, even plainly "totalitarian." To deal meaningfully with the perplexities brought about by the distinction between monism and pluralism (including the particular case of dualism), we need therefore a further distinction that would account not only for *what* is stated about the world or worlds and their reciprocal relations, but that would also account for *who* makes such a statement and *why* (for what purpose and in whose interest?), and *how*, and on the basis of what kind of *authority*. Such a distinction is recommended by certain religious philosophers (most prominently, Martin Buber) or literary theorists (most prominently, Mikhail Bakhtin) as a distinction, on the level of the discourse, between *monologue* and *dialogue* or, more broadly, between a monologic type of consciousness and a dialogic type. By and large, monologism may be seen as having natural affinities with the monistic view and dialogism with the pluralistic view. But under closer examination, this "rule of thumb" allows for outstanding and unexpected exceptions. Thus, Buber's philosophical dialogism is articulated within the framework of the monistic (monotheistic) theological tradition of Judaism. And Bakhtin's aesthetic and ultimately religious dialogism, while hostile to the institutionalized forms of "ideology" (including Christianity), is not only compatible with but actually derived from some of the major tenets of the Christian tradition. As Michael Holquist has convincingly pointed out, Bakhtin's unpublished magnum opus, *The Architectonics of Answerability* "contains in embryo every major idea Bakhtin was to have for the rest of his long life. The whole conception of the work [is] a kind of phenomenological meditation on Christ's injunction to treat others as you would yourself be treated."[4] The fact that Bakhtin's major philosophical-moral work remains unpublished in the USSR (and will probably remain so for the foreseeable future) explains why many of Bakhtin's readers, familiar with his published works (on Dostoevsky, on Rabelais, on the philosophy of language, and on the formalist method in literary scholarship), are generally unaware of the relation between his pluralistic dialogism, rooted in a "heteroglot view of language,"[5] and Christ's fundamental injunction (which may be understood as a formulation of the principle of dialogic equality).[6]

No one summarizes better than Bakhtin the linguistic-stylistic consequences of the consistent monistic-monologic world view: and no one argues
more convincingly about the need to focus attention at long last on the
"centrifugal forces" in the life of language, on the "dialogized heteroglossia"
which has marked the evolution of the novel. Predictably, Bakhtin gives the
novel a philosophical dignity that it has traditionally rarely enjoyed. What
he has to say about the "centralizing" monologic tendencies in the history of
Western linguistics and poetics can be easily generalized to other areas of
knowledge (including the knowledge of knowledge, that is, epistemology):

> Aristotelian poetics, the poetics of Augustine, the poetics of the medieval church,
> of "the one language of truth," the Cartesian poetics of neoclassicism, the ab-
> stract grammatical universalism of Leibniz . . . , all these, whatever their differ-
> ences in nuance, give expression to the same centripetal forces in socio-linguistic
> and ideological life. . . . The victory of one reigning language (dialect) over the
> others, the supplanting of languages, their enslavement, the process of illuminat-
> ing them with the True Word, the incorporation of barbarians and lower social
> strata into a united language of culture and truth, the canonization of ideological
> systems, philology with its methods of studying and teaching dead languages,
> languages that were by that very fact "unities," Indo-European linguistics, with
> its focus of attention directed away from language plurality to a single proto-
> language—all this determined the content and power of the category of "unitary
> language" in linguistic and stylistic thought.[7]

And Bakhtin adds, with specific reference to dialogue: "One might even
say outright that the dialogic aspect of discourse and all the phenomena
connected with it have remained to the present moment beyond the ken of
linguistics."[8] We might note that the phenomena Bakhtin is citing have remained not only beyond the ken of much of modern linguistics and the
philosophy of language, but have also been neglected by modern epistemology and philosophy in general. The recent attention that has been devoted
to them, and that Bakhtin was recommending as early as the mid-1930s,
when he wrote his "Discourse in the Novel," may be a sign that the pluralistic dialogism which lies at the heart of fictional discourse could not be discussed seriously, that is, taking into account its larger philosophical and
axiological implications, before both the positive monism of tradition as well
as the negative monologism of modernity had run their course.

III. Truth As Lying: Negative Monologism and the Alternative of Pluralism

The age of truth "with a big 'T' and in the singular," to which William
James opposed his pragmatism and "radical pluralism" toward the end of
the nineteenth century, has never since managed to come back in a philo-
sophically credible fashion. The subsequent critical age, marked by doubt

and crisis, led to a refinement of earlier strategies of demystification and to a triumph of the "hermeneutics of suspicion" as defined by Paul Ricoeur in his study of Freud. According to Ricoeur, the three masters of the "school of suspicion," Marx, Nietzsche, and Freud, share a general approach to "truth as lying" and a "decision to look upon the whole of consciousness primarily as 'false' consciousness." We remember that "false consciousness" is the standard Marxist definition of "ideology." Eventually, though, Ricoeur believes "all three [masters of suspicion] clear the horizon . . . for a new Truth, not only by means of a 'destructive' critique, but by the invention of a new art of interpreting."[9]

Needless to say, this "new reign of Truth" has never come about. The attempt to revive truth "with a big 'T' and in the singular" by means of absolute suspicion has resulted not merely in failure but, wherever it was pursued along the lines of large-scale "utopian engineering" (to borrow Karl Popper's phrase), in the creation of new, arbitrarily imposed, and rigidly dogmatic forms of "false consciousness."

We also note that the modern ideologies of anti-ideology, including the philosophy of antiphilosophy, whether directly or indirectly, tend to view truth primarily in terms of power. And this applies both to old versions of truth (whose mendacity must be exposed) and to the new "liberating" truth that such ideologies always strive to attain and often proclaim. Interestingly, the terminology of power is all-pervasive and almost obsessive in the discourse of the "masters of suspicion": economic power relations, exploitation, and class struggle in Marx; psychological, ultimately biological power, "censorship," and "repression" in Freud; the paradoxical power of the weak, "*ressentiment*" as the basis of "slave morality," the "will to power," and the advent of the "overman" in Nietzsche. Not surprisingly, the "art of interpreting" invented by suspicion is bound to be, at least potentially, paranoid. This underlying trait of the modern hermeneutics of doubt was noticed and perceptively described by Michael Polanyi in his *Personal Knowledge*.[10] More recently, André Glucksman has attempted from a similar point of view to bring out the common "project of mastery" that forms the obsessive core of the theories advanced by the *maîtres à penser* of modernity (from the German Romantic philosophers, particularly Fichte and Hegel, to Marx and Nietzsche).[11]

Elsewhere, I have characterized the major critical doctrines of the modern age as expressions of "negative monologism."[12] This negative monologism can be translated philosophically as "negative monism." I am aware that this phrase is not unequivocal. It may mean the kind of monism that is attained primarily through a critique of one, or several, or all of the prevailing versions of monism at a given point in the history of philosophy. But it may also mean the special kind of (admittedly metaphorical) "monism of absence" which is implicit in the "deconstructionist" philosophy of Jacques Derrida and his numerous imitators or epigones. The method of deconstruction uses the sometimes loose philosophical equivalents of scientific "demonstrations of impossibility" and explicitly assigns itself the task of discovering and dramatizing the *aporias* of the "metaphysics of presence" and of the "logocentrism" of the whole Western philosophical tradition. This negative monism appears therefore as a monism of negation and of radical agnosticism: to deconstruct is to decenter, displace, dislocate, disseminate, disperse, derealize, fracture, fragment, and to consistently refuse to think in terms of "origins," "originality," "truth," "authority," "authenticity," "legitimacy," "hierarchy," etc. True, the highly sophisticated negation of the idea of unity (in even its minutest aspects and remotest consequences) may in certain respects appear to be close to the recognition of plurality. Furthermore, the very notion of plurality is frequently resorted to, but exclusively for purposes of subversion and disruption of the One, and never for the *affirmation* of the Many. Negative monism in this sense is not inconsistent with a kind of negative pluralism or a pluralism *"en creux,"* in which the apparent "pluralization" or "proliferation" of theories and countertheories is used as a polemical device. The multiplicity that is posited by such pluralism (sometimes with a great display of philosophical imagination) is clearly an empty one: a "doubling" and "redoubling" of absences, an endless repetition, an infinite regress of frames that frame nothing.

But there are, in today's culture, increasingly numerous signs that modernity is rapidly approaching its end (or has it already ended?). One sign is the "pluralist renaissance," a phenomenon whose manifestations are themselves, as we have seen, extremely diverse, indeed so heterogeneous as to frustrate any attempt at generalization. Incidentally, the near-certainty that the effort to unify multiplicity will fail and will eventually be confronted with irreducible "facts" or "fictions" or "worlds" does not mean that such effort should not be undertaken. On the contrary, monistic or reductionist assumptions should be constantly tested and retested against an irreducibility that, in the process of being assailed from all sides, is as open to change, revision, and enrichment as are the hypotheses that challenge it. Authentic pluralism, which is possible only in a dialogic context, has the following remarkable and paradoxical characteristic: it takes monism, in its various versions, quite seriously; not only does it not dismiss but it also welcomes and even encourages it, knowing that the strength of its own theories is conditioned by the strength of those it opposes. Pluralist philosophies can be judged by the degree to which they live up to the great dialogic principle: one must always argue against the strongest case. That is why we should not be surprised to discover that while there is obvious tension between pluralism and monism the two views are not ultimately incompatible. This lack of any fundamental incompatibility can be best understood in terms of dialogy: whatever the specific opinions they want to articulate and test, the participants in a dialogue must observe certain rules if the dialogue is to be pursued in a meaningful and enlightening fashion; mutual respect and the search for a common ground of comprehension—comprehension even of incompatibility or "incommensurability"—is one of these rules. Thus, even the most incompatible ideas or theories are *dialogically compatible* by virtue of simply being presented as alternative solutions to similar, although never quite identical, problems.

Students of pluralist thought have not failed to notice the striking fact that most of the philosophers that can be defined as pluralists are in certain important respects monists. Discussing William James's ambiguous title *A Pluralistic Universe*, a title that taken by itself is not only equivocal but plainly a *contradictio in adjecto*, a declared pluralist like Nelson Goodman points out in his recent book, *Ways of Worldmaking* (1978), that "the issue between monism and pluralism tends to evaporate under analysis. If there is but one world, it embraces a multiplicity of contrasting aspects; if there are many worlds, the collection of them is one. The one world may be taken as many, or the many worlds taken as one; whether one or many depends on the way of taking."[13] One should add that this is so when the issue is analyzed by a pluralist and not, as Goodman puts it a couple of pages later, by his "typical adversary." That adversary is

> the monopolistic materialist or physicalist who maintains that one system, physics, is preeminent and all-inclusive, such that every other version must be reduced to it or rejected as false or meaningless. . . . But the evidence for such reducibility is negligible, and even the claim is nebulous since physics itself is fragmentary and unstable and the kind and consequences of reduction envisaged are vague. (How do you go about reducing Constable's or James Joyce's world to physics?) I am the last person likely to underrate construction or reduction. . . . But reduction in any reasonably strict sense is rare, almost always partial, and seldom if ever unique. The pluralist's acceptance of versions other than physics implies no relaxation of rigor but a recognition that standards different from yet no less exacting than those applied in science are appropriate for appraising what is conveyed in perceptual or pictorial or literary versions.[14]

The last part of the foregoing quotation may serve as a broad introduction to one of the major themes encountered in today's pluralist thinking, namely, the relation between scientific worlds and aesthetic worlds. At long last, the "traditional" conflict between science and art seems to have come to an end, an end that had been not seldom intimated over the last century or so by quite a few great scientists and philosophers of science, as well as by artists and aestheticians, but that somehow failed to be fully recognized. In part, this recognition was prevented by the remarkable stubbornness of "physicalism," the last positive form of monism in the context of the critical or negative monisms that become more and more numerous and sweeping as modernity runs its course. In the meantime, pluralist thought, while accepting science, felt the need to justify and even borrow models from certain types of activity and experience—religious, moral, legal, political, and increasingly aesthetic—which modern scientism had ignored or dismissed as irrelevant to the search for objective truth.[15]

IV. Epistemological Models: Their "Fiduciary" and Ultimately Aesthetic Bases

Once the assumptions and goals of scientism (as distinct from the development of the sciences themselves) came under question, once it became clear that such requirements as total reducibility, absolute uniqueness of truth, total predictability (even in the ideal case represented by the fictional "demon of Laplace"), or perfect linguistic consistency were, even as working hypotheses, untenable, it became possible to discover that the differences among various kinds of human experiences are unbridgeable only within certain frames of reference, and that such frames are not intrinsically preferable to others. There are, then, postcritical and more broadly postmodern frames of reference within which, say, mathematics, religion, and the arts, while preserving all their irreducible differences, can be seen as having highly significant common features. We note that the recognition of such features, rather than being the starting point of a new attempt at reduction, renders possible the resumption of an *intracultural dialogue* that modernity had abandoned. With respect to the relationship between mathematics, religion, and art, for instance, Michael Polanyi advances the "conception of religious worship as a heuristic vision," to be aligned "with the great intellectual systems, such as mathematics, fiction and the fine arts, which are validated by becoming happy dwelling places of the human mind."[16] The following passage can be taken as a good summary of Polanyi's general position:

> In view of the high imaginative and emotional powers by which Christian beliefs control the whole person and relate him to the universe, the specification of these beliefs is much more colorful than are the axioms of arithmetic or the premises of natural science. But they belong to the same class of statements, performing kindred fiduciary functions. We owe our mental existence predominantly to works of art, morality, religious worship, scientific theory and other articulate systems which we accept as our dwelling place. . . . Objectivism has totally falsified our conception of truth. . . . In trying to restrict our mind to the few things that are demonstrable, and therefore explicitly dubitable, it has overlooked the acritical choices which determine the whole being of our minds and has rendered us incapable of acknowledging these vital choices.[17]

Polanyi's fiduciary epistemology does not deny the importance, indeed the indispensability, of external experience in the process of knowledge; but such experience serves only "as a theme for an intellectual activity which develops one aspect of it into a system that is established and accepted on the grounds of its internal evidence."[18] Such systems or frameworks develop into highly complex, articulate, and rigorous structures offering the minds that choose to inhabit them the opportunity to fully exert their "intellectual passions" (the heuristic passion, the persuasive passion, etc.). Validity, then, in any one of these systems is ultimately determined by internal and not external criteria. Obviously, there is no reason to consider the criteria of validity in any one of these systems as being more demanding or strict or exemplary, and therefore deserving to be introduced in all other systems. Furthermore, such criteria are not given once forever: in each one of the great heuristic frameworks, creation and subsequent refinement or reassessment of the whole "explanatory structure" are the rule, and stasis appears always as a temporary exception.

It is my view that Polanyi's general model of a plurality of coexisting heuristic systems, seen as many "happy dwelling places" of the mind, can be better understood if it is considered from an aesthetic vantage point rather than from the religious angle suggested by his insistence on the "fiduciary" basis of knowledge. And this is so, among other reasons, because aesthetic beliefs and judgments have always been more naturally dialogical and tolerant, that is to say, more spontaneously pluralistic. The self-conscious fictionality of the work of art, its traditional freedom from the constraints of literal truth, and its almost universally recognized ludic dimensions account for both the individualistic and the pluralistic vocations of artistic activities.

Polanyi himself is aware of the close connection between his postcritical view of religion and the experience of literature and the arts. "Artistic creation and enjoyment," he writes, "are contemplative experiences more akin than mathematics to religious communion. Art, like mysticism, breaks through the screen of objectivity and draws on our preconceptual capacities of contemplative vision."[19] The essential distinction between aesthetic and other beliefs is not so much that the former tend to be weaker than the latter; aesthetic beliefs can be quite strong, after all. What sets them apart is, I would maintain, the fact that they are rooted in a deeper sense of plurality.

V. Aesthetic Dualism and Pluralism

As I have suggested earlier, ontological dualism (and this is even more so in the case of religious dualism) has led, as a rule, to extremely strong versions of axiological monism. There is, however, one type of dualism that clearly represents a major step in the direction of true pluralism. This is the aesthetic dualism that prepared the emergence of romanticism and, more broadly, constituted perhaps one of the first working models of true philosophic pluralism. The "message" of aesthetic dualism can be summarized in the simple statement that there are two distinct types of beauty—the classic type and the romantic type—and that both of them are *equally legitimate artistically.*

Let us take the "classic/gothic" antinomy as it occurred in English criticism in the second half of the eighteenth century. The major implications of this opposition are illustrated, among many others, by Richard Hurd in his *Letters on Chivalry and Romance* (1772). Hurd speaks of *classic* and *gothic* as two perfectly autonomous worlds, neither of which can be considered superior to the other. Quite naturally, one who approaches the gothic with classical criteria will be unable to discover in it anything except irregularity and ugliness. But this, obviously, does not mean that the gothic has no rules or goals of its own by which its achievements should be judged. "When an architect examines a Gothic structure by Grecian rules," Hurd writes, "he finds nothing but deformity. But the Gothic architecture has its own rules, by which when it comes to be examined, it is seen to have its merit, as well as the Grecian." Hurd, who tries to defend the use of "gothic" fictions in poets like Spenser and Tasso against neoclassical rationalistic attacks, argues that a poem like *The Faerie Queene* must be read and criticized according to the idea of a gothic, not of a classical poem, in order to be adequately understood: "And on those principles, it would not be difficult to unfold its merit in another way than has been hitherto attempted." But even Hurd, as his argument unfolds, turns out to be less of a consistent aesthetic dualist than we might have expected. Going beyond the scope of a mere defense, Hurd's discussion of Tasso concludes with the typically early romantic pronouncement that gothic customs and fictions are superior to classical ones, after all, at least insofar as "poetic truth" is concerned. Hurd says: "The fancies of our modern bards are not only more gallant, but . . . more sublime, more terrible, more alarming, than those of the classic fablers. In a word, you will find that the manners they paint, and the *superstitions* they adopt, are more poetical for being Gothic."[20]

I have used the example of aesthetic dualism not so much for its intrinsic interest as for its didactic clarity. It offers the simplest model of what I understand by axiological pluralism. Whether we are faced with a duality or with a plurality, the obvious problem is always a problem of choice. Preference is unavoidable in the long run, particularly when the alternatives that are presented to us are alternatives of doing something (and even reading or pure aesthetic contemplation is a way of doing something in the Austinian sense in which we always do things with words, and in which even statements that appear as totally "constative" are actually "performative"). What aesthetic dualism or pluralism shows is simply that a choice does not necessarily imply a summary dismissal or ignorance of other available alternatives. On the contrary, when a choice is made in full awareness of the meaning and possibilities offered by other alternatives, the chances are that this choice will be more fruitful, more satisfying, and more insight-producing.

In this sense, any consistent pluralism implies a theory of freedom, and specifically of freedom of thought and discussion. The best formulation of such a theory to date is, I believe, John Stuart Mill's *On Liberty* (1859). According to Mill, "the collision of opinions" always works a "salutary effect." "Not violent conflict between parts of the truth," Mill writes, "but the quiet suppression of half of it is the formidable evil; there is always hope when people are forced to listen to both sides; it is when they attend only to one that errors harden into prejudices, and truth itself ceases to have the effect of truth, by being exaggerated into falsehood." Thus, freedom of thought and discussion is the main precondition of the "mental well-being of mankind."[21] As for truth, in the general sense in which Mill uses this concept, it is always scattered: to attain complete truth is an impossibility; to claim a monopoly on truth is a "formidable evil." We note in passing that, for clarity's sake, Mill also uses a "dualistic" working hypothesis: he divides the truth into two halves, one always more visible and more easily apprehended than the other. There is little doubt, though, that he is one of the first true radical pluralists. And his decisive influence on a typically postmodern philosopher of science like Paul Feyerabend (who applies quite faithfully the Millian theory of the liberty of discussion to the specific problems of the history and philosophy of science), may be interpreted as a sign that Mill's pluralism, a term that he himself never used, is perhaps more fertile today than ever.

VI. Negativity and Relativity: From "Truth" to "Rightness"

Like Romanticism, which both precedes it and renders it possible, aesthetic modernity has been defined in such a wide variety of fashions as to make its very concept almost ungraspable. Some clarity, though, may be gained if we see these definitions as falling within two distinct categories: the first emphasizes the negative values of modernity, singling out such features as antitraditionalism, polemicism, agonism, systematic subversion, nihilism, "dehumanization" (in Ortega's sense), deformation, unpopularity, etc.; the second category, without necessarily underestimating the role of negativity, stresses the positive diversity of styles, languages, and ultimately idiolects that not only coexist within modernity but give it a sort of fluid, changing, unpredictable, though never totally unrecognizable, identity. An example of the second way of approaching modernity, which is on the whole less frequent than the first, is found in the definition of symbolism (for which read modernism) advanced by Edmund Wilson: "Symbolism may be defined as an attempt by carefully studied means—a complicated association of ideas represented by a medley of metaphors—to communicate unique personal feelings."[22] Modernism is seen here as an implicit pluralism rooted in the pursuit of individual expression under conditions of freedom from objectively imposed (positive or negative) constraints. But the problem raised by this and other similar definitions is: How free is the modernist artist to express himself through the complex "medley of metaphors" that Wilson speaks of? The fact is that, even when they recognize the tendency for stylistic pluralization, students of modernism are usually inclined to qualify and limit it by introducing the countertendency toward negativity, crisis, chaos, and even self-destruction.[23]

The will to freedom, uniqueness, visionary self-expression, and revelation of the new is always there in the art of the modernist, but its very condition of possibility seems to be a deep sense of negativity and, indeed, an urge for crisis, destruction, or chaos. That is why modernist (and even more so avant-gardist) experimentalism is primarily an experimentalism of negation. Being of one's time, or preferably in advance of one's time (the claim of the avant-garde), appears the same as adopting an unflinchingly adversarial attitude toward both the past and its numerous deceptive survivals in the present.

Historical relativism, whose first far-reaching intimations date from the eighteenth century, received its most articulate and refined formulations in the Romantic period. But even for the great Romantics, historical conscious-ness—the sense of universal historical relativity or "chronotopicity," to use the term coined by Bakhtin—had only a partially liberating influence and, more often than not, became a principle of tension which, with the advent of modernity, was only increased. What does this principle of tension consist of? What kinds of polarities make it up? To find a convenient answer to such questions is to understand one of the cardinal features of the modern mind. To begin with, let us remark that historical relativism, with its implicit axio-logical pluralism and, at the same time, with its inability to make intercul-tural value judgments, poses a great challenge to our human-all-too-human need for order. The fact remains that the consciousness of historical relativity by itself cannot establish any kind of transhistorical validity of the order of "truth," unique "categorical imperatives," harmony with strict "universal laws," and so forth. For the modern mind, intent on demystification and intracultural criticism, this may be an advantage. But the dangers involved in this stance are also obvious. Unbounded historical relativism often ends up transforming history "with a capital 'H' and in the singular" into a new kind of unpredictable and incoherent God. Hence, among numerous other conse-quences, is the modernist's typically ambivalent attitude toward history, which he perceives as both a locus of hope and a "nightmare."

If we direct our discussion to aesthetic activity taken as a model for other related theoretical activities of the human mind, a more constructive solution of the dilemmas posed by historicism seems to emerge: if there is no general (aesthetic) "truth," if no universally recognized set of rules can be used to determine such "truth," why not resort to certain weaker, but in no way arbitrary, criteria such as "consistency" or "rightness"? Although judgments of consistency or rightness can be tested and retested against similar judg-ments until some kind of consensus is reached, the process—while being as rigorous and exacting as anything—is less exclusive and "coercive" (in Nozick's sense) than the process by which truth in the strict sense is estab-lished. Furthermore, even when we work with the most unambiguous defi-nition of truth, we may be faced with situations in which conflicting truths about the same matter are obtained. As Nelson Goodman points out: "That truths conflict reminds us effectively that truth cannot be the only consider-ation in choosing among statements or versions. . . . Even where there is no conflict, truth is far from sufficient. Some truths are trivial, irrelevant, unin-telligible, or redundant; too broad, too narrow, too boring, too bizarre, too complicated; or taken from some other version than the one in question, as when a guard, ordered to shoot any of his captives who moved, immediately shot them all and explained that they were moving rapidly around the earth's axis and around the sun."[24] We may therefore accept that "a state-ment is true, and a description or representation right, for a world it fits." As Goodman concludes: "Rather than attempting to subsume descriptive and representational rightness under truth, we shall do better . . . to subsume truth along with these under the general notion of rightness of fit."[25]

The concept of rightness of fit is clearly inspired, primarily if not exclu-sively, by fundamental aspects of aesthetic experience. Translated philo-sophically, aesthetic experience does not reject truth in the name of some historical-epistemological relativism or some random plurality of existing (artistic) worlds; what it does is simply to limit the relevancy of truth by spelling out certain larger requirements of appropriateness that apply both to truth and to what Goodman calls "fictional versions" (verbal or pictorial or in a broader sense aesthetic). This means that true versions as well as fic-tional versions are subject to similar criteria of selection by means of which those versions which are too loose, or too rigid, or too banal, or, in a word, too boring, will be eliminated. As we can easily see, within each world or collection of worlds posited by such a pluralistic-aesthetic conception, the notion of rightness of fit (closely connected with the activist notion of "effi-cacy of understanding") not only renders axiological chaos impossible, but introduces positive, if usually competing, standards for establishing articu-late and forceful hierarchies of values. If such hierarchies or schemes are convincing, it is not because they imply (as well they may) some universal thesis or principle, but because, to quote Goodman again, they may have the quality of "calling attention to a way of setting our nets to capture what may be significant likenesses and differences" within one system or another or between systems (pictorial, verbal, etc.).[26] Similar views, although articulated from a "possibilistic" as opposed to "actualistic" perspective, are advanced by Robert Nozick in his *Philosophical Explanations*, a book that ends, signifi-cantly, with a statement entitled "Philosophy As an Art Form." Nozick underscores the notion of the "artistic reshaping" of the world by a philoso-pher who is committed to a vision of truth (and transcendence) that is clearly more closely related to that of artists than it is to the pursuit of those seekers of "knockout arguments" and "proofs" who, perhaps unwittingly, attempt to establish a sort of Cartesian-Orwellian "thought-police." As Nozick re-marks: "The philosopher aimed at truth states a theory that presents a pos-sible truth and so a way of understanding the actual world (including its value). . . . In his artistic reshaping, he also may lift the mind from being totally filled with the actual world. . . . We can envision a humanistic philos-ophy, a self-consciously artistic one, sculpting ideas, value, and meaning into new constellations."[27] Is our age witnessing, due in part to the revival of aesthetic consciousness, a rebirth of old-new philosophy from its analytic "ashes"? From the vantage point of the foregoing remarks, modernism as a vast cultural movement may be seen as illustrating the difficulties and contradictions characterizing the middle point on the road between earlier, predominantly monistic or dualistic world views, and the consistent pluralism and dialogism that our postmodern age seems to be preparing. I have discussed elsewhere some of the outstanding *aporias* of modernist consciousness and their exacerbation in the experimentalism of the avant-garde.[28] Such *aporias* are usually brought about by the clash between the negative monism or monologism of a radically antitraditional attitude (an attitude which views tradition as one enemy) and the unsuspected but real pluralist implications of historical-aesthetic relativism. The category of *relation* itself is certainly not unambiguous, and its modernist interpretation in terms of "will to power" (power of the *cogito* or the self, or conversely, powerlessness and inauthenticity of the self before the Other, whether History, the Unconscious, the socioeconomic Base, etc.) is a possible interpretation, although a narrow one. For the mind of today, which tries to go beyond the restrictions of positive or negative monologism while acknowledging the centrality of the problem of language, dialogic pluralism is the key to a new interpretation of the category of relation. Freed from the inescapably linear unfolding of modernity's concept of time, as well as from the natural attempt to escape that ineluctable linearity (which took the form of various philosophical or scientific abstract schemes of *totally reversible* and ideally controllable concepts of time), historical relativity tends to appear as a vast network of reciprocal determinations in which the irreversibility of certain vital choices creates new patterns of reversibility; it tends to appear as an ongoing process of "creative evolution" without any "objectively" preestablished *telos* or *eskhaton*. Our consciousness exists in a multiplicity of (actual and possible) worlds in perpetual "chronotopical" change.

VII. Conclusion

Instead of a "normal" conclusion that would simply summarize the arguments of the foregoing essay, I would prefer to raise again the problem with which I began: Can we really speak of a pluralist renaissance in today's Western culture? In trying to answer this question I must begin by admitting that a pluralist renaissance in contemporary thought, as I see it, is as much a phenomenon-in-the-making as a desideratum, to both of which I feel committed, but without being able to entertain any kind of certainty with regard to their success. The pluralistic-dialogic frame of mind is essentially fragile. Its delicate balance can be tipped not only by resurgent fanaticisms or intolerant monologic orthodoxies but also by the odd phenomenon of ideologies that work without anyone believing in them. Such ideologies can no longer be defined as forms of "false consciousness." Under totalitarian conditions (and no part of the present world is completely safe from the dangers or "temptations" of totalitarianism), ideology seems to function best when no one believes in it; more than that, belief, and even belief in the ideology's own principles and assumptions, appears as its greatest enemy. Utopia is not the triumph of (rational) belief but, on the contrary, the total interdiction of belief. Wittingly or unwittingly, the great modern philosophies of suspicion and derealization have brought their modest contributions in that direction (the influence of ideas on history being fortunately limited).

In this rather gloomy context, one must note with some cautious optimism that the very fragility of the pluralistic outlook can become an unsuspected source of strength. As we saw earlier, pluralist thought and its immediate consequences (a plurality of world views, a plurality of conflicting beliefs that articulate themselves ever more forcefully and vigorously to become "happy dwelling places of the mind") are possible only on the basis of the type of freedom of expression and discussion that John Stuart Mill defined in *On Liberty*. In spite of numerous limitations, constraints, and risks, such liberty has always existed to some degree, and often to a higher degree than the powers that be would have been prepared to tolerate. And this is so because liberty is not only an idea or ideal, but a fundamental need of human consciousness, and as such one of the factors that have played a direct role—sometimes larger, sometimes smaller, and very often quite invisible at first sight—in the shaping of history.

To come back to our main focus, what consequences could the new (postmodern) pluralism have in the circumscribed area of culture that I have been concerned with in this paper? I will state them very briefly. To begin with, if the trends that I have succinctly and perhaps disjointedly described continue, the chances are that both *inter*cultural and *intra*cultural dialogue will become increasingly active. This dialogue will certainly be more than a dialogue for the sake of dialogue: it will provide new insights into old matters and possible solutions to the new puzzles that the world we live in requires us to solve. The authors of a recent essay in the philosophy of contemporary science, Ilya Prigogine and Isabelle Stengers, suggest that this new kind of dialogism is rendered possible by a rediscovery of a value that did not rank high in the axiology of modernity, namely, the value of respect: respect for nature (restored to its ancient Greek status of *"physis"*) in the physical sciences, and, above and beyond that, cultural respect, in contrast with the earlier cultural suspicion of the moderns. The authors write: "We must learn no longer to patronizingly judge the population of knowledges and know-hows (*"savoirs"*), of the practices, and of the cultures produced by human societies but, on the contrary, how to combine them and how to establish among them new forms of communication which would increase our ability to cope with the unprecedented demands of our age."[29]

The new (postmodern) pluralism also promises, after several centuries of modern scientific "disenchantment of the world," a "reenchantment of the world," another important idea of Prigogine and Stengers. We might add that this process of "reenchantment," which is at the same time a process of "rehumanization," applies not only to the sciences but to other theoretical disciplines and forms of activity as well, including philosophy, the arts, and history itself. In connection with the latter, there are signs that a new historicism is emerging, a historicism that sees the past neither as a normative paradigm (the old traditionalist view) nor as an opponent (the modernist view which conceives novelty exclusively in terms of rupture), nor as a collection of "facts" that should be carefully gathered because one day they may reveal general patterns and universal laws (the positivistic view), nor yet as pure intertextual circularity (the structuralist view, ultimately as sterile as the positivistic approach that it opposes), but rather as a "storehouse" of alternatives and counteralternatives, of stories and counterstories, of smaller and larger narrative scenarios, involving not only individuals but also groups, societies, beliefs, ideas, emotions, myths, and ultimately worlds and "ways of worldmaking." Such a new approach to history, rigorously imaginative and imaginatively rigorous, constitutes, I would argue, one of the great joys and strengths of the pluralist mind.

NOTES

1. For a more comprehensive overview of pluralist thought at the turn of the century, Jean Wahl's *The Pluralist Philosophies of England and America* (London: The Open Court, 1925), is still very useful.

2. The quotation is from Ihab Hassan, *The Right Promethean Fire* (Urbana: University of Illinois Press, 1980), 17. The author refers to a specific work by François Châtelet, Gilles Lapouge, and Olivier Revault d'Allones, *La Révolution sans modèle* (Paris: Mouton, 1975), but the comments and questions occasioned by the reading of this book have an obviously much wider application.

3. Yves Bonnefoy, *Hier régnant désert* (Paris: Mercure de France, 1964), 33.

4. See Michael Holquist, "The Politics of Representation," in *Allegory and Representation: Selected Papers from the English Institute, 1979–1980,* ed. Stephen J. Greenblatt (Baltimore: Johns Hopkins University Press, 1981), 163–83.

5. Ibid. See also Holquist's introduction to M. M. Bakhtin, *The Dialogic Imagination: Four Essays,* trans. Caryl Emerson and Michael Holquist (Austin: University of Texas Press, 1981), xix-xx. The problem of "heteroglossia" is discussed at length by Bakhtin in the fourth essay in the quoted book, "Discourse in the Novel," 259–422. For Bakhtin's theory of dialogue and dialogic consciousness, see also Mikhail Bakhtin, *Problems of Dostoevsky's Poetics,* trans. R. W. Rotsel (Ann Arbor: Ardis Pubs., 1973), especially 87–113 of chap. 4.

6. From a different angle, the link between pluralism and Christianity is also suggested by Wayne Booth in his *Critical Understanding* (Chicago: University of Chicago Press, 1979). For the specifically theological treatment of the question of pluralism, Booth refers to such works as David Tracy's *Blessed Rage for Order: The New Pluralism in Theology* (New York: Seabury Press, 1975); or Hans Urs von Balthasar's *Die Wahrheit ist symphonisch: Aspekte des christlichen Pluralismus* (Einsiedeln: Johannes Verlag, 1972).

7. Bakhtin, *The Dialogic Imagination,* 271.

8. Ibid., 273.

9. Paul Ricoeur, *Freud and Philosophy: An Essay on Interpretation,* trans. Denis Savage (New Haven: Yale University Press, 1970), 32–33.

10. Michael Polanyi, *Personal Knowledge: Towards a Post-Critical Philosophy* (Chicago: University of Chicago Press, 1958), 241.

11. André Glucksman, *Les Maîtres penseurs* (Paris: Editions Bernard Grasset, 1977).

12. See Matei Calinescu, "L'Intellectuel et le dialogue," *Cadmos* 2, no. 7 (1979): 59–83, and "Persuasion, dialogue, autorité," *Cadmos* 3, no. 11 (1980): 16–36.

13. Nelson Goodman, *Ways of Worldmaking* (Indianapolis: Hackett Pub., 1978), 2.

14. Ibid., 4–5.

15. We note that today's scientific discourse has largely overcome the prejudices of "scientism" and may even welcome certain forms of aesthetic self-consciousness. For the latter, see the enlightening collection *On Aesthetics in Science,* ed. Judith Wechsler (Cambridge, Mass.: M.I.T. Press, 1978).

16. Polanyi, *Personal Knowledge,* 280.

17. Ibid., 286.

18. Ibid., 279.

19. Ibid., 199.

20. Quoted after Matei Calinescu, *Faces of Modernity* (Bloomington: Indiana University Press, 1977), 36–37.

21. John Stuart Mill, *On Liberty,* ed. David Spitz (New York: W. W. Norton, 1975), 50.

22. Edmund Wilson, *Axel's Castle* (1931; reprint ed., New York: Charles Scribner's Sons, 1969), 21–22.

23. Cf. Malcolm Bradbury and James McFarlane, *Modernism (1890–1930)* (Baltimore: Penguin Books, 1978), 26–27.

24. Goodman, *Ways of Worldmaking,* 120–121.

25. Ibid., 132.

26. Ibid., 129.

27. Robert Nozick, *Philosophical Explanations* (Cambridge: Harvard University Press, Belknap Press, 1981), 647.

28. Calinescu, *Faces of Modernity,* 95–150.

29. Ilya Prigogine and Isabelle Stengers, *La Nouvelle alliance: Métamorphose de la science* (Paris: Éditions Gallimard, 1979), pp. 294–95.

III.

The Cultural Diversity of Modernism/Postmodernism Dialectics

CINEMAS OF MODERNITY AND POSTMODERNITY

Maureen Turim

Is postmodernity in film exemplified by *Blade Runner? Repo Man? The Terminator? True Stories? Blue Velvet? Subway?* All of the above? Is postmodernity then a genre, a blending of science fiction or the detective story with the *conte morale* for a new age whose participants seem, on the surface, devoid of morality? Or is postmodernism to be found nascent in a certain modernism, in the discursive audio-visual collages that one finds in film and video work by Godard, or in the psychoanalytic reinscriptions of desire found in films by Oshima and Almodovar? Is postmodernism then not a question of filmed architectures and set designs, but perhaps a question of paralleling the postmodern in writing? Or is postmodernity not to be found in film at all, but only in television, or perhaps video? Is it commercial cable television or satellite reception with its remote control multiplicity of viewing options that constitutes the postmodern experience, or is it video art, with its oppositional discourses reinterpreting this medium through its alternative praxes, that deserves that label?

These are the kinds of questions raised by much of the film and video treatments of the notion of the postmodern. I don't think there is any easy answer here, for postmodernity has proved itself the most illusive of constructs, vague and pervasive, carrying contradictory meanings in various usages. I don't like the term and don't normally use it without a lot of qualification aimed at indicating in which of its various incarnations I am summoning it. What follows is my attempt to work through those qualifications. For though I think postmodernism as category is virtually useless, as debate it has taught us much.

Artists and/or Theorists

Postmodernism is a term with strikingly varied applications in different fields. Postmodernism has been used differently by visual artists, musicians, and architects than by theorists, and again in somewhat different ways in the visual arts than in writing or music. For many artists, postmodernism has been a pragmatic means of stylistic and conceptual differentiation from a tradition of form and theory that they otherwise might have simply inherited. It is a way to succeed or supercede the legacy of modernism. It is sometimes a rejection of much of what modernism represented and actualized, sometimes a reaction to the taming and cooptation of modernism. In this sense of inspiration to a new generation of artists, postmodernism usually implies a definition of modernism as one or another form of visual or poetic abstraction in which formal structures are investigated to the detriment of representations; art and writing are no longer referentially engaged, but are preoccupied with their own purist formulations. That this is a very narrow definition of modernism, one constructed only of selected aspects of modernism's many projects, is one of the reasons that the form of postmodernism this view inspires is often an unconscious repetition of many principles already used within various forms of modernism. A return to narrative, to embellishment in architecture, to myth and symbolization is a reaction to a very limited notion of what modernism was.

Yet amongst the reasons postmodernism is so various in each area of artistic practice is that the modernism it comes after can be defined so differently, ranging from the romanticism and realism of the nineteenth century, the abstract movements of the early twentieth century, atonality, the functionalism of design and architecture, geometric abstraction, abstract expressionism, etc. We will come back in more detail to this question of the hazy and multiple definitions of modernism that are seen as preceding postmodernism; for now let's note, as Hal Foster has pointed out, that the notion of postmodernisn as an inspiration to artists has had on one hand a neoconservative cast and on the other a poststructuralist one.[1]

If we assume that the neoconservatives represent not postmodernism but a renewed classicism, the poststructuralist artists can be seen as formulating a postmodernism as an acknowledgment that times have changed and there is something different to be made that has its own logic and imperative. This different logic often involves a response to mass culture and popular forms; it is often an exploration of humor and even whimsy, an irony that is not as focused as is black comedy or surrealism. In architectural terms it has meant a diminished faith in the perfection of Euclidian geometries, which Victor Burgin has argued can be taken as a metaphor to be extended to other postmodernist art, a non-Euclidean, deconstructionist attitude toward representation that he will link to Julia Kristeva's theories of *abjection* (though she of course discusses abjection within modernist literature).[2] A group of recent artists working in the postmodern vein somewhat coalesces as a movement; the post-sixties avant-garde finds a new, if loose, identity by seeing their ideological critiques, image explorations and/or narrative and symbolic innovations framed by a renewal of theories of montage, collage, citation, and reproduction that are felt to be postmodernist. That much of this work echoes constructivism doesn't deny that there is a freshness and a seriousness to the rhythms, colors, attitudes in many of these new works; constructivism is being rethought here, perhaps even unconsciously, perhaps because it now permeates (in transmutation) advertising and the commercial environment. Much of this art displays an eclecticism, a borrowing that mixes modes and confuses receptions. Sometimes it seems that contemporary artists do not pretend to a mastery of themselves as addressors or to a clarity of intention that was somewhat implicit in modernist visions. While the systematic troubling or evacuation of reference of late-modernism is scorned, it is ironically sometimes replaced in this postmodern reaction with a plethora and even a Babel of references that leave the spectator equally troubled as to the meanings of the text.

For film one problem with this functional definition of postmodernism as an artistic reaction against modernism is that some of film's *modernisms were already like postmodernism* as it is being explored in the graphic arts, for example. The introduction of narrative and language into visual representation (photography and painting) is striking in the graphic arts of the past ten years, but in a sense follows from the influence of film, television, and advertising, where those techniques are far more traditional. Barbara Kruger's debt to Jean-Luc Godard's films such as *Deux ou trois choses que je sais d'elle* (1966) in its mixture of advertising graphics with ironic political and philosophical questioning is a case in point. One can solve this apparent problem by identifying an already postmodern concern in Godard, but then we must go back further and say that of Brecht, (his *Mahagonny*, for example) and then perhaps Baudelaire, because the reaction to consumer culture is already there in his poems, etc. As artists have defined postmodernism they have posited a historical break, a difference that constitutes a rupture, but it is one that often misrecognizes the complex history of the art they intend to have left behind.

For theorists, and this includes those artists steeped in theory, these shifts are symptomatic of desires and social conditions that are engaged conceptually. In theory postmodernism becomes a condition, a state of the world after the globalization of exchange and the deconstruction of master narratives that sustained the prior order of things. Though postmodernist theory is split between a tendency toward economically determined periodization (Jameson) and one which largely deviates from this econo-historical model (Lyotard), both tendencies have been "applied" to the production and discussion of contemporary art.[3]

While in artistic practice postmodernism implies a kind of antimodernism, in the theoretical view this is not necessarily the case. Postmodern theory is more conscious of itself as an extension of modernism; it is poststructuralist, but certainly learned its lessons from structuralism. It has more at stake in deconstructing periodization, even that implied by its own "name." The avant-gardes of modernist art usually retain their value in postmodern theory, even as they are being recontextualized as movements of a past whose conditions are no longer those facing the artist today. Lyotard's defi-

nition of postmodernism is, as the unrepresentable in representation, a definition which reformulates what representation might mean in reference to
psychoanalysis. Such a definition is useful for considering the greater and
more reflexive textual incorporation of desire that reorders postmodernist
expression.

For film and video this difference in meaning of postmodernism for artists
and theorists is marked, yet somewhat ambiguous. Very few independent
film or video artists have chosen the term to define their work; it tends to be
used by critics and museums attempting to link film and video art to the
graphic artists whose work they describe using this term. Yet there is a
difference, historically, in the contemporary context in which painters and
photographers on one hand and film and video makers on the other
find themselves. Experimentation in the fifties and sixties in film and the
development of video art itself occurred under the sign of a self-conscious
avant-gardism. Artistic film and video never convincingly was part of the
commercialized gallery and museum scene that so quickly swallowed up
abstract expressionism, geometric abstraction, and all the movements which
followed, including conceptual, performance, and political art despite the
aims of the latter to defeat in one way or another the consumerist and
fetishist aura surrounding the display of art. For film and video artists this
was much less of an issue; there was always only the smallest, most marginal outlets for their work. Avant-garde films were opposed to movies,
video art to television, separated by modes of production, distribution, and
reception, as well as by formal structuration. Even those (primarily European) filmmakers whose modernist works were made for commercial distribution were functioning on the margins of the commercial industries of their
countries, on a reduced scale of investment and profit. Throughout the seventies, when graphic artists were constructing their postmodernism, film and
video artists were still working through their most recent incarnation of an
avant-garde. The aspect of postmodernist art that struggles with the signs of
art as index and object did not have the same currency for film and video
making as it did in the gallery and museum context.[4]

Yet in one sense postmodernism in film and video is sometimes seen as a
relinquishing of interest in a separate avant-garde by artists, a turning away
from oppositional forms to instead integrate with movies and television as
mass culture, even to the extent of taking their energy directly to the marketplace, as it is manipulated by the studios and the record companies in their
control of film distribution and video clip dissemination. Films like Jim
Jarmusch's *Stranger Than Paradise* and Susan Seidelmann's *Desperately Seeking Susan* can be seen as evidence that the kind of filmmakers who a few
years before might have devoted themselves to avant-garde venues instead
began seeking the commercial, international marketplace. If Wim Wenders
can make *Paris, Texas,* if the New German film can successfully take its road
and quest motifs to the United States, then New York filmmakers can also
borrow from European modernism and yet go "Hollywood." Critics

searched for terms to describe avant-garde films' transmutation into commercial property and/or narrative venture, and the label "new narrative" was heard; basically this was less of a postmodern phenomenon than an ongoing attempt by American filmmakers to develop their own modernist movement to correspond to European modernism. John Cassavetes, Woody Allen, and many others after all had paved the way. If there are historical reasons for terming such work postmodern, it must be noted that it is hard to find anything in the semiotics or narrative constructions of these films that was particularly *new* or different from modernist forms.

The theoretical construction of postmodernism also has specific implications for film and video. The commercial film and broadcast television are defining elements of postmodern culture; it is their strategies of financial investment and marketing, pervasive intrusion and monopolization that began earlier in the century to foretell the changes in culture that we distinguish as postmodernist. Some theorists have moved from the quest in the avant-garde for new forms that shape new meanings, to a new, decidedly affirmative investigation of mass culture. The logic seems to be motivated by a desire to move beyond a high/low polarity in our thinking and evaluation of culture. This reassessment of mass cultural expression has often meant embracing soap opera, situation comedy, game shows, music video, science fiction, and action films as the harbingers of a new irony—not the heartfelt, self-conscious, intellectual irony of the avant-garde, but the ironic detachment and shifting before culture, a coolness coupled with great emotional investment, postmodern-buffered love and hate. This is not the postmodernism of Jameson or Lyotard but the postmodernism of Jean Baudrillard, a kind of "love commercial culture because we can't leave it, it's everywhere" approach.[5] Many contemporary feminists and Marxists have also adopted similar attitudes for quite different reasons; they are concerned to validate the attention women and the underclass give to the narratives of commercial culture, and interested in the relevance of these works to the lives in question.[6] In these frameworks modernism and the avant-gardes have been newly scorned for their elitism, and contrasted with the new narrative works, which may be termed postmodernist in this context insofar as they reach out for mass audiences.

The Periodization of Film History

In the past it has been useful for many of us to consider film in terms of differing textual practices: the primitive cinema, before the great adhesion to standardization in the cinematic coding of space and narrative order, the classical cinema with its rules of continuity aimed at producing a filmmaking of narrative seamlessness, the modernist cinema of rupture that breaks with certain of these codes while maintaining much of the flow of event-narration inherent in the classical cinema, and the avant-garde cinema whose break with representational modes of other cinemas is more thorough, for it enters into basic coding of the image, the basic figures of montage, etc. Some of these categories are historically determined. They follow a certain line of succession and development, an art-historical periodization that yields divisions that can be presented on a time line that would look roughly as follows: primitive (1895–1906), early classical (1906–25), classical (1925–55), modernist (1955–75), and potentially, postmodernist (1975–present). The notion of the avant-garde troubles this time line and reveals other troubles inherent in it. The cinematic avant-garde is often conceived of as a punctuative phenomenon, whose intermittent flourishes are partially outside of this history of cinematic coding, through interventions marked by a great flowering in the twenties, a smattering in the forties, and a reemergence throughout the mid-fifties to the present. If the periodization of film history into primitive, classical, and modernist has gained a certain assumed authority, with the avant-garde punctuating this time line of chronological development periodically, there has never been much sense in insisting on the linearity of development of an art whose entire history coincides with modernism in the other arts.

Instead it is possible to see that such periodization fails before a more general fluctuation between the traditional and the modern in the inscription of cinematic form. In this sense, the primitive cinema was already quite avant-garde and the classical often becomes an attempt (by reference to traditional structures of the novel, theater, and its own codes of spatial representation) to tame that avant-garde potential. Various modernisms in film represent a controlled release of the otherness of filmic expression, the frightening newness of its structuration, the challenge of its formal refiguration of prior visual, narrative, and auditory means of signification.

The emergence of postmodernist theory and its application to the theory of the arts therefore signifies a particular quandary for film history and theory. The temptation is to proclaim film was always, from its beginnings, postmodernist, in the sense that it conjoined citation of the traditional with a newness of form and inscription. It was also postmodernist in the sense that its marketing and reception signaled a shifting economy of culture. Video, even more so, tempts us as immediately postmodernist, tied as it is to television's role in the foregrounding of simulacra, vicarious existence, and artificial communities. Yet I would sidestep whatever temptation lurks here, to remind us how both film and video are precisely more complex than this, as is postmodern theory. We cannot so simply make this move, for if we do, the concept of modernism dissolves before us. As in many discussions of postmodernism, we find ourselves forced to ask, what was modernism anyway, and where did it go? If we think we know that in architecture modernism was Mies van der Rohe and in music, Arnold Schönberg, we should remember that the Chrysler building was a more common conception of what constituted modernism, as was jazz. This acknowledgment leaves us without an easy way of conceiving postmodernism in architecture or music.

For film there is a parallel and perhaps exacerbated difficultly in locating and defining modernism; we might choose to foreground as evidences of modernism the temporal displacements of the films of Louis Delluc in the twenties, for example, and their parallels in both the films of Stan Brakhage in the fifties and Alain Resnais in the sixties. Sometimes I get the feeling that Alain Robbe-Grillet's and Resnais's *L'Année denière à Marienbad* (1962) lurks as the singular prototypical instance of modernism in the unconscious of postmodern theorization of film, for it is perhaps the instance in which narrative reaches a certain formal stasis, a graphic repetition and involution that reminds us of the geometric abstractions of high modernist architecture and painting. High modernism is seen as philosophical and formal, restructuring temporality, spatial relationships, and pictorial representation with a dedicated seriousness that consequently limits its commercial acceptance.

Such a notion of filmic modernism would leave out the films of Charlie Chaplin or the film noirs Hollywood produced in the late forties and fifties. However, both lay great claims on modernist sensibilities and modernist structures of reception, in all the terms outlined above (restructuring temporality, spatial relationships, pictorial representation) except that they had great commercial appeal and little self-conscious seriousness (that seriousness can be posited as lying underneath the accessible surface of these texts). If the introduction of the notion of postmodernism teaches us something about modernism, it is that our view of filmic modernism has been perhaps too short-sighted, too aimed at distinguishing challenging texts from accessible texts, too aimed at defining boundaries between high culture and popular culture. However, if we revise our notion of modernism for a more inclusive view of cultural production and its functioning, many boundaries begin to blur, including that between modernism and postmodernism.

Before moving on, then, to a look at the definition of modernism in art and film, let's acknowledge what is significant about the periodization outlined above that perhaps should not be easily dismissed. It is a periodization along two axes, history and textual semiotics. As such it does astutely define some shifts in textual structuration. It is useful, not as an absolute standard, but as a suggestive indication of the historically shifting processes of coding images and discourses. If postmodernism is less convincing as a period than the other periods, it is because unlike modernism, it does not bear within it a strong semiotic difference in structuration. To say as some have that modern texts abstract the referent while postmodern texts disturb the signified is semiotically so oversimplified as to be simply irrelevant. Modernism was seen in the same terms, as a crisis in meaning, as a void in clear signification. Closer analysis of the processes of signification in postmodernist art, films, and video will, I think, find the signifieds less disturbed than they already have been by modernism. The point for the semiotician, however, is that of all aspects of the sign, signifieds are always the most multiple, contradictory, contextual, and always a product of subjective response. We might say that postmodernism recognizes this aspect of semiotic functioning and thematizes it, but that attaches in fact fairly straightforward signifieds to the signs of postmodern art. More problematic for me is the notion that some very obvious significations of some postmodern art, film, and video don't enter into the discussion of these works; the manner in which many of these narratives or images actually formulate straightforwardly some fairly reactionary mythologies is largely ignored. If we can speak of a distinctive process of coding in postmodernism at all, we must talk of mixed codings, mixed to a degree that goes beyond the mixture of coding already there in all the other semiotically distinct textual strategies.

What Is Modernism and Where Did It Go?

Much of what circulates in contemporary theory as a theory of modernism is dependent on definitions derived from analyses of the works of Charles Baudelaire, in which modernism is *not* taken to be a question of form (as it has been elsewhere), but of reference and address. Baudelaire's essay, "The Painter of Modern Life," set the stage for construing modernism as a discourse on modernity and modernization. This is the direction taken up so eloquently by Walter Benjamin.[7] It has been most recently reiterated by Marshall Berman in his *All That Is Solid Melts into Air: The Experience of Modernity* (1982) and T. J. Clark's *The Painting of Modern Life: Paris in the Art of Manet and His Followers* (1984).[8] This definition of modernism is at odds with the received idea of a modernism hermetically encased in its own orientation toward form, and it is not one that will easily cede to a postmodernism whose main purpose is to counteract a supposed absence of referentiality and commentary in modern art.

Theorists of modernism have historically proceeded, though, precisely by establishing boundaries and the criteria for making oppositional distinctions. Consider the boundary Clark proposes in his effort to show the modernity of urbanization and the modernism of cultural expression to be linked. He locates Manet's imagery in the context of Haussmann's redesign of Paris as a modern city and its consolidation of bourgeois industrial, commercial and political power. Clark's championing of Manet as a *critical* modernist is intended to separate his artistic practice from contemporaneous artists whose work is less critical of the restructuring of modern life. This argument rests on Clark's analysis of a lithograph, *Le Ballon*, from 1862 and a painting, *L'Exposition Universelle de 1867*, from that year, which Clark argues comments on the function of the exposition's architectonics within the larger plan of Haussmann. For Clark, the painting suggests that "there are parts of Paris in which it appears that there are no relations, only images arranged in their place" by which he means that the fabric of social life has been transformed into the merely spectacular.[9]

That some painters such as Monet and Renoir present celebratory views of Haussmann's grand boulevards in the years 1873–75 is seen by Clark as "touristic entertainment fleshed out with some low-level demonstrations of painterliness" and as images "untroubled by [their] subject's meanings and not helped by this innocence."[10] This evaluation stems from Clark's renunciation of the "merely spectacular" including, most problematically, photography. In his commentary on *Le Ballon*, he says "It is as if Manet's lithograph is out to show us everything that is supposed not to register on the photographer's plate—the press of identities that cannot be stopped by a shutter (and cannot simply be 'seen')."[11] By extension cinematography is also unlike Manet's painting; these spectacular forms are deemed by Clark unable to reveal anything but surface appearances.

There are two different kinds of problems here. One is the refusal to see that there may have been fundamentally contradictory effects of Haussmannization, including the construction of an aesthetic of urban space in the boulevards, promenades, and gardens that in retrospect seems to have laid the groundwork for much of what today remains liveable and pleasing in contemporary Paris, a matter I take up elsewhere.[12] The other involves the limited ontologies assigned photography and cinematography and the weighted opposition between the spectacular and underlying social realities.

Is the dreaded spectacularity that defies analysis and lacks critical depth to which Clark continually refers a premonition of postmodernism? This rejoins one way of construing the applicability of postmodernism to photography, cinema, and video; these arts which come to us through the camera are seen as postmodern because they reproduce the physical realities before them or are spectacular rather than analytic. That much of the modernist development of these arts is counter to these ontological assumptions, that much of the history of their use is precisely to describe and analyze the life of images as both framed and combinatory is ignored. If one defines the spectacle as that which a mass of people look at together and which distracts or alienates them for concealed relations, it is easy to see how tempting it is to place film in this category. It is, however, a poor assessment of the image, even the image of commercial culture, let alone all camera-produced images.

This constitutes, though, a common reaction to commercial culture with its expansive use of the image and especially great rip-offs that occur as aspects of the modernist and avant-garde movements in film and video are commercialized and appropriated. Mass culture feeds off high culture (the reverse is also true) using tropes and structures of artistic resistance outside of their contexts and without the notions of contestatory textuality that marked their earlier use. According to this scheme, postmodernism can in fact be defined by the type of object represented by a recent MacDonald's commercial that appropriates Bertolt Brecht and Kurt Weill's number from *The Three Penny Opera* for yet another slogan for its establishment, "It's Mac Tonight." Those of you who have seen this commercial recognize the animation of the floating moon singer as embodying the voice of Ray Charles; in one short clip much of modernist culture is reincarnated as an emblem that effaces any other purpose to or history of modernism except as style of the urbane. This commercial was meant to give fast food class. For some with an apocalyptic view, it signifies that tonight is the end of the razor edge of modernism as critique. All oppositional structures can be incorporated into a single culture of commercialism.

The video clip (music television) is often seen as the paradigm of this. For example, E. Ann Kaplan's *Rocking around the Clock: Music Television, Post-Modernism and Consumer Culture* creates a taxonomy of five types of clips, only one of which is the postmodernist clip, (the others are romantic, classic, nihilist, and social activist) but then goes on to argue that in the format of cable play, all clips are equalized through a process of combination of cross-purposes into a blended reception that she also calls postmodernist.[13] This could be supported by the argument that video clips are often themselves meta-commercials, whose discourse puts down the commercial format or attempts to ignore it or explode it, while reproducing its essential function to create desire for a product. Much the same argument has been made concerning the functioning of television in general, as a constant washing over of contradictory messages, leaving no oppositions to stand so that spectators can clearly position themselves. Yet is this new? Was there ever a time in the history of modern culture in which discourses and ideologies did not cross? Doesn't the rapid tempo of music video clips and the continual presence of television simply accentuate modernism in its weave of competing discourses, its barrage of information in newspapers, books, pamphlets, magazines, radio, posters, etc.? Yes and no. As much as I don't believe that the medium has simply become the message, there is a sense in which television can be different from the more discrete textuality we experience in film and print media. While I would argue that many viewers of MTV select and respond to certain clips as texts—they read them, just as ultimately Kaplan does throughout her book—reception often seems to be a changed process in contemporary culture, changed by commercial imperatives and quantitative inundations.

The incorporation of all oppositional structures into a single culture of commercialism is certainly part of what the avant-garde was on guard against. In fact modernism can be construed as a loose association of various avant-gardes, a retrospective collection of small-scale movements of difference. That these movements would eventually be accepted or appropriated is beside the point. They existed to define a historical field of differences, not an eternal one. More than anything else, that impulse is what links the avant-gardes of modernism from the symbolists through the impressionists, supremacists, surrealists, etc. A theory of modernism must incorporate the function of avant-gardes in its formation, and any attempt to define postmodernism must somehow account for this as well. If it is proving difficult to posit something after modernism that is not simply a return to classic structures, a neoclassicism, it is because modernism as the retrospective accumulation of avant-gardes is difficult, by definition, to supercede. We could follow Lyotard and speak of postmodern art and cinema as concurrent with modernism, a flux of uneven developments, but when I try to imagine what this might mean if we come down to cases, I imagine saying that Sergei Eisenstein's *October* (1927) is modernist and Dziga-Vertov's *Man with a Movie Camera* (1929) is postmodernist, or that Robert Bresson's *Mouchette* (1966) is modernist while Jean-Luc Godard's *Deux ou trois choses que je sais d'elle* (1966) is postmodernist. I imagine saying this (the postmodern examples are less sure of master narratives, less unified, less focused on heroics or antiheroics) but I find this type of classification as it becomes reified as a position as problematic as periodization. It reminds me (though it is different) of Peter Wollen's proposal of "two avant-gardes" one which was primarily formal and one which was politically engaged—such divisions are at once too obvious and too blinding. They don't illuminate the ways in which something is obscured on each side to arrive at ostensibly different periods or categories. Beyond this, when an act of implicit evaluation is presented as simple taxonomy, we leave our judgments unchecked.

Theorizing Contemporary Cinema Culture

If we can't simply agree to say, yes, for these reasons we have what we will call postmodern cinema, then how do we theorize contemporary cinema culture? I have already hinted at some major concerns. We should not throw out all the semiotic advances we have made in understanding textuality and the coding of images and sounds. We should not arbitrarily announce that art is now purely indexical, or without historical reference, or "in the realm of simulacra with no gestures toward a signified," or any of the quasi-semiotic formulations being used to describe so-called postmodern texts, without more closely examining the coding of these texts. Before we throw around a term like "new narrative," we should, through narratological study, define what is new about this narrative.

I have suggested that a closer look at historical, material considerations is also needed. How have production, distribution, and reception actually changed? We cannot assume that satellite reception has produced texts that are qualitatively different than those made for broadcast television or that film distribution networks will be transformed by video dissemination, for example. Surely a global economy *is* redefining national culture industries, but that process has been in place throughout the century. We cannot simply assume that a particular change in technology has produced massive shifts in patterns of cultural access or will in the near future. In fact, the pattern of United States domination in cultural exportation has been typical of this century, with some exception before World War I, during World War II itself, and briefly in the sixties. It is perhaps at its strongest today. This pattern has coupled with centralized production within the United States and with a growing concern for creating the self-perpetuation of desire for this type of cultural product alone, to the exclusion of other forms.

This is the context within which genres and remakes continue to repeat formulaic structures, where novelty is limited to superficial matters of style and design. Postmodernism can be just this type of stylistic renovation, an updating of art deco with a high-tech flair. It has often gone unnoticed that the underlying structuration of desire here is not affected. That a number of the commercial feature films spoken about as postmodernist are retrograde in their portrayal of sexual difference and sexist in their portrayal of women is a matter of great concern for me. Their grounding in the sexist genres of film noir and science fiction films may be in part responsible, but it also seems that the glitter of the postmodern design is meant to cover the fictional portrayal of women so as to disguise a reaction against feminism circulating in these texts.

The major contribution, however, of postmodernist theorizing in film and video is I think the questions raised about interactions of cultural production across the schism of popular and high culture.[14] It should now move beyond granting attention and validity to mass-cultural products, beyond allegorical or sympathetic readings of desires elucidated by these texts, into a more critical sense of what we can mean by the textual production and channeling of desire. What is absent from many of the theoretical formulations and the texts that treat the postmodern is a look at creativity in its relationship to desire, to subjectivity, to the psyche. The promise of modernism to transform ideological givens through formal innovation should not be ignored, for modernism had a fundamental respect for creative cognition and the role of the arts as stimulation. While much of the writing on postmodernism attempts to reclaim this aspect of modernism under its own banner, for cinema and video the counterweight of commercial imperatives that fold desire in on consumption of yet another version of the already consumed is indeed heavy.

Postmodernism is perhaps then best seen as a collapse of periodization and the emergence of a great diversity of forms within film, video, art, and culture, coexisting simultaneously. In many ways this diversity and simultaneity of forms and strategies will replay past avant-gardes and the history of modernism, as well as aspects of what might be termed the classical. The consistency and fervor through which one characterizes art movements seems recently to recede; the purism is gone. Instead there is a field of works that, while they share a historical moment, a context, respond to that context with a great range of approaches. The theoretical mistake might be to desire to read this diversity through the same art-historical methods, the same theories of reflection, the same sense of temporal progression and replacement that at least conventionally if superficially described earlier periods. We are perhaps at that place where theory and artistic practice conjoin to face the limitations of this time line and break it, scattering in all directions. If the line of artistic production seems to loop back (rehearse modernism, pastiche earlier forms, replay traditions) more than it leaps ahead, this too may be a part of the refusal to continue the vector of aesthetic developments, a refusal not necessarily voluntary or conscious but itself the most salient evidence that indeed the late twentieth century is finding its own creativity in the astute articulation of the pause and rewind modes.

NOTES

1. Hal Foster, "Wild Signs: The Breakup of the Sign in Seventies Art," in *The Cultural Politics of 'Postmodernism,'* ed. John Tagg (Binghamton, New York: MRTS Press, 1989).

2. Victor Burgin, "Geometry and Abjection," in *Cultural Analysis, Psychoanalysis and Cultural Theory,* ed. James Donald (London: Macmillan, 1987) and reprinted in *The Cultural Politics of 'Postmodernism.'*

3. I discuss the debate implicit in Jameson and Lyotard's positions in "The Cultural Logic of Video," in *Video Art: Theory and Practice* (New York: Aperture, 1989).

4. See Rosalind Krauss, "Notes on the Index," in *The Originality of the Avant-garde and Other Modernist Myths* (Cambridge, Mass.: MIT Press, 1984) for a discussion of the indexical aspect of the representation in postmodernist graphic art and sculpture.

5. See Jean Baudrillard, *L'Amérique* (Paris: Grasset, 1986).

6. See Douglas Kellner, "T.V., Ideology and Emancipatory Popular Culture," *Socialist Review* 45, 1979: 13–53 and Tania Modleski, *Loving with a Vengeance: Mass-produced Fantasies for Women* (New York and London: Methuen, 1982).

7. Walter Benjamin, *Charles Baudelaire: A Lyric Poet in the Era of High Capitalism* (London: NLB, 1973).

8. Marshall Berman, *All That Is Solid Melts into Air: The Experience of Modernity* (New York: Simon and Schuster, 1982) and T. J. Clark, *The Painting of Modern Life: Paris in the Art of Manet and His Followers* (Princeton: Princeton University Press, 1984).

9. Clark, 60–66.

10. Clark, 71–72.

11. Clark, 66.

12. In "The Ambivalent Demonumentalization of Paris," presented at the Society for Cinema Studies conference in April, 1989, to be published in an anthology edited by Scott Nygren, *Cinema's Cities,* I discuss other readings of Haussmannization, including that offered by Antoine Grumbach, "The Promenades of Paris", trans. Marlene Barsoum and Helene Lipstadt, *Oppositions* (Spring 1977): 50–67.

13. E. Ann Kaplan, *Rocking around the Clock: Music Television, Postmodernism and Consumer Culture* (New York and London: Methuen, 1987).

14. See Jim Collins, *Uncommon Cultures: Popular Culture and Post-Modernism* (New York: Routledge, 1989).

The quotation marks are not only the mark of a reservation or distance with regard to a concept or a word. They recall the general quotability, they cite this quotability as a summons, once again not as a formalist neutralization concerned with propriety but as the reminder of the necessary general contamination, of the transplants and irreducible parasitism which affect any theorem.

J.D.

AVANT-GARDE, MODERN, POSTMODERN
THE MUSIC (ALMOST) NOBODY WANTS TO HEAR

Jost Hermand

I.

Anyone who invokes any sort of concept of progress in ongoing discussions of art is immediately castigated by the overwhelming majority of disillusioned, cynical, or so-called realistic critics as being hopelessly naive. This viewpoint, allegedly naive in the face of today's atmosphere of economic, ecological, and nuclear crisis—is regarded at best as a vestige of that simpler past before anyone had heard of Theodor W. Adorno's often cited *Dialektik der Aufklärung* (Dialectic of the Enlightenment). If any notion of the new, progressive, or even revolutionary does crop up nowadays, it is solely on the level of the cheapest marketing slogans, coined by advertising executives who constantly strive to boost consumption by pushing the "brand-new." Thus we all enjoy the blessings of a revolutionary toothpaste, but not of revolutionary art, a total reconception of certain bathroom fixtures, but no longer any subversive dramas or poetry that appeal to the masses.

Yet we know that this was not always the case. There once were times when such concepts as new, rebellious, or even revolutionary still had an undeniable aura, and the best among the artists were proud to be distinguished with these adjectives—when even art, so often belittled as ineffectual, was granted the function of bringing about change. And the key concept connected to this was usually the term "avant-garde."[1] What this phenomenon meant beginning in the early nineteenth century was an art that attempted to base itself on the most progressive social ideas of its own time and strove to develop into progressive conceptions of art corresponding by parallel, analogy, or homology to those social principles; in other words, concepts of art which evinced an inner correlation of aesthetic and social progress. That—and just that—is what was once meant by "avant-garde," whereas purely formal innovations, regardless of whether they were of a technical or aesthetic nature, were viewed as mere "modernism." Thus the status of the avant-gardistic could be claimed by a work of art whose progressive quality was realized both in content as well as in form. By comparison, "modernistic" art was that in which the emphatically progressive became hypostatized on a formal or formalistic plane.

If we proceed from this definition of avant-garde, then there have been only three great avant-garde movements in Europe which have attempted to synchronize sociopolitical and artistic-formal progress, whereas modernism has been an integral component of many bourgeois trends in art over the past 150 years. These are the three time periods in which avant-garde movements came to the fore: 1) the years between 1830 and 1848/49, when the progressive bourgeois artists were oriented toward the revolutionary models of thought such as Left-Hegelianism, Saint-Simonianism, anarchism, socialism, or democratic parliamentarianism, and also tried to convey these basic ideological convictions in their works, which expressed the urge toward a new "realism" and an intense social and political involvement, 2) the years between 1870 and 1889, i.e., between the Paris Commune and the centennial of the French Revolution, when progressive artists for the most part turned to a Naturalism based on Darwinist or social-democratic ideas, and 3) the years between 1905 and 1925 when, set against the most varied revolutions—such as the Russian revolutions of 1905 and 1917 and the German November revolution of 1919—such movements as Cubism, Futurism, Expressionism, Dadaism, Constructivism, and Surrealism developed. In their aversion to bourgeois taste as manifested in Victorian, Bonapartist, and Wilhelminian cultures, these "-isms" radically rejected *all* bourgeois concepts of art and proclaimed instead a politically enriched way of living.[2] In the most general terms, these were the three great periods of the European avant-garde. Everything that occurred along with, in-between, and afterwards in the area of so-called "innovative" art can only be termed "modernism."

The number of writers and painters who joined in these three avant-garde movements is legion. The number of composers who could be considered avant-garde is, on the other hand, hardly consequential (and later we shall hear the reasons for that). In the years between 1830 and 1848/49, Richard Wagner approached the status of a prototype among avant-garde composers.[3] During those years, Wagner read Ludwig Feuerbach, became well-versed in the ideas of the Young Germans and Saint-Simonians, established contact with Heine in Paris in 1840, was interested in the works of Pierre-Joseph Proudhon, counted Georg Herwegh and Mikhail Bakunin among his friends, wrote—as did the young Engels—a *Cola di Rienzi,* in which a Roman tribune incites the populace to revolt against the ruling families, temporarily professed communism in his writing *Das Künstlertum der Zukunft* (Artistry in the future), battled at the barricades in Dresden in 1849, finally had to flee to

Switzerland and there wrote such essays as *Die Kunst und die Revolution* (Art and revolution) in 1849 and *Das Kunstwerk der Zukunft* (Artwork in the future) in 1850, in both of which he turned against the commodification of music and professed a belief in art for all, dedicated to the highest social ideals. Although Wagner later betrayed nearly all these ideas and embraced an obscurantism based on racial theories and an aristocraticism, his earlier ideas long remained the only model for a true avant-garde in music. August Bebel hailed them as "entirely socialistic" in 1879 in his book *Die Frau und der Sozialismus* (Woman under socialism).[4] Even Clara Zetkin and Anatoli Lunacharski praised the young Wagner as late as the 1920s as the illuminating model for a noncommercial, spiritualized art relevant to all of society.[5]

Yet the real development in bourgeois musical life after 1848/49 took a completely different course, as we well know. The so-called "high" music, in today's parlance "serious music," remained a privilege of the upper ten thousand of the population during the Victorian, Bonapartist, and Wilhelminian era. Thus the opera houses and concert halls became the sacred temples of "inwardness secured by force" as Thomas Mann later wrote. Their doors were open only to those who had at their disposal both a large wallet and a soul susceptible to emotional transports. Here they surrendered willingly to feelings and left their brains at the coat-check. Here was the place for zealous idolatry of Tchaikovsky, Grieg, Lalo, Gounod, Bruch, Dvorak, Saint-Saens, Massenet, Fauré, Scriabin; i.e., one wallowed in those overblown works spanning all the way from the *Symphonie pathétique* to the *Poème de l'extase*.

The avant-garde of the Naturalists between 1870 and 1890, oriented toward the natural sciences and social democracy, thought very little of the music of its own era. It perceived the current tone poems and musical dramas to be emotional pomposity without redeeming social value, even to be vain noise and rapture.[6] Thus Heinrich Hart, for example, wrote in 1891 in the *Freie Bühne* (Free stage), the leading journal of the Naturalist avant-garde in Germany, that one should give up music, "for the sake of truth." Music is, he explained apodictically, a "luxury like women and wine." It "intoxicates," "lulls to sleep," "causes chaos and confusion and the soul's decay." Hart continued, it is the lowest form of degradation, pulling down to the "sensual" depths: in short: it is ridiculous, without purpose, and thereby retards further "intellectual growth." "Anyone who has figured out," he stated with avant-garde emphasis, "what it is to be human ought to begin without delay a course in 'music non-appreciation.' "[7]

The message of the small group of Naturalists necessarily fell on deaf ears, at least for most bourgeois music connoisseurs around 1900. For ultimately it was not Naturalism that gained acceptance as the leading art movement in the 1890s, but rather an aestheticism tinged with impressionism and symbolism, showing a special affinity for precisely that sort of purely emotional, sensual, even culinary music decried by the Social Democrats. Yet in spite of this striking continuity, there were also a few new developments in the bourgeois music milieu around 1900. One group of bourgeois composers—including Sibelius, Puccini, Rachmaninoff, and to some extent Richard Strauss—continued to adhere to the emotional pathos of upper-class Victorians, Bonapartists, and Wilhelminians, thus contributing to their enormous popularity with that upper class and even creating an appeal that persists to the present day. On the other hand, during this time of growing aestheticism a smaller group of very serious composers branched off into the esoteric by professing a modernist-oriented secessionism whose chief criteria included aesthetic deviation and the status of social outsider. All those composers between Debussy and the young Schönberg who belonged to this group refused, starting in about 1900, to write any more *Capriccios, Turandots, Valses tristes,* or any of those spirited and sentimental piano concertos which would have ingratiated them with the standard concert and opera audiences drawn from the upper three to four percent of the population. Rather, this second group consciously limited its impact to the "elite," the upper 0.1 to 0.2 percent, or what was termed the connoisseurs. As a young man, for example, Schönberg performed his music only in private recitals, where neither applause nor any signs of disapproval were permitted, musical events that were eerily reminiscent of private poetry readings within the Stefan George Circle.

This, then, in broad terms, was the situation of serious music between 1900 and 1914, at the start of the third and final great avant-garde movement, to which we owe so many aesthetically committed and also aesthetically significant works of literature and painting. Little of the sort is to be found in the serious music produced during those years. The operas and concert halls of that era continued to be the refuges of the culture-conscious bourgeois, who still felt most at home in these "hallowed halls" at a time when, in the realms of literature and painting, one bastion of tradition after the other was falling victim to some avant-garde or modernist trend.

There was no real possibility of turning serious music into a medium for the avant-garde until the numerous technical innovations of the 1920s. Not until the era of radio and the phonograph record, the significance of whose invention nearly matches that of the printing press for literature, did it become possible to lend a broader social character to serious music, in other words to make the music of the upper ten thousand accessible to hundreds of thousands or even millions. Unfortunately scarcely anything of the sort occurred in the 1920s. The reasons for this are obvious: 1) the masses of clerks and factory workers lacked the cultural conditioning to feel any need for such music at all and 2) all these technical innovations were immediately deployed by the political and commercial power elites in the mass media, which primarily sought to manipulate listeners rather than fulfill the program of aesthetic education envisaged by German classicism. Thus between 1923 and 1930, during the period of so-called "relative stabilization," when the arts reflected New Objectivity and the cult of technology, numerous technical achievements fraught with possibilities for broad-based cultural education resulted only in formalistic or phoney and manipulative innovations.

Even the modernistic, elitist music was swept along by this trend toward technologization. This is proven by Schönberg's turn, in approximately 1924, away from the gestural expressiveness of his early works toward a rigidly executed twelve-tone technique which amounts to thorough-going mathematicization of the musical material. Other modernist composers or "Objectivists," as H. H. Stuckenschmidt labeled them at the time, dreamed as early as 1925 of a "colossal orchestrion," that is, a type of super-synthesizer, which someday would supersede the symphony orchestra.[8] Indeed, several serious composers even attempted to design such instruments and put them to the test. Electric pianos come to mind, such as the Neo-Bechstein grand piano or the Welte-Mignon piano, which enjoyed some popularity in the 1920s and which even Stravinsky scored some of his works for. Along with the mechanical piano and the mechanical organ, instruments such as the trautonium, hellertion, vibraphone, and sphere-o-phone caused a great stir at the time. But none of these instruments had a very wide effect. Even the formal innovation of Stravinsky, Bartók, Hindemith, Milhaud, Krenek, and others who attempted to incorporate jazz, folk, exotic, or classical elements, remained a brief episode of high culture and continued to be ignored by the mass of music listeners interested only in popular music from the phonograph, radio, or dance bands. This type of mechanical music was not even appreciated by the conventional concert-goers, who continued to expect music to provide solace, emotional depth, or at least melodiousness, and as a result, this new music had no audience whatsoever.

Of course the situation was even worse for those few composers who supported an ideology that called for change in the system and who wanted to create a truly avant-garde music that would serve both social and aesthetic progress. For their failure the reasons are quite obvious: 1) these composers had access neither to the concert hall nor to the opera, nor even to the mass media, which were largely controlled by the political right or by adherents of the status quo, 2) the masses, whom these composers wanted to address, were not at all prepared for their music, and 3) Marxist aesthetics in the period from Mehring to Lukács centered largely on literature, i.e., the printed word was assumed to be the best means of effective popular education. Thus, during all these years, music remained a secondary concern for the political left. What this camp did have was the applied form of the marches and songs, a vocal music for the class struggle in which the words clearly counted more than the music.

In this category of music on the left, the only exception was Hanns Eisler, who as a student of Schönberg—after joining the Communist Party of Germany—tried to develop from a modernist to a consistent avant-gardist. He thus wrote not only marches or songs for Ernst Busch, but also attempted to compose antibourgeois music of high quality that utilized the bourgeois musical heritage in its most technically advanced form, in the deromanticized, nonbombastic, coldly objective form of Schönberg's twelve-tone technique.[9] Eisler thus belongs to what Werner Mittenzwei has called the "leftist material aesthetics,"[10] which emerged around 1930 and endeavored to appropriate the highest technical standard of bourgeois-capitalistic modes of production, yet simultaneously sought to reshape this standard for the left— as did Brecht, Benjamin, Eisenstein, Piscator, and Heartfield. These practitioners of leftist material aesthetics thus viewed bourgeois modernism above all as an "arsenal of form," as Brecht later put it. Yet even this group failed, due to the Nazis' accession to power in 1933. It was solely in the Popular Front movement between 1935 and 1939 that this group had a final chance to make itself heard. Hanns Eisler, for example, wrote several exile cantatas during these years as well as a *Deutsche Symphonie (German symphony)*, in which he attempted to combine Brechtian texts with Schönbergian twelve-tone technique.[11] But this stylistic mixture was rejected not just by Eisler's Soviet friends (and enemies), but even by Brecht himself. Thus the few avant-garde experiments in music of the thirties faded away unheard. But these were times when even bourgeois modernism was able to prolong its existence only on the fringes. In the United States where they lived, Schönberg and Bartók went virtually unnoticed; in the USSR such composers as Prokofiev and Shostakovich were submitted to repeated rebukes on account of their modernist "pranksterism," as it was called.

II.

In the years after 1945, there were scarcely any signs whatsoever of a new musical avant-garde. In the Soviet-bloc countries, a moderate semimodernism à la Prokofiev, Shostakovich, and Kachaturian dominated in a music scene which attempted to cling to so-called late-bourgeois forms such as opera, symphony, concert, and chamber music. Eisler's theories concerning a truly "socialist musical culture" indeed continued to be discussed—especially in East Germany—but they remained an unfulfilled postulate in the actual musical practice.

In the West, on the other hand, these years witnessed a modernism à la Schönberg, which since 1925 had been of secondary importance within this part of the world, not only in the fascist countries, but also in democracies such as the United States, where in the thirties and early forties such traditional composers as Gershwin and Copland had been more likely to set the tone. As in the pictorial arts of that era, when realist elements were superseded after 1948 by a wave of nonobjectivist painting, the restoration of modernism in serious music also had a Cold War aspect. Nonrepresentationalism in painting corresponded to atonalism in music, and both of these "-isms" were held up as proof of a feeling for freedom and used against any threatening, "totalitarian" restriction. In West Germany, the serious music scene was dominated between 1945 and 1949 by a semimodernist trend à la

Stravinsky, Hindemith, and Bartók. After 1950, virtually everyone de-
manded a restoration of the Vienna School, a movement which centered
principally around the Darmstadt summer workshops, the music festivals in
Donaueschingen, the Musica Viva concerts in Munich, and various late evening music programs broadcast by the radio networks. Adorno provided the
theory for this restoration in his *Philosophie der neuen Musik* (Philosophy of
new music) of 1949, where he ruthlessly consigned Stravinsky and Bartók to
the ash heap of history while describing Schönberg's music as the only
possible "message in a bottle" worthy of being dispatched to uncharted
shores.[12]

A modernist trend long considered defunct, namely the twelve-tone
theory of the early twenties, underwent an unexpected revival during the
early 1950s among listeners interested in serious contemporary music, i.e.,
that legendary 0.1 to 0.2 percent of the population already mentioned. The
revival of twelve-tone music had at least two causes: 1) this musical form, as
mentioned earlier, could be played off extremely well against the "outmoded" tonality of music from the Soviet bloc, where the principle of "being
led on a leash" supposedly prevailed,[13] as Adorno put it, 2) professing one's
long-held admiration for the modernist music of the "Jew" Schönberg provided the desired alibi for many former Nazis, who just a few years earlier
had supported tonality in "German music." Thus for the majority of the
officious to official fanatics of modernism, contemporary serious music after
1950 just couldn't be Schönbergian enough, i.e., it couldn't be elitist, esoteric, formalistic, experimental, or hermetic enough.[14] The motto of these
circles seemed to be: the more unintelligible, the better. The adherents of this
Schönberg revival held in low regard such concepts as the nation, the
masses, or the collective, which they regarded as harbingers of totalitarianism. They no longer felt any concern—as had the avant-gardists—for the
population in its entirety, but rather only for themselves. Thus the journals
of modernist music during those years consistently praised that music whose
atonality and complete lack of melody consciously resisted the popular taste
of the masses.

Two directions taken by this music can be distinguished. On the one hand
there was a snobby, elitist path taken by those who wanted only to be
separate and who took great pride in their areas of specialization, favoring a
"musica reservata" for the very few, as Hans Renner put it on the last page
of his book *Geschichte der Musik* (The history of music) in 1955. The German
music journal *Melos* actually used English to describe this elite tendency as
the "music of the happy few" who wanted nothing more than to serve
music.[15] H. H. Stuckenschmidt claimed in 1955 that all great music is necessarily "esoteric," even "useless," and thus belongs in an "ivory tower."[16] His
ideal at the time was a "music against everyone," completely without purpose, an art-for-art's-sake absolutism which paid homage to and would refuse to compromise with any audience, regardless of how small it may
become.[17] Yet aside from this group there were music theorists such as

Adorno who claimed to see a dialectical element in their very separatism. They saw their marginal position not as a mark of distinction, but rather as a conscious refusal, i.e., a final potential for resistance against the ever more powerful culture industry.

The interplay of these two tendencies in West Germany during the 1950s and early 1960s led within the so-called Darmstadt school to a dictatorship of precisely that modernism, for which Schönberg offered the following theoretical basis in a letter to Willi Schlamm dated June 28, 1945: "If it is art, it is not for the masses. If it is for the masses, it is not art."[18] The first wave in this movement, as mentioned earlier, was a thorough-going restoration of Schönberg's twelve-tone technique. Starting in 1953/54, a wave of punctual or serial music derived from Anton Webern's music joined the movement. This serial music took the mathematicization of the musical material beyond the level of the strict twelve-tone technique by subjecting all remaining musical parameters such as pitch, timbre, intervals, rhythm, etc. to a consistent serialization. Beginning with the mid-fifties—as had happened during the period of "relative stabilization" of the twenties—several technical innovations also played a role, such as the reemergence of bruitism in the framework of Pierre Schaeffer's *musique concrète* as well as the development of electronic music at the Cologne recording studio led by Herbert Eimert and Karlheinz Stockhausen. Any composer at that time who permitted echoes of conventional harmonies, melodies, or tonalities to creep into his works was simply the laughingstock of the Darmstadt clique.

The tyrannical claim to hegemony put forth by the advocates of serial and electronic music was occasionally so extreme that even Adorno began to fear all these sorcerer's apprentices of musical modernism. Looking back on the "heroic years" of new music between 1910 and 1925 when personal innovation had been all-important, Adorno wrote bitterly in 1955 in his essay "Das Altern der neuen Musik" (The aging of new music), that contemporary so-called "music-festival music" is dominated by an "accommodation to the spirit of the times," "radicalism that comes at no cost," even by "sectarian academicism" which merely "manages the new."[19] In place of the "disruptive" music and all that unbridled "subjectivity" found in the earlier representatives of the Vienna School, Adorno argued that serious music since 1950 has been overwhelmed by a terrible normality of the abnormal.[20] Even the most experimental works, Adorno explained, are characterized by observance of a "serial law" or mere "technical trickery" amounting to a "cult of inhumanity."[21] A "critical potential" once present within music is now twisted into something "falsely positive" and results in "false fulfillment" of still unsatisfied desires.[22] When "composing becomes a hobby," the essay continues apodictically, the "idea of progress" forfeits its validity.[23]

Yet Adorno's way of thinking—like that of Hans Magnus Enzensberger in his essay "Aporien der Avantgarde" (Blindspots of the avant-garde)—was shared by very few people. Most liberal music critics in West Germany during the era of the "economic miracle" were firmly convinced (or at least persuaded themselves) that even an empty, upside-down modernism diluted into mere form was still a thousand times preferable to any compromise with concepts of music based on intelligibility, in which they—representing consciously or not the Cold-War mentality suited to the ideology of that economic miracle—saw only a regression to totalitarianism. Indeed, some of these critics were shameless enough to pass off their conscious elitism as "avant-gardistic" without realizing that this classification made a mockery of the revolutionary spirit of earlier avant-garde movements. The historical avant-garde movements had, after all, always been based on a protest against the hypocritical concepts of autonomy held forth by establishment art circles, whereas the self-styled avant-garde of the fifties saw its own specifically avant-garde element precisely in the institutional acceptance of its autonomy.

Thus between 1955 and 1985, despite the warnings of Adorno and Enzensberger, this modernism became established as the most important stylistic formation of the leading social in-group, i.e., as an affirmative art for the establishment which sprang ideologically from a nonconformist conformity. This was an avant-garde without true avant-gardism, which lacked any social relevance, any relation to concrete reality—and which therefore was played up as the ideal art of unrestricted freedom in a formal democracy actually structured on the principle of "repressive tolerance." During these years, the adherents of nonrepresentational painting[24] and atonal, elitist music received the most financial allocations, were granted scholarships, and were constantly awarded prizes by public and private entities. Because of their conscious meaninglessness, these arts did not offend any ideology; indeed, their lack of ideology posed as the only ideology still possible. These arts thus won favor with all parties and social organizations, whether the Social Democrats or the Christian Democrats, unions, or the trendy tycoons in the "Federal Association of (West) German Industry." For this was art that had relinquished any social function, that sought to be nothing but art—and thus did not step on any ideologue's toes. Christian or nationalistic motifs, for example, certainly would have been unable to find that kind of support. But meaningless art was advanced from on-high since it kept out of partisan politics, presented itself as pure, autonomous art, and dispensed with any propagandistic intent, any function, or any concrete *telos* at all. That is why this sort of music remained mere music-festival music or documenta-art-exhibit music addressing the upper 0.1 to 0.2 percent of the population and was not even noticed by the other 99.8 to 99.9 percent.

Thus a paradox evolved that is still with us today. This music was tremendously patronized and prized (especially in West Germany, where high music has enjoyed the benefits of a well-established policy of subsidy from time immemorial), but hardly anyone wanted to hear it. Quite frankly, this was not music at all, but rather only an ideological medium, an alibi for freedom that was to quell any growth of truly avant-garde music. Nothing proves this better than statistics on record store customers and radio music listeners

during the years between 1955 and 1985. The number of prospective consumers of modernistic serious music continually ranked lowest behind the
listeners interested in chamber music and other so-called "opus music." This
was thus a music whose existence was due solely to its snob appeal or to its
function as an alibi.

Until 1967/68 this situation changed little if at all in the higher realms of
contemporary music. Not until then, with the onset of the student unrest,
were there impulses toward an avant-garde in music too. These few modernistic ruptures could not, however, do anything to alter the basic outsider
position of modern serious music and were abandoned after only a few
years. In terms of contents and ideology, the representatives of the avant-
garde focused primarily on the situation of the West European working class
or on the struggles of liberation in the Third World (especially Cuba and
Vietnam). The most important advocate of a music oriented toward the
working class was Luigi Nono, who in such works as *La fabbricca illuminata*
(The transfigured factory) joined in the best avant-garde tradition, the newest technical capabilities (i.e., electronic sounds, bruitistically reproduced factory noises, Schönbergian elements, etc.) with a text that strove to express
the tribulations, hope, and rebelliousness of steelworkers who labored under
inhumane conditions. Mention must also be made of works such as *Das Floß
der Medusa* (The raft of the medusa), the *Sixth Symphony*, and *Voices* by Hans
Werner Henze as examples for seizing the struggles for liberation in the
Third World in the serious music of those years. Like the works of Luigi
Nono, Henze's compositions profess international solidarity as part of a
world-wide alliance against imperialism and colonialism. They simultaneously try to make discernible an internationalism in the melody line without in the process dispensing with the highest technical standard of Western,
modernistic concert music.[25] Other avant-garde composers such as Hartmut
Fladt and Rolf Riehm, on the other hand, followed more closely in the musical style set by Hanns Eisler, whose compositions were rediscovered in West
Germany during those years.[26]

Such avant-garde tendencies were of course vehemently repudiated from
the very beginning by the advocates of elite modernism. Just as earlier in
Hanslick's battle against Wagner, so now, too, there arose a massive defense
of autonomous aesthetics against any aesthetics of heteronomy, which would
seek to employ so-called "extra-musical" means in the creation of music. Thus
Tibor Kneif wrote in 1971 that it was not only "naive" but also downright
"cynical" to fill music "with political or ideological contents."[27] Hans Vogt in
1972 excoriated the political *"engagement"* of Nono, which he termed hopelessly outmoded.[28] In the same year, Helmut Lachenmann vented his spleen
about the "dogma-spouting idiots savants of Marxism-Leninism," in music,
whom he charged with a tendency to "petit-bourgeoisness."[29] Mauricio Kagel
wrote in 1974 that the "new music" struck him as a highly unsuitable means
to "change our social order"[30] and so on and so forth, a message echoed all
the way to the music criticism of H. H. Stuckenschmidt and Carl Dahlhaus.

These composers and theorists of elitist modernism continued to worship at the altar of absolute music and immediately interpreted any musical turn to the real and nonabsolute as a challenge to their own status as would-be "shocking" modernists. As a result, they considered the music of Nono and Henze, with its genuinely avant-garde impulses, a near sacrilege.

Yet these circles actually had no reason to worry. Events unfolded just as they would have wanted. Whereas status quo criticism between 1967 and 1973/74 at least took notice of the avant-garde the following years were completely dominated by the principle of autonomy. And for this there are the following three explanations: 1) the avant-gardists had nearly no chance of gaining access to any sizable orchestras, choirs, opera houses, recording studios, etc., and thus faced the immediate prospect of total exclusion from musical life, 2) in 1973/74 the political change of course in the Federal Republic of Germany known as the "Tendenzwende" became felt in cultural life, and 3) the student movement finally folded after two or three years of "alienated" political activity for workers and the Third World, i.e., students turned to their own egos and thus gave up their specifically avant-gardist notions.

III.

As a result since 1975 this widely recognized modernism has dominated contemporary serious music, which in turn is playing to ever smaller audiences. If we may speak in the terms of Walter Benjamin, who mockingly termed the underlying principle of this modernism a "constant return of the constantly new,"[31] then we must reluctantly point out that attention has been shifted since the mid-1970s from social change to change of styles, trends, and fashion. Just as in modernistic painting since the mid-seventies, abstraction and conceptualism have returned to take the place of a socially critical tendency which had made full use of "realistic" means, so the old formalism came into full force after 1975 in modernistic music as well. Many modernist composers simultaneously attempted to continue developing the stylistic devices worked out by the serial, electronic, aleatoric, or stochastic trends. They defended their incomprehensibility by arguing that musical material automatically undergoes an ineluctable, even inevitable development, which supposedly does not allow resorting back to any exhausted, traditional musical forms (whether harmonic, tonal, or melodic). In West Germany, these views are shared by such serious music composers as Josef Anton Riedl, Nicolaus A. Huber, and Mathias Spahlinger, who are still trying to improve on the technical achievements of the musical style of Webern or Cage. In doing so, they put the chief emphasis on structure, musical abstraction, and minimalistic reduction.

Yet in addition to such modernistic experiments which still draw on the spirit of the old Darmstadt movement by believing in a further logical development of the material revolution, two more modernist directions have developed quite recently. These are labeled postmodern by some critics who lack other definitions or concepts and because it's fashionable. The first of these postmodern trends makes use of archaic, black African, or oriental forms of music. These are then reshaped in the manner of serial techniques of the 1950s or the *ars povera* of the following decade, and are transformed into abstract, monotonous sound structures which, in their provocative uniformity, are intended first to irritate the listener and then to hypnotically absorb the listener. Whereas around 1900 Debussy utilized the whole-note intervals of Indonesia gamelan music as exotic daubs of color, simultaneously keeping it at a certain distance, the tendency in today's postmodern movement is instead to try to transport oneself by meditation into the center of the spirit of the exotic. The theoretical pronouncements of this group often describe this meditation as an intentional repudiation of Eurocentric cultural arrogance. Thus this music is reminiscent of Indian ragas, Japanese Nō music, African drum beats, or Nepalese bells. It is supposed to communicate either the state of religious interiorization or wantonly uncontrolled sensuality. In the United States the hippies were the first to adopt such sounds, which then found their high-culture expression in the music of Terry Riley, Philip Glass, and Steve Reich, whose works—in spite of their staggering length—often show only "minimal variation" and thus are considered by the critics as paradigms of "monotonal" or "gradual" music.[32]

In the 1950s, West Germany's Karlheinz Stockhausen tended toward a religiously tinged music of 'the spheres. He later became one of the first to favor the exotic and at the same time very consciously try to use it as a defense against any concrete political commitments. That is evident as early as 1958 in his work *Stimmung (Tuning in for Six Vocalists)*, composed in "happy" hippy days in San Francisco. He wrote that this meditative music is supposed to illuminate the "interior of the harmonic spectrum" in order to bring to full and simultaneous expression the "beauty of eternity" in the "beauty of sensuality."[33] In such works as *Sternklang* (Stellar Sound) of 1971 and *Der Jahreslauf* (The Course of the Year) of 1977, he endeavored to continue this "tuning." Something similar is at work in such compositions as Peter Michael Hamel's *Samma Samadhi* of 1973 and *Maitreya* of 1974, which like Stockhausen's works are rooted in oriental and occidental sound combinations. All of this is supposed to sound moving, meditative, perhaps even religious—but for the most part it remains a mere experiment in modernistic formalism. In contrast to Asian music, this music does not have any ritual function, it is neither cultic nor collective, but rather only showcases its creators' ambition for formal ingenuity.

The same holds true for the second current within so-called "postmodern" music, which borrows some of its sound material and structure from nineteenth-century Classical and Romantic music. Its borrowings are evident as outright quotations—as is also true for postmodern architectural facades. In this area the most convincing work is being done by those composers whose borrowings do not have the character of literal quotes but rather adopt fundamental, romantic, expressive gestures of a certain work. West German examples of this are the compositions by Wilhelm Killmayer and Wolfgang Rihm, in which such extremes as ecstasy, madness, or even death are conjured up in a neo-neoromanticist fashion. Prime examples are such works as *Schumann in Endenich* of 1972 by Killmayer or the chamber opera *Jakob Lenz* of 1980 and the *Wölfli-Lieder* of 1981 by Rihm, in which displacement into madness dominates, although these works too are haunted throughout by verbatim quotations from Schumann, Brahms, and Mahler. The quote element is absolutely fundamental to compositions such as *Tanzsuite mit Deutschlandlied (Dance suite with the German national anthem)* of 1980 by Helmut Lachenmann, the *Schubert Fantasy* of 1978 by Dieter Schnebel, which is based almost entirely on the first movement of Schubert's *Piano Sonata in G Major*, and the requiem *Prince Igor, Stravinsky* of 1982 by Mauricio Kagel, composed for Stravinsky's funeral and based on an aria from the opera *Prince Igor* by Borodin. The goal of this music is to create a highly serious impression, which has also been the intention of the exotic trend within postmodernism. Yet like the work of the exotic camp, neo-neoromantic music remains mere modernistic experiments in sound, because although the music of Romanticism is indeed quoted, it does not capture the rich world of emotions expressed in Romantic music.

Thus not even these two trends are the highly valued "avant-garde" so often claimed by their managers.[34] A musical avant-garde worthy of the name would, after all, seek to base itself on the progressive "intonations" of its own time.[35] The intonations of non-European cultures or of art music of nineteenth-century Romanticism may very well be just as interesting, "beautiful," or pleasantly soothing as most modernistic sound experiments of the fifties and sixties dominated by choppy, shrill, and dissonant forms—but still they are not avant-garde. For in order to be an avant-garde that keeps the improvement of all society in mind, composers must seize the progressive intonations of their own era, as Beethoven did in his *Eroica*[36] and Berlioz in his *Symphonie funèbre et triomphale*.

But—critics of this concept will begin to object here (if they haven't already)—what exactly *are* the progressive intonations of our own time, similar to the sounds used by Hans Werner Henze in his *Voices* at the start of the 1970s? Are there such voices left at all? Or formulated more radically: where are the progressive movements of our day that could possibly yield such voices? Well, such movements do in fact exist: whether in feminism, the Greens, the remnants of the left, or the peace movement. But have these movements actually brought forth new, progressive voices and intonations—or haven't they instead relied musically on commercial pop in hand-me-down form which they do not even reshape, but merely adopt as is? Thus, in its final hour before being stormed by the police, West Germany's pirate-wavelength alternative radio station "Republic Free Wendland" could think of nothing better to broadcast than a few Walter Mossmann songs and Pink Floyd's "We don't need no education."[37] Aren't these movements capable of making any better music, some voices that would better express their defiance, their desperation, their hope? Don't these movements have any intonations capable of being transformed into "art"? Or is the stereotypical the predominant feature in the music praxis of these movements, as it is in most commercial music? If there truly are only stereotypes at work here, then serious music will never develop the tonal quality that could give it the status of avant-garde music, but will continue to be a cliquish affair of the upper 0.1 to 0.2 percent of the populace. For after all, the artistic avant-garde, an "aesthetics of resistance," does sustain itself on the spirit of the movement from which it springs, from a collective conscience, from a gesture of rebelliousness. But any revolutionary spirit in music can scarcely be discerned nowadays due to the ever widening separation between extreme subjectivity and stereotype-ridden commercialism. There are people who remain unaware of this, there are those who welcome it; but there are also people who regret it, and not just because of the resultant lack of serious music, but also because of the corresponding lack of an ideological *telos*.

Translated by James Keller

NOTES

1. Cf. my essay "Das Konzept 'Avantgarde,' " in *Faschismus und Avantgarde*, ed. Reinhold Grimm and Jost Hermand (Königstein: Athenäum, 1980), 1–19.

2. Peter Bürger, *Theorie der Avantgarde* (Frankfurt: Suhrkamp, 1974) 67ff.

3. Hans Mayer, *Richard Wagner* (Hamburg: Rowohlt, 1959) 14ff.

4. August Bebel, *Die Frau und der Sozialismus*, 9th ed. (Stuttgart: J.H.W. Dietz, 1891) 326f.

5. Cf. Frank Trommler, *Sozialistische Literatur in Deutschland* (Stuttgart: Kröner, 1978), 136–44.

6. Cf. Jost Hermand, *Konkretes Hören: Zum Inhalt der Instrumentalmusik* (Berlin: Argument, 1981), 32ff.

7. Heinrich Hart, "Der Kulturwert der Musik," *Freie Bühne* (1891): 185-211.

8. Cf. Jost Hermand and Frank Trommler, *Die Kultur der Weimarer Republik* (Munich: Nymphenburger, 1978), 324.

9. Cf. Jost Hermand, "Expressionism and Music," in *Expressionism Reconsidered*, ed. Gertrud Bauer Pickar and Karl Eugene Webb (Munich: Fink, 1979), 70ff.

10. Werner Mittenzwei, "Brecht und die Schicksale der Materialästhetik," in *Brechts Tui-Kritik*, ed. Wolfgang Fritz Haug (Berlin: Argument, 1976), 175–212.

11. Cf. my essay "Der Aufmarsch der Dissonanzen: Hanns Eislers 'Deutsche Symphonie,' " *Sieben Arten an Deutschland zu leiden*, ed. Jost Hermand, (Königstein: Athenäum, 1979), 94–110.

12. Theodor W. Adorno, *Philosophie der neuen Musik*, 3rd ed. (Frankfurt: Suhrkamp, 1958), 126.

13. Cf. Theodor W. Adorno, *Dissonanzen: Musik in der verwalteten Welt* (Göttingen: Vandenhoeck and Ruprecht, 1958), 61.

14. Cf. Jost Hermand, "Die restaurierte 'Moderne' im Rahmen der musikalischen Teilkulturen der Nachkriegszeit," in *Musikalische Teilkulturen*, ed. Werner Klüppelholz (Munich: Laaber, 1983), 172–93.

15. *Melos* 27 (1960): 155.

16. H. H. Stuckenschmidt, *Musik eines halben Jahrhunderts: 1925–1975* (Munich: Piper, 1976), 100ff.

17. "Musik gegen jedermann," *Melos* 22 (1955): 248.

18. Arnold Schönberg, *Letters*, ed. Erwin Stein (London: Faber and Faber, 1958), 235.

19. "Das Altern der Neuen Musik," *Der Monat* (1955): 151f.

20. Ibid., 150.

21. Ibid., 153.

22. Ibid., 156, 150.

23. Ibid., 158.

24 Cf. my essay "Restored Modernism: West German Painting in the 1950's," *New German Critique* 32 (1984) 23–41.

25. Cf. Hermand, *Konkretes Hören*, 183f.

26. Cf. *Hanns Eisler, Argument-Sonderband 5* (Berlin: Argument, 1975), 3ff.

27. Tibor Kneif, *Musiksoziologie* (Cologne: Gerig, 1971), 9.

28. Hans Vogt, *Neue Musik seit 1945* (Stuttgart: Reclam, 1972), 54ff.

29. Quote in Ursula Stürzbecher, "Das große Fragezeichen hinter einer gesell-schaftspolitischen Funktion der Musik," *Melos* 39 (1972): 147.

30. Mauricio Kagel, *Tamtam* (Munich: Piper, l975), 67.

31. Walter Benjamin, *Illuminationen* (Frankfurt: Suhrkamp, 1981), 257.

32. Cf. Dieter Schnebel, "Über die experimentelle Musik und ihre Vermittlung," *Melos* 43 (1976): 464.

33. Quote on the album cover of Karlheinz Stockhausen, *Stimmung* (DG 2543 003).

34. It is interesting to note that Stockhausen's *Stimmung* album appeared in the "avant-garde" series.

35. The fundamental work on this is still Boris Assafiev, *Die musikalische Form als Prozeß* (Berlin, 1976).

36. Cf. my essay "Beethoven und Bonaparte: Biographisches und Autobiographisches in der 'Eroica,' " in *Vom Anderen und vom Selbst*, ed. Reinhold Grimm and Jost Hermand (Königstein, 1982), 183–97.

37. Cf. Peter Schleuning and Wolfgang Martin Stroh, "Tätigkeitstheoretische Aspekte musikalischer Teilkulturen: Ein Beispiel aus der Alternativszene," *Musikalische Teilkulturen: 81–107, esp. n. 15.

HAS MODERNIST MUSIC LOST POWER?

Charles Boone

Multiplicity, diversity, and pluralism are catchwords in new music in these closing years of the twentieth century, as they are in all the other fields of creative endeavor. One can also say with assurance that the words apply to the music of this century as a whole and that even the modernist movement itself can be described with them. Because these words have been central to descriptions of recent music, it would seem that: 1) a precise definition of what may (or may not) be a postmodern period is difficult; 2) perhaps we are not ready to make such a definition after all; 3) if postmodernism is indeed in place, perhaps it is simply an extension of the modernist period along with a more completely acknowledged group of diverse byways going along simultaneously.

After the relativizing processes of the sixties occurred, in which one thing became just as good as another, the idea that for composers there exists not just one current—i.e., modernism—but a plethora of currents from which to draw has been recognized clearly. It is now easier to acknowledge that all these many aspects of style and direction in music have been important in many ways over the entire century; but only now at the beginning of the last decade of the 1900s are we starting to come to terms with this fact in some creative ways. We also realize that out of this Babel of possibilities a new period of postmodern style could be emerging. For sure, many diverse streams will continue to flow side by side, but more significantly, at certain points some will begin to run together, causing something completely unexpected and fresh to happen. This is already to be observed, to a certain degree, and it is this plus the renewed and continuing vigor of some of the separate courses that will be considered here.

The era of modernism in music has been a long and exceptionally rich one—its beginnings can be dated from Debussy's *L'Après-midi d'un Faune* (1892–94) or perhaps later from Schönberg's rich creative period around 1909—and is distinguished by an immense catalog of masterworks from the two distinctive periods that preceded and followed World War II. There is no question that this modernist movement has been central to our century; it has seemed to be monolithic both in the breadth of its concerns and in the acknowledgment of its place in history. Nevertheless, during the age of modernism, many other directions were explored, and at least one of these, neoclassicism (both in its forms and tonality), from the early twenties well into the fifties was as all-pervasive as modernism itself.

Now the century-end accounting is beginning to be made and a number of these "other" tendencies are being reexamined and placed in some sort of positive perspective with the modernist mainstream. In music, it is, to a certain extent, the way Jean Baudrillard, in his *America*, describes the position of the United States in today's world: the country has not lost power, it is just that there is no longer any center. The important role of modernism is not just a special effect, however; it is very real, but has now been joined by some other forces as well in the move toward a new style. That in this age of pluralism heroic modernism should be seen as coming to an end, or as is more likely, that shifts are occurring that will suggest new directions which are in fact rooted in the modernist past, seems perfectly reasonable. These new directions are, of course, veiled in the mists of the future and we can only speculate about what will develop. About the immediate past and the present we can be a little more specific.

What seemed to some to be a kind of monolithic modernism that prevailed into the late sixties proves, on closer inspection, to have been as diverse as the composers who produced the work. This is especially true of the prewar masters who did not go untouched by—in fact, actively participated in—all the currents that flowed in music at the time. Schönberg alternated between extended tonal works and atonal-serial writing after devising his method of composing with twelve tones; Berg did likewise, combining atonal and clearly tonal materials while at the same time—notably in *Wozzeck*—employing diverse aspects of classical structuring; Webern never turned his back on serialism after about 1930, but in his works after that time made clear reevaluations and use of classical forms. Stravinsky and Bartók pushed forward into new worlds of harmony and rhythm while simultaneously employing what we today call world music. Stravinsky made the remarkable leap into Apollonian neoclassicism, giving it a legitimacy and status it would not have otherwise had. Certainly, neoclassicism had a much stronger influence on the atonal-serial composers in the twenties and thirties than vice versa (Stravinsky did not begin his flirtation with serialism until three decades later), though in the end there can be no doubt that atonality won out.

The core of early modernist music is generally acknowledged to be the work of the Second Viennese School (Schönberg, Berg, and Webern), plus that of Debussy (who lived well into the twentieth century), Stravinsky, and Bartók. It was out of the products of these fertile intellects that what is thought of as mainstream modernism developed and flourished so notably after World War II. If music goes where the best minds take it—to para-phrase Darius Milhaud—it is no wonder that Pierre Boulez and Karlheinz Stockhausen in Europe and John Cage in America were seminal figures in the explosion of new music after 1945. They, and others, provided not only a large number of ground-breaking compositions but also a good deal of the theoretical commentary that helped clarify and propagate the movement. Their early work grew in very natural ways out of Webern's serial music; just as it has been said that Brahms's First is Beethoven's Tenth, so it is that Boulez's *Sonatine* (1946) and Stockhausen's *Kontrapunkte* (1952-53) can be heard as Webern's Op. 32. Cage's thinking after the war owes a great debt to Webern (and to his studies of oriental philosophy as well), but the methods he developed for structuring his work, the thinking and aesthetic stance behind it, and the sounds themselves offered ways of going forward with rigors other than those of the Europeans' elaborated serialism. A comparison of two works from the early fifties, Cage's *Music of Changes*, for piano (1951) and Boulez's *Structures I*, for two pianos (1951-52) is instructive and quite surprising. It is remarkable to hear that the sounds of these works have as much in common as they do, considering the vastly differing premises from which these composers set about their tasks: *I Ching* vs. total serialism; which is to say, indeterminacy vs. total determinacy.

The work of these composers (Webern, Boulez, Stockhausen, and Cage) alone was enough to provide a clear and optimistic path into music's future in the period 1945–60. So obvious was this path that the cause was taken up by the most significant new music organizers in Europe as well as music faculties there and, to a lesser extent, in the United States Post-Webernian serialism and Cagean indeterminacy were the ways to go.

It should be clear at this point that in the period under discussion, though it was dominated to a very great extent by modernists of various persua-sions, modernism was, in fact, not as monolithic as its enemies—and also its advocates—made it out to be, that a lot of alternatives were being devel-oped, and that, by and large, even the founders of the movement tempered their radical thinking with other points of view. Cross-pollination in various forms began early on when Debussy listened to an Indonesian gamelan for the first time at the 1889 World's Fair in Paris and subsequently used what he heard as inspiration for his own compositions. Members of the Schönberg circle were deeply influenced not only by the poets whose texts they set (Trakl and George, in particular) but also by Viennese contemporaries in other fields (Karl Kraus, the commentator on literary and social matters, and Adolf Loos, the architect). Schönberg made what has recently been recog-nized as a significant contribution to early expressionist painting and worked on compositions which could well have revolutionized music theater had the implications of such pieces as *Die glückliche Hand* (1908–13) been followed up at the time.

Thus it can be said that keeping one eye on history while simultaneously keeping the other on current events—both in music and in other fields—was integral to modernist practice; the work was not created in a vacuum. In the case of Webern, music from Isaac to Mahler and Schönberg—essentially the German tradition—was thoroughly assimilated and distilled before being put back into circulation in the form of compositional thinking of surpassing originality. In his late cantatas, one hears no ostensible trace of Isaac, for example, yet he is there. Without Webern's special insight into four hundred years of music, he would not have done what he did the way he did it; namely, produce an entirely fresh vocabulary, rich in implications, from which composers who followed could build an even newer language of their own. Boulez, Stockhausen, and their associates in the late forties and early fifties clearly were dealing with a kind of history as well, but it did not stretch back over the centuries. For them, the past meant almost entirely Webern. To say that they looked back only a few years to discover their roots is to say that they did not look back at all. This shortness of historical perspective is relatively unusual in the period under discussion—and could easily have been a contributing factor to these composers' unyielding belief in serialism, to their radical experimentation, and to the toughness and singlemindedness of their work well into the sixties.

Postwar modernism remained true to its Webernian, serial beginnings for more than a decade, but by the early sixties, new energy and ideas were beginning to come into the movement. A number of composers who either lived in eastern Europe or who had recently emigrated to the West were composing a music that, to a certain extent, came out of early work by the French-American composer Edgard Varèse. While Webern was writing his highly refined miniatures grounded in the German tradition, Varèse was inventing his own completely individual musical world. His work is descended from Debussy and Stravinsky (in its color, harmony, and blocks of texture), reflecting, of course, his Gallic origins. But in contrast to Webern, Varèse's highly original vision springs from no single, overriding historical source.

As early as 1953 in his *Metastaseis*, the Greek engineer-architect-turned-composer Iannis Xenakis had begun composing music that consisted of dense blocks of massed sonorities in which, unlike Webern's transparent, crystalline structures, the many individual lines disappeared into great chunks of sound. By the early sixties, with the Hungarian Gyorgy Ligeti's *Apparitions* (1958-59) and *Atmosphères* (1961), and Polish composer Krzysztof Penderecki's *Anaklasis* and *Threnody for the Victims of Hiroshima* (1960), a new school of sound-color composers had been born. These dramatic, bold works, along with the music and influence of John Cage, were among the important beginnings of the loosening of serialism's bonds on European modernist music.

A very significant aspect of Ligeti's work at the time, as well as that of his Polish peers, had to do with simplicity and directness of what was heard, something very different from the work of the serialists in the fifties. In *Atmosphères* there were large blocks of easily discernable sound material that went through processes of transformation that could be easily perceived:

long fades from one texture to another, clear movement between areas of greater and lesser density, gradual motion from one register to another, gradual color changes, and so on. With Ligeti, the sounds had an ephemeral, otherworldly quality; with Xenakis, Penderecki, and other Poles the sound was harsh and aggressive. It was even said at the time that Henryk Gorecki's *Instrumental Singing* (1962) seemed to show a new facet of Socialist realism through musical sounds which were as gritty and nasty as the coal mines in the composer's native Silesia. Very rapidly, elements of earlier music that had been off-limits to serial composers began to creep back into the vocabulary. Clear octaves and snippets of melodic material cropped up in Witold Lutoslawski's *Trois Poèmes d'Henri Michaux* (1963) and *String Quartet* (1964), major works that owed more to the spirit and organizational ways of Varèse (the harmony and bold color) and Cage (the indeterminate aspects) than to serial principles. By the time of Ligeti's *Lontano* (1967) and Luciano Berio's *Sinfonia* (1968)—the third movement of which is an immense collage of music ranging from Bach to Boulez, all arrayed over a framework of the third movement of Mahler's Symphony No. 2, something that would have been unthinkable less than a decade earlier—modernist music had moved to a very different place.

During the middle sixties in San Francisco, there emerged a significant new trend that came to be known as minimalism. Late in 1964, the first piece in this idiom, Terry Riley's *In C*, was performed. Quite remarkably, all the elements of subsequent minimalist vocabulary were already present in this splendid work: slow unfolding of materials with gradual transformations from one thing to another, clearly defined pulse, short, easily recognizable motives that are repeated over and over, and a strong sense of tonal center. Whether one views these characteristics as adventures in new territory (not to mention a slap in the face to atonality) or as more reactionary reexaminations of musical ideas long out of fashion could depend on one's point of view. What cannot be denied is that after the almost two decade postwar period, during which atonality and serialism prevailed, with their dissonant harmony, disjunct rhythm, and general feeling of complexity, the arrival of a piece like *In C* seemed to many young composers a breath of fresh air.

Another of the minimalist fathers was Steve Reich, who was also living in San Francisco at the time. His tape composition *It's Gonna Rain* (1965), a critical piece at the beginning of the movement put together shortly after the premiere of *In C*, used a phrase of spoken text as its basic sound material. Reich wanted to see how this would sound when played back on two identical tape loops, but because of the irregular speed of his tape recorders, the loops went slowly in and out of phase, hence the term phase music. This process was analogous to what went on in *In C*, where patterns were repeated over and over to form constantly shifting layers of sound. When Reich went on to write instrumental pieces after this he continued working with this pattern-phase process as well as all the rest of the minimalist vocabulary established in *In C*.

Like the music of the eastern European composers at about the same time, this California minimalism differed significantly from contemporary serial work. Both were more direct and considerably simpler in a lot of ways: both allowed material to transform gradually over long periods of time; both, either immediately or later on, reintroduced vocabulary from preatonal music; both offered ways of composing that made the strictures of serialism unnecessary. The effect of minimalism was recognized very soon in Europe, not least of all by Gyorgi Ligeti himself; in 1976 he composed his *Three Pieces*, for two pianos, the second movement of which is titled "Self Portrait with Reich and Riley (and Chopin is there as well)."

The fifties and sixties marked the beginning of composers' interest in technology as a way of moving forward with their art. Early on, important electronic music studios were established in Cologne, Milan, Paris, New York, and San Francisco where, chief among the finished products were pieces on magnetic recording tape. In the sixties there flourished in addition the ubiquitous rock music in which the main sound sources were electric guitars, plus amplified voices and percussion, all heard through loudspeakers just as tape music was. Already by the mid-sixties it became clear that sound could be produced by computers, thus obviating the need for composers to work with magnetic tape. This not only made many of the traditional analog studio techniques much easier, it also made possible vast resources for sound production and manipulation that had only been dreamed of before. This area of electronic and computer technology was rich with possibilities for the crossovers between rock and concert music that soon began to take place.

Another fascinating possibility for streams to begin flowing together became evident in the early sixties in the conjunction of music and theater. This grew partly out of "happenings" (Cage's *Theater Piece* dates from 1960 and similar events by the visual artists Claes Oldenburg, Jim Dine, George Segal, and Allan Kaprow from about the same time) as well as out of composers' realization that listening to electronic music through loudspeakers with no visual or live components, as one has in traditional musical performance, might be an incomplete experience. During the heyday of the San Francisco Tape Music Center, 1963–66, Morton Subotnick, Pauline Oliveros, Ramon Sender, and others took up this challenge in their innovative experimentation with combinations of theatrical, visual, and musical media. In Europe, Mauricio Kagel was at work on pieces in which the musicians not only played their instruments in highly unusual ways but also engaged in often wild theatrical action, all very carefully notated in the scores. Even Stockhausen himself composed a theater piece in 1961, *Originale*, which used as its musical component his electronic piece *Kontakte* (1959–60).

Starting in the sixties world music became an important part of the thinking of many composers. Terry Riley was off in India learning traditional vocal and drum techniques. Steve Reich was doing likewise in Indonesia and Africa and later studied Hebrew music. Somewhat earlier, both Boulez and Stockhausen had acknowledged music of the Orient and, of course, Cage's thinking has long been bound up with traditional music and philosophy of Japan. Clearly world music provided yet another area for pervasive cross-fertilization.

Nowadays, there is hardly a music school without some sort of program in world music; on the West Coast, for instance, gamelans seem to be everywhere. Similarly, electronic and computer music studios are standard items in music departments. Indeed, equipment is now so small in size and inexpensive that home studios in varying degrees of sophistication are not uncommon. Video equipment, too, has become accessible enough to offer interesting possibilities not only to artists and filmmakers but also to composers wishing to explore ways of combining their music with visual imagery.

There are many fine works by young composers in which some or all of these areas of crossover can be found. Laurie Anderson has had a huge success with concert-theater works that involve music, visuals, and live electronic performance. Robert Ashley has made works that have electronically produced and processed sound plus video and live action. Both Anderson's and Ashley's work shows the influence of popular culture (rock music being as much ethnic-world music in end-of-the-century America as tabla playing is in India, as Reich has pointed out) and is thus important when citing examples of cross-fertilization. Peter Rose (film, video, and performance artist) and David Moss (percussionist) have collaborated on works involving all their various disciplines. One such is *Labys* (1988), a fascinating piece with voices, text, computer animation, video, and stage action. It is visually and sonically superb. Composer Richard Zvonar and theater designer Jill Neff, both Californians, collaborated in 1987 on *OX*, a complex and troubling theater piece on modern and ancient themes using sound, light, visuals, and stage business in stunning manner. Charles Amirkhanian is a composer who uses words and ambient noise instead of musical sounds in his work. Coming out of Gertrude Stein and, perhaps, Kurt Schwitters, he makes works that either exist only on tape or which can be done in live concert situations. They are among the most stimulating and often amusing works in the large catalog of crossover music in the seventies and eighties.

Once the floodgates were opened in the sixties, curious things appeared on the scene that one expected never to see again. One of these was a new romantic movement. Reich's and Riley's relatively small-scale work, with its return to simple tonality and regular pulse, and its almost classical restraint, hardly suggested that in the eighties a full-blown revision in thinking about the nineteenth century would take place. One of the leaders in this trend has been John Adams, who has composed massive works for orchestra (with and without chorus) and is now at work on his second evening-length opera. Though he has been numbered among the minimalists from the very beginning, there are so many things in his work that are not minimal, let alone minimalist, that it seems better to approach his work from other angles. Characteristics other than the working out of patterns in the manner of

Reich and Riley seem more relevant here. Among these is his constant and
overt acknowledgment of composers from earlier times as well as from our
own era. There is the strong sense of looking back to the music of the past—
early Schönberg and the symphonies of Bruckner and Sibelius; the general
eclecticism and the tenor of what is being expressed put a wide space between Adams and the minimalists.

During this time when myriad "neo-" and "post-" movements have been
sprouting and revisionist thinking is made manifest, modernist music in all
its strength and variety has forged onward. Radical concert pieces and instal-
lations have been composed by Alvin Lucier, one of which, *Silver Streetcar
for the Orchestra*, for amplified triangle played live (1988), was a hit at the
1988 New Music America Festival in Miami. Six months before his death in
1987, Morton Feldman completed his penultimate work, *For Samuel Beckett*,
for twenty-three players. This dark and deeply affecting music which is the
sonic equivalent of Mark Rothko's late paintings, not to mention the texts of
Beckett, must surely be counted among the great glories of American music.
Toshio Hosokawa's *Beyond Time*, for violin and string orchestra (1987), is a
piece coming out of late-modernism and Japanese traditional music. It is a
twentieth-century work that deserves to be part of the repertoire of every
enterprising violin soloist. Luigi Nono's *Fragmente-Stille, an Diotima*, for
string quartet (1979–80), is as tough and rarefied a reassertion of modernism,
albeit a pianissimo one, as can be imagined. It is also a moving work of
major proportions and beauty. All these examples are very recent and
are living proof of the vitality of the modernism that has been central to
twentieth-century music.

There is also an audience out there for the great variety of what our
composers are writing, though it must be acknowledged that not all of that
music is intended for the masses. New music groups are scattered all over
the country, and in the major centers, at least—New York, San Francisco,
and Los Angeles, to name the most obvious—most new music events are
well attended by knowledgeable, enthusiastic listeners. The amazing Kronos
Quartet generally sells out their series in San Francisco's twelve-hundred
seat Herbst Theater, and they play regularly in New York and Los Angeles
when they are not appearing abroad. Their repertoire is almost entirely
brand-new music, much of it written especially for them, with sprinklings of
earlier work by Bartók, Schönberg, Carter, and so on. Philip Glass, one of
the major opera composers of the past decades, is booked up with commissions for new work for years to come. Just try getting a ticket for a Glass
concert or for an appearance of Laurie Anderson or Steve Reich and you will
see what it means for a composer in the late twentieth century to have an
immense public success with his or her new music.

If there is to be a new, postmodern trend in music it will surely come out
of all this. It may not be settled in enough yet for us to recognize precisely
what its characteristics will be. Perhaps it will just have to be defined by the
terms multiplicity, diversity, and pluralism which have helped define the

entire century. In any case, the richness of modernism continues, other streams continue, and their blendings continue to make the twentieth century one of the richest and most fascinating in the history of music.

The following is a discography of some of the works and composers mentioned in this paper. Many of the recordings are not listed in current catalogs but should be available in libraries, if not in stores.

John Adams (b. 1947). *Harmonium* (1984). ECM 81465-2.
Charles Amirkhanian (b. 1945). *Mental Radio* (1979–82). CRI 50523.
Luciano Berio (b. 1925). *Sinfonia* (1968). Erato NUM 75198.
Pierre Boulez (b. 1925). *Sonatine* (1946). RCA VICS 1312.
_____ . *Structures* I & I. MACE MXX 9043.
John Cage (b. 1912). *Music of Changes* (1951). Wergo 60099.
Morton Feldman (1926–87). *The Viola in My Life* (1970). CRI S-276.
Gyorgi Ligeti (b. 1923). *Atmosphères* (1961). Wergo 60022.
_____ . *Lontano* (1967). Wergo 60045.
Luigi Nono (b. 1924). *Fragmente-Stille, an Diotima* (1980). DGG 416387-1.
Krzysztof Penderecki (b. 1933). *Anaklasis* (1960). Wergo 60020.
Steve Reich (b. 1936). *It's Gonna Rain* (1965). Electra/Nonesuch 79169-1.
Terry Riley (b. 1935). *In C* (1964). CBS MS 7178.
Karlheinz Stockhausen (b. 1928). *Kontrapunkte* (1952–53). RCA VICS 12398.
_____ . *Kontakte* (1959–60). DGG 138811.
Edgard Varèse (1883–1965). *Déserts* (1954). CBS M 39053.
Iannis Xenakis (b. 1922). *Pithoprakta* (1955–56). Nonesuch 71201.

POSTMODERNISM

EXTENSION OR END OF MODERNISM?
THEATER BETWEEN CULTURAL CRISIS AND
CULTURAL CHANGE

Erika Fischer-Lichte

The controversy surrounding postmodernism which has currently aroused fierce debate in various fields on different levels culminates in the persistent question of whether postmodernism has effected a complete break with modernist traditions, or whether it has, on the contrary, only radicalized the trends first formulated and pronounced by modernism and extended its conclusions. Both viewpoints are vigorously upheld. This is all the more extraordinary since the ground on which the controversy should be discussed is not yet clearly plotted: Does the modernism dealt with here begin with the *Querelle des anciens et des modernes* or with the Enlightenment? With the industrialization of Western Europe or with Nietzsche? Should one see the historical avant-garde movement as an integral component of modernism (as most European critics seem to do), or should modernism be defined by the exclusion of the avant-garde movement (as many American critics would argue)? In attempting to examine the question of whether the "true" *Epochenschwelle* [threshold of an epoch] is to be termed modern or postmodern, one must first secure agreement on these issues.

The most important arguments so far exchanged in the controversy have been collated in a most informative research report entitled "The Postmodern *Weltanschauung* and Its Relation with Modernism" by Hans Bertens. Rather than repeating those arguments here, which in the meantime have become sufficiently well known, I shall take as starting point those elements which refer to postmodernism in literature and examine them from a semiotic point of view.

There is a wealth of argument which concerns literary device. Distinctive characteristics are formulated whose opposites are held to be representative of modernism: indeterminacy, fragmentation, montage, collage, intertextuality, hybridization, the carnivalesque (in the sense of Bakhtin), constructivism, randomness, openness of the form, discontinuity, etc. This catalog which concentrates on the syntactic level of a work, has yet to be completed.

On the semantic level, the presentation of possible worlds, the redefinition of the relationship between time and space, and the dissolution of the self and its boundaries are most frequently referred to. The pragmatic level is conspicuously absent from the argumentation. Here the only discussion is concentrated on the shift of the focus away from the work itself and onto the reader, so that one can only speak of a literary object in the strictest sense as the interaction between the reader and the text.

In addition to this, a string of metasemiotic notions are appealed to, such as the shift of the dominant as epistemological question to the dominant as ontological one (McHale, 1987); from monism to pluralism; from representation to performance; from referentiality to nonreferentiality; or, yet again, the firmly held belief in the self-reflexivity of a literary text and its production. Still largely unclarified remains the status of the various arguments and the interconnections between them: Must all distinctive characteristics be listed in order to be able to speak of a postmodern work, or would it suffice to specify certain chosen ones, and, if so, which? Do they create a structure with one another, within which each fulfills a function, or does one simply enumerate them ad libitum? How can one relate the distinctive characteristics found on the different semiotic levels to one another? Does it make sense simply to list specific literary devices without having analyzed and differentiated their relation to the semantic, pragmatic, or metasemiotic levels?

Apart from these more systematic questions, others arise which stem from the actual methods of procedure. Thus as verification that it is indeed the distinctive characteristics given that differentiate postmodern works from the modern, a literary corpus is created which, despite all its differences in detail, is nonetheless homogeneous in two significant aspects: the examples are predominantly drawn from the narrative genres (short stories and novels) and exclude texts from the historical avant-garde almost entirely. Hence I should like to elucidate the systematic problem of the distinction between postmodernism and modernism by recourse to a body of literature which principally consists of texts of dramatic literature and which will include those of the historical avant-garde movement as it has recently been foregrounded by Peter Bürger (1984). Texts such as *Sphinx and Strohmann* (Kokoschka), *Les mamelles de Tiresias* (Apollinaire), *Le coeur à gaz* (Tzara), *Methusalem* (Yvan Goll), *Le serin muet* (G. Ribemont Dessaignes), and Hugo Ball's texts for the Dada soirées will therefore be referred to as examples of modernist literature. Since Dada was in existence at that time, one must also take it into account. The same of course applies to dramas such as *Mysterium buffo* (Mayakovsky), or *Pobedr nrd solncem (Victory Over The Sun)* (Kručenych), as well as to texts of futurist and constructivist performances.

As a starting point, I have selected a problem which has arisen on the semantic level, and through it, the relation to the syntactic, pragmatic, and metasemiotic levels can easily be established: the area to be examined is the presentation of the individual, the self in modern and postmodern drama.

By way of introduction, I shall cite a somewhat lengthy passage from Bertens's *Forschungsbericht:*

> For Gerald Graff the celebratory mode of Postmodernism is characterized by a "dissolution of ego boundaries"; for Daniel Bell "the various kinds of postmodernism . . . are simply the decomposition of the self in an effort to erase the individual ego," and Ihab Hassan notes that "the Self . . . is really an empty 'place' where many selves come to mingle and depart." For Hoff-mann this movement in the direction of a less defined, less stable identity is even a shift of epistemic proportions: "The perceivable signs of a tendency toward the disappearance of a subjectivity in modern literature become a fact in postmodern works. Thus a radical gap between modern and postmodern literature is reflected in the opposition of two *epistemes:* subjectivity versus loss of subjectivity." The postmodern self is no longer a coherent entity that has the power to impose (admittedly subjective) order upon its environment. It has become decentered, to repeat Holland's phrase. The radical indeterminacy of postmodernism has entered the individual ego and has drastically affected its former (supposed) stability. Identity has become as uncertain as everything else. (Fokkema/Bertens 1986, 46f.)

Aside from the fact that the boundaries of the individual ego were dissolved as early as Strindberg's first dream play *Till Damascus* (1889), it is true to say that modern drama in the early twentieth century was constituted out of the negation of the individual, as the theory here proposes. Pirandello's *Six Characters in Search of an Author,* written and premiered in 1921, for example, can immediately be described as the "Spiel von der Unmöglichkeit des Dramas" (Szondi), since here the possibility of drama is called into question by dramatic characters who no longer have a definable individual ego at their disposal. The "Father" summarizes the problem in the following way:

> My drama lies entirely in this one thing. . . . In my being conscious that each one of us believes himself to be a single person. But it's not true. . . . Each one of us is many persons. . . . Many persons . . . according to all the possibilities of being that there are within us. . . . With some people we are one person. . . . With others we are somebody quite different. . . . And all the time we are under the illusion of always being one and the same person for everybody. . . . We believe that we are always this one person in whatever it is we may be doing. But it's not true! It's not true!

Here we are faced quite clearly with self-reflexion as well as the shift of the dominant from an epistemological question to an ontological one: Since the 'being' (*Sein*) cannot be known or defined by the individual, the question arises how it can then be represented in drama?

Pirandello took recourse in the Baroque topos of role-play and the imma-nent problem of the *Sein-Schein* which he recast in special ways: Each individual does not only act but also *is* the different roles without the possibility of being defined either by the set role itself or even as a persona beyond the role. His being *(Sein)* is the "life that ceaselessly flows and changes" and thus one which knows no boundaries. His appearances *(Schein)* are the different roles which in each case function as the "form" which seeks to "detain it, keep it unchanging."

The literary devices which Pirandello employs to represent dramatically his concept of the self are, among others, intertextuality, irony, and hybridization. Similarly, another so-called classic author of modern drama, Eugene O'Neill, also denies a bound individual ego. In *Mourning Becomes Electra* (1929–31), the characters are introduced almost as replicas of replicas of replicas in a basically unendable stream back to the source. Individuality no longer exists. This characteristic is true on the psychical level and in the physical development of the action.

All the men in the Mannon family, Abe, David, Ezra, Adam, and Orin, share the same facial characteristics: "an aquiline nose, heavy eyebrows, swarthy complexion, thick, straight black hair, light hazel eyes" *(Homecoming,* act 1; *The Hunted,* act 1). The women who marry into the family like Marie Brantome and Christine, or those from the family itself like Lavinia, also share a number of similar physical features: they all have "thick, curly hair, partly a copper brown, partly a gold, each shade distinct and yet blending with the other," "deep-set eyes of a dark violet-blue," "black eyebrows, which meet in a pronounced straight line above her strong nose," "a heavy chin," and "a large sensual mouth" *(Homecoming,* act 1). Furthermore, the male and female members of the Mannon family seem so intertwined that their faces at rest give the impression of a "life-like mask." To these physical similarities, O'Neill ties psychical ones: all the members of the family are driven by incestuous desire. The men all suffer from an Oedipus complex, the women from an Electra or Jocasta complex.

O'Neill uses this system of psychical and physical similarities and equivalents to divest the characters of any individuality: each duplicates the other who is himself a duplication of yet another. There is no "original" and therefore no individual ego. Each repeats one who is repeating another who is repeating another and so on ad infinitum. In fact, not only do they appear as not individual selves, but also rather as seeming substitutes for someone who is absent—as Orin discovered in the war: "Before I'd gotten back I had to kill another in the same way. It was like murdering the same man twice. I had a queer feeling that war meant murdering the same man over and over, and that in the end I would discover the man was myself! Their faces keep coming back in dreams—and they change to Father's face—or to mine" *(The Hunted,* act 3, 304f.). Equally, the characters act as if they are driven by an "other," or are recalling an action initiated by an "other" in the past. In this way, an earlier action is exactly recalled by others, as for example the small gesture used by Ezra, Adam, and Orin on many occasions to try and smooth Marie, Christine, and Lavinia's hair; or alternatively a whole action sequence is repeated as in the case of Orin and Lavinia in the third part of the trilogy (*The Hunted*, act 2, 355f.). In their nature, their desires, their words and deeds, the characters recall others who came before them; they are neither identical among themselves, nor to others—they have no individual self, no definable identity. The self is indeed an "empty place where many selves come to mingle and depart." The most important literary device that O'Neill uses is that of consistently setting the text in its relation to the intertext (Aeschylus's *Oresteia*) and thereby building up a meaning-generating system of differences.

The outstanding feature in both Pirandello and O'Neill of presenting the self as an "empty place" in which widely divergent "roles" (Pirandello) or "others" (O'Neill) can meet, is further radicalized in the Dada movement. Whilst Pirandello and O'Neill in part—principally in terms of language and dramaturgy—employ thoroughly "traditional" literary devices, the Dadaists turn the play into an antiplay, the theater performance into an antitheater; all the traditional devices are parodied, negated, thrown overboard.

In Tristan Tzara's *Le coeur à gaz*, which was premiered in 1921 in the "Salon Dada" in Paris, the dramatic characters are Oreille, Bouche, Oeil, Cou, Nez, Sourcil, a dancer and other characters, who "entrent et sortent ad libitum."

Whilst Strindberg questioned the idea of psychical wholeness in a character by introducing the Doppelgänger, and O'Neill by stressing physical similarities, Tzara on the other hand fragments the human body and defines these isolated parts as the characters of the action. The self becomes literally the "empty space" between the characters of the action. The dialogue between them proceeds as follows:

Oreille:	C'est le printemps, le printemps
Nez:	Je vous dis qu'il a 2 mètres
Cou:	Je vous dis qu'il a 3 mètres
Nez:	Je vous dis qu'il a 4 mètres
Cou:	Je vous dis qu'il a 5 mètres
Nez:	Je vous dis qu'il a 6 mètres

and so on up to 16 meters.

Alternatively, they confront each other with maxims and proverbs which follow senselessly on from each other:

Oreille:	. . . Les hommes simples se manifestent par un maison, les hommes importants par un monument.
Bouche:	Non je veux rien dire. J'ai mis depuis longtemps dans la boîte à chapeau ce que j'avais dire. (171)
Soucil:	"ou", "combien", "pourquoi" sont des monuments. Par example la Justice. Quel beau fonctionnement régulier, presque un tuic nerveux ou une religion. (159)
Cou:	Mandarine et blanc d'Espagne, je me tue Madeleine, Madeleine. (158)

The literary devices employed here can be described as indeterminacy, disconnectedness, randomness, fragmentation, montage, carnivalesque, hybridization; in short, the whole arsenal of distinctive characteristics belonging to postmodernism finds its realization on a syntactic level.

Similar findings can be confirmed on the metasemiotic level. Indeed, here it is more a question of approaching pluralism—to the point where "anything goes." The trend toward loss of referentiality is also clearly to be seen. In Tzara's *La première aventure céleste de Mr. Antipyrine* we find, for example, the following dialogue:

La femme enceinte:	Toundi-a-voua Soco Bgai Affahou
Mr. Bleubleu:	Farafamgama Soco Bgai Affahou
Pipi:	amerture sans église allons charbon chameau synthétisé amerture sur l'église isisise les rideaux dodododo
Mr. Antipyrine:	Soco Bgai Affahou zoumbai, zoumbai, zoumbai, zoum.
Mr. Cricri:	il y a pas d'humanité—il y a les réverbères et les chiens dzinaha dzin aha bobobo Tyaco oahiii hii hii héboum iéha iého
Mr. Bleubleu:	incontestablement. (77)

Here it is clear that the trend toward performance outweighs that toward representation. This is of course also the case to a certain extent of the Dada soreeś and activities which took place rather like happenings. Hausmann, among others, has recorded:

On Sunday, 17th November 1918, Baader attended the morning service at the cathedral in Berlin. As the court chaplain, Dryander, was about to begin the sermon, Baader called out in a loud voice, "Wait! What does Jesus Christ mean to you? Nothing . . ." He wasn't able to go on, there was a terrible tumult, Baader was arrested and a charge of blasphemy held against him. Nothing could be done with him in the end, however, since he was carrying the whole text of his outburst with him in which it continues, "for they do not heed his commands etc." Naturally, all the papers were full of this incident. (Huelsenbeck 1984, 226)

In conjunction with the performative character of the Dada productions and soirées, the concept of the audience as an integral component of the performance was deliberately planned. The Dada chronicler, Walter Mehring, who had himself participated in the sixth performance of the Dada soirée in November 1919, describes how the audience uprising stage-managed by the Dadaists was provoked. Mehring was reciting Goethe's poem *Wanderers Sturmlied* in Dadaist style,

up to a pre-arranged cue when the whole Dada tribe burst onto the podium and bellowed "Stop!" "Stop that rubbish!" they roared, and "Walt" snarled Böff, his monocle jammed in place, "Walt, you're not going to throw these— ah —pearls to such swine?" and "Stop!" yelled the Dada chorus simulta-

neously: "Get out! Ladies and Gentlemen, you are kindly requested to go to
hell . . . if you really want amusement, go to the whorehouse, or (said Huelsenbeck) to a Monas Thann lecture!" and they stepped down from the podium
arm in arm in a chain to face the enraged stalls. (52, German)

From here to Handke's *Offending the Audience* no longer seems such a giant
step.

The literary devices which constitute the syntactic level and the trends
realized on the semantic and metasemiotic levels stand in clear relation to
the pragmatic level which decides and fixes their respective functions: the
intended effect on the reader/spectator is the underlying structural moment.
All the Dadaist activities were directed at an audience. Since the founding of
the Cabaret Voltaire in 1916 in Zürich, they utilized newspaper advertise-
ments and leaflets as an important instrument of self-publicity, to draw public attention. While at first they only aimed to "épater le bourgeois," these
ventures occurred increasingly in the form of an organized assault on the
audience, a "strategy of revolt." The devices shown above were directly
aimed at challenging and re-examining the purely passive attitude of expectation and customary practices of reception in the audience. In this way, they
attempted to dissolve the discrepancies between art and society for the duration of the performance. Theatrical conventions and habits of audience perception were deliberately abused, indeed utterly destroyed. In the end, it
was left to the audience to decide how to react to the Dadaist activities and
happenings, how to arrive at a new understanding of "art" and how to
create a different kind of receptive attitude: the Dadaist performance "work"
only existed in the (mostly aggressive) reaction of the audience; it was the
product and result of a process of interaction between the agents of the
action and the audience.

The Dadaist devices not only operated in the pragmatic dimension, but
also in the semantic dimension. These devices enabled the presentation of
the concept of the world, which they saw as disordered, as chaos.

Reality seemed incalculable, and thus nonrepresentable. Even if one could
admit a fundamental ordering principle to reality, this was in essence beyond
human perception. Life was interpreted as a "vital chaos," and man a clown
hopelessly trapped within it. Only a work which is random, incoherent, hybrid, indeterminant, and nonsequential can function as an adequate reaction
to, or possible way of representing the condition of the world. The Dadaist
activities and the techniques and devices employed to achieve them should
thus be seen in relation to the so-called "culture crisis" (*Kulturkrise*) which, at
the beginning of this century, principally after the First World War, shook the
middle classes in Europe. While the majority of the audience which participated in the Dada soirées, as members of the educated middle class, still
firmly held to the idea of the world and works of art as ordered wholes, the
Dadaists attempted to "decondition" them by leading them to specific reactions through their actions and thus to force new attitudes on them.

The fundamental perception of a far-reaching crisis in Western culture is also characteristic of the "classic" authors of modern theater such as Pirandello or O'Neill as well as for the members of the avant-garde theater before and after the First World War such as Craig, Meyerhold, or Artaud. Artaud thus writes in his third letter "On Language" (9 November 1932):

> Nous vivons une èpoque probablement unique dans l'histoire du monde, où le monde passé au crible voit ses vieilles valeurs s'effondrer. La vie calcinée se dissout par la base. Et cela sur le plan moral ou social se traduit par un monstrueux déchainement d'appétits, une libération des plus bas instincts, un crépitement de vies brûlées et qui s'exposent prématurément à la flamme. (112)

Our thoughts and argumentation so far have led us to three general conclusions:

> 1) The factors that can be called the distinctive characteristics of a postmodern literary work can partly (e.g., Pirandello, O'Neill) or wholly (Dada) be found in works dating from the early twentieth century.
> 2) These factors, which can be related to very different semiotic dimensions, are not separate from each other, but rather create such relations with one another that a structure is formed.
> 3) This structure is in its turn related to the circumstances of the culture crisis, and most particularly to the immanent consciousness of standing at the "threshold of an era" which will either lead to the birth of a new mankind and a new world, or which will lead to catastrophe.

If, therefore, postmodernism cannot be sufficiently distinguished from modernism by the criteria evidence/absence of certain distinctive characteristics, other criteria must be sought. The conclusions of our examination open at least two possibilities. Postmodernism can be differentiated from modernism on the basis of:

> a) the relations made by the distinctive characteristics situated on the different semiotic levels, i.e., on the basis of the structure they form,
> b) the historical, social Zeitgeist of the age to which the structure of relations corresponds.

In this way, Beckett's later dramas (*Play, Not I, That Time, Ends and Odds*), Heiner Müller's plays since *Germania Tod in Berlin,* and the dramas of Peter Handke and Thomas Bernhard can actually be identified through the very distinctive characteristic (which describes postmodern literature in general) that they are open to the reader/spectator: the disintegration of the dramatic characters on a semantic level, for example, or incoherence, randomness, fragmentation, hybridization on the syntactic level, are leveled at the reader/spectator who must himself decide how he will deal with the components offered to him. This can be observed in a very acute way in Robert Wilson's postmodern theatre. In Wilson's mammoth project *CIVIL warS* (1983/84), separate parts of which were produced and premiered in Rotterdam, Marseille, Lyon, Nice, Rome, Cologne, Tokyo, and Milwaukee, different ways of treating language were realized and performed. The texts of the characters' speech, for example, might consist of ready-made phrases from everyday life, ("are you alright," "just leave me alone," "oh come on"), phrases which are on the one hand presented as set scenes in the process of which the text is disconnected and there is no meaning in the dialogue, or on the other hand they are broken up into separate words and phonetic sounds ("are," "you," "alright," "a") and spoken alternately by the dramatic characters often many times over (*CIVIL warS* act 1, scene A).

Here, the manifest refusal to employ language in such a way that the sequence of sounds, words, or sentences yields a cohesive dialogue that will thus make sense, is based on yet another device. In act 4 of *CIVIL warS*, for which Heiner Müller was responsible, literary ready-mades, quotes from world literature are compiled together, (e.g., from *Hamlet, Phaedra, Empedocles*). Single parts of text are broken away from their original contexts and placed nonsequentially next to one another. In fact, the isolated fragments do yield meaning, but not, however, the sequence as a whole.

Another device used to the same effect is that in which the text spoken by the actor is employed as an element of a collage of recorded sound which is as much composed of different but simultaneously spoken texts as it is of shreds of music, sound, and speech. Now, in this context, even the single words and speeches are no longer understandable, but instead solely identifiable as elements of language. To a large extent they are reduced to the distinctive quality of a sound perceived as noise. In this way, the linguistic sign is more or less wholly deconstructed as sign. At first this seems to be a comparable kind of device to that which we have identified in the constructivist, dadaist, and futurist theater experiments: language is almost wholly desemanticized and no longer acts and functions as a sign within the context of the performance. However, while there the desemanticization of language creates a concentration on the quality of sound, in Wilson's case, language is allowed to decay into noise, which because of its multiple and simultaneously transmitted phonetic phenomena can no longer be perceived as a meaningful sign. The desemanticization of language which all three devices considered here effect—even in different ways—is even further advanced through the dissolution of the spoken language on the one hand from a "character" and on the other from the actor's body. The sounds, words, or texts are spoken by the actor at the same time as they are transmitted on tape through a loudspeaker. In this way, they are disengaged from the body of the actor—the language creates its own acoustic space. In so doing, however, language becomes incapable of functioning as the sign of character: speech is deconstructed not only as part of a meaningful dialogue but also as the sign of character. Speech is presented as phonetic phenomena and fragments of text which can neither be linked to one another nor to the body of the actor in a meaning-generating semiosis.

Alongside the desemanticization of language, Wilson presents the desemioticization of the body. Here again he has developed different devices to achieve it. The most important, and one which is especially typical of Wilson, is that he directs the actors to move so slowly that the impression of a slow-motion picture is created. Through this extremely slow motion the spectator's attention is drawn to the process of the movement itself. The spectator perceives gesture as movement, that is, as part of a moving body, and there is no possibility of perceiving it as or interpreting it as the sign for something else (as for example the expression of a role type). The slow-motion technique puts the actor's body on the same level as the objects presented on stage. The actor's body no longer represents or means anything, and finds satisfaction in being presented next to its co-objects. Another device shows the particular use of costume and make-up. In so far as the actor's body can suggest a specific character—as in the German part of *CIVIL warS*, for example, the character Frederick the Great, his mother Sophie Dorothée, an angel, a soldier, the tinman, and Lincoln, or in the American part, Admiral Perry, or a Japanese basket-peddler—it is employed as a quotation, so that characters are barely suggested and do not even begin to be built up dramatically. The separate elements presented by the actor's body such as costume, make-up, gesture, movement in space, and voice do not relate to one another, and thus cannot be integrated by the spectator with one another to provide internal relations that will produce any meaning. On the contrary, they create the potential of many random associative external relations which are almost wholly dependent on the spectator's own universe of discourse. A further device consists of simply employing the actor's body on the stage as bearer or prop of an object being presented, as for example, the bird in *Knee Plays*. Although Wilson has adopted this device from the Japanese theater, where the stagehands dressed in black hold ready the necessary props for the actor, or a glass of water should the actor grow hoarse, or stand ready to light the actor's face when the mime is particularly important, Wilson, in contrast, uses this device to show the unity between the object presented by the actor and the actor's body, thus demonstratively underlining its nonmeaning. The actor's body becomes part of a dream-like image floating by, in that it contains no semantic cohesion.

The single image can now be received on two levels: 1) on the syntagmatic level of the process on stage, which through the lack of internal relations is received as an incoherent sequence of ready-made linguistic and bodily quotations, or meaningless sounds and movements, or at best as a chain of information transmitted in bits; to discover a coherent meaning in the sequence of which is utterly impossible, or 2) on the paradigmatic level of the subjectively triggered chain of associations which integrates the single elements into subjectively asserted and structured areas of meaning and thus allows it to change back into subjective carriers of meaning.

The first level of reception can be linked to the flood of communication brought about by the mass media in that it allows the words to decay into noise and breaks up the succession of events into incoherent pictures so that they can only be perceived as information in bits whose sequence is meaningless. The second level of reception, on the contrary, opens the spectator to the possibility of perceiving the process on the stage as he would his own dream images—as a wonderful, unique, at first foreign world, the single elements of which seem wholly familiar without, however, admitting the possibility of being tied to one another into a superior unit of meaning. If the spectator admits the idea of the concreteness of this world, without needing to bring instant interpretation to it, the associative connections which he can now make release him to new experiences and unlock new possibilities of meaning. This level of reception thus initiates new kinds of perception and constitution of meaning, and is diametrically opposed to the "consumer habit" promoted by the mass media. Similar to the Dada soirées, the work can only be constituted in the interaction between text and spectator.

In the case of Dada, the interaction was aimed at a predominantly educated middle-class audience which was used to tracing specific, if not eternal then at least fixed, meanings in works of art, with the intention of upsetting this expectation and attitude of reception: The audience must be shocked, attacked, and provoked into aggression to get it to engage in any activity at all.

Interestingly, the Dada performances did not even achieve the desired effect in an audience composed mostly of workers who did not bring such expectations with them, and it was for this reason that experiments of this kind were discontinued. The audience at which postmodern drama/theater aims has, on the contrary, long since departed from the expectations and attitudes of reception characterized and fixed by the educated middle classes. It is—as a metropolitan audience—not easily shocked, or made aggressive. Consequently the interaction between text and spectator is realized quite differently: Either the spectator overlays the single elements and their incoherent sequence with meanings which stem from his own historical, social and private, autobiographical experience (he knows in this case that meanings have no fixed, intersubjectively valid values to be conveyed, but that they rather consist of the products of his own imaginative and associative activity); or he refuses to constitute any meanings at all and perceives the bodies, objects, words, and lighting in their concreteness as bodies, words, and lighting without interpreting them as signs of something else, so that, free of the need to bring any meaning to them, he finds satisfaction in the very concreteness of the items presented.

On the basis of these changed attitudes of reception in an audience (as opposed to those brought about by Dada) the distinctive characteristics found on the syntactic, semantic, and metasemiotic levels also take on another function. Fragmentation and collage should not, for example, shock the spectator into perceiving the world which he assumes is interconnected and causal as in fact ruled by incoherence and randomness. Rather, the device should encourage the spectator already oriented toward the principle of randomness to apply his own meaning to the randomly presented single object, without looking to possible links to the meaning he brings it, or to perceive it simply as an object in its concrete fact.

The dissolution of the boundaries of the self on the semantic level should not shock the spectator who believes he has an individual personality by demonstrating the fact that such a supposition of the individual personality is a middle-class fiction, but should rather expose the spectator who is already conscious of the instability of the self to different possibilities of its projection.

The shift of the dominant as epistemological question to the dominant as ontological one does not pursue the goal of sensitizing an essentially rational spectator to the view of the imbalance between the self and the consciousness, but rather confirms to the spectator who has already begun to question his rational consciousness, his rather more concretely directed perceptions.

Thus although we can observe the same distinctive characteristics in modern theater of the early twentieth century as we find in the postmodern, and although in both instances the distinctive characteristics on the syntactic, semantic, and metasemiotic levels only fulfill their function in their relation to the pragmatic dimension, the phenomena we are dealing with are clearly dissimilar. The Zeitgeist to which they belong is fundamentally different.

Whether these differences, however, constitute another *Epochenschwelle* in transition toward postmodernism has yet to be answered. Personally, I believe that the underlying changes on which postmodernism was built had already been fully executed by the end of the nineteenth and beginning of the twentieth centuries: the new perception of time and space, the dissolution of the boundaries of the individual ego, the relativism of rational, logic, causal thinking which in its entirety as *conditio sine qua non* are all evident in postmodern writing and suggest the point of transition into the twentieth century and with it the beginning of modernism.

The essential difference between modernism/avant-gardism and postmodernism seems to lie far more in the fact that the postulate formulated at the beginning of the century as an expression and consequence of a far-reaching culture crisis has in the eighties long been a reality: since the sixties, cultural change has occurred de facto. Thus I would suggest on the one hand to date the *Epochenschwelle* at the outbreak of the culture crisis in art, and on the other hand, plead not to equalize the vast differences between modernism and postmodernism with reference to their very real similarities. Instead, considering that cultural change has long since been effected, it will prove illuminating to define and judge these differences through a kind of functional examination that has been neglected heretofore.

Dada texts translated from the German by Josephine Riley.

BIBLIOGRAPHY

Artaud, Antonin. *Oeuvres Complètes IV.* Paris: Gallimard, 1978.

Bürger, Peter. *The Theory of the Avant-Garde.* Transl. Michael Shaw. Minneapolis: University of Minnesota Press, 1984.

Calinescu, Matei. *Five Faces of Modernity.* Durham: University of North Carolina Press, 1987.

————, and Douwe Fokkema, eds. *Exploring Postmodernism.* Amsterdam: John Benjamins, 1987.

Fischer-Lichte, Erika. "Jenseits der Interpretation." *Kontroversen, alte und neue.* Proceedings of the 7th International Congress of Germanists. Tübingen: Niemeyer, 1986.

———— "Postmoderne Performance: Rückkehr zum rituellen Theater?" *Arcadia* 22, 1 (1987): 191–201.

Fokkema, Douwe, and Hans Bertens, eds. *Approaching Postmodernism.* Utrecht Publications in General and Comparative Literature, vol. 21. Amsterdam: John Benjamins, 1986.

Huelsenbeck, Richard, ed. *Dada—eine literarische Dokumentation.* Reinbek bei Hamburg: Rowohlt, 1984.

Huyssen, Andreas, and Klaus R. Scherpe, eds. *Postmoderne: Zeichen eines kulturellen Wandels.* Reinbek bei Hamburg: Rowohlt, 1986.

Kamper, Dietmar, and Willem van Reijen. eds. *Die unvollendete Vernunft: Moderne versus Postmoderne.* Frankfurt am Main: Suhrkamp, 1987.

McHale, Brian. *Postmodernist Fiction.* New York and London: Methuen, 1987.

Mehring, Walter. *Berlin Dada: Eine Chronik mit Photos und Dokumenten.* Zürich: Arche, 1959.

O'Neill, Eugene. *Three Plays of Eugene O'Neill.* New York: Random House, 1959.

Pirandello, Luigi. *Six Characters in Search of an Author.* Trans. Frederick May. London: Heinemann, 1966.

Tzara, Tristan. *Oeuvres Complètes.* 4 vols. Texte établie, présenté et annoté par Henri Behar. Paris: Flammarion, 1975–1982.

NODALITY OR PLOT DISPLACED
THE DYNAMICS OF SOLLERS'S *H*

David Hayman

It seems axiomatic that an increasing number of books advertising themselves as novels refuse to tell tales. To the extent that such books retain vestiges of plot and narrative discourse, both are attenuated and/or sublimated. Questions of plot, character, setting, and point of view, if not of narrative tension, are displaced by the question of organization, and *that* is most often *nodal*. Such texts are frequently informed by systems of interrelated passages (scenes, images, visions, treatments of topics, etc.) which do not contribute to a coherent and generalized narrative development, but rather break the narrative surface, standing out against or being readily isolable before blending into the verbal context. The passages in question can best be thought of as nodes or clusters of signifiers in "open works."[1]

In their nature and function, fictional nodes will vary from text to text, but generally a major node is a complex, foregrounded moment capable of subdivision and subject to expansion. Typically, a fully developed node will find enriching echoes in other parts of the book. While they need resolve nothing on the level of plot or argument, such echoes gradually contribute to the formation of nodal systems. Nodes tend to be fundamental statements of the textual predicament; so we may expect aspects of a given group of nodes to overlap with those of others, contributing to networks that gradually reveal their significance and simultaneously give the reader a sense of the text's articulation, its essential structure. The latter, while displacing linear discourse by complementing other structuring systems, ultimately reassures by imposing, through a device we may call rhyming or significant redundancy, a more profound, though generally vibrant, order. Thus a text that defies conventions will evolve its own articulation and reveal unexpected but palpable coherence.

Since nodality is most obvious in "difficult," "hermetic," and "revolutionary" texts—structures that tend to be *sui generis*—it is subject to radically distinct applications. There are traces of it in writers as different as Guillermo

Cabrera Infante, Juan Goytisolo, Samuel Beckett, and Alain Robbe-Grillet. It informs Virginia Woolf's *The Waves,* Maurice Roche's *Compact,* and Philippe Sollers's *H.* Before we turn to the practice exhibited in Sollers's remarkable chronicle of 1968 and after, it is worth noting by way of contrast and illustration an aspect of Joyce's enormous and polymorphous-seeming conundrum, *Finnegans Wake,*[2] a text to which Sollers earlier turned for "illumination."[3]

Evidence from Joyce's letters and in the manuscripts suggests that, from the start, that is, even before the elaboration of the pun-filled night language, the *Wake* was to be organized around a group or seminal mini-contexts. These received their initial and clearest formulation in a series of narrative vignettes concerned with different aspects of the Irish condition, character, and history. By extension, they dealt with the human condition through history. Written for the most part before he began working on his chapters, these brief parodic interludes constitute the germ of the book's preliminary and final organization. However, they are interrelated mainly by their broad pastiche/parody tactic and their Irish subject matter. In fact, Joyce took pains to set most of them off one from the other, ultimately placing them strategically at the beginning, middle, and end of his book, thus making gentle mock of Aristotle.

Though by no means the only prime nodes in the completed work, these pastiches are sufficiently foregrounded to constitute significant points of reference for a study of the wakean nodal macro-system and of nodal structures in general. Typically, these are brief, well-defined units with a consistent focus and rhetoric and a logical narrative line to which isolable motifs and refrains contribute. Their narrative content invites elaboration and suggests associations, but such elaboration is never accomplished in the immediate context or in anything resembling a plotted line. Instead, strategically located within the larger chapter structure, other noncontiguous passages extend and complicate the basic sketch in a manner reminiscent of the development of a musical theme.

As we shall see, though Sollers uses nodal strategies, and though some of them involve narrative vignettes, his use of nodes and nodal procedures in *H* reflects a different set of formal concerns. What is significant, however, is that when obliged to establish a framework appropriate to his nonnarrative, but not completely achronological, development, he chose to develop a nodal model. We might add that all of Sollers's mature, postrealist fictions, beginning with *Drame* (1965) are in some sense nodal.[4] It is much to his credit that each, including his work-in-progress, *Paradis,* is structured differently, both from its predecessors and from possible sources.

As the most radical of his completed novels, *H* is a particularly challenging and rewarding text for study from our point of view. While omitting the usual initiatory jacket copy and thus refusing to make its procedures explicit, *H* testifies to an exceptionally elaborate structure which has thus far been ignored. Sollers provides a possible key when he ascribes the mandala-like geometric figure that adorns the book's front cover to Giordano Bruno: "Figura Intellectus . . . Articuli centrum et sexaginta adversus huius tempestatis mathematicus atque philosophos."[5] It is entirely possible that a system of six topics, each developing from some central point and repeated six times, dictates the shape of this subtle and various text. Equally suggestive is the outrageously erotic and, typically, unpunctuated evocation of the Dantesque flower of the *Paradiso*, an evocation touched by a whiff of Hinduism, here applied to a description of the embryonic novel:

> . . . well now my container's growing really page by page it'll have to come with a wing thrust above the peaks to the flowering bubble called asia instatic they say rather than exstatic and me i say correction it's no more within than without since dedans* has for ages been dehors* when it reenters and after all let's be more precise nothing within nothing without no more hands than pockets first anus red four petals square center hole prick second vulva oranged six petals lunar crescent third blue ten petals trio dark red fourth in the heart region resonating with sound though no instrument's there red melody twelve petals golden with solomon's seal fifth within the throat brown sixteen petals while disc eyed forehead lotus two petals central triangle white hole prick recall of first set but naturally one more on the fontanel the occiput at the end of the spinal marrow thousand petals flowered bird overturned regarding from above the summit a little very much passionately not at all violent lightning so what are we waiting for on we go each of us his pamphlet how to tell the spectator from the spectacle lamvamramyamham eclaboussure* that's how you smash . . . (*H*, 179–80)[6]

Sollers's project may well be perceived as a system of juxtaposed vignettes and/or divagations, themselves divisible into six topics, each of which is derived from a central impulse: say autobiography, language, sexuality, psychoanalysis, history, and Marxism. In practice such topics presented in a variety of voices, styles, rhythms, and modes combine to produce what has proved to be a most disturbing text for the general run of readers and critics.

At first glance *H* is very much like an encyclopedia whose entries are both unlabeled and out of sequence. It is remarkable both for the richness of its rhythms, styles, subject matter, and themes and for the unsettling *glissage* effect which tends, aided by the lack of punctuation, to abolish frontiers without doing away with differences, an effect in startling contrast to those of Robbe-Grillet. Repeatedly the reader experiences the loss of context and feels obliged to readapt. The impact is at times dreamlike. Still, as we float, or are tossed, from context to context, image cluster to image cluster, voice to voice, there are moments of recognition, significant echoes, and occasionally we fall upon a clearly defined narrative passage, a conversation, or a bit of coherent exposition—a solid object in a generally fluid development. A second reading reveals much more of this sort of presence and order, a well controlled nodal structure along with a substantial but virtually subliminal narrative development. Above all, this is a process book that takes on dimensions in the course of repeated readings, as reading and text tend increasingly to coincide.

We might further qualify *H* as a novel from which the narrative has been removed. In it we find the traits proper to the sublimated basic design of the traditional novel, but they are foregrounded and organized in accordance with a different sort of logic. Ultimately it is Sollers's particular version of nodal structuration that facilitates our reading, constituting both a source of interest and a very special kind of punctuation. Under its influence we tend to group together units dealing with a given subject, passages that are scattered in what seems a random order throughout the text. It is the sum of these units that defines both a nodal development and a significant elaboration on the theme, though such elaboration would be weak indeed were it seen in isolation.

Within the individual passage we may generally assume an associative linkage, but often the passage-length units are not juxtaposed associatively. Transition is achieved by semantic, stylistic, or syntactic overlaps, as in the following shift from a unit of revolutionary discourse (genre May 1968) to an interview with a Nazi gloating over his power to destroy the Jews, a passage that quickly turns into an infernal vision:

> . . . it's like jesus'd returned reparachuted smack in the middle of all the action guys daubed gaudy with grease paint stomping around in pop communes blessed by cardinal whosehewhat what's to catch is the looks of our chinese comrades when they watch this circus *us and them on one side and not precisely the same and the others on the other pretty clear that ya gotta make a choice one side has to be radically nuts you regret living in that period oh certainly not i think its the make or break moment to establish a position in all quarters on all fronts at once only need to get down to it not let yourself be distracted tie yourself to the mast one more time not tie your hands make up your mind in the face of generalized caution to follow no one* you accept the fact that no one will want it every act even the most tolerant will in fact be a more or less visible slash you place yourself in the fiery circle which means simply i'm implicated in the moment of decision you hear the ghetto being built with enormous haste they ask you for a simple adjective and you refuse have to admit that you're going to take pleasure in the monotonous variety of their contorsions . . . (*H,* 21)

The intersection of the two passages seems to occur at the moment when the Maoist affirmation gives way to an interview. But it is possible to read well into the Nazi passage before noticing the altered topic. At that point the reaction may be one of shock, for the flippant tone of the Maoist has been allowed to blend imperceptibly with a more formal discourse, while retaining its familiar address (the *"tu"*), before leading us from the amusing and off-beat left-radicalism to the apology for the acceptance and even enjoyment of suffering. The topics may be distinct. Indeed they may belong to different nodal strands. But their nature and limits can only be determined after we have read through a passage that is, at first glance, undecidable. (See the italicized passage above.) This use of undecidability is one of the main constants, one of the peculiarities of *H*'s nodal method.

What transpierces the surface of *H* is a record of a historical moment mirrored by the mind in flux of a witness/protagonist who is single, receptive, and singularly observant to the point of bearing witness to his age. The stimulus for this book was May 1968, the climate it engendered and its disillusioning aftermath. Yet Sollers did not set out simply to chronicle that moment of intense hope on the Left. Instead he chose to establish a limited but fluid number of unidentified and highly individualized voices and a sequence of topics that could be heard and returned to repeatedly as the book progressed, coalescing finally into a dynamic ideogram for the period.

A speaker (Sollers?), who seems to be describing this text as a cantata, gives us the best account or its basic procedure: "j'oppose au monologue intérieur le polylogue extérieur."[7] It is precisely to the external polylogue that we must refer when speaking of Sollers's nodality in *H*. This is significant, not only or even because the term serves to distinguish Sollers from Joyce, to whom he refers repeatedly in *Lois* (1971), in *H*, and in his *Paradis* (volume 1, 1981). After all, Joyce innovated a similar tactic for different reasons for the conclusion of "Oxen of the Sun," the chapter styles in the second half of *Ulysses*, and the whole of *Finnegans Wake*, with particular emphasis on chapter II.3 (The Pub). Sollers's term describes with elegance and precision the tactic of casting each cell of this polycellular novel in a distinct but unidentified voice. These are the voices of speech rather than of reflection, and the result is a theatrical procedure that yields dramatic results. Jean-Louis Houdebine is correct in emphasizing a related trait, noting that one of the strategies that separates Joyce's *Wake* from Sollers's *H* and *Paradis* is the substitution of themes for the missing narrative, or rather using the "sequence, repeated essentially on the level of discoursive charges, and hence articulated—especially by rhythm—within other discourses, scientific or philosophical, for example, which bring rational judgement into play as the obligatory 'moment' of reading as well as writing."[8] It is precisely to the clarity of these discourses that we must point, to the rigorousness of their presentation and the demands that that presentation puts on the reader.[9]

May 1968, then. Certainly we hear voices of the epoch, especially in the opening pages of *H*, voices that gradually fade into other contemporary voices as the motion or flow of time carries us into the early 1970s. Beyond that, we have a historical backdrop, a moving one derived from newspaper headlines commented on sardonically by what may be the prime narrator or the authorial persona. The development of these occasional references to strictly contemporary events is chronological: witness this ambiguous but still pointed reference to Yom Kippur of 1972 found near the end of the book: " . . . you can't imagine how hot the sinai is on bare feet in the sand how it is today yom kippur kol nidre golda menhir's troups withdrew after having felled what could be 80 to 100 fedayins . . . what's happened to our revolution . . . " (*H*, 161). This intermittent flow of voices from the retreating present constitutes or takes the place of what would be, in any other novel, a narrative strand. The precise nature of that strand, mingled as its development is with other very different materials and subject to so much variation, is difficult to ascertain, though we may qualify it as contributing to a minor nodal system. Its effect is to turn history into a source of continuity and of narrative suspense. Repeatedly we take our bearings from these historically determined references couched in racy idioms which, by their tonality, bring to mind that other chronicler Céline, while by their placement they suggest the lacework filled with significant holes which Céline used as an image for his procedures. Sollers has gone much further in his use of history, eliminating punctuation and plot, elements so decisive in his predecessor's work.

History is not, however, the primary constituent of Sollers's lacework. It must vie with several others, most obviously with the autobiography both of the author and of his text. On the very first page, in a context suggestive of the writer's study, we find a reference to Sollers as persona followed by allusions to his real name, Philippe Joyaux. In fact, the book opens with a precise, almost new-novelesque description of a personified typewriter (an homage perhaps): " . . . who says hi the machine with its paws pulled into its turtle sides cata socle its keys frozen tonic accents out of line . . . " (*H*, p. 9). Certainly the theme of writing is powerfully present throughout *H*, as it has been in Sollers's other novels,[10] and the account of its composition constitutes one of this book's major nodal systems, even though the process is not presented as a development. Immediately after the description of the typewriter/turtle, we find a typically ambiguous reference to an *"elle"* which could refer to the machine, but soon attaches itself to a woman (perhaps Sollers's wife Julia) who has just dreamed a dream of violence and elevation. The typewriter reference, it appears, was a false, or at least ambiguous, allusion to the persona *"qui dit salut,"* and the use of a vaguely attributed pronoun is designed to introduce the reader to the *glissage* that we have seen organizing and propelling the nodal movement. From the start, then, the world of the author, the book, the lover, the husband, and Philippe Sollers are inextricably intertwined, even though each aspect will constitute a more or less distinct strand in the nodal structure of *H*. The autobiographical system quickly, through the reference to the dream and to the "name of the father," begins to generate a psychoanalytic strand consistent with the author's interest in Lacanian psychoanalytic theory during the years that preceded and followed 1968. Thus on page 1 the process of elaboration has begun, the process which will accommodate all of the other themes and nodes, culminating in a piece of literary music, a cantata, if not in the Dantean rose.

The term cantata, like the image of the exfoliating flower, is evocative, but, despite its use in the novel, it is not descriptive of how *H* is formed and how it informs its apprehension. We could more accurately speak of a system based in the individual node which contributes to a larger strand composed of like elements that tend to complete it. Ultimately strands combine in the reader's mind to form the aggregate that performs the text. We speak of nodal strands in *H* rather than of nodal systems or hierarchies because items of similar importance are usually generated by a given topic. The result is clearly more linear, though within one strand we may find allusions (secondary nodes) to another and though the individual elements tend to be linked by association with others to form a unified network which might be thought of as three dimensional.

As indicated earlier, the book's opening pages constitute an aggregate, overture, or mini-system, a cluster of related matter linked by association and cemented together by repeated references to the topic of the writer's experience. It is the latter that finally constitutes the dominant nodal strand, and any reader familiar with Sollers's background will have little trouble following its development.[11] Readers unfamiliar with that background should be able to discover other emphases or preoccupations. Still, the fact that the writer is speaking of himself in something resembling his own voice will be clear, if not at first, certainly after the passage of two or three such moments, by which time that voice and its range will be both familiar and welcome.

In the opening pages, the autobiographical elements form a cluster interspersed with nodes from other strands, to which they are linked by association or by syntactical *glissage* or both. Thus the passage on pages 9–11 dealing with the author's name and practice is followed by one on the *"événements"* of May 1968. The latter, a fine example of the historical vignette, provides a dynamic overview *through,* as much as *in,* time:

> . . . a hundred thousand on the square today the police say fifteen there goes their helicopter the party gives the same figure a few more perhaps hostile stupefaction closed mind besides where can this lead the workers haven't budged nothing to do about it you can't keep it up comrades it's deadlocked this won't get you anywhere and yet its happening red flags everywhere flapping in the wind sun they snap it's cooler the buildings are beginning to open up the bourgeois to the balconies cameras to eyes archivists shouts the little one who's been singing into his mike the last hour fagged out and dropping in harness [*tombé à la tâche*] defeated you flatten death bound and killed by cowards victory you're the strongest strongest victory you're the strongest your only prayer comrade vengeance vengeance for you for you vengeance vengeance for you the crowd picks it up weakly twenty voices thirty voices old song archaic already bad piece of work mobilization murky nostalgic with ukranian roots totally unsuited to this particular situation they don't know this bit anymore than they do the other couplets of the internationale friend if you fall a friend leaves the shadows to take your place it's beautiful out now the guys in the first rows are hidden by their red roses with the darker portraits it flows splendidly beneath the blue sky with flat silence between the slogans . . . (*H,* 12–13)

This candidly reported bit of fragmented experience with its dominant voice, interrupted by the remarks of organizers, subject to a floating temporality and perspective, illustrates Sollersian concision. Its stenographic rendering recalls Céline's sten-gun delivery, while retaining overtones of the Joycean stream of consciousness which could and did mingle observations and the refrains of songs. It is followed by an argument among *copains* and a passage of reflection on the writer's function in *H*. Though growing quite naturally out of a preoccupation with saying the revolution, the content of these reflections is markedly personal and self-justificatory: " . . . after all you want to write it to do it and write it to take up the volume again you see the adventure novels to bring it over her fold it spread it out bring out new relationships here look i have a mania for climbing live from the tomb i can't really do otherwise it's afterward that the troubles begin . . . " (*H*, 13). The theme of writing is not always and precisely autobiographical, unless we think of the writer as the man and the text as his life. That being the case in *H*, I would relate this passage in pseudodialogue and others dealing with the problem of the text-in-progress to the autobiographical strand.

Though this development is clear and becomes clearer, it is by no means limpid. The reader is obliged to follow the meandering argument or, rather, to assemble and relate the various panels of this immense activated polyptych, pulling together the nodal strands at the same time he/she strings the nodal beads. Punctuation has to be supplied and breaks in the discourse must be noted so that the new topics can be accommodated. Still, the presence of echo passages illustrating the principle of repetition is reassuring, as is the evolving rhythm.[12]

The next passage in *H* seems, at first glance, totally unrelated to writing or revolution; but on inspection, we find it is a creation of the Sollersian voice moving from an ardent defense of his procedures to a reconstitution of the pastoral tradition. The prose development is extraordinarily gentle and convincing. Along with the silent interlocutor, we are taken into a fanciful space, an edenic landscape from which the anxious rhetoric of the preceding passage has been banished, only to reappear when the writer steps out from behind the pastoral mask, dispelling the illusion to explain why we should not do away with such effusions—or, rather, when he shows how his own utterance can contain them:

> . . . it's the depth of the valley you know you can't dismiss it simply because it's elicited a couple of professorial inanities odd how you can stroll through it like an open field avoiding the well-trod paths too obviously dated landmarks too clearly de l'époque as if you had reentered a magnanimous river multiple striated desolving their reference reverence at their phallic base and thus in every second its pain is there and it is not there illuminated in reverse . . . (*H*, 15–18)

After seemingly leaving behind us the revolutionary moment, we suddenly emerge to find ourselves following a funeral cortege winding its way behind the coffin of a fallen comrade to Père Lachaise cemetery. The very next words flowing from our passage are *"continuons si tu veux dans le cime-*

tière." It is the funeral of the revolution. The historical fresco that has provided us with a backdrop for so much of what preceded once again fades, only to sharpen periodically as voices from a chorus of contemporaries intervene, invade the flux of the narrative. Sollers's text is underway, and its reader is implicitly drawn into the flow of its "striated river," not as one might be into the sequentiality of a narrative, but as one might be into life itself conceived of as "suffering blindly from one hour into another hour like the water from a breaker breaking against the breakwater" (*H,* 14).

This effect is sharpened by the reiteration of elements from the longer nodal strands emerging with varying degrees of clarity from the sea of words. There are at least twenty-five passages of varying lengths and importance, and in a variety of voices and modes, contributing to our sense of the writing process and the presence of the writing Sollers, while pointing up the larger project of the text—its desire to rewrite Dante for our times.[13]

The typical Sollersian nodal elements, like those of Joyce, will contain overtones from other strands. In some cases passages belonging to the autobiography/writing strand may even be dominated by or housed in a treatment of a topic belonging to another. Still, the central fact of the organization of *H* is the juxtaposition of related semiautonomous units producing a muted linearity of effect reinforced by the appeals to historical chronology as a parallel for the chronology of the book's development. If we add to this the relatively straightforward, though intellectually demanding, presentation (the refusal to play Joycean wordgames, for example), the result is a considerably less complex overall system in which we find less overlapping, fewer nodal layers, and a more restricted range of nodal topics.

Sollers's choice to anchor his narrative in special historical time and to place his autobiographical persona in the center of his plotless fiction was a determining factor in the generation of the nodal structure. But perhaps the major consideration was the nature of the central problematic of the book— how to write the aftermath of May 1968! For out of that need grew all of the nodal topics, and around Sollers's response are grouped the various strands. In it lies the secret of their interrelationship and the source of the book's dynamic unity. It is finally that process which animates the historical as well as the novelistic vision in the broader sense, that process into which life is breathed by the details of the novel's execution, its *"polylogue extérieur."*

We may question whether narrative interest can persist in a context dominated by meshing systems of significance, but in fact, though *H* is not strictly speaking a narrative, plot persists as a powerful trace element. It is manifested not only by the developing wide-screen historical background, but also, if less overtly, by the various autobiographical elements seen as part of the process of experiencing and recording the evolving present—by Sollers's decision to anchor his text in a specific historical time and to place his autobiographical persona in its center. On this level all of the nodal strands coalesce, and the reader discovers not only a source of interest, but ultimately an engagement in each stage of the text's evolution. Doubtless that engagement is partly a function of the effort required to *dis*engage the components from their context so that their contribution to the whole may better be understood, that they may a reintegrated. But, like so many other successful nonnarrative texts, this *"roman"* is premised on the reader's being conditioned to perceive narrative development as the given of novels, a powerful thirst for balance and coherence that can be assuaged in this case only by the seeming deconstruction and reconstitution of the text's components. It is to the latter process that nodality contributes the necessary building blocks, but it is to the process of distinguishing among those elements, aligning them, and appreciating their conflicts and interrelationships that *H* owes much of its considerable aesthetic interest.

One must not take Sollers more seriously than he takes himself; his books are full of self-mockery. " . . . sol sol sol air let he who has ears hear and who knows how to read should see the meaning deliberately hidden for him . . . you drive them mad with your prophesies parables allegorical in the very heart of a social statement . . . " (*H*, 28), says a hip Christ returned to hand his mantle to a clownish self-baptized sun-air (Sollers) writer. But the joke is sometimes as serious as the assertion. In the following bit of *"polylogue extérieur,"* he projects the image of the great weaver and maker of the world whose project is to write a book like Dante's for our age. The tonality of this passage, so markedly different from that of the earlier autobiography/writing nodes, reflects Sollers's reverence for one of his culture heroes. It also suggests the expressive range of a single nodal line:

> . . . o busy invisible weaver stop one word why these endless labors one moment speak but no the shuttle flies the figures emerge floating from the loom from the rolling mill the vats admit not a second's interruption you would say that production wishes more and more to mime perpetual motion to draw near the heart of nature which established us here and we who contemplate the factory are deafened by its humming it is only when we distance ourselves that we hear the billions of voices that speak through life envelop death death weaves life I am the image I am the carpet I am the machine and the image of the machine and the machination of the image and its sound . . . I must therefore find a crucible in which to melt myself to the point of being no more than a tiny epitome of bone there you are no no what there is of beauty and of terror in man has never yet been mentioned in books no only one author returned from the land of the dead can tell us that it requires only the one who has passed through the flames . . . (*H*, 44–45)

Appropriately the overly reverent pose is repeatedly undercut by irony and finally atomized by what follows on the next page—the advertisement of a pornography merchant which echoes views typical of two other "heroes," Bataille and Sade, in a graphic enactment of the post-Dantesque Inferno.

We discover by reading *H* as a nodal text certain echoes of Joyce as author of and presence in the *Wake*. The principal or prime node of the *Wake* may be the ALP Letter, which stands not only in the place of the *Word* in the universe but also in the place of the *Wake* itself.[14] In a chapter full of strictures on reading (I.5), the following bit of comic jargon is addressed irreverently to the reader:

> You is feeling like you was lost in the bush, boy? You says: It is a puling sample jungle of woods. You most shouts out; Bethicket me for a stump of a beech if I have the poultriest notions what the farest he all mans. Gee up, girly! The quad gospellers may own the targum but any of the Zingari shoolerim may pick a peck of kindlings yet from the sack of auld hensyne. (Joyce, *Wake*, 112)

The letter is, of course, dictated to the Word's highpriest, the darkling Shem, who stands behind it as a persona for Joyce. In effect Joyce's focus on the process of writing, though less frontal, is very close to Sollers's. More importantly, his use of the Letter as a rich and protean image finds its echo in Sollers's use of the autobiographical/writing system which opens and closes and ultimately controls the form of *H.*

Sollers's novel constitutes the negative for Joyce's nodal structure by basing itself in the real and observable, the perception of which is systematically decomposed. If the text conveys the author in the process or writing himself as an integral part of the historical moment he documents, it does so by breaking up that moment and his personal interaction with it into a limited number of nodal strands. Writing himself as history, Sollers found a structural principle that is cognate with that of *Finnegans Wake*. Significantly, he too found in Giordano Bruno, Joyce's "Nolan," an exemplary thinker for whom paradox was the crux. One is reminded of Shaun the post's jaundiced description of his artist brother Shem's act of "writing the mystery of himself in furniture" (Joyce, *Wake*, 184).

There are doubtless all sorts of metaphorical equivalents for the nodal structuration we have been describing. But one that strikes me as particularly apt is the image of the "tangled bank" coined by Darwin and elucidated by Stanley Edgar Hyman, who finds the same idea expressed in Freud's "interwoven chains of association for the separate [neurotic] symptoms that begin to enter into relation with one another."[15] We may see in these chains of images, actions, allusions, etc., an inevitable outgrowth of the refusal to accept the tale, not only as simply the thing told, but also as a possible counter for human experience in an increasingly fragmented world—or rather one whose unity is both real and in constant jeopardy. A writer of unplotted or counterplotted fictions is attempting, consciously or not, to elaborate something resembling a total experience/vision without lapsing into chaotic gibberish. He/she wishes to have it both ways, to present a view that is comprehensive *and* controlled. In general, nodality signals a refurbished and updated baroque sensibility, beleaguered but still vital. We have only begun to study the range and potential of nodal structures, the proliferation of which, like that of paratactics, seems in our times as natural as the fully articulated plot has been until recently. Indeed, it is as a by-product of such established conventions that it finds its intelligibility an era supersaturated with competing orders and the omnipresence of instability and unrest, if not total disorder.

NOTES

1. Umberto Eco, "La Poètique de l'oeuvre ouverte," in *L'Oeuvre ouverte* (Paris: Seuil, 1962), 15–36.

2. James Joyce, *Finnegans Wake* (New York: Viking Press, 1939). For a fuller discussion of Joyce's practice, see David Hayman, "Nodality and the Infrastructure of *Finnegans Wake*," *The James Joyce Quarterly*, 16 (1978): 135–50.

3. See his account of the composition of *Lois* (1972) in *Vision à New York* (interview with David Hayman) (Paris: Grasset, 1981), 112–14.

4. Sollers's more recent "realistic" fiction called *Femmes* (Paris: Gallimard, 1982), could be perceived as another sort of nodal structure, one that is complicated by the introduction of plot and character; this demands elaborate rationalization, for which there is no space here.

5. Philippe Sollers, *H* (Paris: Seuil, 1973), back cover. All translations of this work are mine.

6. *H*, 179-80. The asterisked words, in English in the original, have been translated into French.

7. *H*, 42. It is this striking term, *polylogue*, (with its echoes of Bakhtinian "dialogism") that Julia Kristeva chose as a title for her fine essay on *H*. See "The Novel as Polylogue," in *Desire in Language* (New York: Columbia University Press, 1980). See also Roland Barthes, *Sollers Ecrivain* (Paris: Seuil, 1979), 54.

8. Jean-Louis Houdebine, "La Signature de Joyce," *Tel Quel* 81 (1979), 54. My translation.

9. We may point, along with Houdebine, to the parallel with Dante, whose *Comedy* may also be read as a chronicle of disillusionment in a troubled time and the profile of an age.

10. *Drame* (1965), in particular, comes close to being a poem dedicated to the evocation of the process of its own generation.

11. The reader interested in such matters can consult the volume of interviews, *Vision à New York*; Julia Kristeva's extraordinary essay, "Memoire," *L'infini* 1 (1983): 39–54; and the personal statements that constellate the pages of Sollers's *Femmes*. Such data, though helpful and engrossing, is by no means crucial to an understanding of *H*.

12. I would also suggest, in opposition to the view of Barthes, that thanks to this principle the reader experiences something close to "development (of theme, idea, anecdote, etc.), that is, memory" (*Sollers Ecrivain*, 61). It does not seem necessary for this text to be "without memory," even though Barthes's use of the analogy to atonal music is very suggestive.

13. The passages in question fall on the following pages, which include both the first and the last word: 9–11, 13–14, 15–16, 28–29, 34–35, 42–43, 44–45, 49–50, 66–67, 95–97, 101–102, 103–104, 109–110, 117–118, 119–120, 134–135, 135–136, 139–140, 160, 162–163, 174–175, 176–177, 179–180, 180–181, and 183. Certain of the above which seem to be contiguous are actually separated by elements from other nodal systems.

14. See my "Nodality," 139–143.

15. Stanley Edgar Hyman, *The Tangled Bank: Darwin, Marx, Frazer and Freud As Imaginative Writers* (New York: Grosset and Dunlap, 1966), 32–33, 306–7.

Why not rather be interested in "theoretical" monsters, in the monstrosities which announce themselves in theory, in the monsters who, beforehand, outdate and make comical all classifications or rhythms such as: after New Criticism comes an "ism" and then a "*post*ism," and then again another "ism" and today still another "ism," etc. These last normalizations are themselves monstrous from the perspective of what happens in the most singular and inventive work and texts, in the most idiomatic writings; but these monstrosities are normal. They can be found everywhere.

J.D.

A CORRESPONDENCE ON POSTMODERNISM

Stefano Rosso/Umberto Eco

Rosso: The contemporary debate on literature (especially in the United States, but recently in Italy as well) revolves increasingly around the terms "modern" and "postmodern." There have been numerous attempts to define the term "postmodern"[1] as a "movement" which historically succeeds "modernism," as a "belated" modernism, as a polarity which has always been present in the internal struggles of culture, as the adjective *par excellence* to describe our contemporary "condition," etc. What is your understanding of this term and where do you place your criticism and your recent novel (*Il nome della rosa*)[2] in this spectrum of definitions? Do you think there are relationships among the ways in which the term "postmodern" is used in the areas of 1) architecture (Paolo Portoghesi, Robert Venturi, Denise Scott Brown, and others); 2) the philosophical, aesthetic, and sociological debate which has developed most recently in Italy; and 3) literary postmodernism and narrative theory in the United States?

Eco: All my life I have worked to establish distinctions within the areas covered by umbrella-terms such as iconism, code, presupposition, etc. Naturally I am intrigued by the term "postmodern." It is my impression that it is applied these days to everything the speaker approves of. On the other hand, there seems to be an attempt to move it backwards in time; first it seemed to suit writers or artists active in the last twenty years, then gradually it was moved back to the beginning of the century, then even further back, and the march goes on; before long Homer himself will be considered postmodern.

But I believe that this tendency is to some extent justified. I agree with those who consider postmodern not a chronologically circumscribed tendency but a spiritual category, or better yet a *Kunstwollen* (a Will-to-Art), perhaps a stylistic device and/or a world view. We could say that every age has its own postmodern, just as every age has its own form of mannerism (in fact, I wonder if postmodern is not simply the modern name for *Manierismus* as a metahistorical category). I believe that every age reaches moments of crisis like those described by Nietzsche in the second of the *Untimely Considerations*, on the harmfulness of the study of history. The sense that the past is restricting, smothering, blackmailing us. The historical avant-garde (but here too I would consider avant-garde as a metahistorical category, in the sense in which Renato Poggioli helps us to understand it) tries to settle its accounts with the past. "Down with moonlight," the futurist motto, is a statement typical of any avant-garde; you need only to substitute something appropriate for the moonlight, which for the futurists was the romantic tradition. The avant-garde destroys the past, it disfigures it. The *Demoiselles d'Avignon* represents the typical gesture of the avant-garde; then the avant-garde goes even further. Having disfigured the figure, it erases it, finally arriving at the abstract, the informal, the empty canvas, the torn canvas, the burned canvas. The same thing happens in all the arts; in architecture it is the minimal condition of the curtain wall, of the building as funeral stela, a pure parallelepiped; in literature it is the destruction of the flow of discourse, which leads to the Burroughs-style collage, silence, the empty page. In music it is the passage from atonality to noise, and then to absolute silence (in this sense, the early Cage is modern).

But there comes a moment when the avant-garde can go no further, because it has already produced a metalanguage to talk about its own impossible texts (for example, conceptual art and body art). At this point arises the reaction, which is never simply a reversal. That is to say, at least, a conservative reversal is always possible, but is not a dialectical response to the avant-garde; this retrenchment is the normal production of the midcult and of popular art that always continues, indifferent to the tensions of experimental modes, serving the needs of its own unchanging market.

The postmodern response to the modern consists instead of recognizing that the past—since it may not be destroyed, for its destruction results in silence—must be revisited ironically, in a way which is not innocent. For me the postmodern attitude is that of a man who loves a woman who is intelligent and well-read: he knows that he cannot tell her, "I love you desperately," because he knows that she knows (and she knows that he knows) that that is a line out of Barbara Cartland. Yet there is a solution. He can say, "As Barbara Cartland would say, I love you desperately." At this point, he has avoided the pretense of innocence, he has clearly affirmed that no one can speak in an innocent mode; but he has still told the woman what he wished to tell her—that he loves her, but in an age of lost innocence. If the woman is playing along, she has received a declaration of love just the same. In this case neither of the two interlocutors considers himself innocent; both have taken on the challenge of the past, of the "already-said," of the bracketed. Both are playing consciously and with pleasure at the game of irony. . . . Yet both have managed once again to speak about love.

Irony, metalinguistic play, enunciation to the second power, these are the characteristics of the postmodern. But I might add another. In the case of the

modern, anyone who does not understand the game can only reject it. With
the postmodern it is possible to misunderstand the game, by taking things
seriously. I think this happened with my novel: those who did not catch the
citations, the play on narrative itself, read it as if it were an innocent story.
Which is of course the nature of the risk of irony. There is always someone
who fakes ironic discourse seriously. I think that the collages of Picasso, Juan
Gris, and Braque were modern: for this reason normal people did not accept
them. But the collages that Max Ernst assembled from parts of nineteenth-
century engravings were postmodern: one might read them as a bizarre
short-story, or as the account of a dream, without realizing that they represented a discourse on the art of engraving, and perhaps on the collage form
itself. If this is what we mean by postmodern, it is clear why Sterne and
Rabelais were postmodern, and why Borges must certainly be: why in one
artist the two moments—modern and postmodern—may coexist, or follow
each other at brief intervals, or alternate.

Rosso: As your impulse to equate postmodernism and mannerism suggests,
you seem to be defining postmodernism as essentially an aesthetic phenomenon, a matter of artistic style and form. Do you see the postmodern disruption of received notions of forms as a praxis—an interrogation of the
ontological grounds of traditional art and the cultural and socio-political
institutions these grounds privilege?

Eco: In the first place, I do not think that mannerism is simply an aesthetic
phenomenon. It implies an approach to life, a type of political and religious
behavior, a way of constructing one's psychological and cultural ego. Shakespeare's characters are mannerist heroes; much of the culture that we call
baroque, such as Gracian's *L'oracolo manual*, exemplifies a mannerist ethics,
politics, and praxis. You might say that mannerism is born whenever it is
discovered that the world has no fixed center, that I have to find my way
through the world inventing my own points of reference. Very disturbing,
and naturally "human, all too human." It is the same thing that is happening with a term like postmodern, which for a philosopher like Lyotard is not
just an aesthetic category. I would like to use a general model like the labyrinth, but perhaps we will get to that later. In any case, I would consider
postmodern the orientation of anyone who has learned the lesson of Foucault, i.e., that power is not something unitary that exists outside of us.

People spoke too long of a praxis founded on reason (Vernunft) as if there
were only one "reason." Then they discovered that there was not one "reason," and (in Italy, for example) people began to talk about the crisis of
reason (here in America they probably talk instead about epistemological
anarchism à la Feyerabend). In any case, there is a crisis of reason if we are
referring to the reason of Descartes, Hegel, and Marx. But if we accept the
premise that our behavior in the world ought to be not *rational* but *reasonable*, then I will say (and with a certain satisfaction) that if there is a crisis of
reason, there is no crisis of reasonability. The odd thing is that the great
philosophers—Aristotle, for example—who were long believed the founders

of reason, actually advocated the more human(e) value of reasonability. If this admission makes me a postmodern in the area of philosophy, fine. My friend Gianni Vattimo has discussed for some time the notion of a "soft thought" [*pensiero debole*][3] and I am contributing to the collection of essays that he is preparing on the subject. I trace the origins of this "soft thought" to the failure of certain "strong" modes of thinking to take hold after Aristotle with the late Greek and medieval theories of language. But it is a long story. In any case, let us say that Guglielmo in my novel is not rational but reasonable. This is why he believes in no single truth.

Rosso: You have been working on Joyce for a long time now. After a period of partial silence following your *Le poetiche di Joyce,* you recently published an English translation (*The Aesthetics of Chaosmos: The Middle Ages of James Joyce,* [Tulsa: University of Tulsa, 1982]), in which the parts you added reaffirm your continuing interest in a figure who is considered by some "postmodern" critics as the most significant exponent of "modernism." In the United States, in the field generically defined as "postmodern," there has been an alliance between a literature ("which is the measure of its occasion"[4]) of "open form," or, as it is alternatively put, of "dis-closure" or "destruction," and a literary hermeneutics of a Heideggerian type, reread through the French philosophers. Working from these premises, the attack which Heidegger unleashes on "Western metaphysics" (the "logocentrism of Western culture," as Derrida puts it) is aimed in postmodern literary discussion at authors such as Eliot, Yeats, Proust, etc., and in particular at Joyce, especially the Joyce of *Ulysses.* The Irish writer is accused of retrieving a "will to power over being" in his attitude as "father" of the text, as demiurge, absolute possessor of form, etc. In this perspective, which is inadvertently supported by New Critical readings of his texts, Joyce becomes a philosopher of presence: his metaphysical impulse, which is a desire to "structure," prevents him from seeing reality as temporal process, being as difference. According to these postmodern critics, only certain contemporary writers (for example, John Barth, Robert Coover, Donald Barthelme, Thomas Pynchon, Stanley Elkin, Joseph Heller, Ishmael Reed, etc., whose "fathers" are Borges, Nabokov, and Beckett) manage to break with the tradition of Western metaphysics culminating in modernism and "construct" texts which are "open" or "dis-closive" in form. You wrote a critical book entitled *The Open Work.*[5] How would you defend Joyce against the charge that his texts are closed forms? What constitutes the distinction between open and closed? Your novel surprised many people by its excessive structurality (some critics such as Maria Corti have used the term "closure" to describe it)[6] in an era in which most "postmodern" literature demonstrates instead a deliberate anti-structurality. How would you defend Eco?

Eco: Joyce is a typical example of what I was saying earlier. The *Portrait* is the story of an experiment in modernism. The *Dubliners,* even though it was written earlier, is more "modern" than the *Portrait. Ulysses* is at the border-line. *Finnegans Wake* is already postmodern; at least one could say that it opens postmodern discourse, since to be understood it requires that the "already-said" be not contradicted but reconsidered in an ironic way. But Joyce is a perfect example precisely because he eludes all classification: even in *Ulysses* there is the continual remeditation of the "already-said." In other words the one thing that I would not do is define Joyce as a typical exponent of modernism. But I realize, as I say this, that perhaps I use "modern" and "postmodern" in a different sense from that in which you and others use it. Well, this itself seems to me a postmodern attitude—don't you agree? The postmodern, even that of Lyotard, tends toward a pluralism of categories.

Having said this, naturally I am perplexed by the critical statements you mention. But if there is one thing that cannot be done, it is to teach an initiate of deconstruction how to read a text. If for certain deconstructionists (but can we speak for all of them? Who is handing out the membership cards?) Joyce and Eliot are not "open" and do not see reality as a process and being as difference, that shows that they are reading these authors in a certain way: in a perspective which allows the act of reading to prevail over the texture of the text, what parameter could one use to contest them? On the other hand, do not ask me whether a work is open or closed. I wrote my answer in the preface to the second edition of my *Opera aperta:* I have never seen an open work. I wrote that book not as a critic but as a philosopher. My model was an abstract one: as such it can be incarnated in different ways in different works, but never fully in any single work. It is a way of defining a relationship between a text and its readings. Therefore, by the way, I would be the last person capable of saying whether my own novel is an open work or not. I do not believe, however, that the excessive structurality contradicts the open structure of the work. For example, I have always and clearly considered *Ulysses* to be a book in which the model of the open text plays a major role: but *Ulysses* is extremely structured, it has an iron scaffolding. Apart from the fact that in my book the scaffolding is so ironclad, so evident, as to leave one suspecting that it may be made of *papier-maché.* Like the facades of Las Vegas, to make a "postmodern" reference.

Rosso: Your equation of structure and openness constitutes a curious paradox, which, however, comes to the verge of making sense in your admission that the iron scaffolding of *Il nome della rosa* is so obvious that it activates the suspicion that it may be made of paper. Are you suggesting that the iron scaffolding of Joyce's *Ulysses* and of your novel is thus an intertextual destruction of the iron scaffolding of traditional fictional form?

Eco: Why not? It sounds reasonable. However, I think that in every work of art you need some constraints in order to feel free, to invent some kind of freedom. By the way, recently Harald Weinrich wrote in *Merkur* that my novel is very "open." Some like it open, some like it closed. That is openness.

Rosso: Il nome della rosa appears to be a detective novel but is also a pastiche of theological, political, aesthetic, and philosophical debates, historical references, moral reflections, private jokes with the reader, etc. At the end of the story the "casualness" of the denouement deeply disappoints the reader's expectation of a detective story logic. In recollecting my reading of the text, I realized that the detective plot faded progressively into the background and that a series of elements emerged which were not strictly related to the plot. Meanwhile I was reminded of a reflection of Guglielmo, the *ante-litteram* detective: "Where is all my wisdom? I have behaved like an obstinate man, pursuing an appearance of order, when I should have realized that there is no order in the universe."[7] Your novel has sold more than 500,000 copies in Italy and has been read by a public which is culturally diverse (from academics to detective-novel fanatics).[8] How would you advise a reader to go about investigating the multileveled possibility of reading, of *jouissance* and identification, i.e., everything you call "the textual cooperation of the reader," generated by *Il nome della rosa*? (I am aware that you usually refuse to become the critic of your own novel.)

Eco: Now, this question of yours contributes to the reply that I was giving on the preceding point. You have caught on well (and I thank you) to the play between the appearance of order and the suspicion that there is no order, or rather (as Guglielmo says at a certain point) that there are many kinds of order, and that all of them must be tried in order to reach some (provisional) solution.

I have tried during the past two years to avoid giving interpretations of my book, to avoid becoming the theorist myself. But if you twist my arm, I will tell you that it is no accident that the book begins like a detective novel (and continues to trick the naive reader until the very end so that the naive reader may even fail to realize that it is a detective novel where precious little is discovered, and where the detective is beaten in the end). Now the choice of the detective novel was not accidental. I believe that people like detective novels not because they are full of dead bodies, and not because (as has so often been said) detective novels celebrate the triumph of the final order (intellectual, social, legal, and moral) over the disorder of guilt. It is rather that the detective novel represents a story of pure conjecture. But even a medical detection, a scientific experiment, a metaphysical interrogation are cases of conjecture. After all, the basic question of philosophy (like that of psychoanalysis) is the same one posed by the detective novel: who is guilty? To find out (or to believe that you have found out) you have to conjecture that facts are governed by logic, a logic which has imposed on them a guilty party. Every story of inquiry and conjecture tell us about something we have "dwelt" near forever (do you like my pseudo-Heideggerian quotation?). At this point it is clear why my underlying story (who is the murderer?) branches out into so many other stories, all of them stories of other conjectures, all about the very structure of conjecture itself. One abstract model of conjecturability is the labyrinth. Like any other conjectural space it can be traversed in many ways. Naturally you find your way out of classical labyrinths. But at this point we should specify that there are three kinds of labyrinths. One is the Greek type, that of Theseus. This labyrinth does not allow anyone to lose his way: you enter it and arrive at the center, and then from the center you make your way to the exit. That is why there is the Minotaur at the center; otherwise there would be no point, you would just be out for a harmless stroll. The terror comes in because you do not know where you will come out and what the Minotaur will do. But if you unravel the classical labyrinth, you will find a thread in your hands, Ariadne's thread. The classical labyrinth is its own Ariadne's thread.

Then there is the mannerist labyrinth. If you unravel it, you find in your hands a kind of tree, a root-like structure with many dead ends. There is only one exit, but you can get it wrong. You need an Ariadne's thread to keep from getting lost. This labyrinth is the model of the trial-and-error process.

Finally, there is the network, the structure that Deleuze and Guattari call a rhizome. The rhizome is set up so that each path connects to every other one. It has no center, no periphery, and no exit, because it is potentially infinite. Conjectural space is shaped like a rhizome. The labyrinth of my library is a manneristic labyrinth, but the world in which Guglielmo realizes he is living is already structured like a rhizome, that is, it is structurable but never definitely structured.

And now we come to the public's reaction. I said before that postmodern narrative admits the possibility of a naive reading. It may indeed be possible, but it is not remunerative. That is, an innocent reading of irony is no fun. If I say about someone whom I believe to be an imbecile, "he is really bright," those who understand the irony will enjoy it; if on the other hand, you take my statement seriously, you wonder why in the world I said something so obvious. Now, if anyone read my novel as if it were a simple detective novel, the narrative mechanisms probably worked for him, but I can imagine that his pleasure was minimal. So this innocent reading might explain how someone read the novel, but not why he read it and liked it well enough to pass the word on, triggering that avalanche of 600,000 copies, which neither the favorable press nor the snobbishly negative reaction can otherwise explain. One seventeen-year-old boy told me that he did not understand a word of the theological discussions, but that they helped to stretch out the spatial labyrinth (like the scary music in a Hitchcock film). I think that something like this did happen: even the naive reader sensed that he was up against a story of labyrinths, and not just spatial labyrinths either. We might say that, strangely enough, the most naive readings of my novel were concerned not with its contents (philosophical, political, or religious), and not with the metalinguistic and metanarrative game of its literary references, but with the bare bones of the story, that is, with the fact that the story was not (as it seemed to less naive readers) "closed" within an iron framework, but rhizomatic in structure. Without any form of mediation, the naive reader came to grips with the fact that it is impossible to tell one story. But maybe this is a case of wishful thinking. You should never ask authors this sort of thing, they are such bores. You should let us theoreticians do the talking.

Rosso: How do you account for the "naive" readers getting the "structure" of the novel right and the more sophisticated readers getting it wrong? Does it have anything to do with academically inscribed expectations?

Eco: I never said that there is a way to get my novel wrong.

Rosso: What kind of progression do you think can be traced between *Opera aperta* (1962), *Lector in fabula* (1979), and *Il nome della rosa* (1980)?[9]

Eco: The formulation of the question already contains the answer.

Rosso: On more than one occasion you have claimed that your novel allowed you to talk about "something" (and in "some way") which you would not have been able to express in your essays. Other writers, on the other hand, (for example, Derrida, Deleuze in *Mille plateaux*, not to speak of Blanchot and Lacan) have adopted a style in which the line of demarcation between language and metalanguage is increasingly hard to perceive. What do you think of these two "styles"? Also: you are well known for the speed with which you write books and essays, but you spent many years writing your novel. How do you explain this fact?

Eco: On this point I have very definite views (which does not mean they are not wrong). Anyone who writes essays must work to reduce the labyrinth. He must impoverish the wealth of the real in order to permit definitions, even provisional ones. He must make an effort to reduce the ambiguity. When you want ambiguity to run free, you write poetry or fiction. When theoreticians behave like writers of fiction, I do not like it (even though I might admire what they write as if it were a novel). Our brain is divided into two parts: we can use one or the other, but we always need to know which half we are using. Anything else is a Wagnerian dream of merging the arts, philosophy, religion, everything into a single discourse. I am just an average guy, all those schemes are beyond me.

As for the last part of your question, frankly I do not understand. Every page of my essays has been rewritten at least ten times. Just like every page of the novel. It is only to interviews that I reply in a hurry, because they are a "minor" genre.

Rosso: But isn't the essayist's imperative to reduce the labyrinth a manifestation of the will to power over being (over the differences that time disseminates)? Does, in this way, the essayist become a detective (a *policier*) of the always deviant truth?

Eco: I think that here we would have to trace a typology of the different kinds of essay writing. Consider an essay in organic chemistry. The author must find one formula and one only. If he is of a philosophical bent, he knows that reality is richer than his formula, but the contract he has signed with the reader specifies that he must reduce the labyrinth. On the other hand, a physicist who tells us that light can be explained either in terms of waves physics or in terms of quantum physics, suggests that there is more than one way out of the labyrinth. A philosopher of perception is more than one way out of the labyrinth. But in saying this he reduces it, defines it. In any case, even a scientist who elaborates a hypothesis but shows us how it may be falsified, suggests that the truth can be, as you say, "deviant." But in defining the essayist as a "detective of the always deviant truth," are you not yourself trying to establish a principle, a truth? Are you not, perhaps, collaborating to reduce the labyrinth? Let us try to be honest: there is no mode of essay writing that is not assertive. Only poetry, or narrative, or theater, is truly interrogative and leaves the truth hanging in the balance. A novelist has one of his characters say "I am a detective of the always deviant truth." The reader says, "No, that is not true." And the novelist is satisfied anyway. But if you say this sentence in an essay and I say it is not true, you are dissatisfied. The novelist likes even those who do not believe what he says, but the essayist does not. And if the consent of the reader does not matter to him, he is not an essayist at all, but a novelist in disguise. As I have tried to show.

Rosso: For many years now you have been a tenured professor, you live your normal academic life, you direct a specialized journal of semiotics (*VS*), you have published numerous articles and books of essentially academic interest (e.g., *A Theory of Semiotics*). At the same time you are a regular contributor to *L'Espresso*, one of Italy's most widely read weekly periodicals, you have written several satiric articles in a left-wing newspaper (*Il Manifesto*), you have written some books that have become best-bestsellers (*Il nome della rosa* among them) and now you have collaborated on a movie adapted from your novel.[10] Your interest in both the limited academic culture and the broad phenomena of mass culture makes you a unique kind of intellectual in the United States, where the above-mentioned fields are always religiously separated. What do you think of the "role of the intellectual" today? In what terms do you see the relation between *theory* and *praxis* in the "postmodern epoch"?

Eco: Let me correct you on one point. I am not collaborating on a film from my novel. Jean-Jacques Annaud is preparing the film. We often discuss it, because he asks me for clarification and advice. It seems that otherwise he has a good understanding of the novel and so I trust him. An author is not the right person to transform his own novel into a film.

Your question as such I find rather naive. All intellectuals do the same thing I do—in Italy, Germany, France, Spain, and Latin America (I have no precise information on India and Malaysia). The only place where there is a division of labor between campus and militant culture is the United States. But that is your problem, not mine.

Rosso: Your university training is "hermeneutic" in nature, but in your writings you no longer use this approach. Yet you talk about interpretive processes ("unlimited semiosis," etc.). What is the relationship between your conception of interpretation and that of the phenomenological hermeneutic school of German origin (Heidegger, Gadamer, or in Italy, Vattimo,[11] and others)?

Eco: My university training was not a hermeneutic one. I was a disciple of Luigi Pareyson, but the theory of interpretation that he proposed in his *Estetica* of 1954 (the one that influenced me) was not yet hermeneutic in nature.¹² The hermeneutic Pareyson comes later. At that point interpretation was not considered an act of listening to a voice of being but a reading of formal structures. At least that is the way I read it, and that is why I ventured in the direction of *Opera aperta* and through these considerations toward structuralism and semiotics.

But it is clear that a semiotics of unlimited semiosis has something in common with certain hermeneutic techniques. In the book that I just turned in to Indiana University Press, *Semiotics and the Philosophy of Language*, some mention is made of these problems. Briefly, I might say that a semiotics of unlimited semiosis is based on infinite interpretation, on conjecture and abduction, and on the interrogation of texts as if they were universes and of universes (including the world of our daily experience and that of science) as if they were texts.

With my friend T. A. Sebeok, I have coedited, for the same publisher, a book of essays on the methods of Sherlock Holmes (*The Sign of Three*). In that book there is a chapter on the interpretive methods of Aristotle, Peirce, and Sherlock Holmes, where I try to show that there is no difference between the conjectures of the detective, the philosopher, the scientist, and the reader of a text. But it is equally true that this hermeneutic (if we can call if that) does not necessarily imply in the background a Being that speaks through language. If anything, it is interested in the interpretation of languages as social phenomena. And Being does not speak itself through language because, as Aristotle said, "being is said in many ways." What does this mean? That there is no Being that then speaks. There is a language that speaks Being. And since it says it in many ways, it always speaks through conjectures. What Being might be is always a hypothesis posed by language. Language comes first. But, despite coming first, it is in front of us, with its laws, which are also social laws, conventions, techniques, tactics, strategies. Interpretation is primarily concerned with these mechanisms. Being is only an effect of meaning. Meaning is an effect of culture. The cultural universe is the labyrinth. It is this that we must interpret.

Rosso: Clearly your recurrent word "conjecture" is crucial to your understanding of the interpretive act. I am wondering if you could amplify your understanding of this term by responding to the objection that, say, a Heideggerian or even a Derridean would make to your statement that there is no difference between the conjecture of the detective, the public, the philosopher. Wouldn't a "postmodern" philosopher like Heidegger or Derrida say that the conjecture of the detective in fact annuls its truly explorative possibilities by being guided by an assumed beginning and end, that conjecture in the detective sense of the word is "calculative" and not truly explorative thinking, that it is truly transitive activity?

Eco: I think that we have to distinguish between detectives in novels and real detectives (who are no different from real scientists). Think of what happens in a Rex Stout novel. Nero Wolfe stays at home, gathers the information supplied to him by Archie Goodwin, and then imagines a "possible world" or "possible state of affairs" that accounts for all the evidence at hand. He is not at all sure that the possible world he has imagined corresponds to the real one. It is only a conjecture. In the last analysis, the world he has imagined is logically satisfying—more so than the one in which the crime occurred. Then he calls together all the persons involved in the case, including the guilty suspect, and recounts his possible world as if it were true. If the suspect ever said "This man is mad," Wolfe could not be certain that he had guessed the truth. Instead Wolfe lives in the tranquil world that Rex Stout has created for him, and the suspect is induced by Rex Stout to make a gesture or say a word that betrays him. Therefore Wolfe is sure that the possible world he imagined is identical to the world of reality.

For a real detective or scientist it works differently. The detective or scientist imagines an explanation but cannot yet be sure that it is correct. Nothing guarantees that the order of our ideas corresponds to the order of things (in the sense meant by Spinoza: "*ordo et connexio rerum idem est ac ordo et connexio idearum*"). Peirce said that conjecture is exposed to "fallibilism." A true conjecture is always a wager, a dare. Besides it has to be proven over and over, and often the proofs are mutually contradictory, and so on. . . . The true conjectures are not the ones in detective novels. Those are just representations of thoroughly successful conjectures, which in real life are extremely rare. In real life we first make a conjecture, then we make the conjecture that perhaps our conjecture was correct, and so on, till the conjecture is squared, cubed, ad infinitum. In this sense, in real life as well as in philosophy, the process never ends: there is no closure.

NOTES

1. In the United States on several occasions, among which I will only mention here *Par Rapport* (no. 2, 1979), *New Literary History* (vol. 3, no. 1, 1971) and numerous issues of *boundary 2*; in Italy *aut aut* (nos. 179–80, 1980), *Alfabeta* (nos. 22, 24 and ff., 1981), *Calibano* (no. 7, 1982) and the collection of essays edited by Peter Carravetta and Paolo Spedicato, *Critica postmoderna americana* (Milano: Bomplani, 1984).

2. Umberto Eco, *Il nome della rosa* (Milano: Bomplani, 1980); Eng. trans. William Weaver, *The Name of the Rose* (New York: Harcourt-Brace, 1982).

3. See *Il pensiero debole* ed. Gianni Vattimo and Pier Aldo Rovatti, (Milan: Feltrinelli, 1983).

4. I am referring in particular to the article by William Spanos, "Postmodern Literature and the Hermeneutic Crisis," *Union Seminary Quarterly Review* 34, no. 2 (1979): 119–31. The sentence cited by Spanos is taken from Robert Creeley and Wallace Stevens.

5. Umberto Eco, *Opera aperta* (Milano: Bomplani, 1962).

6. Maria Corti, "E un'opera chiusa" *Espresso* (Oct. 19, 1980), 108.

7. Umberto Eco, *Il nome della rosa*, 495. My translation.

8. *Il nome della rosa* sold 150,000 copies in Germany, 120,000 in France, 50,000 in Spain, and 300,000 hardcover in the United States (before the paperback edition). As of February 1984 the total of the copies sold in the world was about 1,500,000.

9. Umberto Eco, *Opera aperta*, and *Lector in fabula* (Milano: Bompiani, 1979). Translations of parts of these books appeared in *The Role of the Reader: Explorations in the Semiotics of the Text* (Bloomington: Indiana University Press, 1979).

10. Umberto Eco, *A Theory of Semiotics* (Bloomington: Indiana University Press, 1976). Eco signed satiric articles in *Il Manifesto* with the name of "Dedalus" from 1971 to 1975. The movie adapted from *Il nome della rosa* is directed by Jean-Jacques Annaud, the well-known director of *Quest for Fire*.

11. Among the many works of Gianni Vattimo see especially: *Essere, storia e linguaggio in Heidegger* (Torino: Edizioni die "Filosofia," 1963); *Poesia e ontologia* (Milano: Mursia, 1968); *Schleiermacher filosofo dell'interpretazione* (Milano: Mursia, 1968); *Introduzione a Heidegger* (Barl: Laterza, 1971); *Il soggetto e la maschera: Nietzsche e il problema della liberazione* (Milano: Bompiani, 1974, 1979); *Le avventure della differenza* (Milano: Feltrinelli, 1981). In English see: "Bottle, Net, Truth, Revolution, Terrorism, Philosophy" in *Denver Quarterly* 4 (1982): 24–34; "The Shattering of the Poetic World," in *The Favorite Malice*, ed. Thomas J. Harrison (New York: Out of London Press, 1983), 223–35. He was also general director of the *Enciclopedia di filosofia* (Milano: Garzanti, 1981).

12. Luigi Pareyson, *Estetica: teoria della formatività* (Torino: Edizioni die "Filosofia," 1954; 2nd ed. Bologna: Zanichelli, 1960; 3rd ed. Firenze: Sansoni, 1974).

BIBLIOGRAPHICAL NOTE
Reprinted Essays

Jacques Derrida, authorized excerpts "From One Newism to Another through Some Post-isms (New Criticism, Postmodernism, Post-Marxism, Post-structuralism, New Historicism)," in *The "States" of Theory*, ed. David Carroll (New York: Columbia University Press, 1989).

Charles Jencks, "Postmodern vs. Late-Modern," chapters 2–4 of *What Is Post-Modernism?* (London/New York: Academy Editions/ St. Martin's Press, 1986).

C. Barry Chabot, "The Problem of the Postmodern," *New Literary History* 20, no. 1 (1988).

Clement Greenberg, *The Notion of 'Postmodern'* (Sidney: The Sir William Dobell Art Foundation, 1980).

Donald B. Kuspit, "The Unhappy Consciousness of Modernism," *Artforum* (Jan. 1981).

Rosalind E. Krauss, "The Originality of the Avant-Garde," *October* 18 (Fall 1981).

Richard Rorty, "Habermas and Lyotard on Postmodernity," *Praxis International* 4, no. 1 (1984).

Martin Jay, "Habermas and Postmodernism," in Jay, *Fin-de-siècle Socialism and Other Essays* (New York/London: Routledge, 1988).

Susan Rubin Suleiman, "Feminism and Postmodernism," in Suleiman, *Subversive Intent: Gender, Politics and the Avant-Garde* (Cambridge, Mass.: Harvard University Press, 1990).

Gianni Vattimo, "The End of (Hi)story," *Chicago Review* 35, no. 4 (1987).

Peter Koslowski, "The (De-)Construction Sites of The Postmodern," transl. of "Die Baustellen der Postmoderne—Wider den Vollendungszwang der Moderne," in *Moderne oder Postmoderne: Zur Signatur des gegenwärtigen Zeitalters*, ed. Peter Koslowski, Robert Spaemann, and Reinhard Löw (Weinheim: VHC, 1986), 1–18.

Matei Calinescu, "From the One to the Many: Pluralism in Today's Thought," *Innovation/Renovation*, ed. Ihab Hassan and Sally Hassan (Madison: University of Wisconsin Press, 1983).

David Hayman, "Nodality or Plot Displaced: The Dynamics of Sollers's *H*," *SubStance* 43, vol. 8, no. 2 (1984).

Stefano Rosso/Umberto Eco, "A Correspondence on Postmodernism," originally published as Stefano Rosso, "A Correspondence with Umberto Eco: Genova-Bologna-Binghamton-Bloomington, August-September, 1982; March-April, 1983," in *boundary 2*, vol. 12, no. 1 (Fall 1983).

CONTRIBUTORS

CHARLES BOONE is a West Coast composer now based in Houston. His work is published by Editions Salabert, Paris, and has been played by major orchestras and ensembles around the world.

MATEI CALINESCU, Professor of Comparative Literature and West European Studies at Indiana University, Bloomington, has coedited (with D. W. Fokkema) *Exploring Postmodernism* and is author of *Five Faces of Modernity: Modernism, Avant-Garde, Decadence, Kitsch.*

C. BARRY CHABOT is Professor and Chair of English at Miami University. He is the author of *Freud on Schreber: Psychoanalytical Theory*, and is currently completing a study of American literary modernism.

JACQUES DERRIDA is Professor of the History of Philosophy at the Ecole des Hautes Etudes en Sciences Sociales in Paris. His numerous works include *Of Grammatology, Writing and Difference, Positions, Spurs/Eperons, Margins of Philosophy, Glas, Dissemination, The Postcard, Limited Inc.,* and *Of Spirit: Heidegger and the Question.*

UMBERTO ECO is Professor of Semiotics in the Faculty of Letters and Philosophy at the University of Bologna. He is the author of several books on semiotics and reception theory, including *A Theory of Semiotics, The Role of the Reader,* and *Semiotics and the Philosophy of Language.* His *Postscript to the Name of the Rose* is a concise but indispensable contribution to the theory of postmodernism.

ERIKA FISCHER-LICHTE is Professor of General and Comparative Literature at the University of Bayreuth, West Germany. Her publications include *Semiotik des Theaters* ("semiotics of theatre," Engl. translation forthcoming from Indiana University Press), *Problems of a Semiotic Hermeneutics and Aesthetics,* and *History of Drama.*

CLEMENT GREENBERG, art critic, New York. His essays are now assembled in four volumes, *The Collected Essays and Criticism,* edited by John O'Brian. *Art and Culture* became a classic for modernists.

DAVID HAYMAN is Professor of Comparative Literature at the University of Wisconsin, Madison. He is the author of *Ulysses: The Mechanics of Meaning; A First-Draft Version of Finnegans Wake; Reforming the Narrative: Toward a Mechanic of Modernist Fiction;* and *The "Wake" in Transit,* as well as articles on nineteenth- and twentieth-century literature and art.

JOST HERMAND is Vilas Research Professor of German at the University of Wisconsin, Madison. He is the author of *Epochen deutscher Kultur,* 5 vols. (with Richard Hamann), *Interpretive Synthesis: The Task of Literary Scholarship, Konkretes Hören: Zum Inhalt der Instrumentalmusik, Literaturwissenschaft und Kunstwissenschaft, Der alte Traum vom neuen Reich: Völkische Ütopien und Nationalsozialismus, Die Kultur der Bundesrepublik,* and other studies on German culture.

INGEBORG HOESTEREY is Associate Professor of Germanic Studies at Indiana University and has published on twentieth-century German fiction, interrelations of literature and visual art, and on postmodernism. She is the author of

Verschlungene Schriftzeichen: Intertextualität von Literatur und Kunst in der Moderne Postmoderne and editor (with Ann Fehn) of *Critical Narratology* (Princeton: Princeton University Press, 1991).

MARTIN JAY is professor of History at the University of California, Berkeley, where he specializes in Modern European Intellectual History. He is the author of *The Dialectical Imagination, Adorno, Permanent Exiles,* and *Fin-de-siècle Socialism.* He is the editor of *An Unmastered Past: The Autobiographical Writings of Leo Lowenthal* and is senior editor of *Theory and Society.*

CHARLES JENCKS is Adjunct Professor of Architecture at the University of California at Los Angeles, teaches in London at Architectural Association, and writes for various professional publications and *The Observer.* His works include *The Language of Post-Modern Architecture, What Is Post-Modernism?,* and *The New Classicism in Art and Architecture.*

PETER KOSLOWSKI is Professor of Philosophy and Political Economy at the University of Witten/Herdecke, West Germany, and Director of the Forschungsinstitut für Philosophie, Hannover. He has written articles on political philosophy, metaphysics, and economic ethics. His books include *Prinzipien der ethischen Ökonomie, Die postmoderne Kultur, Die Prüfungen der Neuzeit: Über Postmodernität;* he has edited *Gnosis und Mystik in der Geschichte der Philosophie, Moderne oder Postmoderne,* and *Economics and Philosophy.*

ROSALIND E. KRAUSS, Distinguished Professor of Art History at Hunter College, is the author of *Terminal Iron Works: The Sculpture of David Smith, Passages in Modern Sculpture,* and *The Originality of the Avant-Garde and Other Modernist Myths.* She is cofounder and coeditor of *October.*

DONALD B. KUSPIT is Professor of Art History at the State University of New York at Stony Brook and general editor of research publications in art history at the University of Michigan. He is the author of *Clement Greenberg: Art Critic, The Critic As Artist: The Intentionality of Art,* and *The New Subjectivism: Art in the 1980s,* among other titles.

RICHARD RORTY is University Professor of Humanities at the University of Virginia. His most recent book is *Contingency, Irony and Solidarity.*

STEFANO ROSSO teaches American Literature at the University of Bergamo. His interviews conducted with major figures in critical theory for *boundary 2, Critical Inquiry,* and *Alfabeta* as well as for radio are central to the debate on postmodernism, in particular his "Interview with Paul de Man."

JOHN H. SMITH is Associate Professor of German at the University of California, Irvine. He has published *The Spirit and the Letter: Traces of Rhetoric in Hegel's Philosophy of Bildung* and essays on Kleist, Handke, and poststructuralism.

SUSAN RUBIN SULEIMAN is Professor of Romance and Comparative Literatures at Harvard University. Besides many articles and several edited volumes, her works include *Authoritarian Fictions: The Ideological Novel As a Literary Genre* and *Subversive Intent: Gender, Politics and the Avant-Garde.*

MAUREEN TURIM is Associate Professor of Cinema and Comparative Literature at the State University of New York at Binghamton. She is the author of *Abstraction in Avant-Garde Films* and *Flashbacks in Film: Memory and History* as well as numerous articles on film history, theory, and video. She is the editor of a volume of essays, *Film and Literature: Interactions and Transpositions.*

GIANNI VATTIMO is Professor of Philosophy at the University of Torino and the author of critical studies on Aristotle, Nietzsche, Heidegger, and Schleiermacher. More recently he has published *Le avventure della differenza, La fine della modernità* and other works that have appeared or will be forthcoming in English.

INDEX

Absence, monism of, 157, 162–63
Absolute, the, 90, 145–46, 151
Absolute Ego, 145
Absolute (disjunctive) irony, 25–26, 28, 30–31, 36
Abstract art, xiv, 62
Abstraction, 11, 13, 15–16, 202
Academicism/Academism, 44, 149
Adams, John, 213–14
Adorno, Theodor, 87, 88, 122, 151, 192; Habermas on, 84, 106; influence on Habermas, 102, 105; on music, 198–200
Advertising, 122, 179
Aesthetic, the, 56–57, 60, 76, 171
Aestheticism, in art, 194–95
Aesthetic modernism, 168–69
Aesthetic moment (in photography), 69
Aesthetic progress, 192–94, 196
Aesthetic reason, 103–104
Aesthetics, xiv, 13, 106, 148; criteria for, 169–71; dualism and pluralism, 166–68; monistic, 156–57; relativism, 171; standards/value, 44–49. *See also* Art(s); Standard(s); Value(s)
Aesthetics of Chaosmos, The (Eco), 245
Affirmation, 25, 27
Afro-Americans (Blacks), 116, 120, 127–28 n.21
Agonistic Modernism, 13–14, 15, 18
Alienation, 57, 64, 91
Allegory, use by visual artists, 9–11
Alone-standing woman, 124, 130 n.47
Ambassadors, The (James), 68–69
Ambiguity, reduction of, 249
America (Baudrillard), 208
Americanist project, x, xi, xiv
Amirkhanian, Charles, 213
Anarchy, 23, 147–49
Andenken (Recollection), 136, 137–39, 141
Anderson, Laurie, 18, 213, 214
Andre, Carl, 62, 70
Annaud, Jean-Jacques, 250, 253 n.10
Année denière à Marienbad, L' (film), 183
Anti-Aesthetic, The (Foster, ed.), 14–15
Antiphilosophy, 162
Antiquity, 142, 146–47, 149, 156–57
Antireductionists, 89–90
Appearance (*Schein*) and being, question of, 218–19
Appropriateness, 170
Archai, for metaphysics, 137–38
Archaic music, 203
Architectonics of Answerability, The (Bakhtin), 160

Architecture, x, 4–16, 18–20, 31, 42, 148
—avant-garde, 243
—Gothic, 167
—late-modern, xv n.9, 4–16, 18–20
—modern, xii–xiii, 4–14, 16, 18–20, 34–36, 44; difficulty in defining, 182; Habermas on, 105–106; meaning for Greenberg, 42; seen as religion, 12–13
—postmodern, 4–12, 14, 16, 18–20, 100, 177–78; difficulty in defining, 182; as distinguishable from modern, xii–xiii, 34; effect of poststructuralism in, 178; Habermas on, xv n.9, 106; for Jameson, xv n.9, 31–32, 34–35; language of, x; meaning for Greenberg, 42; for Venturi and Brown, 113
Aristotle, 157, 158, 244–45
Ars povera, in music, 203
Art(s), x, 12, 33, 100, 164, 192; avant-garde, 70–71, 243; Dada, 222; as division of culture, 88–90, 103–104; fusion with kitsch as camp, xiv; for Hassan, 23–24; late-modern, 15; modern, 13–14, 50–64, 57–64, 106; periodization, ix, 69; postmodern, 5, 14, 147–49, 165, 173, 186–87; relationship to life-world, 105; in 1890s, 194; in 1920s, 195–96. *See also* Aesthetics; Architecture; Literature; Music; Theater; Visual art(s)
Art-as-making, for modernism, 51, 54–55
Artaud, Antonin, 223
Art criticism, 73, 104
Art-for-art's sake, 46, 47, 198
Ashley, Robert, 213
Atmosphères (Ligeti), 210–11
Atonality, in music, 197–98, 200, 208, 211
Audience, 221–22, 226–27
Austen, Jane, 74, 76
Austin, J. L., 107
Authenticity, 67, 69, 73
Autobiography, as topic in *H*, 231, 234, 235–37, 239
Avant-garde, 13, 145, 187, 192–94, 197, 205; appropriation by, 122–23; disruptivists in tradition of, 29; Eco on, 243; experimentalism as negative, 169, 171; film, xii, 180–82, 185; historical periods, 78–79, 193–94; as metahistorical category, 243; music, 193–94, 196–97, 198, 199–202, 204–205; outdone by the transavant-garde, 147; relationship to modernism, 43, 144, 179, 186, 216; relationship to postmodernism, 17–18, 100, 178; and social philosophy, 95–96; theater, 217, 223–26; video, 180–81, 185; visual arts, 69–79; women in, 114, 128 n.22; yearning for relaxation, 48